Lecture Notes in Computer Science 14468

Founding Editors

Gerhard Goos
Juris Hartmanis

The series Lecture Notes in Computer Science (LNCS), including its subseries Lecture Notes in Artificial Intelligence (LNAI) and Lecture Notes in Bioinformatics (LNBI), has established itself as a medium for the publication of new developments in computer science and information technology research, teaching, and education.

LNCS enjoys close cooperation with the computer science R & D community, the series counts many renowned academics among its volume editors and paper authors, and collaborates with prestigious societies. Its mission is to serve this international community by providing an invaluable service, mainly focused on the publication of conference and workshop proceedings and postproceedings. LNCS commenced publication in 1973.

Bo Nørregaard Jørgensen ·
Luiz Carlos Pereira da Silva · Zheng Ma
Editors

Energy Informatics

Third Energy Informatics Academy Conference, EI.A 2023
Campinas, Brazil, December 6–8, 2023
Proceedings, Part II

 Springer

Editors
Bo Nørregaard Jørgensen 🄳
University of Southern Denmark
Odense, Denmark

Luiz Carlos Pereira da Silva 🄳
University of Campinas
Campinas, São Paulo, Brazil

Zheng Ma 🄳
University of Southern Denmark
Odense, Denmark

ISSN 0302-9743   ISSN 1611-3349 (electronic)
Lecture Notes in Computer Science
ISBN 978-3-031-48651-7   ISBN 978-3-031-48652-4 (eBook)
https://doi.org/10.1007/978-3-031-48652-4

This Springer imprint is published by the registered company Springer Nature Switzerland AG
The registered company address is: Gewerbestrasse 11, 6330 Cham, Switzerland

Paper in this product is recyclable.

Preface

The Energy Informatics.Academy Conference 2023 (EI.A 2023) collected great contributions from researchers and practitioners in various scientific, technological, engineering, and social fields to disseminate original research on the application of digital technology and information management theory and practice to facilitate the global transition towards sustainable and resilient energy systems.

With the whole technical program committee's effort, in total thirty-nine (39) high-quality papers (including full papers and short papers) and three (3) abstract papers were accepted and presented at the conference.

These 42 papers covered the following eight themes, elucidating the breadth and depth of research and development in the energy sector and its convergence with digital technologies:

- AI Methods in Energy
- Data-Driven Smart Buildings
- Energy and Industry 4.0
- Energy and Smart Cities
- Energy Forecasting
- Smart Electricity System
- Smart Energy Device Management
- Smart Heating and Cooling System

Each theme brought forward a wealth of knowledge and novel ideas that promise to shape the future trajectory of energy systems and their integration into digitalization. From exploring innovative technologies and methodologies to discussing practical challenges and future perspectives, the papers enriched the conference's discourse, offering attendees a comprehensive overview of the latest in the field. Consequently, the conference became a fertile ground for exchanging ideas, fostering collaborations, and catalyzing future advancements in the energy sector.

Furthermore, eight keynote speeches provided deep insights and diverse perspectives into the evolving realm of energy and technology:

- "Energy transition in Brazil", by Luiz Carlos Pereira da Silva, University of Campinas, Brazil
- "Artificial Intelligence Applied in the Electricity Sector as a Strategic Investment Theme in the Research, Development and Innovation Program of ANEEL" by Paulo Luciano de Carvalho, Brazilian Electricity Regulatory Agency, Brazil
- "Explainable AI for energy and smart grids: from concepts to real-world applications", by Zita A. Vale, Polytechnic of Porto, Portugal
- "Hierarchies of Controllers for the Future Weather-Driven Smart Energy System", by Henrik Madsen, Technical University of Denmark
- "The importance of supervising energy consumption and production", by Marcelo Stehling de Castro, Federal University of Goiás, Brazil

- "Application of Data Analytics to Electrical Energy Systems", by Walmir Freitas, University of Campinas, Brazil
- "Energy & Digital Agroindustry", by Barbara Teruel, University of Campinas, Brazil
- "Energy Informatics Educational Design", by Bo Nørregaard Jørgensen, University of Southern Denmark, Denmark

Each speaker, with their expertise in various facets of energy systems and technology, enriched the dialogue, fostering a multi-dimensional discussion on the challenges, solutions, and future pathways in the energy sector. Engaging Q&A sessions followed the speeches, further elaborating on the pertinent themes and facilitating an exchange of ideas among the participants and speakers alike.

December 2023

Bo Nørregaard Jørgensen
Luiz Carlos Pereira da Silva
Zheng Ma

Organization

Program Committee Chairs

Jørgensen, Bo Nørregaard	University of Southern Denmark, Denmark
Ma, Zheng	University of Southern Denmark, Denmark
Pereira da Silva, Luiz Carlos	University of Campinas, Brazil

Technical Program Committee Chairs

Attux, Romis	University of Campinas, Brazil
Madsen, Henrik	Technical University of Denmark, Denmark
Rider, Marcos J.	University of Campinas, Brazil
Stehling de Castro, Marcelo	University of Goiás, Brazil
Teruel, Bárbara	University of Campinas, Brazil
Vale, Zita	Polytechnic of Porto, Portugal

Technical Program Committee Members

Ai, Qian	Shanghai Jiao Tong University, China
Angelino de Souza, Wesley	Federal University of Technology, Brazil
Aris, Hazleen Binti	Universiti Tenaga Nasional, Malaysia
Arjunan, Pandarasamy	Indian Institute of Science, Robert Bosch Centre for Cyber-Physical Systems, India
Bergel, Alexandre	RelationalAI, Switzerland
Bonatto, Benedito Donizeti	Universidade Federal de Itajubá, Brazil
Bordin, Chiara	Arctic University of Norway, Norway
Chew, Irene	Monash University, Australia
Christensen, Kristoffer	University of Southern Denmark, Denmark
Dai, Wanyang	Nanjing University, China
Fernandes, Ricardo	Federal University of São Carlos, Brazil
Guillardi Júnior, Hildo	São Paulo State University, Brazil
Howard, Daniel Anthony	University of Southern Denmark, Denmark
Huang, Zhilin	Huaqiao University, China
Liang, An	Hong Kong Polytechnic University, China
Liberado, Eduardo	São Paulo State University, Brazil
Lilliu, Fabio	Aalborg University, Denmark

López, Juan Camilo	Universidade Estadual de Campinas, Brazil
Marafão, Fernando	São Paulo State University, Brazil
Othman, Marini	INTI International University, Malaysia
Qu, Ying	University of Southern Denmark, Denmark
Rajasekharan, Jayaprakash	Norwegian University of Science and Technology, Norway
Roomi, Muhammad M.	Illinois at Singapore Pte Ltd, Singapore
Santos, Athila Quaresma	University of Southern Denmark, Denmark
Shaker, Hamid Reza	University of Southern Denmark, Denmark
Vergara, Pedro P.	Delft University of Technology, The Netherlands
Værbak, Magnus	University of Southern Denmark, Denmark
Watson, Richard T.	University of Georgia, USA
Yussof, Salman	Universiti Tenaga Nasional, Malaysia
Swarup, Shanti	IIT Madras, India

Organizing Committee for Special Session - Digitalization of District Heating and Cooling

Brüssau, Martin	SAMSON Aktiengesellschaft, Germany
Nord, Natasa	Norwegian University of Science and Technology, Norway
Saloux, Etienne	Natural Resources Canada, Canada
Schmidt, Dietrich	Fraunhofer IEE, Germany
Shaker, Hamid Reza	University of Southern Denmark, Denmark
Vallée, Mathieu	National Institute for Solar Energy, France
Yang, Xiaochen	Tianjin University, China

Organizing Committee for Special Session - Data-Driven Smart Buildings

Borkowski, Esther	Institute of Technology in Architecture, Switzerland
Jørgensen, Bo Nørregaard	University of Southern Denmark, Denmark
Saloux, Etienne	Natural Resources Canada, Canada
So, Patrick	Hong Kong Electrical and Mechanical Services Department, China
White, Stephen	CSIRO, Australia

Organizing Committee for Special Session - Digitalization, AI and Related Technologies for Energy Efficiency and GHG Emissions Reduction in Industry

Amazouz, Mouloud	Natural Resources Canada, Canada
Levesque, Michelle	Natural Resources Canada, Canada
Ma, Zheng	University of Southern Denmark, Denmark

Reviewers

Acuña Acurio, Byron Alejandro	University of Campinas, Brazil
Chérrez Barragán, Diana Estefania	University of Campinas, Brazil
Clausen, Christian Skafte Beck	University of Southern Denmark, Denmark
Fatras, Nicolas	University of Southern Denmark, Denmark
Hidalgo Leite, Nathalia	University of Campinas, Brazil
Ito Cypriano, Joao Guilherme	University of Campinas, Brazil
Ma, Zhipeng	University of Southern Denmark, Denmark
Mirshekali, Hamid	University of Southern Denmark, Denmark
Mortensen, Lasse Kappel	University of Southern Denmark, Denmark
Santos, Luiza	University of Campinas, Brazil
Silva, Jessica	University of Campinas, Brazil
Søndergaard, Henrik Alexander Nissen	University of Southern Denmark, Denmark
Tolnai, Balázs András	University of Southern Denmark, Denmark
Vanting, Nicolai Bo	University of Southern Denmark, Denmark

Contents – Part II

Smart Electricity System

Smart Energy Device Management

Smart Heating and Cooling System

Contents – Part I

Energy and Smart Cities

Multi-agent Based Simulation for Investigating Electric Vehicle Adoption and Its Impacts on Electricity Distribution Grids and CO2 Emissions

Kristoffer Christensen [ID], Zheng Ma[(✉)] [ID], and Bo Nørregaard Jørgensen [ID]

SDU Center for Energy Informatics, Maersk Mc-Kinney Moeller Institute, The Faculty of Engineering, University of Southern Denmark, Odense, Denmark
`{kric,zma,bnj}@mmmi.sdu.dk`

Abstract. Electric vehicles are expected to significantly contribute to CO2-eq. emissions reduction, but the increasing number of EVs also introduces challenges to the energy system, and to what extent it contributes to achieving climate goals remains unknown. Static modeling and assumption-based simulations have been used for such investigation, but they cannot capture the realistic ecosystem dynamics. To fill the gap, this paper investigates the impacts of two adoption curves of private EVs on the electricity distribution grids and national climate goals. This paper develops a multi-agent based simulation with two adoption curves, the Traditional EV charging strategy, various EV models, driving patterns, and CO2-eq. emission data to capture the full ecosystem dynamics during a long-term period from 2020 to 2032. The Danish 2030 climate goal and a Danish distribution network with 126 residential consumers are chosen as the case study. The results show that both EV adoption curves of 1 million and 775k EVs by 2030 will not satisfy the Danish climate goal of reducing transport sector emissions by 30% by 2030. The results also show that the current residential electricity distribution grids cannot handle the load from increasing EVs. The first grid overload will occur in 2031 (around 16 and 24 months later for the 1 million and 775k EVs adopted by 2030) with a 67% share of EVs in the grid.

Keywords: electric vehicle · adoption curve · distribution grid · agent-based modeling · multi-agent systems · CO2 emissions

1 Introduction

The transportation sector contributes greatly to CO emissions. For instance, In 2019 cars in Denmark emitted 7.2 million tons of CO2-eq, and the total car fleet in Denmark in 2019 was 2.65 million [1], resulting in an average emission per car of 2.72 tons annually. The car fleet is estimated to increase to about 3.25 million in 2030 [2]. With no change in car emissions, this would result in a total car emission of 8.84 million tons by 2030.

The European Union's climate policies (which Denmark is obligated to), states among other things that emissions from buildings, agriculture, and transportation have

B. N. Jørgensen et al. (Eds.): EI.A 2023, LNCS 14468, pp. 3–19, 2024.
https://doi.org/10.1007/978-3-031-48652-4_1

to be reduced by 30% compared to 2005 levels [3]. In 2005 the CO2-eq. emissions from cars were around 7.1 million tons [2]. This corresponds to a maximum emission level of 4.97 million tons CO2-eq. from cars by 2030, in order to meet the climate goal. Electric Vehicles (EVs) have been prompted to contribute to reducing CO2-eq. emissions in the transportation sector, a minimum of 1.42 million of the car fleet in 2030 has to be EVs to meet the climate goal. Furthermore, EVs are also expected to provide flexibility to the electricity system to leverage the fluctuation due to renewable energy sources [4]. However, EV charging is associated with a CO2-eq. emission due to the energy production is not 100% green [5].

Furthermore, due to the regulations, electricity Distribution System Operators (DSOs) have no access to information on how many EVs, when, and how much EVs will charge in the distribution grids with the increasing number of EVs. Therefore, DSOs are unclear about the loading profile of the distribution grids in the future. Although many studies have investigated EV-caused overloads in distribution grids (e.g., [6, 7]), most studies are based on static modeling or assumption-based simulations without considering the real EV adoption curves. It causes a challenge for DSOs that it is unclear what the overloads in distribution grids will look like with the increasing number of EVs over the years in the future. However, the majority of the literature is based on static modeling or assumption-based simulations without considering the realistic EV adoption curves. It would result in high uncertainty for DSOs to conduct grid planning, especially congestion management.

Therefore, this paper aims to investigate how different adoption curves of private EVs will impact the national climate goals and the consequence to the electricity distribution grids. A multi-agent based simulation with several adoption curves, EV models, driving patterns, and CO2-eq. emission from EV charging is developed to capture the full ecosystem dynamics during a long-term period from 2020 to 2032 with a high resolution (hourly).

Furthermore, the adoption curves, EV models, and driving patterns are all based on national statistics and national market research to ensure the simulation can closely represent the reality to provide a clear and realistic load profile of distribution grids in the future due to EV adoption. The CO2-eq. emissions from consuming electricity depend on the electricity production mix in the grid, thus, the simulation imports and extrapolates hourly electricity consumption emission data. A distribution grid consisting of 126 residential consumers in the city of Strib, Denmark is selected as a case study to investigate the uncertainty of the increasing EVs' impact on the distribution grid with the electricity consumption data for 2019.

The paper outline starts with a background of the Danish electricity system and electric vehicle adoption curve; secondly, the methodology is introduced followed by the case study; thirdly, the scenario and experiment design is presented; lastly, the results are presented followed by the discussion and conclusion.

2   Literature Review

The applications of Multi-Agent Systems (MASs) in the energy domain are increasing as the energy system complexity increases as a result of the green transition [8]. [9] conduct a scoping review of the literature on ontology for MAS in the energy domain. [9] identify the energy domain applications for MAS to be within grid control, electricity markets, demand-side, and building systems. This paper's MAS should represent the energy ecosystem around EV home charging as proposed in [10]. The MAS representation of the ecosystem simulates the impact on the distribution system from the adoption of EVs over time.

The adoption of technology and innovation is a well-covered subject since the innovation adoption theory was first introduced in 1960 by Everett Rogers in his book called "Diffusion of Innovation Theory" [11]. 30 technology adoption theories have been identified [12], and essential elements from the theory are used, such as the S-shaped (logistic function) and the adoption rate curve. Several studies, e.g., [13–17], are conducted using agent-based modeling together with Rogers' adoption theory. Furthermore, [18] and [19] use MAS for investigating the impact of adopting EVs, but do not consider grid loading, tariff schemes, or charging algorithm adoption. [18] uses an ecosystem approach, but the ecosystem does not consider the business part of the ecosystem, hence not considering several flows (e.g., monetary flows). [18] focuses on spatial adoption and does also not consider the business ecosystem perspective. Moreover, [20] investigates the CO2 emissions from charging EVs and compares them with plug-in hybrid EVs and conventional vehicles. The paper applies a static approach using a fixed CO2 intensity of the electricity generation mix to calculate the emissions per km driven by the EV.

3 Methodology

This paper chooses MAS to investigate the ecosystem dynamics, stakeholders' behaviors, and the impacts of increasing EVs on an energy business ecosystem. MAS is chosen since it allows an assembly of several agents with either homogenous or heterogeneous architecture [21] and has been popularly applied to model and simulate complex systems.

The selection of the agent-based simulation tool applied in this paper is based on a comprehensive comparative literature survey of the state-of-the-art in software agent-based computing technology [22]. The survey addresses more than 80 software tools. Classifications are made considering the agent-based simulation tools' scope or application domain and the computational modeling strength against the model development effort. Furthermore, three criteria are defined for the evaluation and selection:

- High to extreme scale of computation modeling strength and simple to moderate model development effort
- The application domains are in a dynamic computational system, business, economics, planning & scheduling, enterprise, and organizational behavior
- Suitable for simulating energy business ecosystems

Among 80 software tools, AnyLogic seems to fit the purpose as AnyLogic's application domains cover power grids, business strategy & innovation analysis. Hence, AnyLogic is chosen as the simulation tool in this paper.

4   Multi-agent Based Simulation Development

There are a vast number of potential scenarios for complex MASs with a wide variety of parameter inputs to investigate an ecosystem. However, in this paper, the focus is to enlighten impacts on the CO2-eq. emissions and distribution grid from increasing EVs. To do so, the ecosystem is translated into a MAS by identifying agents, interfaces, and communications. The identified MAS elements are programmed in the selected software tool AnyLogic.

The agents represent actors and objects in the ecosystem. The communication flows are between roles. Therefore, the roles are represented by Java interfaces (Anylogic is Java-based) holding the interactions related to the role. The agents implement the respective interfaces corresponding to the actor/object and the associated roles.

Figure 1 shows a screenshot of the running simulation which shows an overview of the simulated ecosystem, which is based on the ecosystem presented in [10]. The states of the households and transformer loading are shown in real-time.

The relevant input data for this paper are the adoption curves, EV models, driving patterns, and CO2-eq. emission from EV charging.

Fig. 1. Screenshot of the electric vehicle home charging multi-agent system.

4.1   Danish Electric Vehicle Adoption Curve

Based on Rogers adoption curves and the national statistics [23], the residential EV adoption in Denmark from 2011 to 2021 is shown as the black line in Fig. 2 which is close to a logistic growth with a 52.6% rate shown as the orange line in Fig. 2. The logistic function (Roger's S-curve) running through 124 EVs in 2011 and 16,687 in 2021 is identified using Eq. 1 (orange line in Fig. 2).

$$P(t) = \frac{A}{1 + \left(\frac{A}{P(0)} - 1\right)e^{-rt}} \tag{1}$$

where $P(t)$ is the number of EVs to the time t. A is Denmark's total number of vehicles in December 2021 of around 2.5 million cars for residents [23]. $P(0)$ is the initial value in January 2011 of 124 EVs, and r is the growth rate in percent. The growth rate is identified to be 52.6% in order to match the EV adoption in 2011 and 2021. This results in a population of EVs of 1.3 million by 2030.

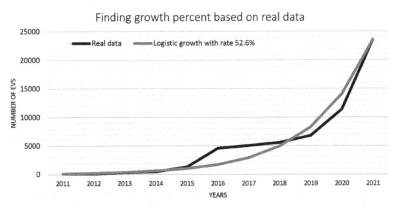

Fig. 2. Growth function estimation based on historical data (orange). (Color figure online)

4.2 EV Models

The EV models are selected as the five most sold EV types in 2019 in Denmark, and the probability of which EV is adopted is based on the purchase share of each type in 2019 (shown in Table 1) [24]. This general approach can be used for other markets by identifying the most popular EV models and their adoption shares.

4.3 Driving Patterns

This research defines the EVs' departure and arrival times based on the significantly decreased and increased electricity consumption data in the mornings and evenings. A significant increase/decrease is defined as 80% above idle hours. Idle hours are calculated as the average load between hours 0 and 5 (at night). Those hours are assumed to represent the idle load of the consumer (consumption when residents are sleeping). When identifying a significant increase in load (indicating residents are awake) between 5 and 9 AM (default), the departure time is set within the hour, which has a load below the significant level (indicating residents have departed). The arrival time is within the hour when the load increases above the significant level between 2 and 10 PM (default). Figure 3 illustrates how departure and arrival are chosen for a consumer.

Suppose no significant decrease or increase in consumption data is detected. The default time is set to a random hour from 5 to 9 AM and 2 to 10 PM for departure and arrival hours, respectively. The same approach applies to systems with similar working cultures, working from around 8 AM to 4 PM.

Table 1. Top five most sold electric vehicles in Denmark in 2019.

EV model	Capacity [kWh]	Mileage [kWh/km]	Maximum charging power [kW]	Percentage of purchased EVs in 2019 [%] [24]
Tesla Model 3 [25]	50	0.151	11	40.5
VW e-Golf [26]	35.8	0.168	7.2	18.0
Hyundai Kona [27]	42	0.154	11	08.3
Renault Zoe [28]	44.1	0.161	22*	06.0
Nissan Leaf [29]	40	0.164	3.68	05.8

*Charging power is limited to the maximum power that can be consumed by each household in Denmark. This limit is typically three phases of 25 Amps (corresponding to approximately 17.3 kW) [30].

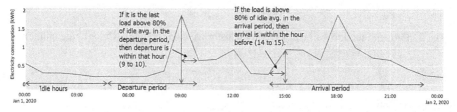

Fig. 3. Example of how the departure and arrival times are chosen.

The distribution of the driving distance per EV is adapted from [31]. The driving distance statistics in [31] are based on 100,000 interview data collected over 15 years for private Danish vehicle users. For simplicity, all EVs will be driven once a day.

4.4 EV Charging CO2-eq. emission

The CO_2-eq. emission from consuming electricity is imported from [32] for DK1 on a 5-min resolution from 2017 to 2020 (4 years). The data is converted to hourly-based (hourly average) to match consumption data. The data are illustrated in Fig. 4.

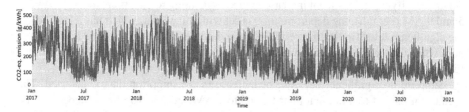

Fig. 4. Data on CO_2-eq. emissions from consuming electricity, from 2017–2020.

The Danish Energy Agency [33] has extrapolated the CO2-eq. emission factor for electricity from 2020 to 2030. The extrapolation is shown in Fig. 5. An exponential regression is made to identify a function that describes the reduction of CO2-eq. emissions from electricity over the years without becoming negative. The Danish Energy Agency's extrapolation is considered a valid calculation used as the reduction factor in the implemented dataset.

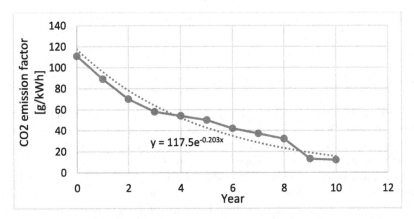

Fig. 5. CO2-eq. emission factor extrapolation over time.

From the exponential regression shown in Fig. 5, the emission factor can be derived by Eq. 2.

$$\text{Emission}_{new} = \text{Emission}_{data} \cdot e^{-0.203 \cdot \text{Year}} \tag{2}$$

where *Emission*$_{new}$ is the new calculated emission accounting for the reduction depending on the simulation time. *Year* is the simulation-years past. Figure 6 shows the data after implementing the emission factor extrapolation during simulation time. The figure shows the emissions reductions over time as the electricity becomes greener, giving a more realistic result on the environmental impact from different scenarios.

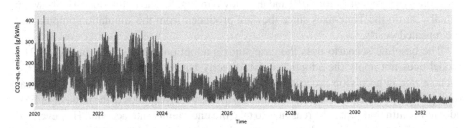

Fig. 6. Repeated data on CO2-eq. emissions from consuming electricity with the implementation of emission factor extrapolation (simulated).

Table 2 shows the results of interest based on the relevant stakeholders' (i.e., the DSO and households) perspective. The output is exported at the simulation end for analysis.

Table 2. Scenario outputs based on the relevant stakeholders.

Stakeholder	Considered output
DSO	• Load Factor (for the day with the first overload) • Coincidence factor (for the first year after overload) • Date and time for the first overload • Number of overloads first year after the first overload
EV users	• Total average of all EV users' average CO2-eq. emissions • Average annual CO2-eq. emissions from charging EVs (kg CO2-eq.)

5   Case Study

The Danish electricity grid is divided into DK1 (Western Denmark - Jutland and Funen) and DK2 (Eastern Denmark - Zealand). The electricity grid is divided into generation, transmission, distribution, and consumption. This paper focuses on the Danish low voltage (400 V) distribution grid. This paper's electricity system boundary starts from the 10 kV/0.4 kV transformer and ends at the residential consumers. The components between the transformer and consumer (i.e., cables, nodes, etc.) are not considered. A distribution grid consisting of 126 residential consumers in the city of Strib, Denmark, is selected as a case study to investigate the uncertainty of the increasing EVs' impact on the distribution grid.

The EV adoption for the area with 126 residents is shown in Fig. 7, which is an extrapolation from the logistic function identified in Fig. 2 (in Sect. 4.1 - Danish Electric Vehicle Adoption Curve). Consumption data for 126 residential consumers are provided by the Danish DSO TREFOR, which operates in the area of Strib.

The data for Strib is available from 2019 to now. However, since this paper uses consumption data to estimate driving behavior, the years with COVID-19 have been excluded, i.e., 2020 and 2021. Therefore, the data is used for 2019 alone. Furthermore, the data has been cleaned for households with EVs, PVs, heat pumps, electric heating, and missing data points. This ensures that the simulation has the actual number of consumer consumption patterns without any distributed energy resources, such as heat pumps. The consumption data is for 2019 and are shown in Fig. 8. The figure does not show the actual year on the Time-axes since they are produced from the simulation outputs and are repeated yearly.

The baseline scenario uses the case study's adoption curve shown in Fig. 7. The model does not apply the adoption curve directly but uses the yearly adoption as the average rate in a Poisson process [34]. This means that the EVs are adopted each year randomly at the given adoption rate, which on average, corresponds to the number of EVs adopted within that year. The reason is to take the uncertainty into account. However, for the scenario of various EV adoption curves, the curves are used directly for comparison purposes.

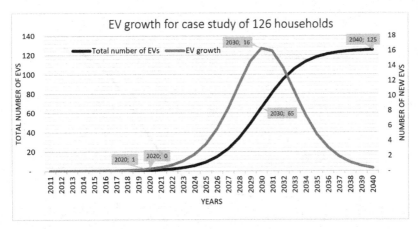

Fig. 7. Adoption curve (black) and adoption rate i.e., electric vehicles adopted per year (green) (Color figure online).

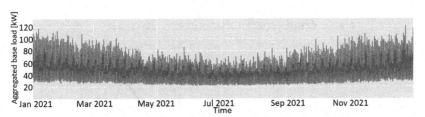

Fig. 8. Aggregated hourly consumption of the 126 consumer consumption data.

6 Scenario Design

Two scenarios are considered in this paper with two EV adoption curves of 775k and 1 million EVs in Denmark by 2030. The scenarios are identified based on the estimation and the political goal by [35], respectively. The two adoption curves are shown in Fig. 9 and Fig. 10, representing the two designed experiments. All simulation experiments start, by default, in 2020 and stop one year after experiencing the first overload. The results considered as key results for this paper are the date for the first overload, the frequency of overloads in the following year, and the average CO2-eq. emissions from charging the EVs. The average total CO2-eq. emissions are calculated for 2031, as this is relevant for the 2030 goal of reducing transport sector emissions by 30%. 2031 has been chosen to see if the goals by 2030 have been achieved in different scenarios.

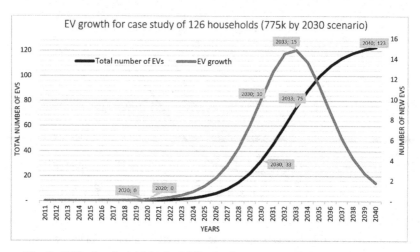

Fig. 9. 775k electric vehicles by 2030 adoption curve applied to the case study.

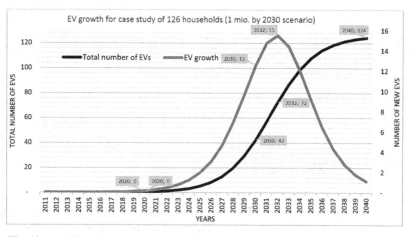

Fig. 10. 1 million electric vehicles by 2030 adoption curve applied to the case study.

7 Results

7.1 Baseline Scenario Results

The baseline scenario is simulated from 2020 to 2032 and simulates the Traditional charging strategy (i.e., charging immediately at arrival). The baseline scenario's EV adoption curve with the Poisson process from the simulation start (2020) to the last simulation year (2032) is shown to the left in Fig. 11. By the end of 2032, 98 EVs are adopted. The distribution of the EV models at the beginning of the last simulation year (January 1, 2032) is illustrated to the right in Fig. 11. The key results for the scenario are shown in Table 3.

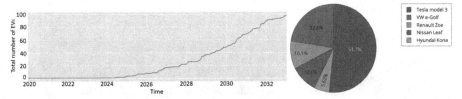

Fig. 11. The total number of adopted electric vehicles from the simulation start (2020) to the simulation end (2032) (left) and the distribution of electric vehicle models at the beginning of the last simulation year (January 1, 2032) (right).

Table 3. Baseline scenario key results.

Date of the first overload	Overloads the year after the first overload	Days with overload	Total EVs when the first overload occurs	Avg. Total CO2-eq. emissions in 2031 [kg]
Oct. 21, 2031, 4 PM	60	41	85	116.37

Figure 12 shows grid information for the day with the first grid overload (October 21, 2031). The first overload in the baseline scenario occurs on October 21, 2031, at 4 PM. A total of 85 EVs are adopted in the grid, with 49 simultaneous charging EVs. The first overload has a size of 1.44 kW above the grid capacity. At this overload, the total charging load is 324.92 kW. The orange line in Fig. 12 shows the total electricity prices and that there is one peak-price period during winter due to the DSO tariff. However, the EVs are not considering the electricity price when charging (Traditional charging strategy, i.e., charging immediately at arrival) and the result from this is 60 overloads (as shown in Fig. 13) the year after the first overload. Nine additional EVs are adopted that year.

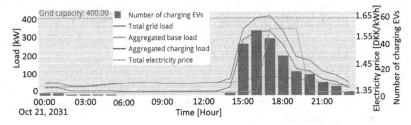

Fig. 12. Details of the day when the first overload occurs in the grid. (Color figure online)

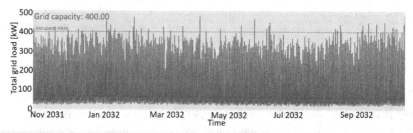

Fig. 13. Total grid loads the year after the first overload (October 21, 2031, to October 21, 2032).

By the end of 2030, 69 EVs were adopted. This resulted in an average annual emission in 2031 of 116.37 kg per EV. The individual emissions vary depending on the driving and charging behavior as evident from Fig. 14.

Fig. 14. The total annual CO2-eq. emissions from charging for 69 EVs in 2031.

7.2 Various Electric Vehicle Adoption Curves Scenario Results

The various EV adoption curve scenario considers the adoption of 775k and 1 million EVs in Denmark by 2030, based on the estimation and the political goal by [35], respectively. This scenario investigates when overloads can be expected with different EV adoptions. To evaluate the two EV adoption curves, the simulation follows the actual EV growth instead of the Poisson process used for the baseline scenario and avoids a situation where one curve adopts faster than another. The result (shown in Table 4) proves that the adoption curve with 1 million EVs by 2030 results in an eight-month earlier overload compared to the adoption curve with 775k EVs by 2030.

The average CO2-eq. emissions are close to the same as in the baseline scenario, which is no surprise since the emission levels are the same, but with fewer EVs adopted. For the 775k and 1 million EVs by 2030 experiments, the number of EVs at the end of 2030 is 30 and 42, respectively.

Both scenario experiments (775k and 1 million by 2030) are adopting slower than the adoption estimated based on the historical data (1.3 million by 2030) used in the baseline scenario. The slower adoption results in around 16 and 24 months later overload. The result indicates that the DSO's planning for dealing with grid overloads should be proactive in that the overloads might happen much earlier than the estimation, especially due to the rapid adoption of other distributed energy resources in the distribution grids.

Table 4. Key results for electric vehicle adoption curve scenario.

Experiment	Overload date	Number of overloads the year after the first overload	Days with overload	Total number of EVs at overload time	Avg. Total CO2-eq. emissions in 2031 [kg]
775k EVs by 2030	October 26, 2033, 4 PM	8	7	71	115.72
1 million EVs by 2030	February 20, 2033, 6 PM	15	10	77	114.21

8 Discussion

It is no supervise, the results show that the adoption curve based on historical data and used in the other scenarios has a faster adoption (1.3 million EVs by 2030) than the 1 million by 2030 adoption curve. The current Danish regulations are following the suggestions to reach 775k EVs by 2030 because reaching 1 million EVs is too costly. However, the Danish authorities are still aiming for 1 million EVs by 2030 and are reconsidering new regulations in 2025 to reach the goal [36].

The reason for considering the curve determined based on historical data for the case study area (Strib) is due to the relation between income and EV adoption as shown in Fig. 15. Figure 15 shows the EV population (left in the figure) and average personal income (right in the figure) for the municipalities in Denmark. The city of Strib (marked by the red circles) is part of one of the municipalities with a relatively high average income. Hence, a faster adoption in the city of Strib than the average adoption of the whole Danish population is expected.

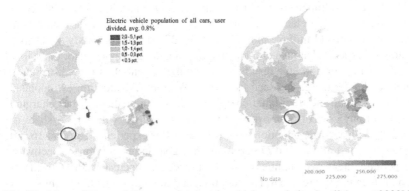

Fig. 15. Maps of Denmark illustrate the electric vehicle population [until August 2020] [37] (left) and the average personal income [DKK in 2017] in the municipalities [38] (right). (Color figure online)

As mentioned at the beginning of this paper, the average CO2-eq. emissions from cars in Denmark were around 2.72 tons annually in 2019. The simulation results showed that for EVs in 2031, the average emission is around 115 kg per EV. At this time, the electricity mix consists of a high share of green production, resulting in low emissions from consuming electricity. With 775k EVs in 2030 out of 3.25 million would result in 6.821 million tons of CO_2-eq. emission (calculation shown in Eq. 3). This does not meet the limit of 4.97 million tons necessary to satisfy the goal of a 30% reduction compared to 2005 emissions.

$$775,000 \cdot 115 \text{ kg} + (3,250,000 - 775,000) \cdot 2,720 \text{ kg} = 6.821 \text{ million tons} \quad (3)$$

For the scenarios with 1 million and 1.3 million EVs, this resulted in 6.235 and 5.456 million tons, respectively. This does also not satisfy the goal, as this requires at least 1.486 million EVs by 2030 to achieve a reduction of 30% of emissions compared to 2005. Alternatively, a larger reduction should be achieved in the other groups of the transport sector, since this calculation only considers passenger cars. As conventional cars also become more efficient, the exact number of EVs needed might be lower.

A faster adoption might help achieve the climate goal, however, this results in new challenges for the DSO. The results show that the current residential distribution grid can manage around 43–49 simultaneous charging EVs depending on the EV models and charging behavior. Each of these experiments uses different randomness (i.e., the random values generated in the simulation differ between scenarios) in the simulation due to the different adoption rates. However, with the conditions presented in the three scenarios, the overload is expected to occur between October 2031 and October 2033. The faster the EV adoption, the faster the grid experiences the first overload, with more frequent overloads following.

9   Conclusion

This paper investigates how different adoption curves of private electric vehicles (EVs) will impact the national climate goals with an example of Denmark's 2030 climate goals and the consequence to the electricity distribution grids. The results show that both considered EV adoptions (1 million and 775k EVs by 2030) will not satisfy the Danish obligation to the European Union's climate goal of reducing transport sector emissions by 30% by 2030. Furthermore, the results show that the current electricity distribution grids cannot handle the increasing load from EVs. With an EV adoption extrapolated from historical data and the traditional charging strategy (immediately start charging at arrival without any control), the overload will occur in 2031 with a 67% share of EVs in the grid. With a slower adoption, the first overload is experienced around 16 and 24 months later for the 1 million and 775k EVs by 2030 goal and estimation, respectively.

This paper enlightens uncertainties from two aspects: an unclear loading profile of distribution grids in the future due to EV adoption, and the indirect CO_2-eq. emissions from charging EVs. As stated in the introduction section, the majority of the literature is based on static modeling or assumption-based simulations without considering the real EV adoption curves and varying CO_2-eq. emissions from charging.

This paper applies multi-agent based simulation with two adoption curves, a common EV charging strategy (Traditional charging), various EV models, driving patterns, and CO_2-eq. emission data to capture the full ecosystem dynamics during a long-term period from 2020 to 2032 with a high resolution (hourly). The research provides a clear load profile of distribution grids as well as the indirect CO2-eq. emissions from EV charging in the future due to EV adoption.

In this research, the financial aspects of EV charging under different price structures are not considered and are recommended for future research to be included e.g., the financial impact from hourly electricity prices with dynamic tariffs. Moreover, this paper mainly focuses on the impact of EV adoption curves on the electricity distribution grids, therefore, only Traditional EV charging strategy is considered in the simulation. However, there are various EV charging algorithms discussed in the literature, e.g., centralized and decentralized EV charging which future research should take into consideration.

Acknowledgments. This research is part of the IEA ES Task 43 "Storage for renewables and flexibility through standardized use of building mass", funded by EUDP (case number: 134232-510227) and Digital Energy Hub funded by the Danish Industry Foundation.

References

1. Statistics Denmark. Statistics on the total number of cars in Denmark (2023). https://www.statistikbanken.dk/statbank5a/selectvarval/define.asp?PLanguage=0&subword=tabsel&MainTable=BIL52&PXSId=228908&tablestyle=&ST=SD&buttons=0. Accessed 26 June 2023
2. Danish Energy Agency: Klimastatus og –fremskrivning 2021 (KF21): Transportsektoren (2021)
3. Danish Energy Agency. Danish Climate Policies (2023). https://ens.dk/ansvarsomraader/energi-klimapolitik/fakta-om-dansk-energi-klimapolitik/dansk-klimapolitik. Accessed 26 June 2023
4. Ma, Z., Jørgensen, B.N.: Energy flexibility of the commercial greenhouse growers: the potential and benefits of participating in the electricity market. In: 2018 IEEE Power & Energy Society Innovative Smart Grid Technologies Conference (ISGT) (2018)
5. Fatras, N., Ma, Z., Jørgensen, B.N.: System architecture modelling framework applied to the integration of electric vehicles in the grid. In: González, S.R., et al. (eds.) DCAI 2020. AISC, vol. 1242, pp. 205–209. Springer, Cham (2020). https://doi.org/10.1007/978-3-030-53829-3_22
6. Habib, S., Kamran, M., Rashid, U.: Impact analysis of vehicle-to-grid technology and charging strategies of electric vehicles on distribution networks – a review. J. Power. Sources **277**, 205–214 (2015)
7. Dubey, A., Santoso, S.: Electric vehicle charging on residential distribution systems: impacts and mitigations. IEEE Access **3**, 1871–1893 (2015)
8. Howard, D.A., Ma, Z., Jørgensen, B.N.: Digital twin framework for energy efficient greenhouse industry 4.0. In: Novais, P., Vercelli, G., Larriba-Pey, J.L., Herrera, F., Chamoso, P. (eds.) ISAmI 2020. AISC, vol. 1239, pp. 293–297. Springer, Cham (2021). https://doi.org/10.1007/978-3-030-58356-9_34
9. Ma, Z., et al.: The application of ontologies in multi-agent systems in the energy sector: a scoping review. Energies **12**, 3200 (2019) https://doi.org/10.3390/en12163200
10. Ma, Z., Christensen, K., Jørgensen, B.N.: Business ecosystem architecture development: a case study of Electric Vehicle home charging. Energy Informatics **4**(1), 9 (2021). https://doi.org/10.1186/s42162-021-00142-y

11. Rogers, E.M.: Diffusion of Innovations. The Free Press of Glencoe (1962)
12. Ma, Z., et al.: Ecosystem-driven business opportunity identification method and web-based tool with a case study of the electric vehicle home charging energy ecosystem in Denmark. Energy Inform. **5**(4), 54 (2022)
13. Christensen, K., et al.: Agent-based decision making for adoption of smart energy solutions. In: 2019 IEEE Sciences and Humanities International Research Conference (SHIRCON) (2019)
14. Værbak, M., et al.: Agent-based modelling of demand-side flexibility adoption in reservoir pumping. In: 2019 IEEE Sciences and Humanities International Research Conference (SHIRCON) (2019)
15. Værbak, M., et al.: Agent-based simulation of implicit demand response adoption for water distribution system reservoirs. In: 2020 IEEE/SICE International Symposium on System Integration (SII) (2020)
16. Christensen, K., et al.: Agent-based simulation design for technology adoption. In: 2020 IEEE/SICE International Symposium on System Integration (SII) (2020)
17. Christensen, K., et al.: Agent-based modeling of climate and electricity market impact on commercial greenhouse growers' demand response adoption. In: 2020 RIVF International Conference on Computing and Communication Technologies (RIVF) (2020)
18. Adepetu, A., Keshav, S., Arya, V.: An agent-based electric vehicle ecosystem model: San Francisco case study. Transp. Policy **46**, 109–122 (2016)
19. Cui, X., et al.: Simulating the household plug-in hybrid electric vehicle distribution and its electric distribution network impacts. Transp. Res. Part D Transp. Environ. **17**(7), 548–554 (2012)
20. Doucette, R.T., McCulloch, M.D.: Modeling the prospects of plug-in hybrid electric vehicles to reduce CO2 emissions. Appl. Energy **88**(7), 2315–2323 (2011)
21. Luna-Ramirez, W.A., Fasli, M.: Bridging the gap between ABM and MAS: a disaster-rescue simulation using Jason and NetLogo. Computers **7**(2), 24 (2018)
22. Abar, S., et al.: Agent based modelling and simulation tools: a review of the state-of-art software. Comput. Sci. Rev. **24**, 13–33 (2017)
23. Statistics Denmark. Transport - Bestanden af personbiler efter drivmiddel, ejerforhold og tid (2022). https://www.statistikbanken.dk/bil611. Accessed 18 May 2022
24. FDM. Tre elbiler snupper hele kagen (2020). https://fdm.dk/nyheder/nyt-om-biler/2020-04-tre-elbiler-snupper-hele-kagen. Accessed 23 Apr 2020
25. Electric Vehicle Database. Tesla Model 3 Standard Range. https://ev-database.org/car/1060/Tesla-Model-3-Standard-Range. Accessed 23 Apr 2020
26. Electric Vehicle Database. Volkswagen e-Golf. https://ev-database.org/car/1087/Volkswagen-e-Golf. Accessed 23 Apr 2020
27. Electric Vehicle Database. Hyundai Kona Electric 39 kWh. https://ev-database.org/car/1239/Hyundai-Kona-Electric-39-kWh. Accessed 23 Apr 2020
28. Electric Vehicle Database. Renault Zoe ZE40 R110. https://ev-database.org/car/1236/Renault-Zoe-ZE40-R110. Accessed 23 Apr 2020
29. Electric Vehicle Database. Nissan Leaf. https://ev-database.org/car/1106/Nissan-Leaf. Accessed 23 Apr 2020
30. Perrig, A., et al.: SPINS: security protocols for sensor networks. Wireless Netw. **8**(5), 521–534 (2002)
31. Wu, Q., et al.: Driving pattern analysis for electric vehicle (EV) grid integration study. IEEE (2010)
32. Energinet. Energi Data Service - CO2 Emission (2022). https://www.energidataservice.dk/tso-electricity/co2emis. Accessed 18 May 2022
33. Danish Energy Agency. Basisfremskrivninger (2020). https://ens.dk/service/fremskrivninger-analyser-modeller/basisfremskrivninger. Accessed 18 May 2022

34. Hossein Pishro-Nik. 11.1.2 Basic Concpets of the Poisson Process. Introduction to probability, statistics and random processes 2022. https://www.probabilitycourse.com/chapter11/11_1_2_basic_concepts_of_the_poisson_process.php. Accessed 17 June 2022
35. The Danish Ministry of Taxation. Markant afgiftslettelse sikrer 775.000 grønne biler (2020). https://www.skm.dk/aktuelt/presse-nyheder/pressemeddelelser/markant-afgiftslettelse-sikrer-775000-groenne-biler/. Accessed 03 Mar 2022
36. Finansministeriet, et al.: Massiv CO2-reduktion og ambition om 1 mio. grønne biler i 2030 (2020). https://www.regeringen.dk/nyheder/2020/massiv-co2-reduktion-og-ambition-om-1-mio-groenne-biler-i-2030/. Accessed 08 June 2022
37. Statistics Denmark. 1 mio. elbiler i 2030 - hvor langt er der endnu? (2020). https://www.dst.dk/da/Statistik/nyheder-analyser-publ/nyt/NytHtml?cid=31064. Accessed 08 June 2022
38. Statistics Denmark. Fakta om indkomster og formue (2019). https://www.dst.dk/da/Statistik/nyheder-analyser-publ/bagtal/2019/2019-02-11-fakta-om-indkomster-og-formue. Accessed 08 June 2022

Brazilian Utilities' Invoice Data Understanding: Extraction, Data Standardization and Consumption Overview from Partner Universities

Hildo Guillardi Júnior[1]([✉])[iD] and Marcelo Stehling de Castro[2][iD]

[1] São Paulo State University (Unesp), São João da Boa Vista, São Paulo, Brazil
h.guillardi@unesp.br
[2] Federal University of Goiás (UFG), Goiania, Goiás, Brazil
mcastro@ufg.br

Abstract. Data plays a crucial role in understanding a scientific problem which includes those related to electrical micro, smart grids, and power consumption. In this scenario, one aspect that requires analysis is the consumption data that can be retrieve into the monthly utility invoices. However, the analysis of utility invoices in Brazil poses an unique challenge due to variations in invoice document formats across different services, utilities and contract types. This article addresses this challenge by developing a software based in Regular Expression to extract and standardized data from diverse invoice models. Through the establishment of a database and the use of a Business Intelligence platform, the retrieval and analysis of pertinent information have been significantly improved. The focus of this article is on understanding and extracting utility invoice data, including electricity, water, piped gas, and telephony services, which have direct or indirect impacts on natural resources and human well-being. The analysis is carried out on public buildings in Brazil, specifically those associated with the São Paulo Center for Energy Transition Studies (CPTEn). The data presented in this paper encompasses consumption invoices from three universities: the State University of Campinas (Unicamp), São Paulo State University campus of São João da Boa Vista (Unesp-SJBV), and the Federal University of Goiás (UFG). It is important to note that all the analyzed information is publicly available under Brazilian law number 12 527 from November 18, 2011.

Keywords: Data understanding · Brazilian utility companies · Brazilian energy market

1 Introduction

Data became an important resource to comprehending various issues, particularly those associated with smart grids [1,2] and the services they offer. These services encompass not only electricity but also other utility services that

B. N. Jørgensen et al. (Eds.): EI.A 2023, LNCS 14468, pp. 20–32, 2024.
https://doi.org/10.1007/978-3-031-48652-4_2

directly or indirectly affect natural resource usage and human well-being, such as water, piped gas, and telephony. Within this context, the monthly consumption data of users, which Brazilian utility companies measure for each type of service, is one of the key datasets that necessitates to analysed.

The analysis of historical consumption patterns, along with future projections, can yield valuable insights and actions to reduce household energy burdens [3]. This analysis can also contribute to enhancing efficiency in resource utilization, including water, energy, and other resources [4]. Moreover, it can inform strategies to decrease costs by aligning consumption with contract conditions and analyzing utility competitors.

While these analyses could benefit all consumers [5], this article focuses on data extraction of invoice documents of selected Brazilian public buildings of the partner universities in the project of the São Paulo Center for Energy Transition Studies (*"Centro Paulista de Estudos da Transição Energética"* - CPTEn), as pilot study to be expanded to other public buildings.

The data presented in this paper is a compilation of consumption invoices for water, piped gas and electricity from the State University of Campinas (Unicamp), São Paulo State University campus of São João da Boa Vista (Unesp-SJBV) and Federal University of Goiás (UFG) for the year 2022. All information presented in those documents are public available under Brazilian law number 12 527 from November 18, 2011 [6].

It is known that the electricity service alone accounts for approximately 51% of the Brazilian public building administration budget [7]. Moreover, there is an ongoing debate about how the government should handle sporadic connections and honor related bills [8,9]. The goal of this work is to understand the data of the invoices related to common services used by public buildings and to provide user-friendly framework of visualization and analysis to enable public administrations to make data-driven policy.

This paper is organized as follows: Sect. 2 provides an introduction to the fundamental aspects of the Brazilian utility market organization and Sect. 2.1 delves into the specifics of the Brazilian electrical market and different contract types. Section 2.2 shows technical trading rules of the invoices data into a proposed database (DB). Section 3 enrolls the consumption of the partner universities in the year of 2022 using the proposed methodology, and Sect. 4 concludes the article.

It is important to highlight that the processes described in this paper were achieved by developing software tools to prune the potential for human error in the data extraction, checking and merging processes.

2   Brazilian Utilities Market

Water, gas, telephony and electricity are considered essential services for the Brazilian population, and the law prohibits private companies from directly monopolizing these sectors. Moreover, there are cases where certain services remain under public control, such as the provision of water services in small cities through municipal autarchies. In other instances, private companies receive government authorization to operate as utilities and are allowed to commercially provide specific services within a designated geographic region.

These utilities bear the responsibility of maintaining the quality standards of the services they offer: ensuring the absence of water impurities, maintaining appropriate gas pressure, ensuring telephony and internet baud-rate, electricity voltage, and keeping service interruptions at a minimum standard. They also have to provide consumers a monthly consumption information in the form of invoices, which can be delivered via mail or through digital channels (Fig. 1).

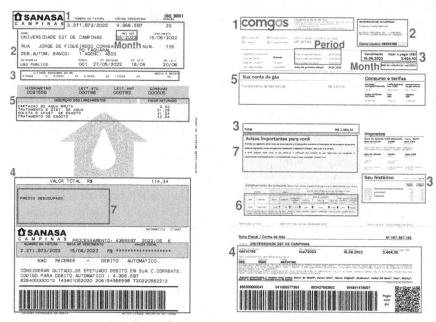

(a) Water SANASA invoice of Unicamp (2022-May).

(b) Piped gas Comgas invoice of Unicamp (2022-May).

Fig. 1. Water and piped gas consumption invoice examples of utilities that supply Unicamp with highlighted data.

In Brazil there are a minimum 27 piped gas companies and over 56 water utility and autarchies [10] operating across 5568 cities. Within the São Paulo State alone, which is the region of interest for the CPTEn, there are 645 cities [11] served by 2 piped gas companies and at least 3 major water companies, excluding the autarchies and municipal water supply authorities. Each utility/company/autarchy/municipal authority is exclusive responsible for a unique region and there is no multiple supply option unless by the internet providers.

As shown in the water (Fig. 1a) and piped gas (Fig. 1b) invoices examples, each utility have it own invoice template but they all contain a minimum information:

1. Utility company identification;
2. User identification;
3. Actual and, sometimes, past consumption (m^3 unit in this case);
4. Monetary amount to pay in Brazilian currency (BRL) and automation data (barcode for bank Automated Teller Machines or it correspondent number sequence);
5. Description of partial costs associated with the service;
6. Service index information: water impurities, gas pressure and temperature;
7. Messages from utility company to consumer.

2.1 Brazilian Energy Market and Contract

The electrical energy market and contract in Brazil, with more than 50 companies [12], is more intricate than the water and gas sectors. The energy contracts vary depending on the consumer category: **Residential consumers** typically have low-voltage connections; **Industrial consumers** can have either low-voltage or high-voltage connections, depending on their energy requirements; **Rural consumers** which including farms, agricultural facilities, and public water pumping consumers, they may have low-voltage or high-voltage connections, depending on their specific needs for water treatment and irrigation. This creates different invoices documents in the same utility (Figs. 2 and 3).

In addition, there are two types of markets: the **Captive market** and the **Free market**, for consumer that may buy kW direct in producer auctions. The tariff structures in both markets consider factors such as consumption levels, time of use, and potential subsidies being split into:

- **Conventional** is the base contract applied to every consumer up to 500kW of power demand in the installation. They stays under the captive market regulation;
- **Seasonal Green** is a contract for bigger consumer that may cause a relevant impact on the power grid. This consumer pay different price of energy (BRL/kW h) in the three-hour sequential time of bigger consumption in Brazil (usually close to 6pm but may vary between Brazilian regions). This contract also pays a amount for energy availability reservation, the maximum kW estimated that the installation may require from the power grid. This type of consumers are connected to the grid under high voltages and it power factor is monitored;
- **Seasonal Blue** is a tariff type for bigger consumer that the seasonal green and it interference affects the grid administration in such way that is required a value of energy demand for the peak-period and other for out such time;
- **White** contract is an optional tariff system introduced by the Brazilian Electricity Regulatory Agency (ANEEL) in 2018 that the Conventional consumer may sign. It ensure a small price (BRL/kW h) out of the peak hour with the disadvantage of bigger price in the peak hour consumption [13].

Although the conventional electricity invoice (Fig. 2a) contain similar information to water and piped gas invoices (1 to 7) with the differences reside on the facts of the consumption being measured in kW h and the service index in min of interruption time. Consumers in the free market (Fig. 2), typically with high energy demand, are forced to chosen between the seasonal contracts. While they pre-pay for a specific amount of energy in kW h, they are still subject to seasonal contracts in terms of transmission and grid usage costs (information 8 to 9).

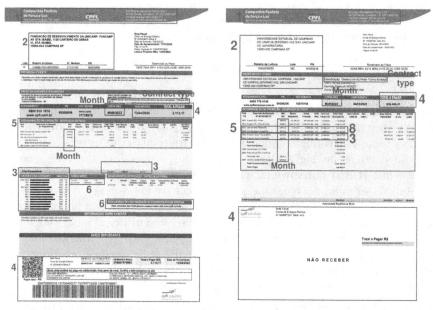

(a) Conventional CPFL invoice of Unicamp (2022-Mar).

(b) Seasonal green free market CPFL invoice of Unicamp (2022-Mar).

Fig. 2. Electricity invoice examples of utilities that supply Unicamp with highlighted base (1 to 7) and specific data (8 to 9).

Additionally the electrical energy invoice have additional charges described as the tariff flags that over price the amount of kW when the Brazilian system of thermometric generation is activated.

The seasonal electricity invoices (Fig. 3) related invoices have a bunch information extra information compared with the conventional one. This extra data are enrolled bellow:

8. Contracted demand (in and out of peak hours for the seasonal blue) and fine by trespass the demand value(s);
9. Reactive power consumption out and inside the peak and/or fine by trespass the power factor restriction value.

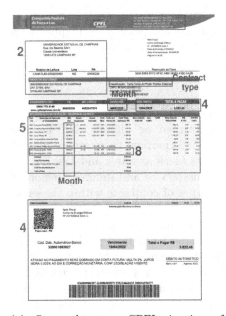

(a) Seasonal green CPFL invoice of Unicamp (2022-Mar, page 1).

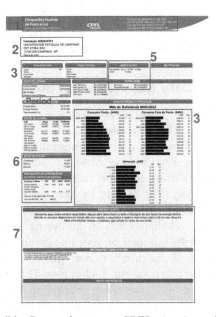

(b) Seasonal green CPFL invoice of Unicamp (2022-Mar, page 2).

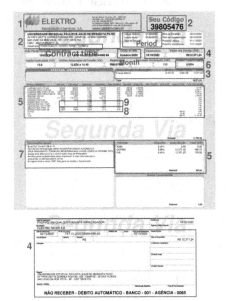

(c) Seasonal green Elektro invoice of Unesp (2022-Oct).

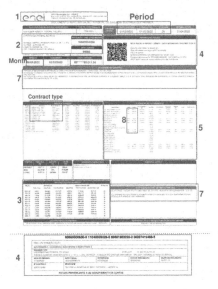

(d) Seasonal blue Enel invoice of UFG (2022-Mar).

Fig. 3. Electricity invoice examples of utilities that supply Unicamp, Unesp and UFG with highlighted base (1 to 7) and specific data (8 to 9).

The energy invoices may also include information about on-site generation. Due to the cost of energy transportation, the utility company typically purchases the generated kilowatts at a lower price than it is sold to consumer.

2.2 Data Extraction and Storage

In Brazil, consumers receive monthly invoices that provide a consumption report. These invoices can be received in printed or digital PDF file *via* email. However, despite containing mandatory information, there are significant variations between invoices for different services (such as water and gas, Fig. 1), invoices from different utilities within the same service and different region of operation (Fig. 3), and invoices for different types of contracts within the same service and utility (Fig. 2).

The challenge lies in analyzing these documents, as it requires extracting data with minimal human interference and standardizing field names to ensure consistent meanings across different utility document models. In this work, Regular Expression techniques [14] were utilized in Python programming language [15] to create extraction modules for each distinct file model that internally execute the follow logic sequence [16]:

1. Converts the PDF file to string;
2. Identify the company (name, address, ...) and it service (water, gas, electricity);
3. Get the user data (name, address, contract / provision number, ...);
4. Extract the consumption and payment values;

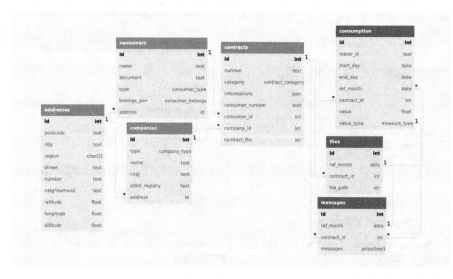

Fig. 4. DB for invoice data store: relational tables (blue) and temporal data (red). (Color figure online)

5. Validate the partial values with total one and other duplicated values present at the document as a safety to check the software integrity;
6. Output the data as standardized JSON that populate DB.

The DB maintains historical consumption records, service indices, and other crucial data extracted from the invoice files. It serves as the foundation for generating analysis. The extracted data is modelled within the DB structure shown on Fig. 4, facilitating efficient retrieval and analysis of information of two types:

- Relational tables (in blue) to keep the relation between `companies`, `consumer`, provision `contracts` and `address`;
- Time series (in red) to store the `consumption` data (consumption it self in each own physical unit, amount paid, service indexes, demand, *etc*), `messages` and link to stored `file` invoice.

The DB organization allows geographic interpretation of the `consumers` and `companies` addresses, `contract` category, company to consumers communication (`messages`), and manual file checking by inspecting the files linked into the `files` table. It is possible get the `consumption` `value` by each period (`start_day` and `end_day`) and even the identification of the physical equipment who measured this data (`meter_id`).

3   Results

The results presented were generated by a DB populated through extracting data from the invoice documents and an automated procedure [17]. The accompanying charts (Figs. 5 to 7) were created using the Microsoft® Power BI™ business intelligence platform.

The charts display the total consumption (m³ or kW h) and amount paid (BRL) by month in the year of 2022 for water services, piped gas and electricity.

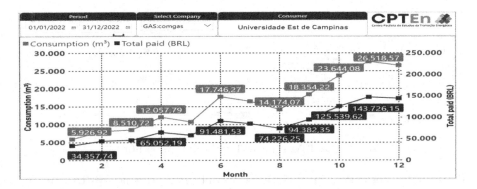

Fig. 5. Piped gas consumption in m³ and monetary in Brazilian currency (BRL) for month at Unicamp, supplied by COMGAS utility.

The analysis take into account that Unicamp have 4 *campi* with the large unique campus and only one with the free market electricity contract, UFG have 5 *campi* and Unesp-SJBV corresponds to only one campus of the numerous *campi* of Unesp present at 24 cities of São Paulo Brazilian Region.

Among the three universities analyzed, only Unicamp has piped gas supply (Fig. 5). The gas is utilized in the main campus located in the (in Barão Geraldo district) to the internal restaurants and hospital services.

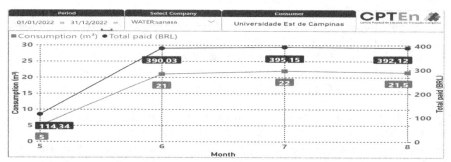

(a) Unicamp, supplied by SANASA water utility.

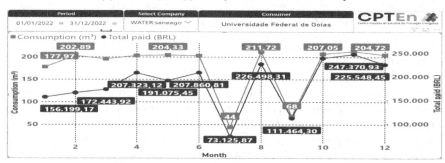

(b) UFG, supplied by SANEAGO water utility.

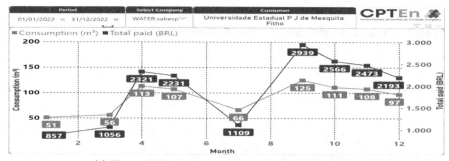

(c) Unesp-SJBV, supplied by SABESP water utility.

Fig. 6. Water consumption in m^3 and monetary in Brazilian currency (BRL) for month at each university and its region utility.

There has been a noticeable increase in gas consumption due to recent investments in green energy renovation projects in the last 3 years [18].

Figure 6 shows the water consumption for the three universities in analysis which reveals some data missing, particularly during the initial months of 2022

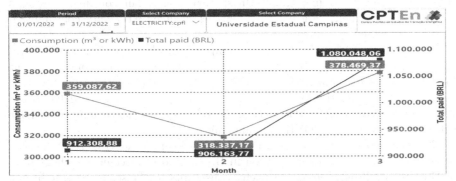

(a) Unicamp supplied by CPFL electricity utility.

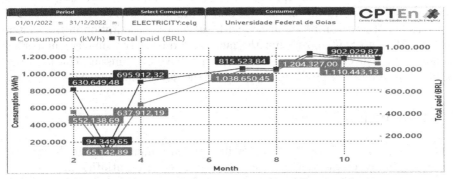

(b) UFG supplied by Enel electricity utility / Equatorial group.

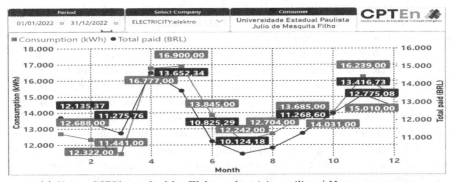

(c) Unesp-SJBV supplied by Elektro electricity utility / Neoenergy group.

Fig. 7. Electricity consumption in kW h and monetary in Brazilian currency (BRL) for month at each university and its region utility.

for Unicamp (Fig. 6a) due some invoice incompatibility with the developed software. It also indicates possible missing data in September for UFG (Fig. 6b), because that is only expected a lower water consumption in July due to the university vacation period. Moreover, an increase in water prices is evident for SANEAGO utility, as the total paid line rate is increasing despite the almost constant consumption line trend. Unesp-SJBV, as small consumer, presents a seasonal component (Fig. 6c) that matches with its electricity consumption (Fig. 7c) discussed in sequence.

Figure 7 shows the electricity consumption of the three universities and despite the missing data, particularly in Unicamp (Fig. 7a), some important insights are possible. For example, UFG presents a increasing consumption rate and a lower value in the March (Fig. 7b), probably caused by the delay in the January vacation, which took place in March, due to the resumption scholar calendar caused by the COVID-19 pandemic.

The seasonal component in Unesp-SJBV consumption (Fig. 7c) evidences the influence of the summer vacation in Brazil (end of December to beginning of March), resulting in lower electricity consumption. Consequently, the higher consumption is observed in April to May, likely attributed to increased demand for air conditioning during the hottest non-vacation months of the year.

This hypothesis can be confirmed with the lower consumption in the winter months (July to September) and the fact that, due to the smaller number of buildings and invoices, Unesp-SJBV does not have any missing consumption data or interpretation problems reported by the developed software.

4   Conclusion

The analysis of utility invoices in Brazil poses an unique challenge due to the variations in invoice file templates across different services, utilities and contract types. However, through the development of a software in Python language with the utilization of Regular Expression techniques, it have been possible to overcome this challenge and extract standardized data from diverse invoice models with not human interference.

The establishment of a DB model has greatly enhanced the retrieval and analysis of relevant information through a Business Intelligence platform. The friendly use of the interface based in charts can empowers the universities to gain valuable insights of its consumption patterns, identify opportunities for reducing energy burdens, improve resource efficiency and optimize cost-saving strategies mainly when talking about pre-paid electricity and demand control.

Despite the missing data, significant consumption trends can still be identified. These include the influence of seasonal variations, the impact of air conditioner usage in Unesp-SJBV, the initiative to transition Unicamp to a greener energy matrix by the extensive use of natural gas and the issues caused in delay of scholar year begin of UFG.

No much can be said about the Unicamp electricity and water consumption due invoices missing and software miss-interpretation. But it can be affirmed that the software's data cross-validation using the partial tables and duplicated values into one document guaranteed that not wrong consumption values was insert into the DB.

Further advancements in this development could lead to a more efficient, sustainable, and data-driven approach to decision-making in energy-saving measures. Moreover, these practices could be expanded to other universities and the Brazilian public sector, ensuring widespread benefits.

Additional tables of environment variables and consumption prevision can be included into the DB allowing data crossing to expanding the consumption planing for a better energy transition.

Acknowledgements. This publication has been supported by Research Foundation of the State of São Paulo (FAPESP) under the grant #2020/16635-9, #2021/11380-5 as part of the effort of the São Paulo Center for Energy Transition Studies (CPTEn) and #2023/11784-4.

References

1. Bhattarai, B.P., et al.: Big data analytics in smart grids: state-of-the-art, challenges, opportunities, and future directions. IET Smart Grid **2**(2), 141–154(13) (2019). https://digital-library.theiet.org/content/journals/10.1049/iet-stg.2018.0261, publisher: Institution of Engineering and Technology
2. Ghorbanian, M., Dolatabadi, S.H., Siano, P.: Big data issues in smart grids: a survey. IEEE Syst. J. **13**(4), 4158–4168 (2019)
3. Drehobl, A., Ross, L., Ayala, R.: How high are household energy burdens (2020)
4. Charlier, D., Risch, A., Salmon, C.: Energy burden alleviation and greenhouse gas emissions reduction: can we reach two objectives with one policy? **143**, 294–313, publisher: Elsevier
5. Ghisi, E., Gosch, S., Lamberts, R.: Electricity end-uses in the residential sector of Brazil. Energy Policy **35**(8), 4107–4120 (2007). https://www.sciencedirect.com/science/article/pii/S0301421507000559
6. Brazilian Government: Law of access to public interest information (in Portuguese) (2021). http://www.planalto.gov.br/ccivil_03/_ato2011-2014/2011/lei/l12527.htm
7. Transparency portal (2023). https://portaldatransparencia.gov.br/funcoes/25-energia?ano=2018
8. Commission approves obligation for the public sector to purchase items with low energy consumption (in Portuguese) (2022). https://www.camara.leg.br/noticias/
9. Proposal obliges the government to pay for water and electricity in street markets (in Portuguese) (2022). https://www.camara.leg.br/noticias/
10. Geller, H., Jannuzzi, G.d.M., Schaeffer, R., Tolmasquim, M.T.: The efficient use of electricity in Brazil: progress and opportunities. Energy Policy **26**(11), 859–872 (1998). https://www.sciencedirect.com/science/article/pii/S0301421598000068
11. Brazilian Institute of Geography and Statistics (IBGE): territorial areas and 2022 census (in Portuguese) (2022). https://www.ibge.gov.br/geociencias/organizacao-do-territorio/estrutura-territorial/15761-areas-dos-municipios.html
12. Piai Paiva, J.C., Jannuzzi, G.D.M., de Melo, C.A.: Mapping electricity affordability in Brazil. Utilities Policy **59**, 100926 (2019). https://www.sciencedirect.com/science/article/pii/S0957178718302431

13. Companhia Paulista de Força e Luz (CPFL): White Tariff (in Portuguese) (2023). https://www.cpfl.com.br/tarifa-branca. Accessed 27 June 2023
14. Stubblebine, T.: Regular Expression Pocket Reference: Regular Expressions for Perl, Ruby, PHP, Python, C, Java and. NET. O'Reilly Media, Inc. (2007)
15. Van Rossum, G., Drake, F.L.: Python 3 Reference Manual. CreateSpace, Scotts Valley (2009)
16. Guillardi Júnior, H.: Utility invoice br - extrator de dados de faturas de concessionárias do brasil (2022). https://busca.inpi.gov.br/pePI/servlet/ProgramaServletController?Action=detail&CodPedido=38963
17. Patil, A., Soni, M.: Hands-on Pipeline as Code with Jenkins: CI/CD Implementation for Mobile, Web, and Hybrid Applications Using Declarative Pipeline in Jenkins (English Edition). BPB PUBN (2021)
18. Partnership between Unicamp and Comgás will reduce greenhouse gas emissions at the university by 10.1% (in Portuguese). https://www.unicamp.br/unicamp/noticias/2022/04/26/parceria-da-unicamp-e-comgas-ira-reduzir-em-101-emissao-de-gases-de-efeito

Distributed Energy Resources and EV Charging Stations Expansion Planning for Grid-Connected Microgrids

Tayenne Dias de Lima[1] , Cleberton Reiz[1] , João Soares[2(✉)] ,
Fernando Lezama[2] , John F. Franco[1] , and Zita Vale[2]

[1] São Paulo State University, Ilha Solteira 15385-000, Brazil
{tayenne.lima,cleberton.reiz,fredy.franco}@unesp.br
[2] GECAD, LASI, Polytechnic of Porto, 4200-072 Porto, Portugal
{jan,flz,zav}@isep.ipp.pt

Abstract. The intensification of environmental impacts and the increased economic risks are triggering a technological race towards a low-carbon economy. In this socioeconomic scenario of increasing changes and environmental concerns, microgrids (MGs) play an important role in integrating distributed energy resources. Thus, a planning strategy for grid-connected MGs with distributed energy resources and electric vehicle (EV) charging stations is proposed in this paper. The developed mathematical model aims to define MG expansion decisions that satisfy the growing electricity demand (including EV charging demand) at the lowest possible cost; such decisions include investments in PV units, wind turbines, energy storage systems, and EV charging stations. The objective function is based on the interests of the MG owner, considering constraints associated with the main distribution grid. A mixed-integer linear programming model is used to formulate the problem, ensuring the solution's optimality. The applicability of the proposed model is evaluated in the 69-bus distribution grid. Promising results concerning grid-connected MGs were obtained, including the enhancement of energy exchange with the grid according to their needs.

Keywords: Energy storage systems · EV charging stations · microgrids planning · renewable generation

1 Introduction

1.1 Motivation

The recent trend toward decentralization and decarbonization of power systems is remarkable. Concern about environmental impacts has driven a strong worldwide movement towards a new era of power systems. Policies such as the Paris Agreement [1] have collaborated and encouraged electric mobility and renewable energy sources as an alternative to carbon-based fuel systems. Thus, in recent years, the adoption of new loads such as electric vehicles (EV), the integration of renewable generation, distributed generation, and energy storage systems (ESSs) has grown worldwide [2]. In this new world

B. N. Jørgensen et al. (Eds.): EI.A 2023, LNCS 14468, pp. 33–48, 2024.
https://doi.org/10.1007/978-3-031-48652-4_3

scenario, the microgrid (MG) concept has emerged. A widely cited definition in the literature was established by [3], defining MGs as follows:

> *"A group of interconnected loads and distributed energy resources within clearly defined electrical boundaries that acts as a single controllable entity with respect to the grid. A microgrid can connect and disconnect from the grid to enable it to operate in both grid-connected or island mode".*

According to this definition, the boundary separating the MG from the main grid must be clearly identified; MGs control their resources and can operate connected to the external grid [4] or in isolated mode [5]. These operation modes have different goals. For example, in the latter, each MG seeks to reduce its own generation cost. On the other hand, MGs that are connected to the grid can interchange electricity with the main grid and/or nearby MGs [6].

According to [7], three main factors have encouraged the development of grid-connected MGs: (1) Economic benefits: MGs can avoid or postpone reinforcements in the distribution grid by integrating distributed energy resources (DERs). (2) Clean energy integration: Renewable energy generation such as photovoltaic (PV) and wind generation depend on weather conditions, and their generation variability can cause problems for power systems. Thus, MGs are designed to deal with this issue, using storage systems to balance generation and loads locally. (3) Energy security: MGs can improve resilience and reliability by providing energy to priority loads such as hospitals, fire departments, and communication systems, among others.

In this context, MGs have emerged as a flexibility tool in active distribution grids and this concept contributes to the EV sustainable charging, since microgrids use renewable energy to charge EVs. A microgrid allows EV users to reduce peak demand on the grid and adapt their energy consumption to times when energy costs are lower. Furthermore, microgrids can simplify EV charging by providing adequate charging facilities, thus making EV charging more affordable [8]. For this purpose, the MG must have an adequate planning and control system to ensure the quality of the energy supply to customers [9]. Therefore, MGs with EV charging stations (EVCSs) play an important role in modern power systems. Thus, appropriate models and methods must be developed to adequately accommodate this new infrastructure.

1.2 Literature Review

MGs can operate autonomously [5] or be connected to the network. This literature review addresses grid-connected MGs [4, 10, 11] and planning of EVCS [12, 13], which are the focus of this paper. A complete review of [4, 10–13] is presented below.

Reference [4] presents a game-based model for the long-term planning of a distribution grid with several connected MGs under the retail electricity market. In that model, the interests of the DSO and MG investors are considered, namely the DSO is responsible for the operation and expansion of the distribution grid. On the other hand, MG investors are responsible for expanding and controlling DERs. The power exchange between the MG and DSO has been addressed. Finally, the bi-level planning problem is transformed into a mixed-integer linear programming (MILP) model easily solved via a commercial solver.

A stochastic multi-objective approach for the expansion planning of a grid-connected MG has been proposed in [10] considering a long-term planning horizon. Such an approach aims to maximize reliability and profit and minimize costs (investment and operation costs). That planning strategy defines the capacity and type of renewable generation, dispatchable generation, and ESSs connected to the MG. As in [4], power exchange with the utility has been modeled in [10], and the problem is solved via the Benders decomposition method.

In [11], a long-term planning model for MGs under uncertainties related to demand growth (including EV demand) has been proposed. The information gap decision theory method was used to deal with these uncertainties. Cost minimization is adopted as the objective function to address costs related to operation and investment, EV charging costs, and power exchange costs between the MG and the main grid. Also, MG expansion alternatives include PV units and ESSs. Then, the problem is formulated as a MILP model and solved via CPLEX.

A mixed integer linear programming model has been proposed to solve the planning of EVCSs in reference [12]. This model considers the multi-period approach and addresses the uncertainties related to EV demand and renewable generation. Planning of EVCS is also covered in [13]. In this proposal, the authors aim to highlight under which conditions the adoption of DERs becomes more convenient compared to investments in network reinforcement. An important contribution of this proposal is to include battery technical properties and degradation in the optimization model.

According to the literature review, it is possible to reach the following conclusions:

- Most of the reviewed works address the interchange of electricity between MGs and the main grid [4, 10, 11]. Also, PV, wind turbines (WT) units, and ESSs are the most adopted DER technologies.
- A DC power flow is used to model the operation of distribution grids [4, 11]. However, such a formulation is unsuitable [14], since these models simplify the operation of distribution grids, ignoring, for example, reactive power flow and power losses [4, 11]. Furthermore, the reference [10] does not consider power flow constraints.
- None of the proposals addresses the fast-charging stations planning in grid-connected microgrids.

In this context, a stochastic optimization model for the planning of grid-connected MGs with DERs and EVCSs is proposed in this work. In contrast to [4, 10–13], this paper addresses the planning of EVCS in MGs. Furthermore, the operation of grid-connected MGs is formulated through an AC power flow (ACPF), [4, 10, 11, 13]. This paper aims to define MG expansion decisions satisfying the growing electricity demand (including EV charging demand) at the lowest possible cost. Such decisions include investments in PV units, WT units, ESS, and EVCS. The objective function of the planning problem is based on the interests of the MG owner, considering constraints associated with the main distribution grid.

A MILP model is used to formulate the planning problem, ensuring the solution's optimality. Finally, Table 1 compares the model proposed here and the previous approaches.

Table 1. Comparison between this work and the previous approaches.

Reference	MG investments				ACPF	Carbon constraint
	PV units	WT units	ESSs	EVCSs		
[4]	✓	✓	✓	–	–	–
[5]	–	✓	✓	–	–	–
[10]	✓	✓	✓	–	–	–
[11]	✓	–	✓	–	–	–
[12]	✓	✓	–	✓	✓	–
[13]	✓	–	✓	✓	–	–
This work	✓	✓	✓	✓	✓	✓

✓ Considered; -: Not considered; WT: Wind turbine; EVCS: ESS: Energy storage system; EV charging stations; ACPF: AC power flow.

1.3 Paper Contributions and Organization

The main objectives and contributions of this paper are:

- A stochastic optimization model for planning grid-connected MGs with DERs and EVCSs, where the grid operation is formulated through an AC power flow.
- A joint planning strategy for EVCSs, PV units, WT units, and ESSs for several MGs. This planning approach model is formulated as a MILP and solved using commercial solvers. Thus, the solutions' optimality is guaranteed.
- Inclusion of environmental constraints in the model, aiming at a low carbon development strategy.

The rest of the work is organized as follows: The proposed model for the MG planning problem and the uncertainty model are presented in Sect. 2. Section 3 describes the case studies and results of the proposed model applied to the 69-bus distribution grid, and conclusions are presented in Sect. 4.

2 Planning Strategy for Grid-Connected MGs with Fast Charging Stations

This section describes the mathematical formulation of the proposed stochastic model for planning grid-connected MGs with DERs and EVCSs. Moreover, the uncertainty model related to electricity demand, electricity price, EV charging demand, solar irradiation, and wind speed is described here. Finally, the proposed optimization model is based on the following assumptions: (i) The grid-connected MG operation is represented by an AC linear power flow model in which the loads are modeled as constant powers; (ii) A set of scenarios represents the annual variation in electricity demand, EV demand, PV generation, wind generation, and electricity price; (iii) The planning horizon is divided into p periods; (iv) The original model is converted to an equivalent MILP model using the piecewise f-function.

2.1 Objective Function

The objective function of the problem is described in (1) and minimizes the following costs: Investments costs (IC_p) (2) related to EVCSs, PV units, WT units, and ESSs. Operational costs (OC_p) (3), related to the operation and maintenance of PV units, WT units, and ESSs, cost of MG load curtailed, and cost of power exchange between MG and the external network. The function $f(\tau, \lambda) = \frac{1-(1+\tau)^{-\lambda}}{\tau}$ permits the estimation of present values.

$$\min \sum_p (I_p + O_p)(1 + \tau)^{-(p-1)\lambda} \tag{1}$$

where:

$$
\begin{aligned}
IC_p = &\sum_r \sum_c (C^{\text{evcs}} x^{\text{evcs}}_{r,p} + C^{\text{ch}}_c N^{\text{ch}}_{r,c,p}) + \sum_u C^{\text{pv}}_u N^{\text{pv}}_{u,p} \\
&+ \sum_w C^{\text{wt}}_w x^{\text{wt}}_{w,p} + \sum_b C^{\text{es}}_b N^{\text{es}}_{b,p}; \forall p
\end{aligned}
\tag{2}
$$

$$
\begin{aligned}
OC_p = &\sum_s \pi_s d_s f(\tau, \lambda) \Bigg(\sum_u C^{\text{op,pv}} P^{\text{pv}}_{u,s,p} + \sum_k C^{\text{op,wt}} P^{\text{wt}}_{k,s,p} \\
&+ \sum_b C^{\text{op,es}-} P^{\text{es}-}_{b,s,p} + \sum_b C^{\text{op,es}+} P^{\text{es}+}_{b,s,p} \\
&+ \sum_m C^{\text{lc}} P^{\text{lc}}_{m,s,p} + \sum_m C^{\text{ep}}_s P^{\text{ex}}_{m,s,p} \Bigg); \forall p
\end{aligned}
\tag{3}
$$

2.2 Constraints

This planning problem is subject to a) Steady-state operation constraints, b) operational limits, c) DERs model, d) EVCS model, and e) environmental constraint, which are described below.

a) Steady-state operation constraints
The set of constraints (4)–(9) defines the steady-state operation of the distribution grid. The active and reactive power balance in the distribution grid is determined by (4) and (5). Constraints (6) and (7) represent the power balance in the MGs. Constraints (8) and (9) represent the application of Kirchhoff's second law. Constraint (10) determines that the power exchange between the distribution grid and each MG is equal to the power flow between the branch that connects the grid to the MG; if $P^{\text{ex}}_{m,s,p} < 0$, the MG will supply power to the grid, otherwise ($P^{\text{ex}}_{m,s,p} > 0$) the grid will supply power to the MG. Finally, the model is originally a nonlinear expression that is linearized by utilizing the piecewise f-function to determine the sum of $(P_{ij,s,p})^2 + (Q_{ij,s,p})^2$, employing Γ blocks. This linearization is described in detail in [15].

$$
\begin{aligned}
&\sum_{kg} P_{kg,s,p} - \sum_{gj}(P_{gj,s,p} + R^L l_{gj} I^{\text{sqr}}_{gj,s,p}) + P^s_{g,s,p} \\
&= P^D_{g,p} + P^{\text{ex}}_{m,s,p}; \forall g, s, p, m \in m^c
\end{aligned}
\tag{4}
$$

$$\sum_{kg} Q_{kg,s,p} - \sum_{gj}(Q_{gj,s,p} + X^L l_{gj} I^{sqr}_{gj,s,p}) + Q^s_{g,s,p} \tag{5}$$
$$= Q^D_{g,p} + P^{ex}_{m,s,p}; \forall g, s, p, m \in m^c$$

$$\sum_{km} P_{km,s,p} - \sum_{mh}(P_{mh,s,p} + R^L l_{mh} I^{sqr}_{mh,s,p}) + P^{pv}_{m,s,p} + P^{wt}_{m,s,p} + P^{es+}_{m,s,p}$$
$$- P^{es-}_{m,s,p} + P^{lc}_{m,s,p} = P^D_{m,p} f^D_{s,p} + D^{evcs}_{m,s,p} + P^{ex}_{m,s,p}; \forall m, s, p \tag{6}$$

$$\sum_{km} Q_{km,s,p} - \sum_{mh}\left(Q_{mh,s,p} + X^L l_{mh} I^{sqr}_{mh,s,p}\right) + P^{pv}_{m,s,p} + P^{wt}_{m,s,p}$$
$$+ Q^{lc}_{m,s,p} = Q^D_{g,p} + Q^{ex}_{m,s,p}; \forall m, s, p \tag{7}$$

$$V^{sqr}_{i,s,p} - V^{sqr}_{j,s,p} = [2(R^L P_{ij,s,p} + X^L Q_{ij,s,p})l_{ij}$$
$$+ Z^{L2} l^2_{ij} I^{sqr}_{ij,s,p}]; \forall i, s, p \tag{8}$$

$$V^{sqr}_{j,s,p} \hat{I}^{sqr}_{ij,s,p} = f(P_{ij,s,p}, \Gamma) + f(Q_{ij,s,p}, \Gamma); \forall ij, s, p \tag{9}$$

$$P^{ex}_{m,s,p} = \sum_{gm} P_{gm,s,p}; \forall m \in m^c, s, p, \tag{10}$$

b) Operational limits

Equations in the set (11)–(15) determine the operational limits for the distribution system. By constraints (11) and (12), respectively, voltages at nodes and current through circuits are bound. Constraints (13) and (14) define the active and reactive power flow limits through circuit *ij*. Moreover, the square of the apparent power ($\varrho^{sqr}_{d,s,p}$) supplied by the substation is determined by (15).

$$\underline{V}^2 \le V^{sqr}_{i,s,p} \le \overline{V^2}; \forall i, s, p \tag{11}$$

$$0 \le I^{sqr}_{ij,s,p} \le \overline{I^2_{ij}}; \forall ij, s, p \tag{12}$$

$$|P_{ij,s,p}| \le \overline{VI}_{ij}; \forall ij, s, p \tag{13}$$

$$|Q_{ij,s,p}| \le \overline{VI}_{ij}; \forall ij, s, p \tag{14}$$

$$\varrho^{sqr}_{n,s,p} = f(P^s_{n,s,p}, Q^s_{n,s,p}, \Gamma); \forall n, s, p \tag{15}$$

c) DERs model

Constraints (16)–(25) represent the operation and investment limits of DERs. Constraint (16) limits the number of PV units in each candidate bus. The limits of active and reactive power by PV units are shown in (17) and (18). There will only be one WT unit installed at each bus, according to constraint (19). The operational limits of active/reactive power by WT units are presented in (20) and (21). The number of ESSs that can be allocated to each bus over the course of the planning period is limited by constraint (22). Additionally, according to the converter's capacity, constraints (23) and (24) provide limits on an ESS's charging and discharging power. Finally, constraint (25) is used to estimate the charging and discharging processes of an ESS in each time block.

$$\sum_p N_{u,p}^{\text{pv}} \leq \overline{N}_u^{\text{pv}}; \forall u \tag{16}$$

$$0 \leq P_{u,s,p}^{\text{pv}} \leq f_s^{\text{pv}} \overline{P}_u^{\text{pv}} \sum_{t=1}^{P} N_{u,t}^{\text{pv}}; \forall u, s, p \tag{17}$$

$$\left| Q_{u,s,p}^{\text{pv}} \right| \leq P_{u,s,p}^{\text{pv}} \text{tg}\left(\cos^{-1}\left(\varphi^{\text{pv}} \right) \right); \forall u, s, p \tag{18}$$

$$\sum_p x_{w,p}^{\text{wt}} \leq \overline{N}_u^{\text{pv}}; \forall w \tag{19}$$

$$0 \leq P_{w,s,p}^{\text{wt}} \leq f_s^{\text{wt}} \overline{P}_w^{\text{wt}} \sum_{t=1}^{P} x_{w,t}^{\text{wt}}; \forall w, s, p \tag{20}$$

$$\left| Q_{w,s,p}^{\text{wt}} \right| \leq P_{w,s,p}^{\text{wt}} tan\left(cos^{-1}\left(\varphi^{\text{wt}} \right) \right); \forall w, s, p \tag{21}$$

$$\sum_p N_{b,p}^{\text{es}} \leq \overline{N}_b^{\text{es}}; \forall b \tag{22}$$

$$0 \leq P_{b,s,p}^{\text{es}-} \leq \sum_{t=1}^{P} P_b^{\text{es}} N_{b,t}^{\text{es}}; \forall b, s, p \tag{23}$$

$$0 \leq P_{b,s,p}^{\text{es}+} \leq \sum_{t=1}^{P} P_b^{\text{es}} N_{b,t}^{\text{es}}; \forall b, s, p \tag{24}$$

$$\sum_{s^{\varpi}} d_s \left(\eta^{\text{es}-} P_{b,s,p}^{\text{es}-} - \frac{1}{\eta^{\text{es}+}} P_{b,s,p}^{\text{es}+} \right) = 0; \forall b, bl, p \tag{25}$$

d) EVCS model

Constraint (26) ensures that only one charging station will be allocated for each bus. The number of EV chargers assigned to each bus is limited by constraint (27). Constraint (28) ensures that an EVCS's maximum capacity is not exceeded by the EV charging demand. Besides, the demand at charging stations coincides with the demand from EVs in each MG, according to constraint (29) Finally, constraint (30) ensures that at least one EVCS is installed in each MG.

$$\sum_p x_{r,p}^{\text{evcs}} \leq 1; \forall r \tag{26}$$

$$\sum_p N_{r,c,p}^{\text{ch}} \leq \overline{N}_c^{\text{ch}}; \forall r, c \tag{27}$$

$$D_{r,s,p}^{\text{evcs}} \leq \sum_{t=1}^{P} N_{r,c,t}^{\text{ch}} P_c^{\text{ch}}; \forall r, c, s, p \tag{28}$$

$$\sum_{r \in Mi} D_{r,s,p}^{\text{evcs}} = \sum_{m \in Mi} D_{m,s,p}^{\text{ev}}; \forall r, M, s, p \tag{29}$$

$$\sum_{r \in Mi} x_{r,p}^{\text{evcs}} \geq 1; \forall M, p \tag{30}$$

e) Environmental constraint

Carbon emissions related to energy supplied by the grid are limited by (31).

$$\sum_p \sum_n \zeta_n^s P_{n,s,p}^s \leq \overline{EM}; \forall n, s, p \tag{31}$$

2.3 Uncertainty Model

Uncertainties related to electricity demand, solar irradiation, wind speed, and electricity price are modelled through discrete scenarios by using historical data. The uncertainty related to the EV charging demand is modelled using the algorithm presented in [15]. Scenario reduction is necessary to achieve computational tractability. For this purpose, the k-means method (available in MATLAB) has been used. This approach, which is frequently used to solve planning problems [16], preserves the correlation between uncertain data. Details of the uncertainty model are described in [15].

3 Numerical Results

A 69-bus distribution grid has been employed to evaluate the proposed optimization model. This adapted network has a nominal voltage of 12.66 kV, a planning horizon of ten years (two periods of five years each), and three MGs. The allowed voltage ranges are 0.95 p.u (lower limit) and 1.05 p.u (upper limit). The chargers installed in EVCSs have capacities of 50 kW (fast charger) and 150 kW (super-fast charger) at USD 28,401 and USD 75,000, respectively [17]. MGs can sell their surplus generated energy, and when the power provided by the DERs in the MGs is insufficient to meet their demand, the MGs can buy energy from the grid. The ESS has the energy to power (E/P) ratio of 4 h with a capacity of 250 kW/1000 kWh, an investment cost of USD 241,750 (USD 189/kWh and USD 211/kW) [18]. In addition, all data used in the case studies are available in [19].

In AMPL, the mathematical model was implemented, and CPLEX was employed to solve it. The simulations were performed using a DELL PowerEdge T430 computer with an Intel Xeon E5-2650 processor and 64 GB of RAM. The following case studies were used to analyze the proposed model:

Case I) Planning strategy considering islanded MGs.
Case II) Planning for grid-connected MGs without investments in ESS.

Case III) Similar to Case II, with the difference of considering investment in ESSs.

Regarding carbon emissions, the proposed planning obtained the following results: no carbon emissions (Case I), 8742.99 tons (Case II), and 8488.34 tons (Case III). Moreover, the computational time for Cases I, II, and III was 2005.48 s, 79.92 s, and 396.13 s, respectively. A summary of the main costs of the proposed planning is presented in Table 2. Note that Case III, which includes investments in PV units, WT units, EVCSs, and ESSs, obtained the lowest total cost. Cases I and II costs are 391.59% and 1.71% higher than Case III, respectively.

Table 2. Summary of main costs for Cases I, II, and III.

Case	I	II	III
Investment costs (10^3 USD)			
PV units	10,385.70	13,899.00	15,368.00
WT units	19,451.06	16,000.00	16,000.00
EVCSs	545.00	495.87	495.87
ESSs	3,618.36	–	300.22
Total investment	34,000.12	30,394.87	32,164.09
Operational costs (10^3 USD)			
DER O&M	2,043.68	277.84	366.02
MGL	13,372.39	621.71	0.00
Total operational	15,416.07	899.55	366.02
Cost of energy exchange between the MG and external grid (10^3 USD)			
EPG	0.00	664.34	657.54
ESG	0.00	19,123.32	20,568.33
Balance	0.00	18.458,98	19,710.79
Total cost	49,416.19	12,835.44	12,619.32

In contrast to Case III, Case I defines the planning decisions for islanded operation of MGs. This case without external grid support had the highest investment cost, with a difference of approximately 3,605.25 10^3 USD and 1,836.03 10^3 USD compared to Cases II and III, respectively. Furthermore, this case had a significantly higher cost of load curtailment (13,372.39 10^3 USD) compared to cases II (621.71 10^3 USD) and III (no load curtailment). Another important result in Table 2 is the cost of energy exchange between MGs and the external grid. Note that the MG sells much more energy than it buys from the grid; thus, in the energy transaction with the distribution network, the MG obtained a profit of 18.458,98 10^3 USD (Case II) and 19,710.79 10^3 USD (Case III), respectively. In Case I, there is no energy exchange with the grid since the MG operates in islanded mode. Finally, Table 3 summarizes the investments made for each case.

Table 3. Investment plans for cases I, II, and III

Case	I	II	III
PV units (bus i, units, period p)	28, 1, 1; 36, 3, 1; 38, 1, 1; 39, 2, 1; 45, 1, 1; 46, 2, 1; 53, 6, 1; 54, 3, 1; 55, 4, 1; 56, 6, 1; 57, 4, 1; 58, 4, 1; 59, 3, 1; 60, 6, 1; 61, 9, 1; 62, 1, 1; 63, 3, 1; 36, 1, 2; 37, 1, 2; 38, 4, 2; 40, 1, 2; 46, 1, 2; 53, 4, 2; 54, 2, 2; 55, 2, 2; 57, 1, 2; 58, 2, 2; 59, 1, 2; 60, 1, 2; 61, 28, 2; 62, 3, 2; 63, 1, 2;	28, 50, 1; 46, 2, 1; 53, 71, 1;	28, 56, 1; 46, 2, 1; 53, 78, 1;
WT units (bus i, period p)	35, 1; 42, 1; 63, 1; 31, 2; 43, 2; 65, 2;	31, 1; 42,1; 63, 1; 65, 1;	31, 1; 42,1; 63, 1; 65, 1;
ESS (bus i, units, period p)	28, 1, 1; 45, 1, 1; 56, 1, 1; 60, 1, 1; 61, 1, 1; 62, 1, 1; 63, 3, 1; 60, 2, 2; 61, 2, 2; 62, 3, 2; 63, 1, 2;	-	53, 2, 2
Quick EV charger (bus i, units, period p)	55, 2, 1; 28, 2, 2; 46, 3, 2;	28, 1, 1; 46, 1, 1; 53, 1, 1;	28, 2, 1; 46, 2, 1; 53, 2, 1;
Super-fast EV charger (bus i, units, period p)	55, 1, 1; 28, 2, 2; 46, 2, 2;	28, 1, 1; 46, 1, 1; 53, 1, 1;	28, 2, 1; 46, 2, 1; 53, 2, 1;

The power exchange between MGs and grid is illustrated in Fig. 1, highlighting the power exchanged in each scenario and planning period for Cases II (Fig. 1.a) and III (Fig. 1.b). Analyzing this figure, some important issues can be highlighted:

- In both cases in period 1, the MGs buy energy from the grid in scenarios 10, 12, 14, 15, 26, 29, and 32; these scenarios are critical for MGs since there is no energy generation by PV units. Also, the energy provided by other DERs technologies is not enough to supply the demand. Thus, grid support is needed to ensure the energy supply in the MGs.

- In period 2, the demand growth causes an increase in energy purchase in scenarios 10, 12, 14, 15, 26, 29, and 32 in Case II. Furthermore, in scenarios 16, 27, and 30 the MGs buy energy from the grid, in contrast to period 1. In addition, it is important to highlight that the energy sale by MGs in period 2 is reduced due to the increased demand.

- In general, in period 2, the demand growth causes an increase in the purchase of energy from the grid, except for scenarios 12 and 14, which in Case 3 reduce the power supplied from the grid to the MG compared to period 1 (from 504.71 kW to 441.9 kW in scenario 12; from 536.62 kW to 232.32 kW in scenario 14), due to an investment of 2 ESSs in period 2 of Case III.
- In contrast to Case II, Case III invested in ESSs in period 2. As a result, Case III is less dependent on grid support, reducing energy purchases compared to Case II, in period 2. On the other hand, Case II generally sells more energy in scenarios with photovoltaic generation due to the lack of storage systems. Thus, MGs in Case II sell the excess energy produced by photovoltaic generation since this energy cannot be stored.
- All scenarios in which the grid supplies energy to the MGs are critical (solar irradiation is zero). Therefore, there is no energy generated by the PV units.

Finally, Fig. 2 illustrates the investment plan for Case III that provided the best outcomes in terms of the problem's objective function. Note that most investments are made in period 1. On the other hand, period 2 has only investment in two ESSs at bus 53.

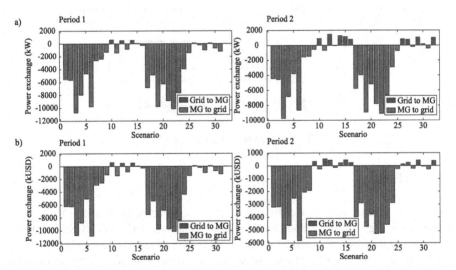

Fig. 1. Power exchange between MGs and the external grid for a) Case II and b) Case III.

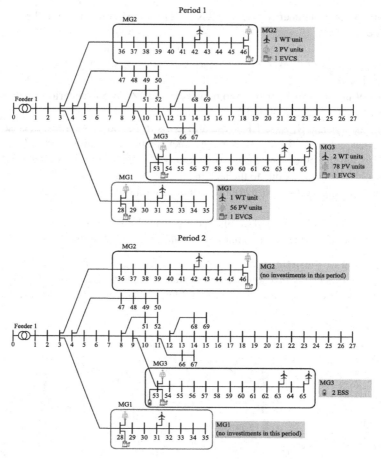

Fig. 2. Investment plan for Case III.

4   Conclusion

A stochastic optimization model for planning grid-connected microgrids (MGs) with distributed energy resources and electric vehicle charging stations (EVCSs) has been proposed in this paper. This model seeks to define MG expansion decisions, aiming at a low-carbon development strategy. Therefore, only clean generation alternatives were considered in the MG investment plan. The proposed model was tested and validated using the 69-bus distribution grid.

The current planning strategy has obtained promising results concerning grid-connected MGs. Parallel operation (grid connected operation) benefits MGs, allowing them to exchange energy with the external grid according to their needs or interests. The MG can sell the energy if the renewable generation units have excess production. On the other hand, in critical scenarios of low generation and high demand, the MG can buy energy from the grid. Additionally, integrating MGs into the grid allows adding more renewable energy sources (RES), contributing to environmental goals. The results also emphasize the importance of integrating RES with energy storage systems (ESSs). Using ESSs, MGs become more empowered and less dependent on network support.

This planning proposal can be easily adapted according to the planner's interests. For example, the adopted objective may maximize the MG investor's profit considering the revenues related to the energy transaction in the local and/or retail markets. Finally, future research may include: (i) Aspects related to reliability since MGs can be a promising strategy to improve continuity and quality of energy service; (ii) Energy transactions between MGs under a competitive market environment; (iii) Collaborative planning between DSO and MGs that meets the interests of both players, highlighting the impact of MGs on the expansion of the distribution system; (iv) Battery degradation model and its impact on planning decisions.

Acknowledgments. The present work has received funding from the Brazilian Federal Agency for Support and Evaluation of Graduate Education (CAPES) and through the FCT Portuguese Foundation for Science and Technology (2019.00141.CBM). We also acknowledge the work facilities and equipment provided by GECAD research center (UIDB/00760/2020 and UIDP/00760/2020) to the project team and CEECIND/00420/2022 (Joao Soares grant). Also, the Brazilian team acknowledges the scholarships granted from the Brazilian Federal Agency for Support and Evaluation of Graduate Education (CAPES), in the scope of the Program CAPES-PrInt, process number 88887.310463/2018-00, Mobility number 88887.570741/2020-00. Moreover, was supported by other Brazilian institutions, the Brazilian National Council for Scientific and Technological Development (CNPq)-Grant No. 409359/2021-1 and the São Paulo Research Foundation (FAPESP)-grants 2015/21972-6, 2018/08008-4, and 2022/03161-4.

Nomenclature

Indices and sets:

$b/u/r/w$	Index of possible locations for ESS/PV/EVCS/WT units allocation.
c	Index of EV charger types.
g/m	Index of grid/ MG buses.
$i/k/h/ij$	Index of buses/circuits.
M	Set of MGs.
m^c	Index of MG buses connected to the distribution grid.
n	Index of substation buses.
p/t	Index of planning periods.
s/s^{ϖ}	Index of scenarios/scenarios s contained in block ϖ.

Parameters:

ζ_i^s	Energy emission rate supplied by grid.
$\eta^{es+/-}$	Efficiency rate of charging and discharging for ESSs.
λ	Number of years in each planning period.
π_s	Probability of scenarios.
$\varrho_{i,p}$	Apparent power demand at node i and period p.
τ	Interest rate.

Γ — Number of discretization blocks.

C_c^{ch} — Cost of EV charger type c.

C_s^{ep} — Cost of energy exchange between MGs and external grid at node i.

C_b^{es} — Cost of ESS.

C^{evcs} — Installation cost for EVCS.

C^{lc} — Cost of MG load curtailment.

$C^{op,es+}$ — Costs associated with ESS discharge process operation and maintenance.

$C^{op,es-}$ — Costs associated with ESS charge process operation and maintenance.

$C^{op,pv}$ — Costs associated with PV unit operation and maintenance.

$C^{op,wt}$ — Costs associated with WT unit operation and maintenance.

C_u^{pv} — Cost of PV unit at bus u.

C_w^{wt} — Cost of WT unit at bus w.

$D_{m,s,p}^{ev}$ — EV aggregated demand, at bus m, scenario s, and period p.

d_s — Duration (hours) of scenario s.

$\overline{EM}$ — Maximum limit of CO_2 emissions.

f_s^D — Demand factor of scenario s.

f_s^{pv} — PV production factor of scenario s.

f_s^{wt} — WT production factor of scenario s.

$\overline{I}_{ij}$ — Maximum current of circuit ij.

l_{ij} — Length of circuit ij.

$\overline{N}_c^{ch}$ — Maximum number of EV chargers type c to be installed.

$\overline{N}_b^{es}$ — Maximum number of ESS to be installed at node b.

$\overline{N}_u^{pv}$ — Maximum number of PV units to be allocated at node u.

P_c^{ch} — Capacity of EV charger type c.

$P_{i,p}^D / Q_{i,p}^D$ — Active/reactive power demand at node i and period p.

$\overline{P}_b^{es}$ — Maximum active power capacity of ESS at bus b.

$\overline{P}_u^{pv}$ — Active power capacity of PV units at bus u.

$\overline{P}_w^{wt}$ — Active power capacity of WT units at bus w.

$\overline{V}/\underline{V}$ — Upper and lower voltage limits.

$R^L/X^L/Z^L$ — Conductor resistance/reactance/impedance.

Continuous variables:

$\varrho_{i,s,p}^{sqr}$ — Square of the apparent power provided by the substation at bus i, scenario s, and period p.

$D_{r,s,p}^{evcs}$ — Charging demand in EVCS at bus r, scenario s and period p.

$I_{ij,s,p}^{sqr}$ — Square of current through circuit ij in scenario s and period p.

$P_{ij,s,p}$ — Active power flow through circuit ij for conductor a in scenario s and period p.

$P_{b,s,p}^{es-/+}$ — Active power stored/ provided of ESS at bus b, scenario s, and period p.

$P_{m,s,p}^{ex}$ — Active power injected/absorbed by MGs at bus m, scenario s, and period p.

$P_{m,s,p}^{lc}$ — Active power related to load curtailment at bus m, scenario s, and period p.

$P_{u,s,p}^{pv}$ — Active power injected by PV at node u, scenario s, and period p.

$P_{w,s,p}^{wt}$ — Active power injected by WT at node w, scenario s, and period p.

$P^s_{i,s,p}$ Active power supplied by substation at node i, scenario s, and period p.

$Q_{ij,s,p}$ Reactive power flow through circuit ij in scenario ω and period p.

$Q^{ex}_{m,s,p}$ Reactive power injected/absorbed by MGs at bus m, scenario s, and period p.

$Q^{lc}_{m,s,p}$ Reactive power related to load curtailment at bus m, scenario s, and period p.

$Q^{pv}_{u,s,p}$ Reactive power injected by PV at node u, scenario s, and period p.

$Q^s_{i,s,p}$ Reactive power by the substation i at node d, scenario s, and period p

$V^{sqr}_{i,s,p}$ Square of the voltage at node i, scenario s, and period p.

Integer and binary variables:

$N^{ch}_{r,c,p}$ Integer variable representing the number of EV chargers at node r, type c and period p.

$N^{es}_{b,p}$ Integer variable representing the number of ESS at node b and period p.

$N^{pv}_{u,p}$ Integer variable representing the number of PV units at node u and period p.

$x^{evcs}_{r,p}$ Investment variable representing the installation of an EVCS at node r and period p.

$x^{wt}_{w,p}$ Investment variable representing the installation of an WT units at node w and period p.

References

1. United nations climate change (2019). https://unfccc.int/process-and-meetings/the-paris-agr eement/the-paris-agreement. Accessed 10 Oct 2019
2. IRENA: Future role of distribution system operators (2019). https://www.irena.org/-/media/ Files/IRENA/Agency/Publication/2019/Feb/IRENA_Landscape_Future_DSOs_2019.pdf? la=en&hash=EDEBEDD537DE4ED1D716F4342F2D55D890EA5B9A#:~:text=In. The future%2C DSOs will, and communication technologies (ICTs). Accessed 14 Feb 2023
3. Ton, D.T., Smith, M.A.: The U.S. department of energy's microgrid initiative. Electr. J. **25**, 84–94 (2012). https://doi.org/10.1016/j.tej.2012.09.013
4. Boloukat, M.H.S., Foroud, A.A.: Multiperiod planning of distribution networks under competitive electricity market with penetration of several microgrids, Part I: modeling and solution methodology. IEEE Trans. Ind. Inform. **14**, 4884–4894 (2018). https://doi.org/10.1109/TII. 2018.2807396
5. Hajipour, E., Bozorg, M., Fotuhi-Firuzabad, M.: Stochastic capacity expansion planning of remote microgrids with wind farms and energy storage. IEEE Trans. Sustain. Energy **6**, 491–498 (2015). https://doi.org/10.1109/TSTE.2014.2376356
6. Zidan, A., Gabbar, H.A.: Scheduling interconnected micro energy grids with multiple fuel options. In: Smart Energy Grid Engineering, pp. 83–99. Elsevier (2017)
7. Hirsch, A., Parag, Y., Guerrero, J.: Microgrids: a review of technologies, key drivers, and outstanding issues. Renew. Sustain. Energy Rev. **90**, 402–411 (2018). https://doi.org/10.1016/ j.rser.2018.03.040
8. Mohan, H.M., Dash, S.K.: Renewable energy-based dc microgrid with hybrid energy management system supporting electric vehicle charging system. Systems **11**, 273 (2023). https:// doi.org/10.3390/systems11060273
9. Reiz, C., De Lima, T.D., Leite, J.B., et al.: A multiobjective approach for the optimal placement of protection and control devices in distribution networks with microgrids. IEEE Access **10**, 41776–41788 (2022). https://doi.org/10.1109/ACCESS.2022.3166918

10. Shaban Boloukat, M.H., Akbari Foroud, A.: Stochastic-based resource expansion planning for a grid-connected microgrid using interval linear programming. Energy **113**, 776–787 (2016). https://doi.org/10.1016/j.energy.2016.07.099

11. Sun, K., Li, C., Peng, Q.: Planning of microgrid based on information gap decision theory. In: 2020 IEEE 4th Conference on Energy Internet and Energy System Integration (EI2), pp. 144–149. IEEE (2020)

12. de Lima, T.D., Franco, J.F., Lezama, F., et al.: Joint optimal allocation of electric vehicle charging stations and renewable energy sources including CO2 emissions. Energy Inform. **4** (2021). https://doi.org/10.1186/s42162-021-00157-5

13. Bordin, C., Tomasgard, A.: SMACS model, a stochastic multihorizon approach for charging sites management, operations, design, and expansion under limited capacity conditions. J. Energy Storage **26**, 100824 (2019). https://doi.org/10.1016/j.est.2019.100824

14. de Lima, T.D., Soares, J., Lezama, F., et al.: A Risk-based planning approach for sustainable distribution systems considering EV charging stations and carbon taxes. IEEE Trans. Sustain. Energy, 1–14 (2023). https://doi.org/10.1109/TSTE.2023.3261599

15. De Lima, T.D., Franco, J.F., Lezama, F., Soares, J.: A specialized long-term distribution system expansion planning method with the integration of distributed energy resources. IEEE Access **10**, 19133–19148 (2022). https://doi.org/10.1109/ACCESS.2022.3146799

16. Baringo, L., Conejo, A.J.: Correlated wind-power production and electric load scenarios for investment decisions. Appl. Energy **101**, 475–482 (2013). https://doi.org/10.1016/j.apenergy.2012.06.002

17. Nicholas, M.: Estimating electric vehicle charging infrastructure costs across major U.S. metropolitan areas. Int. Counc. Clean Transp. (11) (2019)

18. Mongird, K., Viswanathan, V., Balducci, P., et al.: Energy storage technology and cost characterization report I Department of Energy (2019)

19. De Lima, T.D., Reiz, C., Soares, J., et al.: Distributed energy resources and EV charging stations expansion planning for grid-connected microgrids: Study data (2023). https://docs.google.com/spreadsheets/d/1sUFRBoEwLYr47LSAD0NABv4bz0lyoJ90/edit?usp=sharing&ouid=116642585806249513780&rtpof=true&sd=true. Accessed 10 May 2023

Energy Forecasting

Comparison of Inputs Correlation and Explainable Artificial Intelligence Recommendations for Neural Networks Forecasting Electricity Consumption

Daniel Ramos, Pedro Faria[✉], and Zita Vale

GECAD - Research Group on Intelligent Engineering and Computing for Advanced Innovation and Development; LASI - Intelligent Systems Associate Laboratory, Polytechnic of Porto, Porto, Portugal
{dados,pnf,zav}@isep.ipp.pt

Abstract. The energy sector explores various paths to improve the energy management of buildings. Nowadays a frequent path is to schedule load forecasting activities due to the accessibility of reliable forecasting algorithms. Data scientists usually take advantage of a large historic of consumption with weekly patterns and sensors data presenting a higher correlation with the consumption variable. However, specialists in the explainable artificial intelligence area focus on studying the positive or negative impact of each variable to the prediction accuracy. In this paper, a correlation analysis evaluates in the first stage the most reliable sensors to be used during training and forecasting tasks. In the second stage, the Local Interpretable Model-Agnostic Explanations (LIME) explainable artificial intelligence method is applied to determine which features have a stronger positive or negative influence on the prediction accuracy. The training and forecasting tasks are supported in this paper by the forecasting algorithm Artificial Neural Networks. In the case study, a historic of two years and six months is used to estimate the consumption values of a targeted week considering periods of five minutes. The results section calculates the confidence of each sensor to the prediction accuracy provided by LIME method and compares the obtained insights with the correlation analysis. The results and conclusions sections state that the two sensors more correlated with the consumption variable either contribute negatively to the prediction performance or do not contribute at all on most test targets.

Keywords: Energy Management · Energy Sector · Explainable Artificial Intelligence · Prediction Accuracy

1 Introduction

The forecast of consumption patterns plays a crucial role in the energy management of buildings on different levels including the demand-side management [1]. In [2], for example, prediction activities are scheduled to optimize the energy dispatch of building energy systems for demand response. It is worth noting that the incentive of demand

© The Author(s), under exclusive license to Springer Nature Switzerland AG 2024
B. N. Jørgensen et al. (Eds.): EI.A 2023, LNCS 14468, pp. 51–62, 2024.
https://doi.org/10.1007/978-3-031-48652-4_4

response programs leads to the improvement of power grid flexibility and the reduction of energy costs [3].

Several forecasting algorithms of the machine learning field may be applied in various sectors of the building including ARIMA, SARIMA, XGBoost, and Random Forest [4]. Deep learning applications from the artificial intelligence domain can be enumerated as well for forecasting tasks including Artificial Neural Network, Deep Belief Network, Recurrent Neural Network, Elman Neural Network, Deep Recurrent Neural Network, Convolutional Neural Network and Nonlinear Autoregressive Network [5].

The prediction of electricity consumption in smart homes is approached in [6] with the support of past consumption data, inhabitants' actions and activities, and environmental data. The electricity consumption forecasting of office buildings is approached in [7] with the support of an artificial intelligence approach based on forecasting algorithms including artificial neural networks, support vector machines hybrid fuzzy inference systems, and Wang and Mendel's fuzzy rule learning method. The prediction of the aggregated load for residential and commercial buildings is approached in [8] with the support of artificial neural networks to compare the fore-casting performance of recurrent and non-recurrent networks. A hybrid deep learning model consisting of convolutional neural network and recurrent neural network is proposed in [9] to predict hourly energy consumption for smart buildings.

Obtaining reliable predictions is important to guarantee efficient energy management as well as to reduce energy costs [10]. It is possible to improve the forecasting accuracy in smart buildings with the support of feature selection strategies [11]. Another solution to reduce the forecasting error consists in optimizing the hyperparameters of the forecasting algorithm models [12]. The evaluation of forecasting models is valued in [13] as the selected forecasting model puts in question if it results in lower errors than other forecasting model alternatives. Explainable artificial intelligence (XAI) plays a crucial role in the interpretability of various forecasting algorithms [14]. Some explainable artificial intelligence (XAI) techniques are indicated in [15] including SHapley Additive exPlanations (SHAP), and Local Interpretable Model-Agnostic Explanations (LIME).

The motivation of this paper consists on understanding if the sensors more correlated with consumption patterns have a very positive contribution to the prediction performance with the support of the LIME explainable method. The sensors correlation analysis has been studied previously by the authors of this paper in [16]. This paper takes advantage of the LIME analysis on first stage to understand which features contribute most to the prediction performance with Artificial Neural Networks. The second stage is focused on the motivation of this paper which is to understand if the sensors more correlated with the consumption patterns had a very positive contribution to the prediction performance as seen through the LIME analysis. The use of Artificial Neural Networks in this scientific paper resides in resulting in lower forecasting errors than other forecasting algorithms such as K-nearest Neighbors as concluded in [16]. An annual historic of past consumption and sensors data with weekly patterns is trained to predict energy consumption patterns for a target week contextualized for periods of five minutes with the support of Artificial Neural Networks. The correlation analysis has been studied with the support of the Excel software while the training and the prediction with Artificial Neural Networks and the LIME explainable method have been run with Python programing language. These two crucial tasks have been supported by Python libraries including tensorflow and LIME respectively.

Following this introduction, Sect. 2 explains the different steps of the proposed methodology. Afterwards, Sect. 3 details the case study. Then, Sect. 4 displays the results. Finally, Sect. 5 presents the main conclusions of this research.

2 Methodology

This section explains the different steps of the proposed methodology. These include as illustrated in Fig. 1 the access to a historic dataset composed of consumptions and sensors data, a correlation analysis procedure, the training of data with the support of artificial neural networks algorithm, and a LIME analysis of the features contribution to the prediction performance.

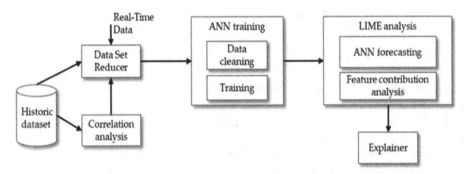

Fig. 1. Proposed two-stage methodology diagram.

The real-time data involves all the consumption and sensors data from an electrical building monitored in IoT devices contextualized for periods of five minutes. The historic dataset is composed of consumptions and sensors data for the intended peri-od for training and forecasting activities. The correlation analysis evaluates the sensors with higher influence on the consumption variable that should be added to the training data. The data set reducer excludes the sensors data not presenting a high correlation with the consumption variable.

The data resulted from the data set reducer procedure goes through a data cleaning procedure that reorganizes the data structure and values incoherencies to prepare the data for training and forecasting tasks and furthermore to improve the data reliability. The new data structure consists of consumptions and sensors data reorganized in an unique spreadsheet with consumption and sensors values associated to different data features separated in various columns. These data features consist of the following variables: year, month, day of the month, day of the weeks, hour, and minutes. Moreover, the content of the spreadsheet is contextualized for periods of five minutes from Monday to Friday. The data cleaning procedure has also detection and correction functions to improve the reliability of data. Firstly, the detection and correction of missing data gathers all the periods of five minutes lacking consumption or sensor values in the spreadsheet and associates these records with new values corresponding to previous entries. Secondly, duplicated records defined by the same data features are detected and transformed into unique records composed of the average of the consumption and sensors data. Lastly, the detection of outliers gathers records with consumption and sensors incoherencies described by incorrect readings made by the IoT devices. The detection of outliers is supported by the mean and standard deviation calculations as presented in Eq. 1 and Eq. 2 and validated with the if-then condition presented in Eq. 3.

$$M = \frac{\sum_{NPExact=NPActual-NPFrame}^{NPActual} V(NPExact)}{NPFrame} \tag{1}$$

- M – mean of V in NPFrame
- V(NPExact) – consumption/sensor value at NPExact
- NPActual – current number of period
- NPFrame – number of periods used as frame
- NPExact – exact number of period

$$SD = \sqrt{NPFrame^{-1} * \sum_{NPExact=NPActual-NPFrame}^{NPActual} (V(NPExact) - M)^2} \tag{2}$$

- SD – standard deviation of V in NPFrame
- M – mean in NPFrame
- V(NPExact) – consumption/sensor at NPExact
- NPActual – current period
- NPFrame – number of periods used as frame
- NPExact – exact number of period

$$V(n) \geq M + \varepsilon * SD \vee V(n) \leq M - \varepsilon * SD := V(n) = \frac{V(NPExact - 1) + V(NPExact + 1)}{2} \tag{3}$$

- V(NPExact) – consumption/sensor value at NPExact
- ε – error factor
- M – mean in NPFrame
- SDC – standard deviation of V in NPFrame
- NPActual – current period
- NPFrame – number of periods used as frame
- NPExact – exact number of period

The average and standard deviation are calculated for the consumption variable and for a frame used as basis respectively in Eq. 1 and Eq. 2. Afterwards, an if-then condition presented in Eq. 3, checks if the value of the consumption or sensor variable at an exact period is higher or equal to the calculated mean plus an error factor times the calculated standard deviation. The condition presented in Eq. 3 also checks if the value of the consumption or sensor variable at an exact period is lower or equal to the calculated mean minus an error factor times the calculated standard deviation. If the if-then condition presented in Eq. 3 is verified. Then the value the of the consumption or sensor variable at the exact period is replaced by the average of the value occurring in the previous and following periods. In the aftermath of the cleaning operations, a training function trains most of the data with the support of artificial neural networks algorithm. The value considered for the error factor was 2. The reason of why artificial neural network algorithm is applied is because this forecasting algorithm is recommended to deal with large amounts of data while other such as k-nearest neighbors and random forest despite their advantages are not so good to deal with big data.

The LIME analysis proposed in this methodology is supported by the theorical and practical explanations provided by [17]. Firstly, LIME is supported by a forecasting function to estimate consumption values for a large sequence of short periods with artificial neural networks algorithm. Secondly, a feature and contribution analysis integrated in LIME analyzes which features contributed positively or negatively to the prediction performance. The positive features contribution to the prediction performances means that the values of the features influence the prediction performance with a higher accuracy. On the other hand, a negative features contribution to the prediction performance means that the respective feature values influence a lower prediction accuracy. Afterwards, an explainer function takes place to compare the features contribution insights obtained with the two approached strategies: LIME analysis, and correlation study.

3 Case Study

The historical data of this case study is composed of consumption and sensors records monitored in a building with the support of IoT devices. The considered dataset for cleaning, training and forecasting activities is composed of a large historic from 22 May 2017 to 15 November 2019. This dataset is reused according to previous work developed from the authors of this paper. Furthermore, it should be noted that the prepared version of the dataset for cleaning, training, and forecasting activities is contextualized for periods of five minutes. Furthermore, it should be noted that although the monitored data is saved to the building database for periods of ten seconds, the prepared version of the dataset for cleaning, training, and forecasting activities is the result of data transformations from periods of ten seconds to periods of five minutes. Therefore, the training and forecasting procedures are contextualized for periods of five minutes. The building is composed of three zones, each one with three different rooms, each one with three different rooms. The training and forecasting activities occur for zone 1 of the building. The IoT sensors presented in zone 1 of the building are:

- One air quality sensor;
- One temperature sensor;
- One humidity sensor;
- One CO_2 sensor;
- Four movement sensors;
- Three door status indicators;
- Seven light power indicators.

The weekly consumption from 22 May 2017 to 15 November 2019 is illustrated in Fig. 2 considering a total of 1440 periods of five minutes due to the weekends exclusion. The reason about the weekends exclusion is because of the low consumption activity during the weekend. Furthermore, a total of 150 weeks illustrate the weekly consumption profile with unique and random colors. The consumption activity from week to week tends to result in different behaviors. This observation is clear in Fig. 2 as the consumption activity of each week highlighted with an unique color differs from the consumption activity of other weeks highlighted by other colors.

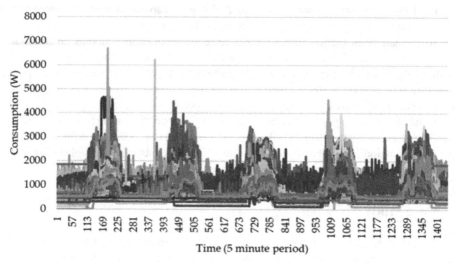

Fig. 2. Weekly consumption profiles from 22 May 2017 to 15 November 2019 contextualized for periods of five minutes and zone 1 of the building.

4   Results

This section presents all the results following the theorical explanation of the methodology and the detailing of the case study. Subsect. 4.1 explains the artificial neural networks configuration. Subsect. 4.2 compares the sensors contribution to the prediction performance with the support of LIME method to compare with the insights of a correlation analysis that concludes the sensors with higher influence on the consumption variable.

4.1   Forecasting

The ANN forecasting algorithm trains all the historic of consumptions and sensors data except the last week for periods of five minutes. Therefore, the time horizon of the training data is described by all periods of five minutes from 22 May 2017 to 8 November 2019. Furthermore, the selected sensors added to the input of the training data are the ones with higher correlation as concluded in the Subsect. 4.3. Therefore, the selected sensors are CO_2 and light intensity. The ANN architecture is composed of the parameterization model resulting in lower forecasting errors through different trial and errors scenarios as researched previously by the authors of this paper in [18]. Hence, ANN architecture is composed of a multilayered model with an input layer with twelve neurons connected to all the neurons of the first of two sequential hidden layers, each one with sixty-four neurons. The first and second hidden layer have their neurons connected to all the neurons of the other layer. Finally, all the neurons of the second hidden layer are connected to the only neuron presented in the output layer. The reason that ANN is configured with twelve neurons in the input layer is that the input of the training data is composed with ten consumption values contextualized for sequential periods of five minutes, and the two selected sensors known as light intensity and CO2 occurring in the same period of five minutes as the last consumption input. Furthermore, the reason that ANN is configured with only one neuron in the output layer is that the training output is composed of only one consumption contextualized for a period of five minutes. The epochs parameterization of ANN is assigned to five hundred. This means that ANN will apply the feedforward algorithm (to train the output) and the backpropagation algorithm (to update the weights) five hundred times. The epochs parameterization was assigned to the indicated value since the volume of consumption and sensors data is very high. Therefore, it is crucial to train both the feedforward and backpropagation algorithms many times. It should be noted however that an early stopping procedure is added to the ANN architecture to stop automatically the training before reaching the final five hundred times if no training improvements are detected within 20 sequential epochs. The method used for the feedforward algorithm is the gradient descent method with learning rate assigned to 0.001. The reason that the learning rate is very small is to allow a rigorous search for local minimums to improve the training accuracy of the variable.

4.2 Explanations

The LIME results expressing the positive and negative confidence of each one of the features (consumptions, light sensor, and CO2) are presented in Fig. 3 for scenario 1 and for twenty four different test targets with artificial neural networks algorithm.

The positive and negative confidence are marked respectively in orange and blue. Moreover, the consumptions labeled as C0 to C9 correspond to sequences of consumption input values precede the output consumption contextualized on periods of five minutes. The light sensor (labeled as DALI_LIGHT) and the CO2 (labeled as CO2) precedes the output consumption contextualized in a period of five minutes. The configuration of LIME uses an exponential kernel to calculate the Euclidean distances, and the mode assigned to the regression level to deal with quantitative measures.

The consumptions marked as C1, C4, C5, C6, C7 and C8 contribute more positively to the prediction. On the other hand, the consumptions labeled as C2, C3, and C9 contribute more negatively to the prediction. It is also worth noting that the light sensor and CO2 contribute negatively to most test targets. Some exceptions where the light sensor contributes positively to the prediction correspond to the test target labeled as t12 with the value 4.03, and to the test target labeled as t17 with the value 1.48. An exception where CO2 contributes positively to the prediction correspond to the test target labeled as t6 with the value 7.24.

Three test targets were selected to study the positive and negative impact for each feature in detail as provided by LIME method. To study with higher precision, a bar plot illustrates in Fig. 4, 5 and 6 the positive and negative impact of each feature respectively for the following test targets: t1, t12, and t24.

	C0	C1	C2	C3	C4	C5	C6	C7	C8	C9	DALI_LIGHT	CO2
t1	-27.80	27.61	40.30	23.00	-25.45		15.44	-19.12	-11.01	17.49		-8.68
t2	379.69	136.85	-6.30	-40.09	83.14	51.95		101.63	21.00	-24.75		12.73
t3	379.68	148.04	-11.99	-61.54	63.65	40.07	13.91	122.12	17.38	-31.23		
t4	29.19	137.15	-78.84	14.36	8.13	-40.41		114.19	8.65	-36.50	-7.15	
t5	38.12	-26.16	39.05	24.53	-19.69	-14.54		111.80	6.33	13.34		-19.56
t6	380.50	132.91	-72.10	-48.97	74.49	21.32		-12.94	-21.59		-4.50	7.24
t7	-109.60	-45.11	34.71	11.50	12.24	-9.89		16.61	22.52	-30.97	-13.89	
t8	393.25	129.17	-91.14	-55.37	75.60	29.98		119.58	23.28	-31.46		-24.87
t9	-21.63	32.68	18.63	23.60		12.62	-12.66	-22.79	7.52	-23.96		-15.57
t10	371.63	152.90	-45.19	-39.84	94.62	42.92	19.00	124.95		-29.98		18.37
t11	-24.74		49.73	26.00	-39.63	-33.14	10.04	-43.16	15.19	13.84		8.65
t12	104.03	-43.99	46.90	27.96	-10.58	37.65	21.21	-24.05			4.03	-3.17
t13	376.88	138.70	-78.03	-67.22	63.83	28.98		135.81	18.12	-24.35	-16.07	
t14	383.54	106.53	-64.96	-40.67	65.55	32.56	22.55	114.56	5.78	-33.35		
t15	-93.54	-39.29	40.41	13.13		9.10	6.46		14.70	-19.51	-2.90	-17.59
t16	391.40	125.93	-32.93	-59.15	74.44	32.48	-10.64	115.19	12.83	-33.09		
t17	-27.06	7.72	47.91		11.94	6.42		-13.50	-11.03	-3.75	1.48	-10.88
t18	389.65	137.69	-51.41	-46.94	81.20	43.12	12.38	112.19	17.35	-31.20		
t19	389.18	140.19	-78.37	-55.22	73.38	43.78		113.09	21.53	-44.39		-11.48
t20	396.85	128.50	-49.08	-54.73	70.94	14.15	15.42	-21.40	10.80			-12.59
t21	377.72	142.91	-23.93	-51.17	67.25	36.34		124.67	17.50	-26.24		-11.47
t22	379.83	144.75	-41.81	-56.38	78.75	26.41		115.44	14.02	-37.84	-9.92	
t23	387.38	139.87	-75.35	-50.14	75.02	37.82	6.52	122.67	15.69	-25.64		
t24	393.86	142.40	-79.13	-55.15	86.89	36.34	16.63	109.35	23.53	-36.44		

Fig. 3. LIME positive and negative confidence of each feature for scenario 1 and for different test targets with artificial neural networks algorithm.

Figure 4 shows that the features contributing more positively to the prediction are the consumptions marked as C2 with the value 40.30, C1 with the value 27.61, C3 with the value 23.00, C9 with the value 17.49, and C6 with the value 15.44. Moreover, the features that contribute more negatively to the prediction are the consumptions marked as C0 with the value 27.80, C4 with the value 25.45, C7 with the value 19.12, C8 with the value 11.01, and CO_2 with the value 8.68.

Figure 5 shows that the features contributing more positively to the prediction are the consumptions marked as C2 with the value 46.90, C5 with the value 37.65, C3 with the value 27.96, C6 with the value 21.21, and the light sensor with the value 4.03. Moreover, the features that contribute more negatively to the prediction are the consumptions marked as C0 with the value 104.03, C1 with the value 43.99, C7 with the value 24.05, C4 with the value 10.58, and CO_2 with the value 3.17.

Figure 6 shows that the features contributing more positively to the prediction are the consumptions marked as C0 with the value 393.86, C1 with the value 142.40, C7 with the value 109.35, C4 with the value 86.89, C5 with the value 36.34, C8 with the value 23.53, C6 with the value 16.63. Moreover, the features that contribute more negatively to the prediction are the consumptions marked as C2 with the value 79.13, C3 with the value 55.15, and C9 with the value 36.44.

As seen previously, the correlation analysis shows that light sensor and CO_2 are the variables with a stronger influence on the consumption, respectively with the values 0.8484 and 0.5403.

The correlation analysis studies the sensors with a stronger influence on the consumption variable. Table 1 studies the correlation of all the sensors with the consumption variable considering the time horizon and the context of the data detailed in the case study. These sensors are indicated in Table 1 evidencing the total PV, light intensity,

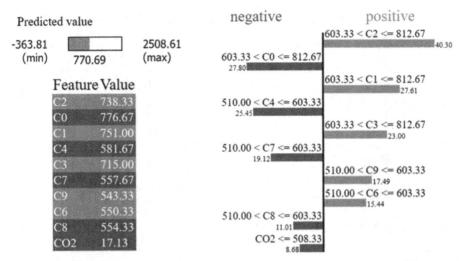

Fig. 4. LIME positive and negative confidence of each feature for scenario 1 and for different test targets with artificial neural networks algorithm.

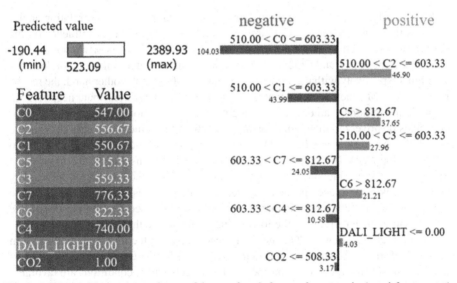

Fig. 5. LIME positive and negative confidence of each feature for scenario 1 and for target t1 with artificial neural networks algorithm.

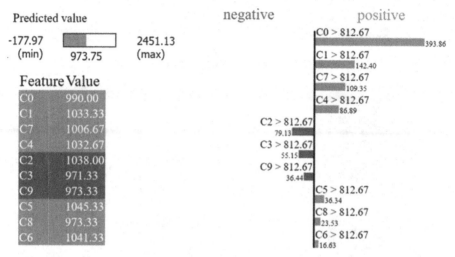

Fig. 6. LIME positive and negative confidence of each feature for scenario 1 and for target t24 with artificial neural networks algorithm.

CO_2, air quality, temperature, humidity, and light consumption. The correlation analysis shows that light sensor and CO_2 are the variables with a stronger influence on the consumption, respectively with the values 0.8484 and 0.5403. The correlation analysis shows that light sensor and CO_2 are the variables with a stronger influence on the consumption, respectively with the values 0.8484 and 0.5403. On the other hand, the results provided by LIME method show that the light sensor and CO_2 contribute negatively to the prediction or none at all on most test targets. A few exceptions where the light sensor contributes positively to the prediction is for t12 (with the value 4.03) and t17 (with the value 1.48). An exception where CO_2 contributes positively to the prediction is for t6 (with the value 7.24). The negative contribution of the light sensor and CO_2 on most test targets is understandable since artificial neural networks is the considered forecasting algorithm. Taking into account that the indicated algorithm is very effective for large volumes of data, the consumption inputs separated in a large sequence of periods of five minutes will contribute more to the forecasting performance than the sensors data.

Therefore, the adding of CO_2 and light sensor values to the input data will result in excessive information that will result in negative contribution to the forecasting performance on most test targets. Only on specific test targets where conditions are favorable to the sensors data, the adding of this additional data to the input will result in positively contribution to the forecasting performance.

Table 1. Correlation matrix of consumption and sensors data from 22 May 2017 to 15 November 2019 contextualized for zone 1 and periods of five minutes.

	Correlation							
Total consumption	1							
Total PV	0.3374	1						
Light intensity	0.8484	0.3681	1					
CO2	0.5403	0.4918	0.5677	1				
Air Quality	−0.2064	−0.3193	−0.2665	−0.2831	1			
Temperature	0.4178	−0.0132	0.2487	−0.0037	0.2205	1		
Humidity	0.0679	0.044	−0.0305	−0.0377	0.2348	0.296	1	
Light consumption	0.3376	0.2738	0.468	0.4154	−0.2326	−0.0568	−0.2516	1

5 Conclusions

This paper evaluates the sensors contribution to the forecasting performance of a building installed with IoT devices to compare the obtained insights with a correlation analysis studied previously by the authors of this paper. This evaluation conducted with the support of LIME analysis and the artificial neural networks forecasting algorithm concludes that the insights obtained are incompatible with the correlation analysis. The LIME analysis concludes that CO_2 and the light sensor have a positive contribution only on a small number of test targets. The insights of the correlation analysis contradict the observations of the LIME analysis since CO_2 and the light sensor had a stronger influence on consumption patterns than other sensor variables. This however can be explained since artificial neural networks are successful on dealing with large volumes of data. Therefore, the training of artificial neural networks will give more importance to the input consumptions contextualized in sequential periods of five minutes than the CO_2 and the light sensor occurring in the same period of five minutes that the last input consumption takes place. It is understandable therefore that the adding of CO_2 and light sensors data to the input will contribute positively to the forecasting performance only on specific test targets. As future work, the authors of this paper intend on researching with higher precision the conditions of the test targets that result in more accurate performances considering the sensors usage. Moreover, the authors of this paper intend to use additional explainable artificial intelligence methods to analyze the sensors contribution to the prediction performance.

Acknowledgments. This work has received funding from the EU Horizon 2020 research and innovation program under project IoTalentum (grant agreement No. 953442). The authors acknowledge the work facilities and equipment provided by GECAD research center (UIDB/00760/2020) to the project team. Daniel Ramos is supported by national funds through Fundação para a Ciência e a Tecnologia (FCT), Portugal government, Fundo Social Europeu

(FSE), and Por_Norte, with PhD grant reference 2022.12944.BD. Pedro Faria is supported by FCT, with grant CEECIND/01423/2021 CIND.

References

1. Khalil., M., McGough, S., Pourmirza, Z., Pazhoohesh, M., Walker, S.: Machine learning, deep learning and statistical analysis for forecasting building energy consumption — a systematic review. Eng. Appl. Artif. Intell. **115** (2022)
2. Li, H., Wang, S.: Two-time-scale coordinated optimal control of building energy systems for demand response considering forecast uncertainties. Energy **253** (2022)
3. Wang, H., et al.: A data-driven load fore-casting method for incentive demand response. Energy Rep. **8**(4), 1013–1019 (2022)
4. Hadri, S., Naitmalek, Y., Najib, M., Bakhouya, M., Fakhri, Y., Elaroussi, M.: A comparative study of predictive approaches for load forecasting in smart buildings. Procedia Comput. Sci. **160**, 173–180 (2019)
5. Abdulrahman, M., et al.: A review on deep learning with focus on deep recurrent neural network for electricity forecasting in residential building. Procedia Comput. Sci. **193**, 141–154 (2021)
6. Cuncu, E., Manca, M., Pes, B., Riboni, D.: Towards context-aware power forecasting in smart-homes. Procedia Comput. Sci. **198**, 243–248 (2022)
7. Jozi, A., Pinto, T., Marreiros, G., Vale, Z.: Electricity consumption forecasting in office buildings: an artificial intelligence approach. In: 2019 IEEE Milan PowerTech, Milan, Italy, pp. 1–6 (2019)
8. Almalaq, A., Edwards, G.: Comparison of recursive and non-recursive ANNs in energy consumption forecasting in buildings. In: 2019 IEEE Green Technologies Conference(GreenTech), Lafayette, LA, USA, pp. 1–5 (2019)
9. Jayashankara, M., Shah, P., Sharma, A., Chanak, P., Singh, S.K.: A novel approach for short-term energy forecasting in smart buildings. IEEE Sens. J. **23**(5), 5307–5314 (2023)
10. Rana, M., Sethuvenkatraman, S., Goldsworthy, M.: A data-driven approach based on quantile regression forest to forecast cooling load for commercial buildings. Sustain. Cities Soc. **76** (2022)
11. González-Vidal, A., Jiménez, F., Gómez-Skarmeta, A.: A methodology for energy multivariate time series forecasting in smart buildings based on feature selection. Energy Build. **196**, 71–82 (2019)
12. Khalid, R., Javaid, N.: A survey on hyperparameters optimization algorithms of fore-casting models in smart grid. Sustain. Cities Soc. **61** (2020)
13. Somu, N., Kowli, A.: Evaluation of building energy demand forecast models using multi-attribute decision making approach. Energy Built Environ. (2023)
14. Moon, J., Rho, S., Baik, S.: Toward explainable electrical load forecasting of buildings: a comparative study of tree-based ensemble methods with shapley values. Sustain. Energy Technol. Assess. **54** (2022)
15. Chung, W., Liu, C.: Analysis of input parameters for deep learning-based load prediction for office buildings in different climate zones using eXplainable artificial intelligence. Energy Build. **276** (2022)
16. Ramos, D., Teixeira, B., Faria, P., Gomes, L., Abrishambaf, O., Vale, Z.: Use of sensors and analyzers data for load forecasting: a two stage approach. Sensors **20**(12), 3524 (2020)
17. Radečić, D.: LIME: How to Interpret Machine Learning Models With Python. betterdata-science.com/lime/
18. Ramos, D., Khorram, M., Faria, P., Vale, Z.: Load forecasting in an office building with different data structure and learning parameters. Forecasting **3**, 242–255 (2021)

Deep Learning Models to Estimate and Predict the Solar Irradiation in Brazil

Wesley A. Souza[1]([✉]) [iD], Augusto M. S. Alonso[2] [iD], Luiz G. R. Bernardino[3] [iD],
Marcelo F. Castoldi[1], Claudionor F. Nascimento[4] [iD],
and Fernando P. Marafão[3] [iD]

[1] DAELE, Federal University of Technology - Paraná (UTFPR), Cornélio Procópio,
PR, Brazil
wesleyangelino@utfpr.edu.bra
[2] EESC, University of São Paulo (USP), São Carlos, SP, Brazil
[3] ICTS, São Paulo State University (UNESP), Sorocaba, SP, Brazil
[4] DEE, Federal University of São Carlos (UFSCar), São Carlos, SP, Brazil

Abstract. Solar irradiation is the backbone of photovoltaic power technologies and its quantization allows to optimize energy generation. However, solar irradiation can be difficult to detect, mostly due to the design and disposition of sensors, as well as their high cost. To address this limitation, this paper proposes a deep neural network-based model to estimate global solar irradiation by only relying on weather data, focusing on applications targeting the Brazilian territory. The model uses a deep neural network trained with data from the Brazilian National Institute of Meteorology (INMET), which includes 606 nationwide weather stations and over 39 million hourly records of meteorological variables cataloged from years 2010 to 2022. Thus, in this paper *i*) a deep neural network is used to estimate irradiation, and *ii*) a long short-term memory is used to predict solar irradiation considering different time granularities: 5 min, 30 min, 6 h, and 1 day. The results show a small error between the measured irradiation data and the calculated results with regard to the following six meteorological variables: time, temperature, relative humidity, wind speed, precipitation, and atmospheric pressure. Moreover, experimental validations conducted using a weather station set up by the authors demonstrate that the proposed models can accurately predict solar irradiation. Thus, the developed model stands as a promising approach for applications within the Brazilian perspective, improving the efficiency and reliability of solar energy generation.

Keywords: Solar irradiation · Deep learning · Weather station · Weather quantities

List of Abbreviations

AI	Artificial Intelligence
ANFIS	Adaptive Neuro-Fuzzy Inference System

© The Author(s), under exclusive license to Springer Nature Switzerland AG 2024
B. N. Jørgensen et al. (Eds.): EI.A 2023, LNCS 14468, pp. 63–82, 2024.
https://doi.org/10.1007/978-3-031-48652-4_5

ANN   Artificial Neural Network
ARMA   Autoregressive Moving Average
A-P   Angstrom-Prescott
DL   Deep Learning
DNN   Deep Neural Network
GAN   Generative Adversarial Networks
GEP   Gene Expression Programming
GRNN   Generalized Regression Neural Network
GRU   Gated Recurrent Unit
INMET   Brazilian National Institute of Meteorology
LSTM   Long Short-term Memory
MAD   Median Absolute Deviation
MAE   Mean Absolute Error
MAPE   Mean Absolute Percentage Error
MLP   Multilayer Perceptron
MSE   Mean Squared Error
PV   Photovoltaic
RBF   Radial Basis Function
RBFNN   Radial Basis Neural Network
RF   Random Forest
RNN   Recurrent Neural Network
SVM   Support Vector Machine
WRNN   Wavelet Recurrent Neural Networks

1   Introduction

The availability of energy supply is crucial for the economic and social development of any country, and producing electricity by means of sustainable generation sources has been playing a pivotal role in meeting the expected world demand for energy. Photovoltaic- (PV) and wind-based energy sources are examples of alternative resources that have supported the reduction of fossil fuel usage and decreased the need for nuclear power installations. Consequently, due to the advancement of such technologies, the world is becoming less dependent on power generation means, which may harm the environment or human life while producing electricity [1]. Hence, such alternative sources are shedding light on the new energy paradigm [2].

Particularly in Latin America, PV power plants have presented an accentuated growth since the past decades; for instance, now accounting for 2.47% of Brazil's total power generation [3]. PV-based technologies rely on the physical nature of solar radiation, depending directly on the irradiation performance to attain efficient energy conversion and/or utilization. The more one knows about the irradiation patterns in a certain territory, the more adequate the PV-based energy can be processed. Thus, quantifying solar irradiation is of paramount importance in several scenarios, such as power generation and utility markets, heat load distribution in buildings [4], PV system analysis and installation [5], agricultural applications [6], as well as irrigation systems [7].

Solar irradiation, measured in W/m^2, varies throughout the day at any given geographic location, mainly due to the earth's movement and the chaotic effects of the atmosphere [8]. With regards to Brazil, it has the world's highest potential for solar energy generation, given that a large part of its territory is located in the equatorial and tropical zones [9].

Measuring such irradiation is challenging due to its cost, maintenance requirements, and technical demands for calibration of sensors [10,11]. Several approaches have been proposed in the literature to address this issue, considering empirical models, mathematical formulations, and satellite-based data. Recently, the development of artificial intelligence (AI) algorithms to predict and estimate solar irradiation profiles at specific geographical locations has also been commonly evidenced [4–7,12,13]. Gao, Miyata and Akashi highlighted in [14] that most of the solar-related research findings available worldwide applied long short-term memory (LSTM), autoregressive moving average (ARMA), and multilayer perceptron (MLP) as a basis for solar irradiation forecasting algorithms.

Many research works have focused on artificial neural networks (ANN) for either predicting or forecasting solar irradiation, such as the one conducted by Yadav and Chandel [15], Shaddel, Javan, and Baghernia [16], and Zhang et al. [8]. In particular, Zhang et al. [8] and Salazar et al. [9] reviewed and compared various models, such as MLP, radial basis function (RBF), and wavelet recurrent neural networks (WRNN), in terms of estimation type and time scale.

For what concerns the Brazilian perspective, ANN-based applications focused on solar irradiation quantization are still limited, being particularly targeted only for a small number of areas or regions. Some research efforts have investigated ANN techniques for solar irradiation prediction in local scenarios, such as in Fortaleza - Ceará [17], Seropédica - Rio de Janeiro [18], Petrolina - Pernambuco [9,19], and Botucatu - Sao Paulo [20]. However, Brazil is a geographically extensive country with a significant north-to-south extension, and it lacks research on a generalist model to predict solar irradiation throughout the entire region.

Motivated by such a scientific gap, this paper presents two main contributions to fulfill the need to estimate solar irradiation in any location within the Brazilian territory. First, a model based on a deep-learning neural network (DNN) is developed to estimate solar irradiation based on the following attributes: daytime, temperature, humidity, atmospheric pressure, wind speed, and hourly precipitation. As a second contribution, a dynamic model is proposed to forecast daily irradiation based on locations' latitude, longitude, and month of the year.

A DNN is used as a regressor for the former model, and its performance is compared with other estimation techniques. The latter (i.e., dynamic) model uses a Recurrent Neural Network (RNN) based on the LSTM principle, allowing solar irradiation prediction for different time scales ranging from 5 min to 24 h. It is worth highlighting that this study utilizes data from 606 meteorological stations managed by the Brazilian National Institute of Meteorology (INMET) to train and evaluate the proposed models, considering the datalogging period between 2010 and 2022.

This paper reads as follows. Section 2 presents the process of choosing and implementing DNN and LSTM for the estimation and forecasting process of solar irradiation. Section 3 presents information about the database provided by INMET, the data munging process, and the results attained from the ANNs' model. In addition, it is presented performance analyses for short, medium, and long-term estimation and forecasting of irradiation, also considering comparisons with previous works from the literature. Section 4 presents the final considerations about the proposed models, their limitations, and future work proposals.

2   Artificial Neural Network Techniques for Solar Irradiation

ANNs are bio-inspired computational models capable of representing complex knowledge, maintenance, and generalization processes using the relationship between input and output data [6,12]. The basic unit of an ANN is the neuron, and models known as synapses interconnect the multiple units of neurons. A tuning value is associated with such synapses comprising the ANN, known as the weight factor.

The first ANNs were idealized in 1943 [21]; however, practical models were implemented in applications only after 1986, with the construction of an MLP with backpropagation [22]. An MLP is an ANN architecture comprising an input layer, one or more hidden layers, and an output layer, as shown in Fig. 1a. The MLP uses the supervised learning concept called backpropagation in the training process and can solve the nonlinearity of the input data to perform pattern recognition or estimation [6].

Since the MLP milestone, deep learning (DL) has progressed because of the computational evolution in the last decades and the possibility of increasing the number of hidden layers and neurons [23], as shown in Fig. 1b. Therefore, new architectures of ANNs were developed for several purposes, such as regression, supervised classification, computer vision, speech recognition, natural language processing, and audio detection [24].

Many research efforts present techniques for solar irradiation forecast. For instance, Wang et al. [25] conducted a study on daily solar radiation prediction comparing three ANN architectures: the MLP, generalized regression neural network (GRNN), and radial basis function neural network (RBFNN). The models were developed using as attribute input the air temperature, relative humidity, air pressure, water vapor pressure, and sunlight duration measured from 12 weather stations in different climate zones. Based on the results, they found that the MLP and RBFNN models provide better accuracy than GRNN.

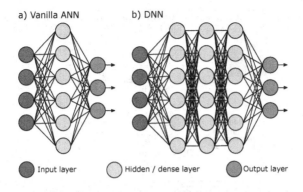

Fig. 1. ANN and DNN comparison.

Belaid and Mellit [26] developed a method that uses a support vector machine (SVM) to predict daily and monthly global average solar irradiation in an arid climate (Ghardaia, Algeria), taking as input the temperature, maximum sunshine duration, and the extraterrestrial solar radiation. For these quantities, the correlation coefficient ranged from 0.894 to 0.896, and the prediction error of approximately 7.5%.

Mehdizadeh et al. [27] conducted a study comparing gene expression programming (GEP), ANN, adaptive neuro-fuzzy inference system (ANFIS), and 48 empirical equations to estimate daily solar radiation in Kerman, Iran. The authors reported that the scenarios based on meteorological parameters and sunlight in ANFIS and ANN showed better accuracy than empirical models.

For the Brazilian scenario, ANN-based applications relating to the solar irradiation context are still limited. However, some studies have presented ANN approaches for solar irradiation prediction focusing on the regions of Fortaleza - Ceará [17] and Seropédica - Rio de Janeiro [18], achieving an accuracy of 89.7%. Salazar et al. [9] have developed a time series-based method to identify the solar irradiation in the equatorial near-zone and obtained a median absolute deviation (MAD) equivalent to 1.4% in the validation at a weather station installed in Petrolina - Pernambuco - Brazil. Carneiro et al. [19] used an ensemble learning method based on crest regression achieving mean absolute percentage error (MAPE) values of 14.191% also in Petrolina - Pernambuco - Brazil. Silva et al. [20] applied SVM, Angstrom-Prescott (A-P), and ANNs to estimate solar irradiation: the first achieved the best result while comparing to the A-P and ANN models, achieving a R^2 of 0.806.

Based on some studies found in the literature [17,25,27], ANNs provide significant capacity to predict solar irradiation. ANNs can estimate solar irradiation based on meteorological quantities and predict future irradiation based on historical events. Thus, this paper presents both models for obtaining solar irradiation, with the steps depicted in Fig. 2 and detailed in the Subsects. 2.1, 2.2 and discussed in Sect. 3.

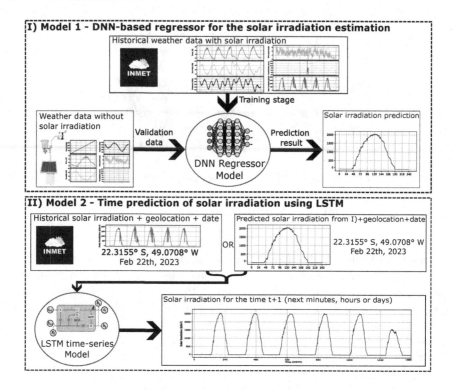

Fig. 2. The proposed ANN models.

2.1   Model 1 - DNN-Based Regressor for the Solar Irradiation Estimation

We assume this model as linear regression, in which a numerical value (target value or dependent variable) is obtained as a function of input values (attributes or independent variables), as presented in Eq. (1). Target values are continuous, meaning they can take any numerical value within the real number domain. In the literature, linear regression is used in various applications, such as stock market price forecasting, house price forecasting, sales forecasting, and others [28]. With regards to linear regression applications, using DNNs as regressors is helpful since they can learn the complex relationship between attributes and the target, mainly due to the presence of the activation function in each layer [6].

$$Y = \beta_0 + \sum_{n=1}^{N} \beta_n X_n + \epsilon \tag{1}$$

where:
Y is the numerical value of the dependent variable. It is this value that is wanted to be predicted;
β_0 is the intercept on the Y-axis when all input attributes are zero;

β_n are the fitness coefficients for the attribute n. In ANN's case, these values are calculated to indicate the effects that each attribute causes for the most accurate prediction of Y;

X_n is the n-th independent variable;

N is the number of independent variables in the regression model;

ϵ is the model error, which shows the difference between the real and the predicted value;

One must take into account the following considerations to build the linear regression model using DNN:

- Build a sequential ANN architecture;
- Define the quantity and neurons of the dense layers;
- Assign a performance metric (loss function) based on numerical error calculation, such as the mean absolute error (MAE), which is calculated according to Eq. (2);
- Defining the output layer with a single neuron, having as activation function the linear function $[f(x) = x]$;

$$MAE = \frac{1}{n} \sum_{i=1}^{n} |y_i - \hat{y}_i| \tag{2}$$

in which:

i is the sample;

n is the total number of samples;

y_i is the true or real value of the dependent variable;

$\hat{y}_i$ is the value of the dependent variable predicted by the regression model.

The second model is a forecasting process for future events, and it is based on another ANN architecture, as presented in the following subsection.

2.2 Model 2 - Time Prediction of Solar Irradiation Using LSTM

Vanilla ANN cannot perform time series prediction, depending on a previous data history to predict the next instant [29]. On the other hand, RNNs are well-known for achieving solid results in many applications with time series and sequential data [30]. The most well-known RNN structures, such as the LSTM and the gated recurrent unit (GRU), can capture the long-term temporal dependencies in variable-length samples [31]. Another distinguishing characteristic of RNNs is that they share parameters across each network layer. In addition, while feed-forward networks have different weights across each node, RNNs share the same weight parameter within each network layer. Such weights are still adjusted through the backpropagation and gradient descent approaches to facilitate reinforcement learning.

Since the previous outputs obtained during training leave an information base, the RNN model supports predicting future outputs as a function of the input attributes (X_t). Note that this occurs with the help of the previous outputs (h_t), as presented in Fig. 3.

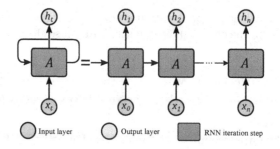

Fig. 3. Introducing the iterative process of an RNN.

LSTM is an RNN technique that can learn long-term dependencies, especially in sequential or seasonal prediction problems. LSTM has feedback connections that can process the entire data sequence and single data points. Each iteration of the LSTM network presents the data vector as input and two output data for each iteration:

- X_t is the input vector;
- C_t is the memory state cell, which maintains its state over time, considered as an output with memory;
- h_t is the time series output value.

Information can be added to or removed from the state C_t, regulated by input, forgetting, and output gates, presented after the layer applications shown in Fig. 4. These gates allow information to flow in and out of the cell, thus allowing memory propagation to the next iteration. The sigmoid layers (Fig. 4) present output numbers between zero and one, in which the former means that "nothing should be carried forward", and the latter means that "everything should be carried forward".

For constructing the solar irradiation prediction model, the number of steps represents the input layer (which corresponds to hourly data) and the attributes. We have the solar irradiation output in the output layer.

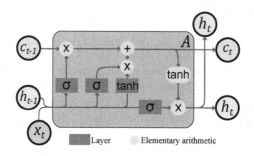

Fig. 4. Iterative process of an LSTM network.

Considering the structures of the two models, Sect. 3 presents the construction of the ANNs to estimate and predict solar irradiation and perform the models proposed in this work.

3   Methodology and Results

3.1   INMET Meteorological Station Data

The study comprised within this paper uses the meteorological database from the Brazilian National Institute of Meteorology (INMET), which is available at [32]. In this database, namely BDMEP, each data sample corresponds to the collection of meteorological variables collected at every hour or every six hours, being separated into individual files for each of the 606 meteorological stations distributed throughout Brazil, as shown in Fig. 5. Each file is composed of a header containing information about each meteorological station, as well as a structured set of samples of the collected meteorological variables. The dataset used in this study considers the interval between 01/01/2010 and 31/12/2022, as presented in Table 1.

Fig. 5. Localization of the meteorological stations used in this work.

Table 1. Composition of each file in the BDMEP dataset.

Name	Unit/Format
Header	
Region of the country	
State	
Code (WMO)	
Latitude	°
Longitude	°
Altitude	m
Foundation date	dd/mm/yy
Data	
Date	YYYY-MM-DD
Time	HHMM UTC
Hourly precipitation	mm
Atmospheric pressure at station level	mB
Maximum atmospheric pressure in the previous hour	mB
Minimum atmospheric pressure in the previous hour	mB
Global radiation	kJ/m^2
Air temperature	°C
Dew point temperature	°C
Maximum temperature in the previous hour	°C
Minimum temperature in the previous hour	°C
Maximum dew point temperature in the previous hour	°C
Minimum dew point temperature in the previous hour	°C
Maximum relative humidity in the previous hour	%
Minimum relative humidity in the previous hour	%
Relative humidity	%
Wind direction	°
Maximum wind gust	m/s
Wind speed	m/s

Data preprocessing and cleaning are considered relevant step, as it enhances the quality of the information, assists in decision-making, and improves the machine learning model [33]. As a first step in data preprocessing, only momentary quantities that do not depend on the previous time were considered, resulting in 11 quantities. Furthermore, the data from all 606 meteorological stations were merged, resulting in 39,656,352 samples.

Subsequently, data cleaning was performed [34], with the removal of samples with reading errors, missing data, duplicate data, and removal of outliers, considering the empirical rule of 3σ [35], resulting in 36,433,601 samples, which represents approximately 91.87% of the initial dataset.

After the data preprocessing and cleaning step, the data is used in the training stage for modeling and constructing the solar irradiation estimation tool, as presented in Subsect. 3.3.

Considering the data presented in Sect. 3.1, the method and the results of the studies are presented in the following subsections. We consider two main scenarios for the results: *i)* the estimation of solar irradiation based on indirect meteorological quantities; and *ii)* the prediction of solar irradiation based on geolocation and date.

3.2 Estimation of Solar Radiation Based on Other Meteorological Variables Applying Model 1

In this first scenario, the focus is given to the solar radiation estimation applying Model 1, presented in Subsect. 2.1, and the target data was initially normalized using the *Z-score* technique [36]. After that, we conducted a k-fold cross-validation ($k = 5$) analysis to evaluate the efficacy of deep learning-based models on the BDMEP dataset. Cross-validation is a widely recognized technique for assessing machine learning model performance [37]. In 5-fold cross-validation, the dataset is divided into five equal subsets, where four subsets are employed for model training, and the remaining subset is employed for model validation. This procedure is repeated five times, using a different subset for validation. The model's generalization performance is accurately assessed by averaging the performance metrics over the five folds. Cross-validation aids in ensuring that the models do not overfit and can effectively generalize to new data.

The DNN architecture is presented in Fig. 6. As input data for the DNN, six variables were considered: hour, precipitation, atmospheric pressure, temperature, humidity, and wind speed. The output layer corresponds to the value of solar radiation. In all intermediate layers, the ReLu activation function was used [38], and the linear function $f(x) = x$ was used in the output layer. The optimizer of the model is the "Adamax".

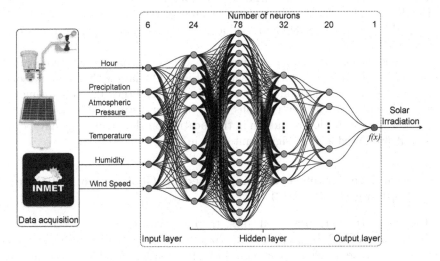

Fig. 6. DNN architecture with the best parameters.

In order to present the best results, a grid search was performed, which is a technique that searches for the best parameters for the machine learning model. For the DNN, a grid search was performed for the number of neurons (n) in the i-th hidden layer and the number of layers (i), where $n = 20, 24, 28, ..., 66, 72, 78$ and $i = 2, 3, 4, 5$. At this stage, k-fold cross-validation was also considered, with $k = 10$ [37].

With the DNN configuration presented in Fig. 6, the training process was performed with a limit of 100 epochs. Additionally, the stabilization of MAE was considered as the stopping criterion. Figure 7 presents the learning curve of the DNN implemented in this study.

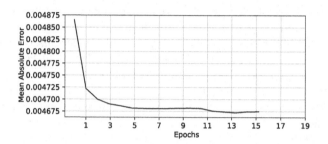

Fig. 7. DNN learning curve.

For the test data, the data for the year 2022 (i.e., until 10/30/2022) were considered, which can be accessed at [32]. Therefore, through such data, the mean absolute error equivalent to 9.34 kJ/m^2 was obtained in the study. To verify the system's dynamics in estimating solar irradiation, the results are presented in Fig. 8 for two real scenarios: 1) Xanxerê-SC-Brazil station, which is a member of BDMEP; and 2) IBAURU9 station, located in Bauru-SP-Brazil, which was developed by the authors [39] and used as a scenario of data not seen previously by the DNN model.

The model could predict irradiation behavior, as demonstrated by comparing the actual and estimated values presented in Fig. 8. On days with maximum solar radiation, the model could follow the approximate trend (i.e., note the estimated and actual curves in the lower graphs of Fig. 8). Furthermore, the model could still follow the irradiation reduction in the location on cloudy or rainy days, even though it presented a more significant error in the estimation.

3.3 Solar Irradiation Forecasting Based on Geolocation and Date Applying the Model 2

At this stage, the data presented in Sect. 3.1 was considered for Model 2, presented in Subsect. 2.2, being then normalized using the Z-score technique, which has the advantage of using a common normalization for variables with different standard deviations [40]. The training data corresponded to data between 2010

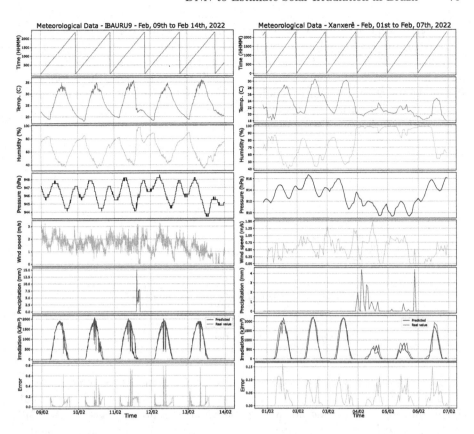

Fig. 8. Result of solar irradiation estimation for Bauru-SP-Brazil and Xanxerê-SC-Brazil stations.

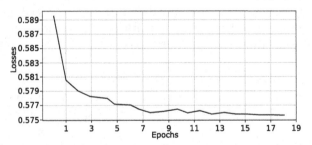

Fig. 9. LSTM learning curve.

and 2021, while the data from 2022 was used for testing. The target inputs are the solar irradiation information, the geolocation, and the date. The output of the model is the predicted irradiation at the next time step t. Moreover, the learning curve is shown in Fig. 9, presenting a final loss of 0.576.

Different time granularity was considered in this result. For the prediction for the next 5 min, the model presents an MAE equivalent to 18.91 kJ/m^2; for the next 30 min, 33.15 kJ/m^2; for the next hour 43.64 kJ/m^2; and for the prediction for 24 h, the MAE corresponds to 91.52 kJ/m^2. Figure 10 shows the response of the model for the next hour of irradiation prediction, and the system can track the real solar irradiation. A valley is visible around 17:00 due to the appearance of a cloud, which caused a significant decrease in solar irradiation. The model did not follow the real value, but it did follow the trend when the sun returned.

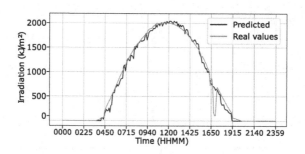

Fig. 10. One-day prediction results from the LSTM.

Figure 11 shows the 24-hour forecast made by the model for a sequence of seven days. There is also a slight delay between the predicted and the actual signal, but the forecast had adequate generation tracking for days of full solar irradiation. On the sixth day, there was a cloudy and rainy day, and the model had a higher error but still captured the decrease in irradiation for the day. On cloudy days, solar irradiation is diffuse, elusive and typically between 10 and 25 percent of its normal value on sunny days [41]. The proposed model tries to adjust values according to historical data without high accuracy, but presents a decrease in the solar irradiation estimation.

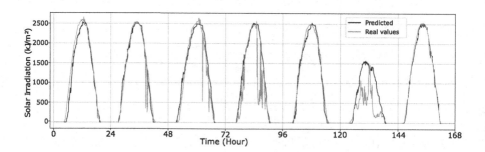

Fig. 11. 7-day prediction results from the LSTM.

3.4   Method Comparison and Discussion

This section considers techniques commonly found in the literature aiming at comparing the two proposed scenarios. The data used for testing and validating the methodologies was obtained from INMET, being identical to that presented in Sect. 3.1. A Macbook Pro, model A1990, with an Intel i9 9980H processor, 16GB of RAM and a Radeon Pro 560 × 4GB video card, was used to compute the comparison analyses of the results.

Model 1 - Comparison. According to Gao, Miyata, and Akashi [14], deep learning-based models have demonstrated outstanding ability for predicting solar irradiation, with LSTM demonstrating superior assertiveness performance compared to other techniques. However, it is necessary to verify the performance of the two scenarios proposed in this paper using methodologies from the literature. In addition to the DNN proposed in this project, traditional machine-learning regression techniques used in the literature for estimating solar irradiation from meteorological quantities were contrasted. Support Vector Machine (SVM) [42,43], Random Forest (RF) [42,44], and MLP [6,42,45,46] are the techniques used in the comparison with the results displayed in Table 2. The results indicate that the DNN approach had a lower MAE for the prediction scenarios. The MLP, which is another neural network architecture, presented the second-best performance. Moreover, the RF approach had the worst results, confirming the findings of Gao, Miyata, and Akashi [14]. On the other hand, while SVM has the best efficacy in training and testing regarding computational time, its error rate is nearly twice that from the DNN.

Table 2. Model 1 - Regression model comparison to estimate the solar irradiation.

Method	MAE	train(s)	test(s)
DNN - Model 1	**14.86**	74,736	102.3
MLP	18.42	20,375	75.4
RF	104.89	17,759	**21.2**
SVM	28.25	**13,302**	245.7

Note in Table 2 that Model 1 provided results comparable to the current state of the art, presenting the lowest MAE of all evaluated methods. Thus, based on such results, the DNN is recommended. One of the DNN's disadvantages, however, is that it has one of the highest computational costs. As demonstrated in Sect. 3.3, another disadvantage is the behavior on cloudy and rainy days. A potential solution to such an issue is to either use generative adversarial networks (GAN) or consider balanced data for what concerns sunny, cloudy, and rainy days, aiming at providing the model with generalized adjustments.

Model 2-Comparison. The efficacy of four statistical and machine learning tools for global solar irradiation forecasting was analyzed and compared during this study. Gao, Miyata, and Akashi [14] demonstrate that ARMA [47,48], MLP [49], and LSTM [14,50,51] are the most popular and appropriate models for the prediction of future solar irradiation. The Kalman filter [52] was also used to perform such a comparison. Table 3 displays the results taking into account various future time granularities, such as 5 min, 30 min, 6 h, and 1 day. Note that the Kalman filter produced the best results for the 5 min and 1 day baselines, while the LSTM produced the best results for 30 min and 6 h instances. With regards to neural network-based architectures, the LSTM and MLP demanded the most time to train, while the Kalman filter presented the faster training process. During the test, ARMA had the fastest time. Hence, the Kalman filter is recommended for the smallest and largest granularities. On the other hand, based on the data analyzed in this paper, the LSTM is recommended for the intermediate granularities of 30 min and 6 h. The presented comparative analyses corroborate the findings of Yu, Cao, and Zhu [50], who concluded that the LSTM is not recommended for a 24-hour granularity model.

Table 3. Model 2 - Time-series prediction comparison of solar irradiation.

	MSE					
Method	5 min	30 min	6 h	1 day	train(s)	test(s)
LSTM - Model 2	18.91	**33.15**	**43.64**	191.52	6,971.3	23.55
ARMA	22.37	36.54	61.11	102.54	533.5	**12.50**
Kalman's filter	**18.11**	35.04	48.31	**122.50**	101.4	88.52
MLP	58.44	98.104	114.88	157.30	7,392.8	45.77

At last, note that Model 2 produced results that are similar or better than achieved by the state-of-the-art, with regards to the mean squared error (MSE): a ranking near the best one was obtained for 5 min; it was the lowest one for the 30-minutes and 6-hour predictions; although it was the worst performance for the 1-day forecast. As an inherent disadvantage, Model 2 presents one of the highest computational costs for training. Nonetheless, Model 2's performance could be improved by taking into account additional input attributes, such as the weather data displayed in Model 1. Moreover, minimizing the number of input samples may enhance training performance.

4   Conclusion

Quantifying solar radiation is essential for a range of applications, from solar energy generation to building thermal management, agriculture, and irrigation. However, measuring this magnitude poses technical and operational challenges, making its real-time use difficult.

This work presented the use of a database of 606 Brazilian weather stations collected by INMET between 2010 and 2021 to develop two deep learning-based models. The first model is a DNN-based method that estimates solar radiation across Brazil based on hourly temperature, humidity, atmospheric pressure, wind speed, and precipitation data. The second model is an LSTM-based method that predicts future solar radiation for intervals of 5 min, 30 min, 1 h, and the entire day.

Our results demonstrate that both models accurately estimate and predict solar radiation. The first model has an MAE of 9.34 kJ/m^2, while the second model has an MAE of 1.89 kJ/m^2, 3.31 kJ/m^2, 4.36 kJ/m^2, and 31.52 kJ/m^2 for predicting the next 5 min, 30 min, 1 h, and 24 h, respectively.

Our findings demonstrate that DNN modeling can adequately identify solar radiation using indirect meteorological variables, while the LSTM model can adapt well to a prediction system, producing close-to-real results with geographic coordinates, the previous radiation level, and the month of the year as inputs. These results indicate the potential of deep learning-based methods for estimating and predicting solar radiation in Brazil, considering the successful performance of the model with over 39 million hourly data points from 606 weather stations nationwide.

Future work involves utilizing adversarial generative networks to improve the prediction performance on rainy or cloudy days and exploring RNA applicability in intelligent meter immersion to aid solar generation management and prediction.

Acknowledgements. The authors are grateful for the financial support provided by the Coordenação de Aperfeiçoamento de Pessoal de Nível Superior (CAPES) through the Social Demand scholarship (DS), Araucaria Foundation and by the Federal University of Technology – Paraná (UTFPR), campus Cornelio Procopio.

References

1. Adedoyin, F. F., Bekun, F. V. & Alola, A. A. Growth impact of transition from non-renewable to renewable energy in the EU: The role of research and development expenditure. Renewable Energy 159, 1139–1145. ISSN: 0960–1481 (2020)
2. Brodny, J., Tutak, M.: Analyzing similarities between the european union countries in terms of the structure and volume of energy production from renewable energy sources. Energies **13** (2020) ISSN: 1996– 1073
3. EPE (Brasil). Balanço Energético Nacional 2022: Ano base 2021 In Portuguese. Tech. rep. (2022)
4. Wang, Z., Hong, T., Piette, M.A.: Building thermal load prediction through shallow machine learning and deep learning. Appli. Energy **263**, 11468 (2020). ISSN: 0306–2619
5. Notton, G., Voyant, C., Fouilloy, A., Duchaud, J.L., Nivet, M.L.: Some applications of ANN to solar radiation estimation and forecasting for energy applications. Appli. Sci. **9**, 2076–3417 (2019)
6. Antonopoulos, V.Z., Papamichail, D.M., Aschonitis, V.G., Antonopoulos, A.V. Solar radiation estimation methods using ANN and empirical models. Comput. Electr. Agricult. **160**, 160–167 (2019). ISSN: 0168–1699

7. Ali, B.: Comparative assessment of the feasibility for solar irrigation pumps in Sudan. Renew. Sustainable Energy Rev. **81**, 413–420 (2018). ISSN: 1364–0321

8. Zhang, J., Zhao, L., Deng, S., Xu, W., Zhang, Y.: A critical review of the models used to estimate solar radiation. Renew. Sustainable Energy Rev. **70**, 314–329 (2017). ISSN: 1364–0321

9. Salazar, G., Gueymard, C., Galdino, J.B., de Castro Vilela, O., Fraidenraich, N.: Solar irradiance time series derived from high-quality measurements, satellite-based models, and reanalyses at a near-equatorial site in Brazil. Renew. Sustainable Energy Rev. **117**, 109478 (2020). ISSN: 1364–0321

10. Rocha, A.B.d., Fernandes, E.d., Santos, C.A.C.d., Diniz, J.M.T., Junior, W.F.A.: Development of a real-time surface solar radiation measurement system based on the internet of things (IoT). Sensors **21**, 3836 (2021). ISSN: 1424–8220

11. Bayray, M., et al.: Measured solar irradiance data for resource assessment at four sites in Geba catchment, Tigray, North Ethiopia. Data Brief **40**, 107836 (2022). ISSN: 2352–3409

12. Khosravi, A., Nunes, R., Assad, M., Machado, L.: Comparison of artificial intelligence methods in estimation of daily global solar radiation. J. Cleaner Product. **194**, 342–358 (2018). ISSN: 0959–6526

13. Zang, H. et al. Estimation and validation of daily global solar radiation by day of the year-based models for different climates in China. Renewable Energy **135**, 984–1003 (2019). ISSN: 0960–1481

14. Gao, Y., Miyata, S., Akashi, Y.: Multi-step solar irradiation prediction based on weather forecast and generative deep learning model. Renewable Energy **188**, 637–650 (2022). ISSN: 0960–1481

15. Yadav, A.K., Chandel, S.: Solar radiation prediction using Artificial Neural Network techniques: a review. Renew. Sustain. Energy Rev. **33**, 772–781 (2014). ISSN: 1364–0321

16. Shaddel, M., Javan, D.S., Baghernia, P.: Estimation of hourly global solar irradiation on tilted absorbers from horizontal one using Artificial Neural Network for case study of Mashhad. Renew. Sustain. Energy Rev. **53**, 59–67 (2016). ISSN: 1364–0321

17. Barros Silva, A.W. et al. Methodology based on artificial neural networks for hourly forecasting of PV plants generation. IEEE Latin America Transactions **20**, 659–668 (2022)

18. Oliveira, J.M., Santos, D.D.S., Da Silva, R.M.: Predição da radiação solar global usando modelos de redes neurais artificiais. Revista Mundi Engenharia. Tecnologia e Gestão **4** (2019). ISSN: 2525–4782

19. Carneiro, T.C., Rocha, P.A., Carvalho, P.C., Fernández-Ramírez, L.M.: Ridge regression ensemble of machine learning models applied to solar and wind forecasting in Brazil and Spain. Appli. Energy **314**, 118936 (2022)

20. da Silva, M.B.P., Francisco Escobedo, J., Juliana Rossi, T., dos Santos, C.M., da Silva, S.H.M.G.: Performance of the Angstrom-Prescott Model (A-P) and SVM and ANN techniques to estimate daily global solar irradiation in Botucatu/SP/Brazil. J. Atmospheric Solar-Terrestrial Phys. **160**, 11–23. (2017). ISSN: 1364–6826

21. McCulloch, W.S., Pitts, W.: A logical calculus of the ideas immanent in nervous activity. Bull. Math. Biophys. **5**, 115–133 (1943). ISSN: 1522–9602

22. Rumelhart, D.E., Hinton, G.E., Williams, R.J.: Learning representations by back-propagating errors. Nature **323**, 533–536 (1986). ISSN: 1476–4687

23. Ng, A., Ngiam, J., Foo, C.Y., Mai, Y.: Deep learning. In: CS229 Lecture Notes, pp. 1–30 (2014)

24. Kim, K.G.: Book review: deep learning. hir **22**, 351–354 (2016)
25. Wang, L., et al.: Solar radiation prediction using different techniques: model evaluation and comparison. Renew. Sustain. Energy Rev. **61**, 384–397 (2016). ISSN: 1364–0321
26. Belaid, S., Mellit, A.: Prediction of daily and mean monthly global solar radiation using support vector machine in an arid climate. Energy Conversion Manag. **118**, 105–118 (2016). ISSN: 0196–8904
27. Mehdizadeh, S., Behmanesh, J., Khalili, K.: Comparison of artificial intelligence methods and empirical equations to estimate daily solar radiation. J. Atmospheric Solar-Terrestrial Phys. **146**, 215–227 (2016). ISSN: 1364–6826
28. Dixon, M.F., Halperin, I., Bilokon, P.: Introduction. In: Machine Learning in Finance, pp. 3–46. Springer, Cham (2020). https://doi.org/10.1007/978-3-030-41068-1_1
29. Joshi, V., et al.: Accurate deep neural network inference using computational phase-change memory. Nat. Commun. **11**, 2473 (2020). ISSN: 2041–1723
30. Ismail Fawaz, H., Forestier, G., Weber, J., Idoumghar, L., Muller, P.-A.: Deep learning for time series classification: a review. Data Mining Knowl. Dis. **33**, 917–963 (2019) ISSN: 1573–756X
31. Murad, A., Pyun, J.-Y.: Deep recurrent neural networks for human activity recognition. Sensors **17**, 2556 (2017). ISSN: 1424–8220
32. INMET. Banco de Dados Meteorológicos do INMET In Portuguese (2022). https://bdmep.inmet.gov.br/
33. Ilyas, I.F., Chu, X.: Data Cleaning. Association for Computing Machinery, New York (2019). ISBN: 9781450371520
34. Van den Broeck, J., Argeseanu Cunningham, S., Eeckels, R., Herbst, K.: Data cleaning: detecting, diagnosing, and editing data abnormalities. PLOS Med. **2** (2005)
35. Zhao, Y., Lehman, B., Ball, R., Mosesian, J., de Palma, J.-F.: Outlier detection rules for fault detection in solar photovoltaic arrays. In: Proceedings of the IEEE Applied Power Electronics Conference and Exposition, pp. 2913–2920 (2013)
36. Patro, S., Sahu, K.K.: Normalization: A preprocessing stage. arXiv preprint arXiv:1503.06462 (2015)
37. Souza, W.A., et al.: Selection of features from power theories to compose NILM datasets. Adv. Eng. Inform. **52**, 101556 (2022). ISSN: 1474–0346
38. Eckle, K., Schmidt-Hieber, J.: A comparison of deep networks with ReLU activation function and linear spline-type methods. Neural Netw. **110**, 232–242 (2019). ISSN: 0893–6080
39. Tavares, K., Alonso, A.M.S., Souza, W.A.: Estimating solar irradiance system using meteorological quantities and deep neural networks (In Portuguese). Peer Rev. **5**, 225–238 (2023)
40. Zhang, Z., Cheng, Y., Liu, N.C.: Comparison of the effect of mean-based method and z-score for field normalization of citations at the level ofWeb of Science subject categories. Scientometrics **101**, 1679–1693 (2014). ISSN: 1588–2861
41. Armstrong, S., Hurley, W.: A new methodology to optimise solar energy extraction under cloudy conditions. Renew. Energy **35**, 780–787 (2010). ISSN: 0960–1481
42. Voyant, C., et al.: Machine learning methods for solar radiation forecasting: a review. Renew. Energy **105**, 569–582 (2017). ISSN: 0960–1481
43. Zendehboudi, A., Baseer, M., Saidur, R.: Application of support vector machine models for forecasting solar and wind energy resources: a review. J. Cleaner Prod. **199**, 272–285 (2018). ISSN: 0959–6526

44. Fouilloy, A., et al.: Solar irradiation prediction with machine learning: forecasting models selection method depending on weather variability. Energy **165**, 620–629 (2018). ISSN: 0360–5442
45. Ahmad, A., Anderson, T., Lie, T.: Hourly global solar irradiation forecasting for New Zealand. Solar Energy **122**, 1398–1408 (2015). ISSN: 0038–092X
46. Yousif, J.H., Kazem, H.A., Boland, J.: Predictive models for photovoltaic electricity production in hotweather conditions. Energies **10** (2017). ISSN: 1996–1073
47. Reikard, G.: Predicting solar radiation at high resolutions: a comparison of time series forecasts. Solar Energy **83**, 342–349 (2009). ISSN: 0038–092X
48. Yang, D., Jirutitijaroen, P., Walsh, W.M.: Hourly solar irradiance time series forecasting using cloud cover index. Solar Energy Solar Res. **86**, 3531–3543 (2012). ISSN: 0038–092X
49. Alfadda, A., Rahman, S., Pipattanasomporn, M.: Solar irradiance forecast using aerosols measurements: a data driven approach. Solar Energy **170**, 924–939 (2018). ISSN: 0038–092X
50. Yu, Y., Cao, J., Zhu, J.: An LSTM Short-term solar irradiance forecasting under complicated weather conditions. IEEE Access **7**, 145651–145666 (2019)
51. Srivastava, S., Lessmann, S.: A comparative study of LSTM neural networks in forecasting day-ahead global horizontal irradiance with satellite data. Solar Energy **162**, 232–247 (2018). ISSN: 0038–092X
52. Gupta, A., Gupta, K., Saroha, S.: A review and evaluation of solar forecasting technologies. In: Materials Today: Proceedings of International Conference on Materials and System Engineering, vol. 7, pp. 2420–2425. 2214–7853 (2021)

Computational Approaches for Green Computing of Energy Consumption Forecasting on Non-working Periods in an Office Building

Daniel Ramos, Pedro Faria$^{(\boxtimes)}$, Luis Gomes, and Zita Vale

GECAD - Research Group on Intelligent Engineering and Computing for Advanced Innovation and Development; LASI - Intelligent Systems Associate Laboratory, Polytechnic of Porto, Porto, Portugal
{dados,pnf,log,zav}@isep.ipp.pt

Abstract. The energy management of electrical buildings takes an active role in the energy market. Researchers tasked with the primary goal of reducing the energy costs take advantage of machine learning algorithms to predict how much energy should be bought and sold in the market ahead of time. Some researchers take account green computing approaches to reduce the energy cost spent in forecasting roles and ensure the environmental sustainability of computing devices. In this paper two forecasting algorithms known as k-nearest neighbors and artificial neural networks train an annual historic with energy consumptions and sensors devices data to predict several energy consumption values of a target week for non-working periods of either five minutes or hour schedules. The green computing area is highlighted in this paper by studying the influence that decisions intended on decreasing the energy of the CPU processing unit on forecasting activities may have in the forecasting accuracy. Such decisions include changing the training and forecasting schedule of five minutes to hour periods and excluding the retraining using updated data from the test set. The conclusions of this paper clarify that scheduling forecasts for non-working hours with the support of k-nearest neighbors algorithm contextualized for periods of five minutes results in lower errors than artificial neural networks. However scheduling forecasts for periods of five minutes instead of hour periods also results in higher energy and time dedicated for cleaning, training, and forecasting tasks.

Keywords: environmental sustainability · forecasting algorithms · green computing

1 Introduction

Energy consumption forecast is very important for adequate management of energy resources, namely in the smart grids context. This raises the possibility of consumers to have great benefits form the participation in Demand Response (DR) programs [1, 2].

Moreover, nowadays, several buildings equipped with photovoltaic and renewable energy systems are certified with green building schemes [3]. This is because many governments provide incentives to promote green building practices in the construction sector as means to improve the energy sustainability [4]. This explains the strong link between the building information modelling and the green building certification systems in the energy area [5]. Several energy sources are widely used to supply demand in microgrids, therefore ensuring the robust and stable control of microgrids especially in green buildings [6]. The smart grids technology control is fundamental when environmental issues are a threat studied by several investigations including the CO2 emissions and the energy savings [7]. The rise of electric vehicles and integrated photovoltaics in smart buildings is a promising opportunity for green computing applications to maximize the green energy produced by photovoltaic units, thus reducing climate change issues [8]. Therefore, the adoption of energy trading strategies in distributed energy systems of smart systems should reflect the consumer behavior and energy in sustainable environments [9]. This is why green data centers are powered by renewable energy and have their technology infrastructure and computing devices readapted to use the minimum number of servers [10]. Green electronics may promote the energy savings based on the electronic factors, for example, an eco-friendly laptop takes into account the price, battery, shell, central processing unit, monitor, storage device and keyboard [11]. The government role on environmental supervision of smart cities is fundamental to promote the use of low-carbon environmental protection [12]. While minimizing carbon emissions guarantees green building environments, an additional green computing factor considers the minimization of non-renewable energy to maintain sustainable building environments [13]. However, data centers are threatened by the expensive costs and intermittent availability of renewable energy, thus optimization algorithms are usually the solution to minimize the costs in data centers [14]. The blockchain integration in smart grids energy applications requires high computation and communication complexity, thus greener and computational-friendly auctions are recommended to carry out the decentralized energy trading [15].

This paper continues the green computing research developed in a recent publication to lower the energy costs while forecasting energy consumptions of an electrical building for different non-working periods [16]. Moreover, this paper reuses the proposed configurations of artificial neural networks and k-nearest neighbors algorithms and the selected sensors to be added to the annual historic of energy consumptions as concluded previously by the authors of this paper [17]. The goal of this paper is to analyze how decreasing the energy costs in cleaning, training and forecasting activities affects the forecasting accuracy. Therefore, alternatives from five minutes to hour schedules and from historic retraining to using the historic previously saved in disk storage are considered in this paper in different trial and error scenarios. Similar research has been studied recently in [18] studying how it is possible to lower the forecasting energy costs for working periods instead. The forecasting algorithms artificial neural networks and k-nearest neighbors are selected in this paper regarding non-working periods to compare the forecasting accuracy and energy and time dedicated for cleaning, training, and forecasting tasks with recent research developed by the authors of this paper regarding working periods in [18]. Following this introduction, Sect. 2 presents the methodology, then Sect. 3 proceeds with the case study, afterwards Sect. 4 presents the results, and finally Sect. 5 presents the main conclusions.

2 Methodology

The methodology illustrates and explains all required steps to forecast different electricity consumption values for a long sequence of short periods. The data transformations, the training of an historic of electricity consumptions and sensors devices, the forecasting of different electricity consumption values and the performance evaluation of forecasting errors and the total energy cost are among the methodology steps.

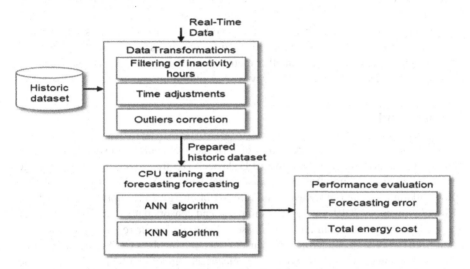

Fig. 1. Proposed methodology.

The methodology illustrated in Fig. 1 evidences an historic dataset with consumption and sensor values monitored in an electrical building contextualized in different short periods. The sensors featured in the historic dataset correspond to CO_2 and binary values representing light activity or light absence in the electrical building respectively assigned to the values one and zero. The data transformations intend on simplifying the historic dataset to train and forecast electricity consumption values under non-working hours where no duties are scheduled in the electrical building. These non-working hours correspond to behaviors after 6 p.m. and before 11 a.m. during Monday to Friday and all the hours between 12 a.m. and 11 p.m. during the whole weekend. The data transformation may also perform time adjustments to convert periods of five minutes to hour schedules. Average calculations reassign the twelve values contextualized in five minutes periods of each hour to a single value representing the energy consumption and sensors behavior of a particular hour. The outliers' correction is another data transformation technique that checks possible energy consumption inconsistencies for non-working hours and corrects these anomalies to logical values with non-working energy consumption behaviors. The rules to detect and correct outliers follow the logic researched by the authors of this paper in [R1]. Moreover, the data transformation rules to the historic dataset follow the same logic for the real-time data. After the outliers detection and correction, the final version of the prepared historic dataset is obtained and sent to be trained and forecasted with the CPU device. The historic of energy consumption and sensors data is trained with the artificial neural networks and k-nearest neighbors algorithms. Afterwards, energy consumption values are predicted for an entire week with the artificial neural networks and k-nearest neighbors algorithms using the CPU device. The training and forecasting of data are contextualized for non-working periods of either five minutes or hour schedules relying on the context defined previously for data transformations. The artificial neural networks and k-nearest neighbors' configuration for training and forecasting tasks follows the same logic defined by recent research written by the authors of this paper in [R1]. The performance evaluation analyzes the forecasting error for non-working hours using the Symmetric Mean Absolute Percentage Error (SMAPE) metrics. The authors of this paper reuse the calculation method used for recent research which explains also why SMAPE is more effective than other metrics for this context [R1]. The performance evaluation also calculates the total energy cost spent on training and forecasting tasks.

3   Case Study

The case study analyzes the forecasting effectiveness of energy consumptions in five minutes and hour schedules with the CPU device. The train dataset involves a large historic of energy consumption and sensor values from 22 May 2017 to 10 November 2019 while the test dataset focus on the forecast of energy consumption patterns from 11 to 17 November 2019. Energy consumption and sensors data from 2020 and 2021 was excluded from the train and test datasets due to the lower reliability in data as a result from COVID-19 pandemic. The sensors selection involves CO_2 values and binary values indicating either light activity on the electrical building with the value one or no light activity on the electrical building with the value zero instead. Moreover, the energy consumption and sensors data used in the train and test datasets for the period from 22 May 2017 to 17 November 2019 involves only non-working hours where no duties are schedules for the electrical building. Thus, only hours after 6 p.m. and before 11 a.m. during Monday to Friday and all the hours from 12 a.m. to 11 p.m. during the weekend are considered. The training and forecasting of energy consumption and sensor values are scheduled for five minutes or hour contexts relying on the defined context. Thus, the training dataset considers a total of 198144 observations for five minutes periods and a total of 16512 observations for hour schedules. The test dataset features a total of 1536 observations for five minutes periods and a total of 128 observations for hour schedules. Non-working hours for the training and test datasets present energy consumption usual behaviors between 500 and 600 kWh. Similar training and forecasting datasets are illustrated in recent research written by the authors of this paper and contextualized for working hours in [18].

4   Results

The results analyze the influence of alternating between periods of five minutes and hour schedules for non-working hours and the training strategy on the forecasting accuracy and the time dedicated for cleaning, training and forecasting activities. Two forecasting algorithms support the energy consumption forecasts from 11 to 17 November 2019 including the artificial neural networks and the k-nearest neighbors' algorithms with the effort of the CPU processing unit. The forecast of energy consumptions of an electrical building is scheduled for non-working hours with four different trial and error scenarios labeled from A to D as identified in Table 1. The forecasting error is displayed in Table 1 as well using the SMAPE metrics. All these scenarios use a training set from 22 May 2017 to 10 November 2019 to forecast energy consumptions of a building on 11 to 17 November 2019 for non-working hours. Scenarios A and C feature training and forecasting periods of five minutes while scenarios B and D feature training and forecasting periods scheduled for different hours. The training of energy consumptions and sensors devices data patterns may be processed in two different ways, either retraining the algorithm continuously in RAM for each target period or saving previously to disk storage to be loaded in RAM later during the forecasting of energy consumptions from 11 to 17 November 2019. Moreover, the training and forecasting of energy consumptions are run with the CPU device.

Table 1. Forecasting scenarios scheduled for non-working hours and SMAPE errors using the CPU device.

Scenario	Period	Training	SMAPE KNN (%)	SMAPE ANN (%)
A	5 min	Training update for each target period	2.61	7.51
B	1 h	Training update for each target period	6.52	7.33
C	5 min	Loaded from storage disk	2.19	6.91
D	1 h	Loaded from storage disk	5.72	6.10

The four scenarios identified previously in Table 1 compare the forecasting errors with the SMAPE metric to identify the forecasting deviations to the real energy consumptions considering schedules of five minutes on scenarios A and C and schedules of hour periods on scenarios B and D. The symmetric mean absolute percentage errors presented on Table 1 for the four scenarios initially show that forecasting electrical consumptions for all five minutes periods for non-working hours and with k-nearest neighbors' algorithm is more precise than forecasting for hour periods for non-working hours and with k-nearest neighbors. This is evidenced by the SMAPE forecasting errors provided by k-nearest neighbors algorithm for periods of five minutes in scenarios A and C, respectively 2.61 and 2.12% and the same forecasting errors for hour schedules in scenarios B and D, respectively 6.52 and 5.72%. On the other hand, the forecasting algorithm artificial neural networks result in more precise forecasts for hour schedules as evidenced by SMAPE forecasting errors in scenarios B and D, respectively 7.33 and 6.10%, while the same forecasting errors for five minutes periods in scenarios A and C correspond respectively to 7.51 and 6.91%. Nevertheless, the k-nearest neighbors forecasting algorithm evidences lower forecasting errors than artificial neural networks in all scenarios from A to D. The retraining in RAM results in lower forecast effectiveness both for five minutes periods and hour schedules. Retraining with five minutes periods result in SMAPE errors of 2.61 and 7.51% respectively for k-nearest neighbors algorithm and artificial neural networks. The forecasts of energy consumptions for five minutes periods loading the k-nearest neighbors and artificial neural networks training from disk storage and no retraining result in SMAPE errors respectively of 2.19 and 6.91%. Retraining with hour periods result in SMAPE errors of 6.52 and 7.33% respectively for k-nearest neighbors algorithm and artificial neural networks. The forecasts of energy consumptions for hour periods saving the k-nearest neighbors and artificial neural networks training to disk storage and no retraining result in SMAPE errors respectively of 5.72 and 6.10%. It is understandable that the use of k-nearest neighbors algorithm results in lower errors than artificial neural networks recalling that the training and forecasts are developed for non-working periods. Therefore, the historic and the target data present data with low activity and low dispersion which does not work with high precision for artificial neural networks. This is because artificial neural networks is an artificial intelligence algorithm that can only work with high accuracy if big data is considered on the historic dataset. Moreover, since there is a low dispersion of data k-nearest neighbors will eventually handle the data better than artificial neural networks for non-working periods. The time dedicated for data cleaning operations, training activities concerning the period from 22 May 2017 to 10 November 2019 and forecasting activities concerning the period from 11 to 17 November 2019 is studied for the scenarios A to D as evidenced in Table 2. Moreover, the energy spent on cleaning, training and forecasting activities is studied as well for each scenario in Table 2.

Table 2. Forecasting scenarios scheduled for non-working hours and training and clean time and energy spent using the CPU device.

Scenario	Period	Training	Train time (KNN)	Train time (ANN)	Train and clean time	Energy (Wh)
A	5 min	Training update for each target period	2584.86	486084.75	906913.25	23.54
B	1 h	Training update for each target period	24.53	4347.01	5358.55	0.31
C	5 min	Loaded from disk storage	1.89	142.11	431.91	0.42
D	1 h	Loaded from disk storage	0.09	49.47	139.21	0.04

The time dedicated for k-nearest neighbors and artificial neural networks training and forecasting and the sum of the two variants with the time dedicated for cleaning operations show that scheduling forecasts for periods of five minutes and retraining the algorithms dedicates much more time as evidenced by scenarios A and B. The time dedicated for train and cleaning operations is nearly 906913 s with retraining and five minutes periods as evidenced in scenario A. A similar analysis evidences retraining and hour schedules resulting in a cleaning and training time of nearly 5359 s as evidenced in scenario B. No retraining result in cleaning and training times of nearly 432 and 139 s respectively using five minutes periods and hour schedules in scenarios C and D. The time dedicated for the training and forecasting of energy consumptions is much higher for artificial neural networks than k-nearest neighbors presenting a difference of 483500 s for scenario A, 4322 s for scenario B, 140 s for scenario C and 49 s for scenario D. Thus, using retraining and five minutes periods increases the difference in the training and forecasting of artificial neural networks and k-nearest neighbors.

The energy spent in each trial and error scenarios is much higher for periods of five minutes than hour schedules due to the need to process much more data during cleaning, training and forecasting activities. This is clear when identifying the energy spent by five minutes scenarios including scenario A with a total of 23.54 Wh, and the energy spent by scenario C with a total of 0.42 Wh. These values are much higher than hour schedule scenarios including scenarios B and D with respectively 0.31 and 0.04 Wh. The retraining of data evidenced in scenarios A and B influence also more energy spent in cleaning, training and forecasting activities with totals of respectively 23.54 Wh and 0.31 Wh. These values are much higher than the energy spent on scenarios C and D where there is no retraining with values of respectively 0.42 and 0.04 Wh.

5 Conclusion

This paper studies the forecasting accuracy for hours where the energy consumption has non-working hours and the computational time and energy influence on cleaning, training and forecasting activities. This influence is analyzed alternating trial and error scenarios between periods of five minutes and for the different hours. Moreover, the retraining in RAM for each test target and the loading of the training from the disk storage with no retraining are two additional options studied as well to test the cost on spending higher computational time and CPU energy while considering retraining. The SMAPE forecasting errors and the forecasting accuracies for the different scenarios show lower forecasting errors using k-nearest neighbors algorithm compared to artificial neural networks. It is possible to guarantee much lower forecasting errors using k-nearest neighbors if five minutes periods are considered. However, the use of periods of periods of five minutes instead of hour schedules increases considerately the time dedicated in cleaning, training and forecasting tasks and the CPU energy spent on these tasks as well. Moreover, it is noted that considering retraining for non-working hours is less effective as the forecasting errors are higher and the computational time and energy spent by the CPU is also much higher than saving the training previously to storage disk. As for the limitations of this paper, it is clear that there is a reduced number of forecasting algorithms to support the insights regarding the scenarios with higher forecasting accuracy and lower energy and time spent in forecasting activities. Therefore, future research intends on adding more forecasting algorithms other than artificial neural networks and k-nearest neighbors.

Funding. This work has received funding from the EU Horizon 2020 research and innovation program under project IoTalentum (grant agreement No 953442). The authors acknowledge the work facilities and equipment provided by GECAD research center (UIDB/00760/2020) to the project team. Daniel Ramos is supported by national funds through Fundação para a Ciência e a Tecnologia (FCT), Portugal government, Fundo Social Europeu (FSE), and Por_Norte, with PhD grant reference 2022.12944.BD. Pedro Faria is supported by FCT, with grant CEECIND/01423/2021 CIND.

References

1. Ramos, D., Faria, P., Gomes, L., Vale, Z.: A contextual reinforcement learning approach for electricity consumption forecasting in buildings. IEEE Access **10**, 61366–61374 (2022)
2. Faria, P., Vale, Z.: Distributed energy resource scheduling with focus on demand response complex contracts. J. Mod. Power Syst. Clean Energy **9**(5), 1172–1182 (2020)
3. Chan, L.S.: Neighbouring shading effect on photovoltaic panel system: its implication to green building certification scheme. Renew. Energy **188**, 476–490 (2022)
4. Saka, N., Olanipekun, A.O., Omotayo, T.: Reward and compensation incentives for enhancing green building construction. Environ. Sustain. Indic. **11** (2021)
5. Olanrewaju, O.I., Enegbuma, W.I., Donn, M., Chileshe, N.: Building information modelling and green building certification systems: a systematic literature review and gap spotting. Sustain. Cities Soc. **81** (2022)
6. Jonban, M.S., et al.: Autonomous energy management system with self-healing capabilities for green buildings (microgrids). J. Build. Eng. **34** (2021)
7. Lamnatou, C., Chemisana, D., Cristofari, C.: Smart grids and smart technologies in relation to photovoltaics, storage systems, buildings and the environment. Renew. Energy **185**, 1376–1391 (2022)
8. Guzmán, C.P., Arias, N.B., Franco, J.F., Soares, J., Vale, Z., Romero, R.: Boosting the usage of green energy for EV charging in smart buildings managed by an aggregator through a novel renewable usage index. IEEE Access **9**, 105357–105368 (2021)
9. Kim, H., Choi, H., Kang, H., An, J., Yeom, S., Hong, T.: A systematic review of the smart energy conservation system: from smart homes to sustainable smart cities. Renew. Sustain. Energy Rev. **140** (2021)
10. Haddad, M., et al.: Combined IT and power supply infrastructure sizing for standalone green data centers. Sustain. Comput. Inform. Syst. **30** (2021)
11. Liao, C., Chuang, H.: Determinants of innovative green electronics: an experimental study of eco-friendly laptop computers. Technovation **113** (2022)
12. Sun, M., Zhang, J.: Research on the application of block chain big data platform in the construction of new smart city for low carbon emission and green environment. Comput. Commun. **149**, 332–342 (2020)
13. Su, Y.: Smart energy for smart built environment: a review for combined objectives of affordable sustainable green. Sustain. Cities Soc. **53** (2020)
14. He, H., Shen, H.: Minimizing the operation cost of distributed green data centers with energy storage under carbon capping. J. Comput. Syst. Sci. **118** (2021)
15. Hassan, M.U., Rehmani, M.H., Chen, J.: Optimizing blockchain based smart grid auctions: a green revolution. IEEE Trans. Green Commun. Netw. **6**(1), 462–471 (2022)
16. Vale, Z., Gomes, L., Ramos, D., Faria, P.: Green computing: a realistic evaluation of energy consumption for building load forecasting computation. J. Smart Environ. Green Comput. **2**, 34–45 (2022)
17. Ramos, D., Khorram, M., Faria, P., Vale, Z.: Load forecasting in an office building with different data structure and learning parameters. Forecasting **3** (2021)

18. Faia, R., Faria, P., Vale, Z., Spinola, J.: Energy forecast in buildings addressing computation consumption in a green computing approach. In: 9th International Conference on Energy and Environment Research (2022)

Solar Energy Forecasting: Case Study of the UNICAMP Gymnasium

Gleyson Roberto do Nascimento[1]($\boxtimes$) (ID), Hildo Guillardi Júnior[2] (ID), and Romis Attux[1] (ID)

[1] University of Campinas (UNICAMP), Campinas, São Paulo, Brazil
g043801@dac.unicamp.br, attux@unicamp.br
[2] São Paulo State University (UNESP), São João da Boa Vista, São Paulo, Brazil
h.guillardi@unesp.br

Abstract. Within the spectrum of studies conducted by the São Paulo Center for Energy Transition Studies (CPTEn), time series from the Photovoltaic Energy Plant of the UNICAMP Multidisciplinary Gymnasium (GMU-PV) were analyzed. This plant is associated with the first implementation of a photovoltaic system in the context of the Sustainable Campus Project (PCS) at UNICAMP - as a consequence, it originated the most extensive and robust time series in the project.

The research, structured according to the Cross Industry Standard Process for Data Mining (CRISP-DM) methodology, aimed to identify the patterns and parameters associated with the energy production of the aforementioned photovoltaic system. Based on Machine and Deep Learning techniques, forecasting models were developed to maximize the use of available resources and promote the sustainability of this energy system at UNICAMP.

In evaluating the results, it was observed that the most effective model was the Orthogonal Matching Pursuit (OMP) built from the Python low-code library, PyCaret. This regression machine learning model led to a coefficient of determination (R^2) of 0.935 494 and a root mean square error (RMSE) of 8.561 679.

Keywords: Solar Energy Forecasting · Machine Learning · Deep Learning

1 Introduction

The United Nations Climate Change Conference of 2022 (COP27) [1] recently examined the progression of global temperature and the impacts resulting from CO_2 usage. The agreements and protocols established the aim of controlling

Supported by DeepMind Scholarship Programme, São Paulo Center for Energy Transition Studies (CPTEn), Research Foundation of the State of São Paulo (FAPESP) under grants #2021/11380-5 and #2020/16635-9 and Coordenação de Aperfeiçoamento de Pessoal de Nivel Superior - Brasil (CAPES) - Finance Code 001.

B. N. Jørgensen et al. (Eds.): EI.A 2023, LNCS 14468, pp. 92–107, 2024.
https://doi.org/10.1007/978-3-031-48652-4_7

CO_2 emission sources, promoting an extensive transition to less environmentally damaging renewable energy sources.

In alignment with this global endeavor, the São Paulo Center for Energy Transition Studies (CPTEn) [2] was founded to conduct multidisciplinary research and development of technological solutions for the transition to renewable energies with minimal environmental impact in the Brazilian state of São Paulo. Despite the fact that the Brazilian energy matrix is primarily renewable (hydroelectric power - 56.8% [3]), it still has a significant environmental footprint.

The University of Campinas (UNICAMP), in whose campus CPTEn is based, is a public university; hence, it has the obligation to seek an efficient use of its financial resources and to protect the environment. Electricity costs at the university, accounting for annual expenses exceeding 30 million reais (5.45% of the current University budget [4]), have surpassed those related to water and sewage since 2019. With an approximate monthly consumption of 5000 MW h of electrical energy, UNICAMP has chosen to participate in the Free Energy Market, allowing the contracting of a more cost-effective energy band.

According to [5], each MW h produced in the National Interconnected System (SIN) resulted in the emission of 0.3406 tCO_2 in 2022. Consequently, UNICAMP, when contracting 6000 MW h of electric power from SIN, co-contributes to the emission of 2043.60 tCO_2 into the atmosphere. To mitigate this issue, the Sustainable Campus Project (PCS) [6] was introduced at UNICAMP, taking charge of the installation of the Photovoltaic Energy Plant of the UNICAMP Multidisciplinary Gymnasium (GMU-PV) (see Fig. 1), a solution with a power of 336 kWp. Presently, PCS oversees six Plants with a combined installed power of 534 kWp.

Fig. 1. Photovoltaic Energy Plant of the UNICAMP Multidisciplinary Gymnasium (GMU-PV).

The GMU-PV, located at latitude -22.815 070 and longitude -47.071 253 in Campinas, Southeastern Brazil, operates in a high-altitude tropical climate and hosts five inverters of the INGECON SUN 100TL 55 kW model [7]. Each of these is connected to ten strings containing 26 photovoltaic modules of the Canadian Solar CS6K-270 model, with each module having a power output of 270Wp and an efficiency of 16.98% [8].

In this context, it became essential to expedite and structure the energy transition at UNICAMP. This justifies the rationale of this work: to analyze photovoltaic electric energy production data series, thus providing an overview of energy production to guide decisions affecting existing Photovoltaic Power Plants and the installation of new ones. It analyzes GMU-PV production system and evaluates created forecasting models in order to seek more realistic generation values through use of Python programming language version 3.10.12 and Google Colaboratory notebooks.

2   CRISP-DM Methodology

The Cross Industry Standard Process for Data Mining (CRISP-DM) [9] (Fig. 2) is one of the most widely disseminated methodologies for Machine/Deep Learning and Data Science projects in general. In this paper, the following topics will be addressed: Business Understanding, Data Understanding, Data Preparation, Modelling and Evaluation.

Fig. 2. CRISP-DM Methodology Diagram.

2.1   Business Understanding

The developed models seek to address two inquiries: 1) feasibility of developing a photovoltaic energy production forecast model with the available data from GMU-PV; 2) whether the forecast results could help achieve the objectives of CPTEn by optimizing energy contracting and aiding in the energy transition, leading to a less impacted environment.

In this context, two types of data are expected to be crucial: photovoltaic energy production and climate conditions. In accordance with [10,11], three time series forecasting techniques could be applied to address these questions: 1) a univariate method using only the target for forecasting; 2) a multivariate method incorporating features and the target for forecasting; 3) a regression method using only features to determine the target. Machine/Deep Learning models and traditional techniques like Seasonal Autoregressive Integrated Moving Average (SARIMA) were considered. According to [12,13], the performance of the models could be evaluated using metrics such as Mean Absolute Error (MAE), Mean Squared Error (MSE), Root Mean Square Error (RMSE), Mean Absolute Percentage Error (MAPE), and Coefficient of Determination (R^2). The model with the best performance across most of these metrics was selected as the most suitable.

2.2   Data Understanding

For the analysis, GMU-PV data from May 4, 2019 to April 15, 2023, as well as climatic data from [14], were used. Given the disparity in sampling between the two data sources, it was necessary to convert both into daily samples. This was achieved by taking the average value of variables of the photovoltaic energy production and climatic condition.

Upon analyzing the target variable Energy (kW h) and decomposing this time series into trend, seasonal, and residual components, Fig. 3 was obtained. In addition to this procedure, the target variable was also subjected to the Augmented Dickey Fuller (ADF) and Kwiatkowski-Phillips-Schmidt-Shin (KPSS) tests [15] to assess its nature as a time series. For the ADF test, if the test statistic result is below zero and the p-value is less than 0.05, the null hypothesis is rejected, indicating that the target is stationary. Conversely, with the KPSS test, if the test statistic result is above zero and the p-value is less than 0.05, the null hypothesis is rejected, suggesting that the target is non-stationary. As

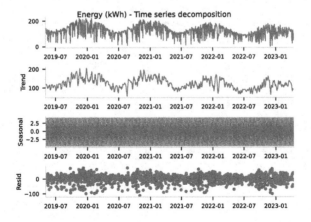

Fig. 3. Decomposition of the time series of the target variable Energy (kW h).

shown in Table 1, there is a duality in results, implying that the target variable is difference stationary.

Table 1. ADF and KPSS Test Results.

Test	Test Statistic	p-value	Result
ADF	$-2.866\ 094$	0.049 435	Stationary
KPSS	1.287 349	0.010 000	Not Stationary

Furthermore, using [16], it is possible to analyze the main statistics of the target variable, as depicted in Fig. 4, and check that these data do not follow a normal distribution, so suitability is required for application in some AI models.

For the other numeric variables in this dataset, which include: Phase I Voltage, Phase II Voltage, Phase III Voltage, Phase I Current, Phase II Current, Phase III Current, Frequency, Active Power, Reactive Power, Cos Phi, Voltage (DC), Current (DC), Power (DC), Energy (kWh), Downward Irradiance, Photosynthetically Active Radiation Total, UVA Irradiance, UVB Irradiance, UV Index, Temperature, Dew/Frost Point, Relative Humidity, Precipitation Corrected, Surface Pressure, Wind Speed, Wind Direction, Wet Bulb, Specific Humidity, proceeded with a decomposition into trend, seasonal, and residual components.

Subsequently, the ADF and KPSS tests and the Pearson Correlation Coefficient Matrix were applied, as shown in Fig. 5. Given the strong correlation observed among numerous variables, the implementation of Feature Engineering [17] became essential for optimizing Machine Learning models, including those like SARIMA.

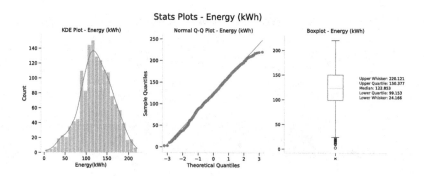

Fig. 4. KDE Plot, Normal Q-Q Plot and Boxplot of the target variable Energy (kW h).

Pearson Correlation Coefficient Matrix

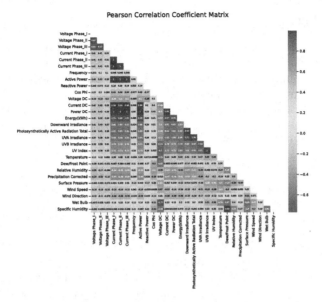

Fig. 5. Pearson Correlation Coefficient Matrix of variables dataset.

2.3 Data Preparation

The photovoltaic solar energy production dataset comes directly from the monitoring software of the inverter supplier while the climatic dataset that originates from Prediction Of Worldwide Energy Resources (POWER) Project by NASA, in this way, no type discrepancies, redundancies, missing, or excessive outliers were identified. Nevertheless, the regulations outlined in Module 8 of Electric Energy Distribution Procedures in the National Electric System (PRODIST) [18] mandate a power grid frequency between 59.9 and 60.1Hz. Frequencies outside this values lead to the system disconnecting from the electrical grid. As all outliers identified in the dataset resulted from disconnections due to frequency alterations, these outliers were removed. The total percentage of outliers in the dataset amounted to 0.3%.

After excluding this data, the only process performed was the resampling of the 72 593 hourly observations to daily sampling. Through the Pandas library [19], variables were resampled by their averages, and the two data sources were joined to create a single dataset with 1443 observations, 27 numeric float-type features, 1 numeric float-type target, and 1 datetime variable.

Finally, due to the difference in scale among the variables and to optimize the convergence of the models, the Scikit-Learn library [20] was used to perform standard scaling. Moreover, the dataset was divided into training (713 observations = 50%), validation (300 observations = 20%) and test (430 observations = 30%) sets.

2.4   Modeling

Considering the presence of variables with a high degree of correlation (Fig. 5), feature engineering is important. However, for the selected Machine and Deep Learning models and libraries, the original features was retained, as these methods internally handle feature engineering.

Additionally, to prevent overfitting, models underwent cross-validation through the TimeSeriesSplit (ts_splits) feature of the Scikit-Learn library, and, in the case of Deep Learning, Early Stopping and Dropout have also been implemented.

Another strategy adopted was hyperparameter optimization using Random Search and fine-tuning with Grid Search for Machine Learning models, and HParams [21] for Deep Learning models. As mentioned, three distinct approaches were used, as explained:

Univariate Time Series: In this methodology [10], only the target variable Energy (kW h) is used and the datetime variable is the data index. The concept involves predicting a value based on a number of previous points and a distance from the point to be predicted. Using the Darts library [22], which specializes in time series and combines classic models like SARIMA, Machine and Deep Learning models, and carries out a low-code process for the sequential computation of all models available in the library.

As the ADF and KPSS tests classified the series as difference stationary, differentiation for a better result in terms of prediction was considered in models that, like SARIMA, can use differentiation.

After submitting the train, validation and testing datasets to the available models, the Machine Learning model XGBoost Regressor yielded the best results. Next, the hyperparameter optimization process was carried out by Random Search and fine-tuning with Grid Search, the best model hyperparameters contemplated: lag = 10, n_estimators = 100 and Input as ndarray (1,).

The evaluation metrics of this model for the test data are presented in Table 2, and Fig. 6 presents the performance of the prediction compared to the actual Energy (kW h) data.

Table 2. XGBoost Regressor model results from the Darts Library.

MAE	MSE	RMSE	MAPE	R^2
29.335 376	1346.605 155	36.696 119	0.524 371	−0.185 010

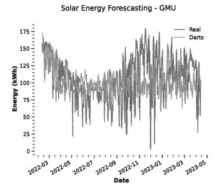

Fig. 6. Solar Energy Forecasting - GMU-PV (using models from Darts).

As the results with this approach were not fully convergent for the analyzed hyperparameters in relation to the test data, this approach could not be considered as the final model.

Multivariate Time Series: In this methodology [10], all variables in the dataset is involved. The concept also involves predicting by a number of previous points as previous. The best result was obtained with the NeuralProphet library [23].

While the original Prophet uses an additive model to decompose time series into trend, seasonality, and holiday components, NeuralProphet adds the ability to use neural networks to model these components, providing the ability to capture non-linear relationships in the data.

Thus, upon submitting the train, validation and testing datasets to the model, the best model contemplated a lag of 1 point to predict the immediately subsequent one. The final hyperparameters are: `growth` = `'off'`, `num_hidden_layers` = 4, `d_hidden` = 4, `learning_rate` = 2e-2, `loss_func` = `'MSE'`, `epochs` = 64, `ts_splits` = 6 and Input as ndarray (27,).

The evaluation metrics of this model for the test data are presented in Table 3, Fig. 7 represents the training and validation loss, confirming that no overfitting occurred. Finally, Fig. 8 presents the performance of the prediction compared to the actual Energy (kW h) data.

Table 3. Results of the NeuralProphet Model.

MAE	MSE	RMSE	MAPE	R^2
1.895 517	6.012 676	2.452 076	0.552 482	0.161 024

Although the results with this approach were convergent for the analyzed hyperparameters in relation to the test data and no overfitting was detected, as the metrics results and graphs performed low, this approach could not be considered as the final model.

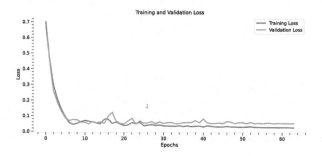

Fig. 7. Training and Validation Loss (using NeuralProphet model).

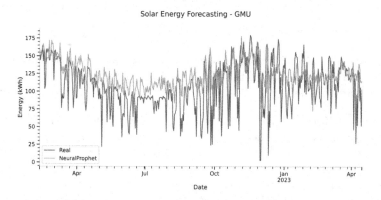

Fig. 8. Solar Energy Forecasting - GMU-PV (using NeuralProphet model).

Regression: In this methodology [11], two modelling approaches are used: 1) Machine Learning models: all regression models available in the low-code PyCaret library [24], the regression model of Conformal Prediction [25] from the Mapie library [26], as well as the Prophet [27] model developed by Facebook; 2) Deep Learning models: Convolutional Neural Network (CNN) [28], Long Short-Term Memory (LSTM) [29] and Transformer [30].

PyCaret library brings together the Machine Learning regression models available from the Scikit-Learn library, in addition to automating the use of these models serially. Moreover, for cases like this one, where strongly correlated features exist, the library performs Feature Engineering and cross-validation with splits parts of the series. Upon applying the train, validation and testing datasets to the aforementioned models, the Orthogonal Matching Pursuit (OMP) [31] linear regression technique proved to be the most effective. The following hyperparameters were used: `fit_intercept` = `True`, `n_nonzero_coefs` = `None`, `normalize` = `'deprecated'`, `precompute` = `'auto'`, `tol` = `None`, `ts_splits` = 6 and Input as ndarray (27,).

Conformal Prediction [32] is implemented through a two-regressor framework: one for the regression task itself, and another to evaluate the performance of the first and assign a conformity score, thereby improving its result, regardless of the algorithm employed in the initial regressor. In this paper, the Random Forest Regressor was selected as the primary regressor, given its inherent ability to perform Feature Engineering. The Mapie Regressor was applied as a secondary measure, a feature of the Mapie library [26].

Upon applying the train, validation and test datasets to the model, and after hyperparameter optimization, the following hyperparameters were obtained for the Random Forest Regressor: `n_estimators` = 2, `max_depth` = 5, `ts_splits` = 6 and Input as ndarray (27,).

Prophet is a additive Machine Learning model, developed by Facebook, where time series are viewed as a combination of trend, seasonality, and holiday components. The trend component captures the non-periodic evolution over the long term, seasonal components capture periodic effects, and holiday components capture the effects of irregular events that occur on scheduled dates. It is a flexible trend model that can accommodate both linear and logistic growth trends.

Upon applying the train, validation and test datasets to the model, and after hyperparameter optimization, the following hyperparameters were obtained: `changepoint_prior_scale` = 0.4, `growth` = 'linear', `n_changepoints`= 25, `changepoint_range` = 0.8, `ts_splits` = 6 and Input as ndarray (27,).

Convolutional Neural Networks (CNN) [33] for unidimensional cases (1D CNNs) represent an adaptation of the traditional Convolutional Neural Networks (CNNs), specifically configured to handle sequential or temporal data. Analogous to standard CNNs, 1D CNNs use convolution operations to extract features from a dataset, however, instead of operating on a 2D matrix of pixels like in an image, they process a unidimensional sequence of data.

The Deep Learning architecture described here was developed in Tensorflow Keras [34] via HParams [21] obtain the optimizing architecture in Fig. 9, with the training and validation loss shown in Fig. 10. The selected hyperparameters were: `loss` = MSE, `optimizer` = RMSprop, `learning_rate` = 1e-4, `epsilon` =1e-16, `metrics` = RMSE, `ts_splits` = 6 and Input as tensor (27,1).

Fig. 9. CNN architecture used.

Long Short-Term Memory (LSTM) [35] are a specific variant of Recurrent Neural Networks (RNNs) designed to circumvent the problem known as "gradient vanishing", making them effective in learning long data sequences. Due to their ability to retain information from previous data points, LSTMs are particularly suitable for time series regression tasks, a crucial attribute for predicting future values in such a series.

The Deep Learning architecture in question was implemented in Tensorflow Keras. Upon submitting the train, validation and test datasets to the model and optimizing hyperparameters, the final architecture was arrived at, as shown in Fig. 11, with the training and validation loss displayed in Fig. 12. The selected hyperparameters were: loss = MSE, optimizer = RMSprop, learning_rate = 1e-5, epsilon = 1e-12, metrics = RMSE, ts_splits = 6 and Input as tensor (27, 1).

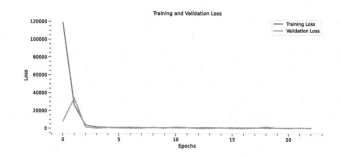

Fig. 10. Training and Validation Loss (using CNN model).

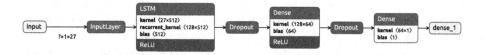

Fig. 11. LSTM architecture used.

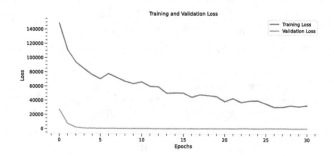

Fig. 12. Training and Validation Loss (using the LSTM model).

Transformers [36] are a neural network architecture originally designed for Natural Language Processing (NLP) tasks, such as automatic translation, in which they have achieved remarkable success. However, their application has also extended to time series regression tasks, where they exhibit significant performance. One of the distinct features of Transformers is their ability to model complex dependencies over time, stemming from their capability to weigh the importance of different data points within the input sequence.

The aforementioned Deep Learning architecture was implemented in Tensorflow Keras. Following the submission of the train, validation and test datasets to the model, and the hyperparameters optimization, the final architecture was obtained, as illustrated in Fig. 13, with the corresponding training and validation loss displayed in Fig. 14. The adjusted hyperparameters were: loss = MSE, optimizer = Adam, learning_rate = 1e-3, epsilon = 1e-12, metrics = RMSE, amsgrad = True, head_size = 56, num_heads = 4, ff_dim = 4, ts_splits = 5 and Input as tensor (27, 1).

Fig. 13. Transformer Architecture used.

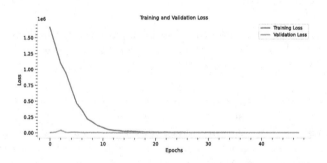

Fig. 14. Training and Validation Loss (using the Transformer model).

Hence, the results obtained from the use of regression models are summarized in Table 4, and additionally, Fig. 15 presents the forecasting performance of the models compared with the actual Energy (kW h) data.

From this, it can be observed that all the presented models converged and achieved good results on the established metrics, despite the LSTM model exhibiting an underfitting case, as illustrated in Fig. 12. However, out of the three approaches considered for this paper, this was the most successful one, with the Orthogonal Matching Pursuit (OMP) Machine Learning model from

Table 4. Regression Models Results Table.

Model	MAE	MSE	RMSE	MAPE	R^2
PyCaret	6.317 669	73.302 349	8.561 679	0.127 132	0.935 494
Conformal	6.746 395	83.538 955	9.139 965	0.120 461	0.926 486
LSTM	8.755 827	109.929 299	10.484 717	0.142 408	0.903 262
Prophet	9.424 195	126.971 854	11.268 179	0.155 440	0.888 265
Transformer	8.496 331	133.023 516	11.533 582	0.110 105	0.882 940
CNN	9.713 513	133.339 422	11.547 269	0.141 591	0.882 662

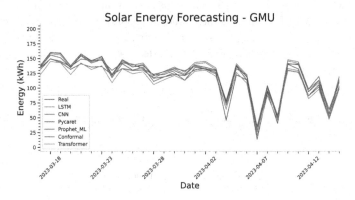

Fig. 15. Solar Energy Forecasting - GMU-PV (using Regression Models).

the PyCaret Library demonstrating the best performance and, consequently, being selected as the final model to be implemented in production.

2.5 Evaluation

Out of the three proposed strategies, there was no convergence in the univariate time series analysis. On the other hand, convergence was observed in the multivariate analysis, but with lower performance compared to the regressive approach. Using three distinct Machine Learning regression models [24,25,27] and three others through Deep Learning [28–30], R^2 values ranged between [0.882 662; 0.935 494], demonstrating significant efficacy and potential for research questions analysis.

The most effective model, Orthogonal Matching Pursuit (OMP), is commonly used for retrieving sparse signals from noisy measurements and involves approximating the fit of a linear model with constraints imposed on the number of non-zero coefficients. As a forward feature selection method, it approximates the ideal solution vector with a fixed number of non-zero elements.

$$\arg\min_{w} ||y - Xw||_2^2 \text{ subject to } ||w||_0 \leq n_{\text{nonzero\_coefs}} \tag{1}$$

Alternatively, the orthogonal matching pursuit can aim for a specific error rather than a specific number of non-zero coefficients. This approach can be expressed as:

$$\arg\min_{w} ||w||_0 \text{ subject to } ||y - Xw||_2^2 \leq \text{tol} \tag{2}$$

In the context of this paper, OMP predominantly behaves as a greedy algorithm. This means the algorithm consistently selects the best available orthogonal vector without necessarily considering future consequences. As a result, the best global solution might not always be found, but rather an optimal local one. While this approach might result in a suboptimal solution, an advantage lies in the algorithm is typical efficiency and simplicity in implementation.

When comparing it to other analyzed alternatives, OMP shows better performance, since greedy algorithms in seasonal time series, with minimal structural variation and reduced data volume, are not very compromised, the local optimal solution leading to more interesting metrics than in the other models evaluated.

Finally, for this model and datasets, the features of greatest importance were DC Voltage (0.35) and Wind Speed at 10m height (0.08).

3 Conclusions

Regarding the research inquiries, with the available data from the GMU-PV, it was possible to implement a model with an R^2 of 0.935 494 and an RMSE of 8.561 679, for a variable with an average of 123.08 kW h. This result is promising for future forecasts and enables a contract in the Free Energy Market with seasonal clauses, taking into account the cyclical variation presented by Fig. 3.

Given the need to resample the data to a daily average, since data acquisition from the original sources varied, the number of data points in the dataset dropped to 1443. Of these, 50% were used for training, 20% for validation, and 30% for testing. Therefore, even with measures taken to prevent overfitting/underfitting, such as Cross Validation, Dropout and Early Stopping, models tested with more complex architectures experienced a slight decrease in performance due to the reduced data volume. However, in the broader context, this difference did not exceed 5% in the R^2 metric, for example.

In the process of resampling for daily averages by variable, the results obtained can be deemed conservative. However, there is the possibility of creating a range of values considering the lower limit as the daily resample by the minimum value (pessimistic projection) and the upper limit by the daily resample by the maximum value (optimistic projection).

Finally, it is feasible to extend this methodology to other Photovoltaic Plants of the University, thereby enhancing the robustness and reliability of the results. These findings could be instrumental in planning new installations.

If the robustness of the model is validated with data from the other Photovoltaic Plants of the University, it will move to production and undergo testing during the Deployment phase of the CRISP-DM Methodology. Only after receiving positive feedback from the University community will it solidify its role as a management tool. This would contribute to reducing the use of high environmental impact energy, aligning with the primary objectives of CPTEn and PCS.

Acknowledgement. The authors thanks the Research Foundation of the State of São Paulo (FAPESP) for supporting the research under grants #2021/11380-5 and #2020/16635-9 also the support from São Paulo Center for Energy Transition Studies (CPTEn), DeepMind Scholarship Program and Coordenação de Aperfeiçoamento de Pessoal de Nivel Superior - Brasil (CAPES) - Finance Code 001. R. Attux thanks CNPq (proc. 308811/2019-4).

References

1. COP27: United nations climate change conference of 2022 (2022). https://cop27. eg/. Accessed 01 Feb 2023
2. CPTEn: São Paulo Center for Energy Transition Studies (2023). https://cpten. unicamp.br/en/home-english/. Accessed 01 Feb 2023
3. Balance, N.E.: National energy balance 2022 (in portuguese), p. 12 (2022). https://www.epe.gov.br/sites-pt/publicacoes-dados-abertos/publicacoes/ PublicacoesArquivos/publicacao-675/topico-638/BEN2022.pdf. Accessed 01 Feb 2023
4. AEPLAN: PDO Unicamp 2023 (in portuguese), p. 12 (2023). https://www. aeplan.unicamp.br/wp-content/uploads/sites/5/2023/03/pdo_unicamp_2023. pdf. Accessed 01 Feb 2023
5. Ministry of Science, T., Innovation: Emission factors - sirene (in portuguese) (2023). https://www.gov.br/mcti/pt-br/acompanhe-o-mcti/sirene/dados-e- ferramentas/fatores-de-emissao. Accessed 01 Feb 2023
6. Campus, S.: Sustainable campus - solar power plants (2023). https://campus- sustentavel.unicamp.br/pv/. Accessed 01 Feb 2023
7. Ingeteam: Ingecon sun 100tl (2023). https://www.ingeteam.com/en-us/sectors/ photovoltaic-energy/p15_24_624_450/ingecon-sun-100tl.aspx. Accessed 01 Feb 2023
8. Canadian solar datasheet cs6k-p (2023). https://www.solar-electric.com/lib/wind- sun/Canadian_Solar-Datasheet-CS6K-P.pdf. Accessed 01 Feb 2023
9. Wirth, R., Hipp, J.: CRISP-DM: towards a standard process model for data mining. In: 4th International Conference on Practical Application of Knowledge Discovery and Data Mining, Manchester, pp. 29–40 (2000)
10. Wei, W.: Time Series Analysis Univariate and Multivariate Methods. Pearson Modern Classics for Advanced Statistics Series. Pearson Education (2019). https:// books.google.com.br/books?id=_v-xswEACAAJ
11. Bowerman, B., O'Connell, R., Koehler, A.: Forecasting, Time Series, and Regression: An Applied Approach. Duxbury Advanced Series in statistics and Decision Sciences. Thomson Brooks/Cole (2005). https://books.google.com.br/books? id=2Yc_AQAAIAAJ
12. Hastie, T., Tibshirani, R., Friedman, J.: The Elements of Statistical Learning: Data Mining, Inference, and Prediction. Springer, Heidelberg (2009). https://doi. org/10.1007/978-0-387-84858-7
13. Murphy, K.P.: Machine Learning: A Probabilistic Perspective. MIT Press, Cambridge (2013)
14. Project, N.P.: Data access viewer (DAV) (2023). https://power.larc.nasa.gov/data- access-viewer/. Accessed 15 Apr 2023
15. Seabold, S., Perktold, J.: Statsmodels: econometric and statistical modeling with python. In: 9th Python in Science Conference (2010)

16. Peng, J., et al.: DataPrep.EDA: task-centric exploratory data analysis for statistical modeling in python. CoRR abs/2104.00841 (2021). https://arxiv.org/abs/2104.00841
17. Dong, G., Liu, H.: Feature Engineering for Machine Learning and Data Analytics, 1st edn. CRC Press Inc., USA (2018)
18. Module 8 revision 8 of prodist (in portuguese), p. 20 (2023). https://antigo.aneel.gov.br/documents/656827/14866914/M%C3%B3dulo8_Revisao_8/9c78cfab-a7d7-4066-b6ba-cfbda3058d19. Accessed 01 Feb 2023
19. The pandas development team: pandas-dev/pandas: Pandas (2020). https://doi.org/10.5281/zenodo.3509134
20. Pedregosa, F., et al.: Scikit-learn: machine learning in Python. J. Mach. Learn. Res. **12**, 2825–2830 (2011)
21. Petrochuk, M.: HParams: hyperparameter management solution (2019). https://github.com/PetrochukM/HParams
22. Herzen, J., et al.: DARTS: user-friendly modern machine learning for time series. J. Mach. Learn. Res. **23**(124), 1–6 (2022). https://jmlr.org/papers/v23/21-1177.html
23. Triebe, O., Hewamalage, H., Pilyugina, P., Laptev, N., Bergmeir, C., Rajagopal, R.: NeuralProphet: explainable forecasting at scale (2021)
24. Ali, M.: PyCaret: an open source, low-code machine learning library in Python (2020). https://www.pycaret.org. PyCaret version 1.0.0
25. Gammerman, A., Vovk, V.G., Vapnik, V.: Learning by transduction. In: Proceedings of the 14th Conference on Uncertainty in Artificial Intelligence, pp. 148–155 (1998)
26. Taquet, V., Blot, V., Morzadec, T., Lacombe, L., Brunel, N.: MAPIE: an open-source library for distribution-free uncertainty quantification (2022). Submitted 25 July 2022
27. Taylor, S.J., Letham, B.: Forecasting at scale. Am. Stat. **72**(1), 37–45 (2018)
28. O'Shea, K., Nash, R.: An introduction to convolutional neural networks. CoRR abs/1511.08458 (2015). https://arxiv.org/abs/1511.08458
29. Hochreiter, S., Schmidhuber, J.: Long short-term memory. Neural Comput. **9**(8), 1735–1780 (1997)
30. Vaswani, A., et al.: Attention is all you need. In: Advances in Neural Information Processing Systems, pp. 5998–6008 (2017)
31. Mallat, G., Zhang, Z.: Matching pursuits with time-frequency dictionaries. IEEE Trans. Signal Process. **41**(12), 3397–3415 (1993). https://ieeexplore.ieee.org/document/258082
32. Balasubramanian, V., Ho, S.S., Vovk, V.: Conformal Prediction for Reliable Machine Learning: Theory, Adaptations and Applications. Newnes (2014). Google-Books-ID: pgfUAgAAQBAJ
33. Li, Z., Liu, F., Yang, W., Peng, S., Zhou, J.: A survey of convolutional neural networks: analysis, applications, and prospects. IEEE Trans. Neural Netw. Learn. Syst. **33**(12), 6999–7019 (2022)
34. Chollet, F., et al.: Keras (2015). https://keras.io
35. Han, L., Jing, H., Zhang, R., Gao, Z.: Wind power forecast based on improved long short term memory network. Energy **189**, 116300 (2019). https://www.sciencedirect.com/science/article/pii/S0360544219319954
36. Lin, T., Wang, Y., Liu, X., Qiu, X.: A survey of transformers. AI Open **3**, 111–132 (2022). https://www.sciencedirect.com/science/article/pii/S2666651022000146

Smart Electricity System

Gossen's First Law in the Modeling for Demand Side Management: A First Heat Pump Case Study

Chang Li[✉][iD], Kevin Förderer[iD], Tobias Moser, Luigi Spatafora, and Veit Hagenmeyer[iD]

Karlsruher Institut für Technologie, Kaiserstraße 12, 76131 Karlsruhe, Germany
{chang.li,kevin.foerderer,tobias.moser,luigi.spatafora,
veit.hagenmeyer}@kit.edu

Abstract. Gossen's First Law, also known as the law of diminishing marginal utility, describes the decreasing marginal utility gained from an increased consumption of a good or service and this is observed in various areas. This paper proposes the hypothesis that Gossen's First Law also holds in the modeling for Demand Side Management. It motivates the exploration of how the utility of a model depends on its complexity in this context, in order to provide a guideline that helps developing more simple and efficient models. We then propose a methodology for this investigation and apply it to a ground source heat pump in a stand-alone house. For this purpose, four mathematical models are developed with different degrees of simplification based on a detailed mathematical model. The model complexity is then quantified, and the simulation results are compared with actual measurement data to explore the utility of each model. The first results are in line with our hypothesis. Finally, we outline the next steps to provide more results and thoroughly verify the hypothesis.

Keywords: Demand Side Management (DSM) · Distributed Energy Resources (DER) · Ground Source Heat Pump (GSHP) · Modeling

1 Introduction

The total energy consumption of private households in Germany has only slightly increased by 3.7% from 2010 to 2018. In the meantime, the use of renewable energy has significantly increased by 26.3% and accounted for more than 14% of all kinds of energy sources [4]. On the way to a sustainable energy supply, higher flexibility in the overall system is of increasing importance due to rising shares of renewable energies. In addition to adapting production to renewable energies, there is also the possibility of adapting the electricity load to electricity production, also known as Demand Side Management (DSM) [8]. Load-changing ability is usually provided by so called Distributed Energy Resources (DERs), such as battery energy storages. Due to the energy transition, buildings will contain more and more electricity-related components such as heat pumps, solar systems, charging stations for e-mobility and fuel cell systems as home power plants. Thus, there are plenty of different models for DSM applications with varying degree of complexity. However, when modeling such components and their synergies for DSM, it is often unclear how detailed they need to be for the purpose of DSM since there is always an interaction effect between the utility and complexity of a model.

As seen in many modeling-based works, energy system models are generally categorized into three types: white box, gray box and black box [15]. White box models are based on detailed physical entities of a system and the laws of physics such as the thermodynamics, e.g., [1,5]. On the contrary, black box models do not focus on the physical properties of a system and instead are data-driven by lots of empirical datasets, e.g., [1,22]. Gray box models, which fall between the other two, consider the physical structure of a system by using simplified models such as low-order ordinary differential equations, e.g., [9,22]. Each kind of the modeling categories has its own characteristics and results in different complexities and utilities. To build white box models, a lot of expertise on specific physical systems is required. For a whole system of different mechanical, thermal or electrical components, the effort for modeling is enormous and the expansibility is limited, whereas the details, especially the interactions between them, are well contained. In contrast, the details of an energy system in black box modeling are neglected. However, massive highly resolved datasets such as load profiles are necessary for a good modeling. Although some advanced algorithms can make the results of black box models accurate enough for specific use cases, the lack of details can raise concerns on its reliability and interpretability. When we only focus on the non-transient interaction between major elements, the physical structure of a system may be simplified in order to build balanced gray box models.

A complex model can usually provide more meaningful results than a simple model, but the effort required to modeling it increases accordingly. The question of how to strike a reasonable balance when modeling for DSM considering interaction between complexity and utility, to the best of our knowledge, is still not answered in the literature. Mainly inspired by Gossen's First Law in economics and by research results in other modeling applications, e.g., in Building Information Modeling (BIM) [16], we want to propose the hypothesis that in general the complexity-utility relationship in the field of DSM modeling could be represented by a diminishing marginal utility curve, too. In this context, a method is needed for quantifying the complexity and the utility, in order to illustrate the complexity-utility relationship.

In order to verify the proposed hypothesis, four mathematical models of a Ground Source Heat Pump (GSHP) with different degrees of simplification are derived. All four models are used to calculate the electrical load profile with different number of measurement inputs and then compared with ground truth i.e. the electrical power consumption by high precision sensors in the circuit. By analyzing the Mean Absolute Percentage Error (MAPE Mean) and the Maximum Absolute Percentage Error (MAPE Max), the utility of different models is quantified for the purpose of plotting the diminishing marginal utility curve.

The remainder of the paper is divided into four parts. Several related works are concluded in the following Sect. 2. In Sect. 3, a brief description of the infrastructure used for measurement is given. Then the method and ideas for quantifying complexity and utility of DSM modeling as well as visualizing the relationship between them are defined and explained in Sect. 4. Section 5 presents the four developed mathematical models, along with the detailed reference model. Section 6 presents, analyses and discusses the simulation results and measurement data. Finally, the main conclusions and plans for future work are highlighted in Sect. 7.

2   Related Work

In recent years, there has been an increasing amount of literature on modeling of demand response or DSM technologies. For instance, in [26] a modeling framework for 4 types of individual devices which are expected to participate in future demand-response markets are introduced. The purpose is to pursue their optimal price-taking control strategy under a given stochastic situation. The models are differentiated into 4 types which are optimal and generic. Therefore, modeling of specific systems and synergies between different systems are not investigated. In 2013, a more generic taxonomy for modeling flexibility in Smart Grids are defined in [21], which divided all systems into three categories and used them to optimize and solve flexibility problems in Smart Grids. This type of modeling approach simplifies the modeling process and improves optimization efficiency. However, the challenges of considering different influencing factors in real energy systems such as temperature are not solved since the models are too abstract. For this reason, the models are hard to be directly applied to real energy systems on the demand side.

In contrast, [12,20,25] used very detailed theoretical models and complex numerical techniques such as Lax-Wendroff finite difference approximations for a specified system i.e. heat pump and its subsystems. These models are capable of delivering accurate results, however, yield very high complexity and low performance, which limits the application in DSM.

In summary, we conclude that models of varying degree of complexity have different utilities, as mentioned in Sect. 1. However, there is no, to the best knowledge of the authors, straightforward investigation of the effect of model complexity on model utility in DSM. Hence, it's necessary to investigate the relationship between the utility and complexity of a model in order to provide a better reference for different DSM applications.

3   Measurement System Infrastructure

Analyzing the utility of different models relies on accurate real-world measurement data, which are provided by our measurement system infrastructure. This section first briefly introduces the floor plan and setup of our LLEC (Living Lab Energy Campus) buildings [10] to give an overview of their spatial layout and their heating matrix setup. Subsequently, the technical and software infrastructure that makes time series data from LLEC available is described.

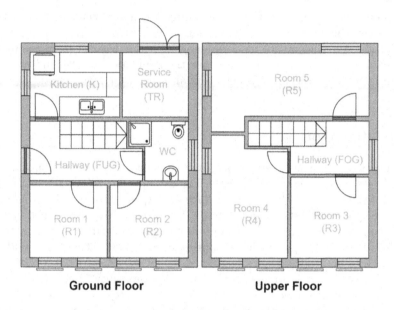

Ground Floor   **Upper Floor**

Fig. 1. Schematic floor plan of the LLEC house

3.1   Overview and Setup of Living Lab Energy Campus

Within the facilities of the Energy Lab 2.0 [13], three free-standing single-family houses have been purpose-built and equipped with a large variety of automation hardwares to allow for the use of advanced modern energy solutions [10]. All houses share the same two-story floor plan with several normal rooms, kitchen and restroom, as shown in Fig. 1. But they differ in the choice of heating source. Each room is equipped with a range of different kinds of sensors and actuators, e.g., room climate sensors, heat flow meters, motorized windows, and smart thermostats, with only minor differences in equipment between the houses. The hardware is addressed by a PLC (Programmable Logic Controller), which handles control requests from external systems and automatically collects, filters and stores measurement data in our database. The latter process will be explained in more detail in the next subsection.

This paper focuses the LLEC house which uses a GSHP together with a hot water tank for the house heating and domestic hot water supply. Figure 2 shows the schematic heat matrix of the overall heating system along with the electrical circuit installed in the experimental LLEC house. The GSHP has its own internal sensors to determine the hot water flow rate, the supply and return temperature of water and brine as well as other datapoints.

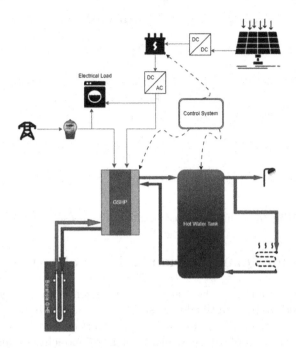

Fig. 2. Schematic heat matrix and electrical circuit of the experimental LLEC house

Furthermore, additional external sensors for water temperature and flow rate are installed to build a redundant measurement system to ensure more useful characteristics such as self-calibration, error compensation and the recovery of lost information.

3.2 Technical Infrastructure for Measurement Acquisition and Storage

The measurement system architecture is shown in Fig. 3 and consists of separate tools for collecting, processing, and storing timeseries data, with the relevant systems being shown in green. The data source in our experiments is the PLC, which acquires data in regular intervals via different bus systems or analogue inputs. In the new protocol version, the data is then formatted as JSON and sent to a MQTT (Message Queuing Telemetry Transport) Broker with a datapoint-specific topic. The data is subsequently received by a data logger service subscribed to the MQTT topic, parsed, and pushed to our InfluxDB database via its REST (Representational State Transfer) interface. This new architecture allows to easily select the required inputs for different models via their respective topics and to choose the datasets for the validation and analysis of the simulation results.

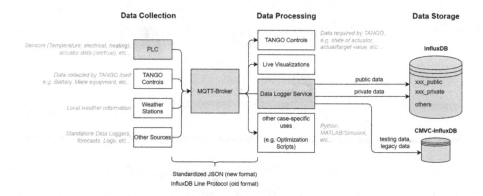

Fig. 3. Technical infrastructure of the measurement

4   Method for Quantification and Visualization

As with Gossen's First Law, the marginal utility itself is an inherently abstract concept and needs to be quantified first, such as income [14], in order to illustrate its relationship with consumption or other properties. Similarly, the method for quantifying the complexity and utility of DSM modeling is also crucial to visualize the interaction between them. This section discusses separately what kinds of quantitative options for complexity and utility are available and then explains those that have been chosen in the present work.

4.1   Quantification of Complexity

In computer sciences complexity is measured in various ways, such as required time, number of operations, or required memory. They do depend on the specific algorithms, their implementation, and the hardware they are running on. For modeling we need other measures. Different from computational complexity theory or information theory, this work focuses on the modeling of physical structure or dynamical processes of energy components in DSM applications. Thus, an appropriate method for quantification appliable for all possible system components is required.

In [2,3,11] different time scales are used in energy systems of different complexity. In the process of modeling, if transient processes within a system are non-decisive, we could neglect the details and use larger time scale to simplify the whole process. However, this option cannot differentiate the complexity of the same model because different time scales can also be chosen during the simulation for the same model.

Besides choosing different time scales, another option to quantify complexity would be by the power range that can cover the range from milliwatt (mW) to gigawatt (GW). Different power ranges would have an impact on dynamic responses of the model, leading to more complex model and corresponding controls [6]. However, the limitations of this option are also significant because the power range is generally determined for a given energy system. Therefore, the power range of a model cannot always be artificially changed to quantify its complexity.

A third way of quantifying complexity could be based on the number of required parameters in models. On a structural basis, any model is a combination of different input and output parameters. Furthermore, for the same model, the number of parameters could be adjusted according to the study objectives or experimental conditions, so that models of different complexity can be built.

Among the three methods mentioned above, the third method has the best applicability and feasibility. Based on that, the included parameters of a model, i.e. the number of applied parameters, has been chosen to quantify the complexity in our work.

4.2 Quantification of Utility

The main goal of DSM applications is to improve the flexibility of a power system [8]. In this context, the methods for the quantification of utility are as same as those for quantifying flexibility in DSM applications. In [19] four typical ways for quantifying flexibility in DSM, namely load-shifting, peak shaving, reduction of energy use and valley filling, are explained and summarized. In [7] two more specific approaches i.e. daily primary energy use and daily energy costs are used to show the improved and quantified flexibility.

In addition, it is worth noting that the accuracy of a model must first be verified through offline simulations before the model is used to analyze flexibility in DSM applications. According to ISO 5725-1, the general term "accuracy" describes the closeness of a measurement to the true value [18]. Based on this definition, we can quantitatively describe the accuracy of a model with the help of some useful metrics in descriptive statistics, such as max error, Root-Mean-Square Error (RMSE) and Mean Absolute Percentage Error (MAPE).

This work focuses on the accuracy of different models in an offline simulation and uses quantified accuracy to represent utility of models. In order to reduce the impact of absolute values on the accuracy analysis, MAPE Mean and MAPE Max are used for the analysis in this work. It's worth noting that the Mean and Max after MAPE are meant to distinguish between the two MAPE abbreviations as described in Sect. 1. More details are given in Sect. 6.

5 Ground Source Heat Pump and Heat Pump Storage Modeling

In this section we introduce the employed models and discuss different options for modeling a GSHP and heat pump storage with varying degree of detail that we used for the evaluation of utility and complexity. The operating principle of a GSHP for house space heating and hot water supply is based on a reverse Carnot thermodynamic cycle [24], which means the thermal energy at the output consists of two parts i.e. environmental energy and driving energy. Depending on the source of different energy, models can vary accordingly. This work focuses on a Ground-Coupled Heat Pump (GCHP), a subset of GSHP, with vertical U-tubes as Ground Heat Exchanger (GHE). In this case, heat transfer takes place in three subsystems: GHE in borehole, heat pump and heat pump storage. The following subsections develop and explain mathematical models with different complexity for each subsystem.

5.1   Thermal Model of Borehole Ground Heat Exchanger

Building and validating a detailed theoretical model of a borehole GHE requires too many geometric and thermal properties [23, 25] which is beyond the scope of the present work. Alternatively, if we only focus on the inlet temperature T^{in} and outlet temperature T^{out} of the borehole GHE, we can easily use the specific heat capacity of brine c_b and the mass flow of brine $\dot{m}_b$ to calculate the temperature change at different times as follows:

$$T_t^{out} = T_{t-1}^{in} + \frac{P_{Q,t-1}^{abs}}{c_b \cdot \dot{m}_b} \tag{1}$$

where $P_{Q,t-1}^{abs}$ is the absorbed thermal power at time $t-1$, which is also the difference between thermal power $P_{Q,t-1}^{hp}$ and electrical power of the GSHP $P_{el,t-1}^{hp}$ at the same time and calculated in (2).

$$P_{Q,t-1}^{abs} = P_{Q,t-1}^{hp} - P_{el,t-1}^{hp} \tag{2}$$

5.2   Thermal Model of Heat Pump

In contrast to the GHE, the GSHP is modeled with varying degree of detail and complexity. As mentioned before, heat pumps operate upon a reverse Carnot cycle involving four steps. In a detailed, physical model we would describe each step and the associated physical processes. However, in the context of DSM, models are much more abstract. Therefore, we focus on more abstract models based on COP (Coefficient of Performance), which is typically used to characterize heat pump's overall performance. This value is influenced by many factors in actual operation such as the supply/return temperature, outdoor temperature. In [20] a linear data-fitting equation was used for calculating the COP of the GSHP taking the outlet temperature of borehole GHE and indoor temperature into consideration. Similarly, this work employs a second-order polynomial regression in consideration of outdoor air temperature T_t^{env} to calculate the declared COP and declared heat power P_{dh} in kW at medium partial load based on the data sheet of the heat pump manufacturer [17] in (3) and (4). The R-squared value of the regression is 0.9902 and 0.9972 respectively.

$$COP_t^{cal} = -0.0007 \cdot (T_{t-1}^{env})^2 + 0.0983 \cdot (T_{t-1}^{env}) + 3.8429 \tag{3}$$

$$P_{dh} = 0.0009 \cdot (T_{t-1}^{env})^2 - 0.1992 \cdot (T_{t-1}^{env}) + 3.4164 \tag{4}$$

For the subsequent combination of different models with varying degree of detail in Sect. 6, we can further simplify (3) and (4) by neglecting the effect of outdoor temperature and consider COP as well as P_{dh} as a constant as follows:

$$COP^{const.} = 3.8429 \tag{5}$$

$$P_{dh}^{const.} = 3.4164 \tag{6}$$

Alternatively, we can calculate the COP directly with the measured thermal and electrical data over a period of time and obtain an average value as follows:

$$COP^{avg} = \frac{1}{n} \sum_{1}^{n} \frac{P_{Q,t}^{hp}}{P_{el,t}^{hp}} \tag{7}$$

The thermal power $P_{Q,t}^{hp}$ is measured and calculated with (8), where c_w, ρ_w and $\dot{V}_w$ are the specific heat capacity, density and volume rate of water respectively. The difference between supply temperature and return temperature is represented by $(T^{supply} - T^{return})$.

$$P_{Q,t}^{hp} = c_w \cdot \dot{V}_w \cdot \rho_w \cdot (T_{t-1}^{supply} - T_{t-1}^{return}) \tag{8}$$

5.3 Thermal Model of Heat Pump Storage

As the central storage for thermal energy, the temperature and corresponding energy changes have a significant impact on the overall system. This work uses a multi-layer hot water tank with negligible heat loss as the central storage for domestic hot water and space heating. Assuming the density and the specific heat capacity of hot water as constant, the thermal energy change in the storage between two successive time steps is calculated as follows:

$$\Delta Q_s = c_w \cdot V_s \cdot \rho_w \cdot (T_t^{mean} - T_{t-1}^{mean}) \tag{9}$$

where V_s is the volume of the hot water tank and $(T_t^{mean} - T_{t-1}^{mean})$ denotes the average temperature change of hot water, which are determined in (10) with the assumption that the temperature is evenly distributed in each layer at every time step:

$$T_t^{mean} = \frac{T_t^u + T_t^m + T_t^l}{3} \tag{10}$$

In (10), we use three temperature sensors placed in the upper, middle and lower layer of the hot water tank to measure the temperature of each layer, assuming that each of these temperatures represents one-third of the total capacity.

6   Results and Discussions

In this section, the models are first classified based on the number of required parameters by combining different mathematical models presented in Sect. 5. Then, various models are used to perform offline calculations of the load profile and analyze the results together with the measurement. Lastly, the section concludes with a discussion of the hypothesis mentioned at the beginning of this work.

6.1   Model Classification and Geometric-Thermal Parameters

Table 1. Model classification with respect to parameters

Model Class	Combination	Number of required Parameters
Model A	(1)(2)(7)(9)(10)	11
Model B	(7)(8)	6
Model C	(5)(8)	5
Model D	(3)(6)	3

Table 2. Overview of the applied parameters to each model class

Parameter	Model A	Model B	Model C	Model D
T^{supply}		x	x	
T^{return}		x	x	
$\dot{V}_w$		x	x	
COP^{avg}	x	x		
$\dot{m}_b$	x			
T^{out}	x			
T^{in}	x			
T^u	x			
T^m	x			
T^l	x			
ρ_w	x	x	x	
c_w	x	x	x	
c_b	x			
V_s	x			
T^{env}				x
$P_{dh}^{const.}$				x
COP^{cal}				x

This subsection aims to classify the mathematical models based on the number of required parameters by combining different models presented in Sect. 5. We introduce four different model classes (A, B, C, and D) with decreasing complexity in terms of the number of parameters required. Model A utilizes (1) and (2) to calculate the absorbed thermal power in the brine directly. The result is then combined with (7) to calculate the electrical power of the heat pump. And furthermore, the energy change in the heat pump storage is also taken into account by calculating (9) and (10). Model B combines (7) and (8) to compute the consumed electrical power of the heat pump without consideration of the energy change in the storage. Furthermore, Model C uses a constant COP to estimate the $P_{el,t}^{hp}$. Finally, a constant declared heat power is obtained in the simplest Model D. Table 1 presents this classification and the number of required parameters. An overview of the individual parameters that apply to the four model classes is given in Table 2. Furthermore, Table 3 lists the fixed thermal and other parameters, where the specific heat capacity of brine is taken from the technical diagram provided by the heat pump manufacturer and based on a 20 vol% mixture of Tyfocor.

Table 3. Fixed thermal and volume parameters

Parameter	Value
Hot water tank volume V_s	920 L
Specific heat capacity of water c_w	4186 J/(kg·°C)
Density of water ρ_w	0.988 kg/L
Specific heat capacity of brine c_b	3940 J/(kg·°C)

6.2 Results and Utility Comparison

Table 4. Comparison of MAPE Mean and MAPE Max

	MAPE Mean	MAPE Max
Model A	0.68%	0.82%
Model B	1.65%	5.55%
Model C	1.80%	4.54%
Model D	8.07%	17.32%

For the simulation and analysis, we have selected a typical winter day in February and recorded the sensor data for 24 h continuously. The data are then collated in a 60-min interval for the off-line load profile simulation. The initial value of the electrical power of the GSHP is set to the first value of the measurement. Figure 4 shows the simulation results of different models along with the differences between them and the measurement. The diagram shows that the results of Model A are almost identical to the measured results, whereas Models B and C show large deviations at some points in time, such as $t = 10$ and $t = 15$. This behavior could be caused by ignoring the energy change in the heat pump storage. To describe the overall statistic features of simulation results, we calculate the MAPE Mean and the MAPE Max, yielding the results presented in Table 4. Model A, with the most parameters, has the lowest MAPE Mean of 0.68% as compared to the other three simplified models. Furthermore, the MAPE Max by using Model A is also the minimum in all cases. It is worth noting that although the MAPE Max of Model B is larger than that of Model C, the MAPE Mean of it is still smaller than the MAPE Mean of Model C. As for Model D, the simplification leads to the largest error among the other models.

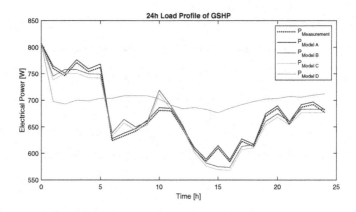

Fig. 4. Comparison between model simulation results and measured values

To quantify the utility of these models, the following formula is defined to calculate and describe the accuracy, i.e., utility of the model:

$$U = (1 - (\text{MAPE Mean})) \cdot 100 \tag{11}$$

where U represents the utility of a model in natural number that is not greater than 100 and MAPE Mean is the mean absolute percentage error of the model simulation results compared with the measurement. With this definition, we illustrate the relationship between the utility and complexity of four different GSHP models in Fig. 5. This demonstrates that the results are basically in line with our hypothesis mentioned in the Sect. 1. However, regarding the limitations of data points, the graph line is not as smooth as an approximated diminishing marginal utility curve by using regression methods which is also presented in orange dashed line in Fig. 5.

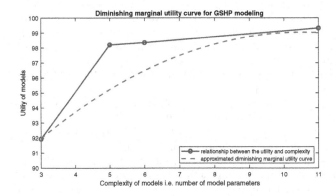

Fig. 5. Diminishing marginal utility curve based on the complexity of models

7 Conclusion

The present paper introduces a first study to investigate diminishing marginal utility in DSM modeling based on Gossen's First Law in economics. We model a GSHP in a stand-alone house with four different kinds of complexity to simulate the electrical load profile of the heat pump. A comparison between the simulation results and the measurement is carried out and then analyzed using metrics such as MAPE Mean. By defining a formula to quantify the utility of GSHP modeling and drawing the resulting curve showing the relationship between the utility and complexity, we reinforce the hypothesis. The results appear consistent with the diminishing marginal utility curve and provide a promising basis for future work. Future research should explore other possibilities of quantifying the utility of models based on flexibility. For this purpose, models with different complexity should be integrated into a control system to influence the future load profile. Moreover, more prominent and more general modeling approaches for DER flexibility found in the literature should be compared. Furthermore, future research could examine the synergy of more complex DSM by combining more subsystems in a model e.g. PV-systems and battery storage.

Acknowledgement. A special thanks to the anonymous peer reviewers for their insightful comments and pertinent feedback. This work was supported by the Energy System Design (ESD) Program of the Helmholtz Association (HGF) within the structure 37.12.02.

References

1. Anvari, M., Proedrou, E., Schäfer, B., Beck, C., Kantz, H., Timme, M.: Data-driven load profiles and the dynamics of residential electricity consumption. Nat. Commun. **13**(1), 4593 (2022)
2. Bao, Z., Zhou, Q., Yang, Z., Yang, Q., Xu, L., Wu, T.: A multi time-scale and multi energy-type coordinated microgrid scheduling solution-part i: model and methodology. IEEE Trans. Power Syst. **30**(5), 2257–2266 (2014)

3. Bao, Z., Zhou, Q., Yang, Z., Yang, Q., Xu, L., Wu, T.: A multi time-scale and multi energy-type coordinated microgrid scheduling solution-part ii: optimization algorithm and case studies. IEEE Trans. Power Syst. **30**(5), 2267–2277 (2014)
4. Bundesamt, S.: Energy consumption. https://www.destatis.de/EN/Themes/ Society-Environment/Environment/Material-Energy-Flows/Tables/energy- consumption-households
5. Chiasson, A.D.: Advances in modeling of ground-source heat pump systems. Ph.D. thesis, Oklahoma State University (1999)
6. De Brito, M.A., Sampaio, L.P., Luigi, G., e Melo, G.A., Canesin, C.A.: Comparative analysis of MPPT techniques for PV applications. In: 2011 International Conference on Clean Electrical Power (ICCEP), pp. 99–104. IEEE (2011)
7. De Coninck, R., Helsen, L.: Practical implementation and evaluation of model predictive control for an office building in brussels. Energy Build. **111**, 290–298 (2016)
8. Energie-Agentur, D.: Studie: roadmap demand side management (2016)
9. Frahm, M., Langner, F., Zwickel, P., Matthes, J., Mikut, R., Hagenmeyer, V.: How to derive and implement a minimalistic RC model from thermodynamics for the control of thermal parameters for assuring thermal comfort in buildings. In: 2022 Open Source Modelling and Simulation of Energy Systems (OSMSES), pp. 1–6. IEEE (2022)
10. Hagenmeyer, V., et al.: Information and communication technology in energy lab 2.0: smart energies system simulation and control center with an open-street-map-based power flow simulation example. Energy Technol. **4**(1), 145–162 (2016)
11. Jiang, Q., Wang, H.: Two-time-scale coordination control for a battery energy storage system to mitigate wind power fluctuations. IEEE Trans. Energy Convers. **28**(1), 52–61 (2012)
12. Keeling, S., Butcher, K.: Ground source heat pumps (2013)
13. KIT: Energy lab 2.0. https://www.elab2.kit.edu/
14. Layard, R., Mayraz, G., Nickell, S.: The marginal utility of income. J. Publ. Econ. **92**(8–9), 1846–1857 (2008)
15. Mauser, I., Mueller, J., Foerderer, K., Schmeck, H.: Definition, modeling, and communication of flexibility in smart buildings and smart grid. In: International ETG Congress 2017, pp. 1–6. VDE (2017)
16. McArthur, J.: A building information management (BIM) framework and supporting case study for existing building operations, maintenance and sustainability. Procedia Eng. **118**, 1104–1111 (2015)
17. NIBE: Installateurhandbuch nibe f1155. https://www.nibe.eu/assets/documents/ 24306/331341-5.pdf
18. per a la Normalització, O.I.: Accuracy (trueness and Precision) of Measurement Methods and Results. International Organization for Standardization (1994)
19. Péan, T.Q., Salom, J., Costa-Castelló, R.: Review of control strategies for improving the energy flexibility provided by heat pump systems in buildings. J. Process Control **74**, 35–49 (2019)
20. Peralta, D., Cañizares, C.A., Bhattacharya, K.: Ground source heat pump modeling, operation, and participation in electricity markets. IEEE Trans. Smart Grid **13**(2), 1126–1138 (2021)
21. Petersen, M.K., Edlund, K., Hansen, L.H., Bendtsen, J., Stoustrup, J.: A taxonomy for modeling flexibility and a computationally efficient algorithm for dispatch in smart grids. In: 2013 American Control Conference, pp. 1150–1156. IEEE (2013)
22. Picard, D., et al.: Comparison of model predictive control performance using grey-box and white box controller models (2016)

23. Ruiz-Calvo, F., De Rosa, M., Acuña, J., Corberán, J., Montagud, C.: Experimental validation of a short-term borehole-to-ground (b2g) dynamic model. Appl. Energy **140**, 210–223 (2015)
24. Sarbu, I., Sebarchievici, C.: General review of ground-source heat pump systems for heating and cooling of buildings. Energy Build. **70**, 441–454 (2014)
25. Śliwa, T., Gonet, A.: Theoretical model of borehole heat exchanger (2005)
26. Turitsyn, K., Backhaus, S., Ananyev, M., Chertkov, M.: Smart finite state devices: a modeling framework for demand response technologies. In: 2011 50th IEEE Conference on Decision and Control and European Control Conference, pp. 7–14. IEEE (2011)

Measurement of the Wood Stove Impact on the Electric Power Consumption of a Norwegian Detached House

Abolfazl Mohammadabadi[1]([✉]) [iD], Øyvind Skreiberg[2] [iD], and Laurent Georges[1] [iD]

[1] Department of Energy and Process Engineering, Norwegian University of Science and Technology (NTNU), Kolbjørn Hejes vei 1B, 7034 Trondheim, Norway
abolfazl.mohammadabadi@ntnu.no

[2] SINTEF Energy Research, Sem Sælands vei 11, 7034 Trondheim, Norway

Abstract. Wood stoves are commonly used as space heating systems in Norwegian houses. However, the specific impact of wood stoves on electric power remains relatively unexplored and is investigated in our study. We also aim to reveal the coincidence between the wood stove operation and the use of electric appliances during the different hours of the day, as it directly impacts the total electric power of the dwelling. Detailed field measurements have been performed in a detached house equipped with a wood stove and electric radiators in the cold climate of Trondheim, Norway. As expected, the use of the wood stove leads to a significant reduction of the space-heating power. However, as wood stoves are operated manually, there are still periods when the electric radiators are operated at maximum power. Nevertheless, we discovered a positive correlation between the usage of the wood stove and electric appliances. It means that when occupants are active, they extensively use their electric appliances and are more likely to use the wood stove simultaneously. Consequently, the peak power of electric appliances does not coincide with the peak power of the electric radiators so that total electric power of the dwelling is reduced by using the stove.

Keywords: Wood Stove · Space Heating · Electricity Consumption

Nomenclature

P_{sh} Space heating power for the electric radiators
P_e Electric power of the smart meter (AMS)
P_{app} Power of the electric appliances
$PT100$ Platinum sensor with 100 Ω resistance at 0 °C
T_i Indoor temperature
T_s Surface temperature of the stove
T_p Pipe temperature of the stove

B. N. Jørgensen et al. (Eds.): EI.A 2023, LNCS 14468, pp. 126–138, 2024.
https://doi.org/10.1007/978-3-031-48652-4_9

1 Introduction

Wood stoves are an integral part of space heating in Norway, with nearly half of the Norwegian households equipped with wood stoves, as shown by a survey conducted by Norsk Varme in 2016 [1]. In terms of regulatory requirements, the building code in Norway, currently TEK 17, states that small residential buildings must either be equipped with a chimney or a water-borne heating system [2].

With the advancement of technology and population growth, the need for energy is increasing. In European residential houses, space heating accounts for almost two-thirds of the total building energy consumption [3]. Electricity stands as the most widely used energy source in Norwegian buildings [4]. During the cold seasons, space heating power requires a large amount of electricity to be transmitted using the grid. The grid must be able to transmit this load, maintaining a balance between supply and demand. The widespread usage of wood stoves in Norway provides an opportunity to lower the pressure on the electricity grid during peak periods, especially in the mornings and evenings when demand is at its highest. Consequently, proper operation of wood stoves has the potential to reduce the risk of blackouts and the need for costly grid expansions.

In addition, the utilization of wood stoves can play a vital role in meeting the space heating needs of households using the renewable energy produced by logs or pellets. Norway possesses a plentiful and valuable wood resource, which can be effectively utilized to decrease dependence on electricity.

It is important to highlight that wood stoves differ from other space heating sources, such as electric radiators and heat pumps, in terms of their operational characteristics. While most heating options are equipped with thermostats allowing users to set the desired indoor temperatures, wood stoves are manually operated and thus heavily rely on the behavior of the individuals.

Active involvement and awareness of users in properly operating the wood stove can significantly enhance its efficiency. In such cases, the full potential of a wood stove is exploitable. Therefore, user behavior and knowledge play a vital role in maximizing the benefits of having a wood stove as a part of the heating system. In a study conducted by Thalfeldt et al. [5], the impact of various wood stove-related user behaviors was examined using building performance simulation (BPS). These behaviors included factors such as the set-point temperature, the wood stove power modulation, the energy in each batch of wood, and the opening of internal doors within the building. However, this study did not specifically investigate the reason behind using the stove and the times when the stove was utilized.

Georges et al. [6] investigated the contribution of a single wood stove to the overall space heating of a passive single-family house in cold climates using BPS. Although it can be possible to cover the heating needs for a passive house, it is challenging to only use one wood stove to heat an entire house when the building is less insulated. A study conducted in the project iFleks [7] divided 5,000 households from six cities across Norway into two groups: control and price. They tested various hourly artificial electricity prices throughout the day, ranging from NOK 1/kWh to NOK 30/kWh, with different time profiles. The study revealed that 6 to 11% of the participants reduced their consumption. The individuals took several actions, such as turning off the heating in unoccupied rooms, lowering the indoor temperature, or shifting showering times to hours with lower prices, but they also prioritized wood stoves over electric heating.

Kipping et al. [8] investigated the effect of various heating systems on the hourly electricity consumption of Norwegian households using smart meter data combined with occupant surveys. In houses equipped with both electric radiators and wood stoves, 60% used their wood stove as the main source of space heating, 30% of those households used the wood stove as an additional heat source and the remaining 10% as coziness. The results indicated that the use of wood stoves led to a significant reduction in the hourly electricity consumption for space heating.

Felius et al. [9] examined wood stove usage habits and motivations based on survey data. In the responses obtained from the questionnaires, it was found that more than 50% of the respondents mentioned that one of their reasons for using the fireplace was its coziness, while approximately 20% used it exclusively for that purpose. Additionally, most of the participants (over 75%) affirmed that the fireplace offered a quick way to heat their homes. Typical schedules of wood stove operation were identified and incorporated into a BPS model of a typical Norwegian single-family detached house. The aim was to assess the influence of stove user behavior on energy use and the risk of overheating. The results demonstrated that using a wood stove could potentially save up to 32% of the electrical energy required for space heating.

Except for Kipping et al., the existing literature primarily consists of simulation-based research where the user behavior is fixed. For instance, Felius et al. [9] modeled the user behavior using a fixed deterministic hourly time schedule for the wood stove operation. Furthermore, they also assumed a fixed daily schedule for electric appliances. Therefore, our contribution differs by presenting a field study based on real data collected from loggers and sensors. No simplification is done for the user behavior regarding the wood stove and electric appliances operation. This also enables us to investigate the coincidence in time between these two activities, a factor that directly influences the total electric power of the dwelling.

Using detailed field measurements, the paper aims to reveal the processes leading to the reduction of the total electric power of the building when using a wood stove. Again, the answer to this question is not obvious due to the key influence of user behavior. To the best of the authors' knowledge, this question has never been addressed in the scientific literature. The overall purpose is to enable informed decisions and strategies for optimizing power usage at the grid scale.

2   Materials and Methods

2.1   The Test House

The house that has been studied is located in Trondheim, Norway. It is a detached house with a concrete foundation and wooden walls with double-paned windows. The roof is made of concrete slabs, and the floor is covered by wooden parquets. The house is naturally ventilated. It comprises two floors and a basement. The first floor accommodates a kitchen, a bathroom, a bedroom, and a living room. The second floor consists of a bathroom and three bedrooms. The residents of the house are individuals affiliated with NTNU University, including Ph.D. and exchange students. Space heating on the first floor is performed using three 1 kW electric radiators and one wood stove. The electric radiators are equipped with a local on-off controller. This means that when the desired temperature is reached, the radiators turn off, and when the temperature drops below a set threshold, they turn on again (i.e., hysteresis control).

In Norwegian houses, electric radiators (or panels) are commonly used for space heating [10]. In our study, the occupants actively utilized the wood stove as their primary source for space heating.

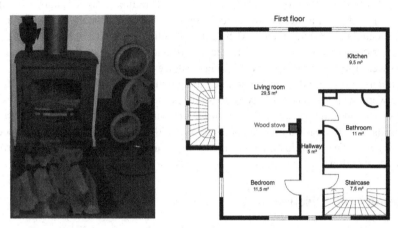

Fig. 1. The first-floor plan featuring the wood stove on the right and a photo on the left showcasing the wood stove and three electric fans.

The wood stove is situated in the living room (as shown in Fig. 1). Additionally, there are two electric radiators located in the living room and one in the bedroom. In order to circulate the air generated by the stove to the second floor, the occupants employ three electric fans, as indicated in Fig. 1. It is important to note that these fans are solely used for air circulation and do not contribute to heating.

2.2 Data Collection

The data collection for this study took place during the winter season, specifically from February 28th, 2023, to April 6th, 2023. In order to assess the impact of the wood stove on electricity consumption and understand user behavior, the period was divided into two segments. During the initial period, spanning from February 28th to March 21st, occupants were allowed to utilize both the wood stove and the three electric radiators for space heating. The second segment, which lasted for nearly one week from March 22nd to March 28th, the occupants were not allowed to use the wood stove, leaving the electric radiators as the only option for space-heating. The brief duration of this second period is due to the limitation of time as we were approaching the end of the heating season.

2.3 Sensors and Data Loggers

In this study, a total of 10 temperature sensors were utilized indoors, along with one sensor to measure the outdoor temperature. These indoor sensors were strategically placed throughout the house, including the bedrooms, bathrooms, living room, and kitchen. The precision of these sensors is within ±0.1 °C. The recorded temperature data was conveniently accessible through a cloud dashboard or a mobile app. The temperature sensors recorded measurements at intervals of five minutes.

To monitor the power consumption of each electric radiator, Zigbee smart mini plugs were employed, with a measurement accuracy of ±1%. Additionally, a Zigbee logger was connected to the smart meter (ALS) of the dwelling using its HAN port to track the total electricity consumption of the house at a frequency of every two seconds. These loggers were linked to a Raspberry Pi 3 via a Zigbee gateway.

In order to measure the surface and flue temperatures of the wood stove, two PT100 sensors were installed. The purpose of these two sensors was to identify when the stove was in operation rather than to get an accurate measurement of the surface temperature. These sensors had a wide temperature range of −200 °C to 400 °C and were connected to two loggers. The recorded data was then transmitted to the cloud dashboard through a Wi-Fi connection.

3 Results and Discussion

To initiate this section, a general description of the building and stove operation during the measurement period is given prior to analyzing the electricity consumption in more detail. The temperature readings are represented by the box plots in Fig. 2 that present the hourly-averaged value recorded throughout the experiment. The recorded minimum and maximum outdoor temperatures were −13.5 °C and 16.7 °C, respectively. The measured indoor temperatures during the experiment were between 15.8 °C and 23.7 °C. The average indoor temperature was recorded at 19 °C, while the average outdoor temperature was measured at 0 °C. In this study, we will not incorporate outdoor temperature to explain the user behavior due to the limited measurement period. To establish a correlation between outdoor temperature and electricity consumption for heating, measurement data for a longer period than one month is required, as seen in other studies [11].

Figure 3(A) illustrates the hourly-averaged pipe temperature at various hours of the day throughout the experiment. It is clear that the stove is typically initiated for operation from 17:00 until midnight. In Fig. 2(B), the stove is depicted as being in operation, and this representation is based on the condition that its pipe temperature is above 35 °C. Using this Boolean information, it was possible to evaluate the probability of stove operation for each hour of the day.

As previously mentioned, the electric radiators are equipped with an on-off thermostat. As the radiator power was recorded with a one-second sampling interval, each on-off cycle was recorded. A time average of one hour is applied to filter out the short-term dynamics of this local controller and the building fabric. For instance, a linear regression between the hourly space heating power and the hourly outdoor temperature proved to be valid in the literature [11]. In addition, shorter time intervals (lower than 15 min) are of lower interest to the grid company and the end users. The grid companies typically seek

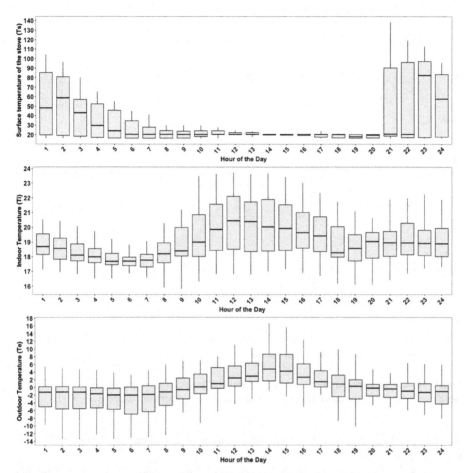

Fig. 2. Hourly-averaged indoor and outdoor temperature, and surface temperature of the stove displayed at various hours of the day for the entire duration of the experiment.

hourly electric power aggregated for several buildings, while the households currently pay their monthly bills according to their electricity use but also the maximum hourly electric power, measured during the previous month [12]. Figure 4 provides a clearer understanding of this phenomenon. The on-off controller causes abrupt jumps between 0 and 3 kW while hourly-averaged data provides a (more) continuous variable. For the remainder of the paper, hourly-averaged data will be used consistently.

Figure 5(A) presents the relationship between space heating power (P_{SH}) and total electric power (P_e). The data points are categorized into circles and triangles, representing periods when stove usage was allowed and prohibited, respectively. On the right side of the figure, we predominantly observe triangles, indicating a peak P_e and P_{SH} of ~5 kW and 1.2 kW, respectively. This peak of 5 kW represents the worst-case scenario observed during the one-month experiment. As we move to the left, triangles transition into circles,

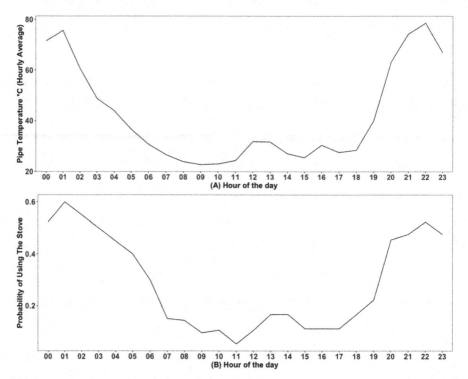

Fig. 3. Hourly pipe temperature averaged throughout the experiment period (A). Probability of stove usage assuming the stove in operation when surface temperature exceeds 35 °C (B).

meaning that P_{SH} is reduced when the stove is in operation. In the very left part, the peak P_e is approximately 4 kW while P_{SH} is nearly zero.

Figure 5(B) and Table 1 explain the correlation between the total power (P_e) and the power of electric appliances (P_{app}). As clearly shown in the graph and table, when the use of the stove is allowed, a significant drop in the intercept of the linear regression between these two variables is observed.

Analyzing Fig. 6 indicates that when the user is permitted to utilize the stove, they actively employ it, as evidenced by the space heating box plots.

The final explanation relates to the correlation between the space heating power (P_{sh}) and the power of appliances (P_{app}). As expected, Fig. 7 confirms a significant negative correlation between these two variables when the user was permitted to use the stove. To quantify this trend, we include three common correlation coefficients: Kendall, Pearson,

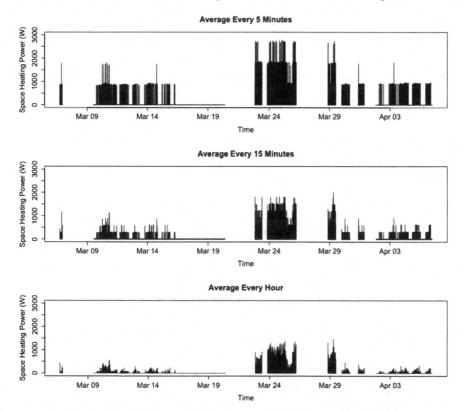

Fig. 4. Space heating power (P_{SH}) averaged for different time intervals.

Table 1. The coefficients of linear regression between the power of appliances (P_{app}), and the total power (P_e) in two different scenarios

Coefficient	Electric panels only	Wood stove and panels
Intercept	925	136
Slope	0.99	0.96

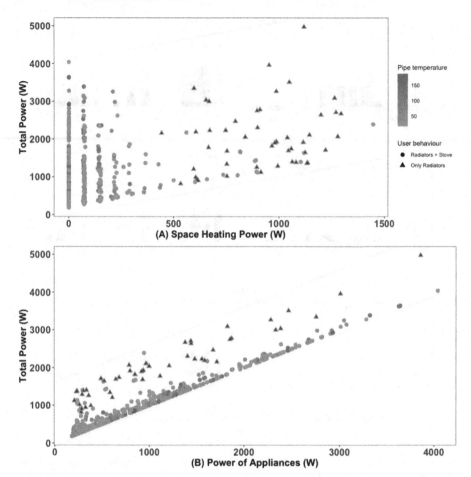

Fig. 5. The relationship between the power of electric appliances (P_{app}) and the total power (P_e) in figure (A). The relationship between space heating power (P_{sh}) and the total power (P_e) in figure (B).

and Spearman [13]. Kendall and Spearman are non-parametric rank correlation coefficients used to assess the strength and direction of the monotonic relationship between two variables, while Pearson correlation measures the linear correlation between two sets of data. Table 3 provides the numerical calculation of these correlations. According to Fig. 7, when the wood stove was allowed to be used, when users were highly active using appliances (while being at home and awake), they also actively used the stove, resulting in low space heating power, and vice versa.

Conversely, when users were not allowed to use the stove, there was no meaningful correlation between these variables, as indicated in Fig. 7 and confirmed by Table 2.

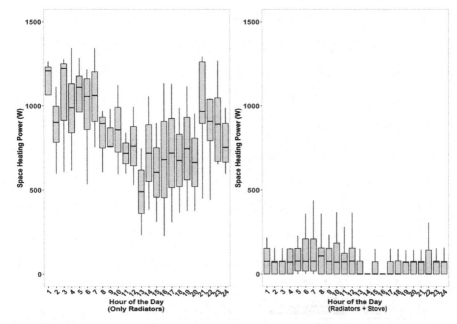

Fig. 6. Comparison of the hourly space heating power with and without the wood stove use.

Table 2. The correlation between the power of electric appliances and space heating during the period when users can utilize only the panels.

Correlation	Estimate	P-value
Spearman	−0.08	0.48
Kendall	−0.05	0.49
Pearson	−0.04	0.74

Table 3. The correlation between the power of electric appliances and space heating during the period when users can utilize the stove.

Correlation	Estimate	P value
Spearman	−0.21	0.00
Kendall	−0.15	0.00
Pearson	−0.18	0.00

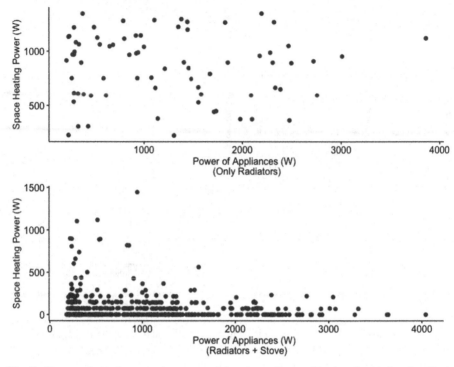

Fig. 7. The correlation between the power of electric appliances (P_{app}) and space heating (P_{sh}).

4 Limitations and Future Work

The analysis of the occupants' behavior, as depicted in Figs. 2 and 3, revealed certain peculiarities in their usage patterns of the wood stove and electric appliances. These patterns may be attributed to the occupants' unique lifestyle, which differs from a typical family. To validate the findings and ensure their generalizability, future studies should encompass a broader range of households with diverse user habits.

Furthermore, it is noteworthy that the house under examination was equipped with only three 1kW electric radiators, which should be insufficient for adequately heating a two-storey house with 151 m² area. Typically, this kind of dwelling has 5.3 to 6 kW of installed space heating power [14]. In further research, it is recommended to investigate different types of houses that feature various ventilation systems and space heating units, such as heat pumps and mechanical ventilation. This will enhance our understanding of the interplay between household characteristics, heating technologies, and occupant behavior.

Finally, it should be noted that the duration of the period when only the electric radiators are in use and the period when both the wood stove and the radiators are in use should be equivalent. It was also observed that the outdoor temperature was milder during the period when the users exclusively relied on the radiators, as opposed to the period when they had the option to use the wood stove. These parameters should be kept the same to ensure a better comparison between the two scenarios.

5 Conclusions

During the period when the use of the wood stove was permitted, we observed a clear negative correlation between space heating power (P_{sh}) and the power of appliances (P_{app}). This indicates that when people were active, they used their appliances extensively and were more likely to use the stove, resulting in lower total electricity consumption (P_e) when the stove was part of the heating strategy. Grids are designed to face the most severe events, here represented by the maximum hourly total power ($P_{e, max}$) measured during the experiments. When the user could not use the stove, $P_{e, max}$ was the sum of the maximum hourly power for appliances ($P_{app, max}$) and the maximum hourly power for the radiators ($P_{SH, max}$). Intuitively, one could have initially expected the same behavior when the wood stove was allowed to be used as there were always periods when occupants did not (or forgot) to use the stove. However, when the users were allowed to use the stove, the maximum hourly total power ($P_{e, max}$) was equal to the maximum hourly power for the appliances only ($P_{app, max}$). In other words, $P_{e, max}$ has been decreased by $P_{SH, max}$, even though the electric radiators have been operated at high instantaneous power during this period. Since grid tariffs are currently determined based on the $P_{e, max}$ recorded during the previous month, our measurement shows that the use of a wood stove can lower electricity bills [12]. This study also underscores the potential of wood stoves to reduce electric power consumption during mornings and evenings, thus reducing the stress on the electricity grid. These conclusions will become more evident with longer measurement periods, such as an entire cold season or consecutive cold seasons in multiple houses.

Acknowledgement. This research was conducted as part of the SusWoodStoves project, which is a knowledge-building Project for the Industry financed by the Research Council of Norway and the industry.

References

1. Norsk Varme OPPDATERT STATISTIKK 2016. Norsk Varme. https://norskvarme.org. Accessed 20 June 2023
2. Building technical regulations (TEK17): Norwegian Building Authority. https://www.dib k.no. Accessed 20 June 2023
3. Eurostat. https://ec.europa.eu/. Accessed 20 June 2023
4. An electric Norway – from fossil to electricity. Statnett. https://www.statnett.no. Accessed 20 June 2023
5. Thalfeldt, M., Skare, A.B., Georges, L., Skreiberg, Ø.: Parametric energy simulations of a nordic detached house heated by a wood stove. In: 12th Nordic Symposium on Building Physics, pp. 1–7. E3S Web of Conferences, Tallinn, Estonia (2020)
6. Georges, L., Skreiberg, Ø., Novakovic, V.: On the proper integration of wood stoves in passive houses: investigation using detailed dynamic simulations. Energy Build. **59**, 203–213 (2013)
7. iFleks–Første resultater fra fase 1 (vinter 2020). Statnett. https://www.statnett.no. Accessed 20 June 2023
8. Kipping, A., Trømborg, E.: Hourly electricity consumption in Norwegian households–assessing the impacts of different heating systems. Energy **93**, 655–671 (2015)

9. Felius, L.C., Thalfeldt, M., Georges, L., Hrynyszyn, B.D., Dessen, F., Hamdy, M.: 1st Nordic conference on Zero Emission and Plus Energy Buildings. IOP Conference Series: Earth and Environmental Science, Trondheim, Norway (2019)

10. Varmepumper reduserer utgiftene til strømavhengige nordmenn. Statistics Norway. https://www.ssb.no. Accessed 21 June 2023

11. Ding, Y., Brattebø, H., Nord, N.: A systematic approach for data analysis and prediction methods for annual energy profiles: an example for school buildings in Norway. Energy Build. **247**, 111160 (2021)

12. Heide, V., Thingbø, H.S., Lien, A.G., Georges, L.: Economic and energy performance of heating and ventilation systems in deep retrofitted Norwegian detached houses. Energies **15**(19) (2022)

13. Moore, D.S., McCabe, G.P., Craig, B.A.: Introduction to the Practice of Statistics, 10th edn. W. H. Freeman, New York (2021)

14. IEA HPP Annex 32 – Economical Heating and Cooling Systems for Low-Energy Houses. State-of-the-Art Report NORWAY. https://www.sintef.no. Accessed 05 Sept 2023

Market Abstraction of Energy Markets and Policies - Application in an Agent-Based Modeling Toolbox

Florian Maurer[1,2]([envelope]) [ID], Kim K. Miskiw[3] [ID], Rebeca Ramirez Acosta[1] [ID],
Nick Harder[4] [ID], Volker Sander[2] [ID], and Sebastian Lehnhoff[1] [ID]

[1] University of Oldenburg, Oldenburg, Germany
maurer@fh-aachen.de
[2] University of Applied Sciences Aachen, Heinrich-Mußmann-Straße 1, 52428 Jülich, Germany
[3] IISM KIT, Karlsruhe, Germany
[4] INATECH, Freiburg, Germany
https://uol.de,https://fh-aachen.de

Abstract. In light of emerging challenges in energy systems, markets are prone to changing dynamics and market design. Simulation models are commonly used to understand the changing dynamics of future electricity markets. However, existing market models were often created with specific use cases in mind, which limits their flexibility and usability. This can impose challenges for using a single model to compare different market designs. This paper introduces a new method of defining market designs for energy market simulations. The proposed concept makes it easy to incorporate different market designs into electricity market models by using relevant parameters derived from analyzing existing simulation tools, morphological categorization and ontologies. These parameters are then used to derive a market abstraction and integrate it into an agent-based simulation framework, allowing for a unified analysis of diverse market designs. Furthermore, we showcase the usability of integrating new types of long-term contracts and over-the-counter trading. To validate this approach, two case studies are demonstrated: a pay-as-clear market and a pay-as-bid long-term market. These examples demonstrate the capabilities of the proposed framework.

Keywords: energy market design · agent-based simulation · market modeling

1 Motivation

The importance of a well-functioning energy market for a stable economy becomes further apparent, as the recent energy crisis in Europe challenges the current energy market design. The needed adjustments to existing energy markets are discussed by regulatory stakeholders [1] as well as in current research [2]. The latter highlights the need for simulating the effects of a particular market mechanism to evaluate proposed changes to the design. A well-established simulation technique for this purpose is agent-based modeling. Instead of providing a central solution it allows a fine representation of individual agents' behavior and adjusts the behavior when new bidding options arise [3], making it the right tool for this task.

In line with the increased necessity of simulating markets, the research around energy market designs has evolved significantly through better data availability, the increase of computational power and access to relevant open-source software libraries for general energy system modeling [4,5]. Consequently, recent research provides a variety of new theoretic concepts in the field of energy market mechanisms, like pricing schemes for Vickrey Clarke Groves auctions [6,7], transactive energy markets [8] or local energy markets [9]. Investigating new market mechanisms can be done with morphological boxes, a well-known technique for exploring the market design space. However, these new market mechanisms require further standardization of how the design space can be put into practice. Similarly, current research states that "there is an emerging need for standardized and realistic test beds for market mechanisms" [9] to test theoretical concepts in a setting with special assumptions, such as the data available in market agents, as also noted in [10,11]. Yet such a standardized investigation and comparison of different energy market designs is not supported by widely used frameworks. Unfortunately, the lack of a generic agent-based framework results in tools that represent the behavior of a particular market and which are, therefore, not interoperable or comparable and often one-off solutions [12]. Many important research questions need a comprehensive market simulation framework. Here, we identify a research gap for a tool enabling the standardized exploration of the design space for energy markets. By providing a software tool to move from a conceptual market design to a ready simulation, researchers can more efficiently explore new market mechanisms, overcoming the technical challenges associated with rising design complexity.

The proposed methodology is derived from current publications in the field of energy market abstractions, ontologies, and existing simulation tools. In conjunction with the benefits of a common abstraction provided by ontologies, a novel market abstraction framework focusing on the integration of currently evaluated market mechanisms and contracts is developed. Currently, discussed mechanisms of complex contracts like Contract for Differences (CfD) and Power Purchase Agreements (PPA) [13,14] as well as concurrent markets are considered by the developed model, resulting in the core contribution of this paper: a methodology for modeling different market designs through a flexible configuration of the particular properties of the analyzed scenario. Accounting for current and future market complexity, the abstraction capabilities are shown by comparing an energy-only market with a market design containing a second market that includes long-term options.

This paper is structured as follows: The latest work on energy market abstractions, in the field of ontologies is evaluated and compared to the functionality of existing market simulations in Sect. 2. Subsequently, a categorization and requirements of market abstractions are derived from a morphological box app-roach. In conjunction with the common abstraction provided by ontologies, the novel market abstraction framework is developed and presented in Sect. 3. The market abstraction is then applied in a case study in Sect. 4. Finally, a conclusion is given in Sect. 5.

2 Related Work

Looking at existing energy market simulation tools with varying focus, the first need is to specify the scope of a market design. In literature, a market design is described through different marketplace institutions, rules, and customs, which induce different strategies and produce a variety of outcomes [15]. By taking the scope of existing market simulations and market designs into account, the rules can be specified as changes to the incentives of agents. Taking descrip-tions of energy market designs from [16] leads us to the definition of an energy market design as the sum of all possible trading options, including subventions, promotions and customized incentives through policies. It also points out that a market design can include several marketplaces offering different bidding options to agents with varying clearing schedules and properties.

Of the publicly available energy market simulation tools, most focus only on a single specific given market [17]. Hence, they are not inherently designed to evaluate different market mechanisms. The approaches that attempt to compare market mechanisms can be divided into simulation frameworks, which provide the toolset to model energy markets, and market abstraction models, which provide an abstraction layer for the definition of different energy market designs [18]. To detail this, the following paragraphs will discuss the related models and their scope - starting with simulation frameworks.

The needed elements of simulation frameworks are the availability of a trans-parent evaluation mechanism to model comparative simulations with different market mechanisms. For this, open access and interoperability are similarly cru-cial, so that the scientific community can contribute and verify results from the framework or reuse the results [4]. Considering future possible market designs, frameworks need to include the calculation of power flow and grid congestion for the comparison of nodal markets [29]. Having a scalable solution that can run on a distributed cluster is a feature, which also supports future use cases with a high model complexity [30]. Support for new mechanisms like conditional contracts and bilateral contracts between agents is also needed in modern mar-ket simulation tools. An overview of existing tools and their adherence to the requirements is given in Table 1.

AMIRIS is an agent-based energy market model developed to explore and simulate future energy market characteristics [31,32]. The focus of AMIRIS is on the modeling of the day-ahead-spot market on an hourly basis. Furthermore, it supports the use of basic predefined contracts, like Contracts for Differences (CfD) or the market premium, yet the supported market design is unflexible and not readily substitutable. Similarly, PowerACE is an agent-based simulation

Table 1. Overview of existing agent-based market simulation frameworks and their relevant properties, Legend: ○ – not applicable, ◐ – partly applicable, ● – fully represented

model	year	market process	open source	interoperability	distributed system	grid consideration	supports contracts	market comparability
AMES [19]	2008-now	SCUC/SCED	●	◐	◐	◐	○	○
AMIRIS [20]	2016-now	DA, ID, DV	●	○	●	○	●	○
ASAM [21]	2021-now	DA, ID, RE	●	○	○	◐	○	○
FlexAble [22]	2020-2023	DA, DHM, CRM	●	○	○	○	○	◐
GSY-e [23]	2016-now	LEM	●	●	●	○	○	○
lemlab [24]	2021-now	LEM	●	◐	◐	○	○	○
MASCEM [25]	2012-now	DA, ID, RE, DV	○	●	◐	◐	◐	◐
ÃČãÄŞkoFlex [26]	2014-2017	DA	○	○	○	◐	○	○
PowerACE [27]	2014-now	DA	○	○	○	◐	◐	○
USEF [28]	2016-2017	USEF	●	○	○	◐	○	○
Proposed (ASSUME)	2023-now	Various Mechanisms	●	●	●	●	●	●

model that captures operation and investment decisions for dispatchable power plants in the European electricity system. It models the reserve and day-ahead market and was extended to also capture different market design choices such as capacity remuneration mechanisms [33] or market splitting [34]. The AMES toolbox on the other hand focuses on the modeling of Security-Constrained Unit Commitment (SCUC) and Security Constrained Economic Dispatch (SCED) as it is commonly used in parts of the USA. While providing a simulation for nodal markets with a clearing based on marginal costs, it does not allow modeling pay-as-clear auctions or subventions [19,35]. The Universal Smart Energy Framework (USEF) contributes a new artificial market design, which defines new market participants and roles for a deregulated energy market [28]. The corresponding simulation tool [36] is a one-off development, which is used to showcase the new market design. It does not allow comparing the new design to existing approaches and did not receive further development after the first publication, even though the contribution of this modern market design approach is still relevant [18]. FlexAble is a modern market simulation written in Python, which investigates the interaction of an Energy-Only Market, a District-Heating Market and a Control-Reserve Market for modeling of the German electricity market [22], but does allow comparing other markets than the defined. The simulation toolbox MASCEM allows modeling different energy market designs and tries to solve the comparability of simulations while having an interface to different energy markets [25]. Unfortunately, it is not available as open source and there has not been recent development of it.

The research behind the MASCEM model builds the bridge to the second category - the market abstraction models. They developed a market ontology for the interoperability of multi-agent-based modeling [37], as well as an ontology, which defines how bidding agents can interact with a given market agent [38,39]. Market Abstractions are usually derived from ontologies since they provide a common understanding of the knowledge domain. Generally, they are not interoperable without integration work [40] or do not have a respective simulation model tied to the ontology at all [41]. The energy market ontology proposed in Santos et al. [40] provides basic definitions of bidding behavior in energy-only markets, for example for NORDPOOL, MIBEL and EPEX markets. It also integrates a simulation, which does not support the full scope of a market design by the aforementioned definition. Instead, it fits into a subset of the approach provided in this paper by focusing on a single market or trading option, e.g., the Day-Ahead-Market in Europe.

As mentioned before, notable abstractions and generalizations are often part of an ontology. The Open Energy Ontology (OEO) takes a more generalized approach, which does not only focus on markets but tries to provide a consistent interfacing language to energy modeling [41]. Relevant ontologies for the energy domain are discussed in [42]. Some are focusing on facility data like the one given by Tomasevic et al. [43]. An ontology for the integration of flexible devices into smart grids is provided by SARGON [44], which is an extension to the smart application ontology SAREF [45]. As both are more related to the integration of individual buildings, they can not be used to model market interactions. Ontologies aid understanding in energy system modeling, but a standardized implementation for market simulations is not yet established. The proposed model uses the findings from research on existing ontologies and provides needed features for the simulation and evaluation of different energy market designs.

The provided market abstraction model makes it possible to model various energy market designs and mechanisms, providing a comparable evaluation, while using the agent-based simulation framework mango-agents [46]. At the time of writing, this is the first market abstraction, that provides such features, while the aforementioned frameworks are not focusing on modeling multiple concurrent bidding options and market complexity to this extent.

3   Market Abstraction Model

The following section utilizes the top-level market abstraction categories obtained from the morphological box approach, which incorporates key characteristics of different energy markets as shown in [47,48]. Morphological analysis proves valuable in creating diverse designs for a specific artifact [49], in our case electricity market characteristics worldwide. For instance, variations in the degree of competition can be observed, with some markets being vertically integrated while others allow competition in both wholesale and retail sectors. Market designs can involve either a central scheduling and dispatch process to model an Energy Only Market (EOM), or bilateral contracts with power exchange for investigating long-term market (LTM) interactions. Furthermore, since different markets may employ distinct price formation mechanisms, it is essential to define the corresponding price formation method, such as pay-as-clear, pay-as-bid, or other approaches. These characteristics serve as categories in Table 2 which were then detailed into the configuration items. Therefore, all different combinations of market models that result from the morphological box should be mappable to our proposed market configuration, so that comparative simulations with different market designs are possible. Currently, additional information on requirements to bid on other markets is missing but can be enabled by extending the market configuration with additional fields, restricting the current version to fields needed to model the core of the market design.

Table 2. Description of the parameters used to configure a single trading option/market extended from [47,48]. The configuration of multiple market products allows for extensive configuration of trading options.

category	market config item	description
market product	product type	energy or capacity or heat
	market products	list of available trading products
	volume unit	string for visualization
	price unit	string for visualization
opening & duration	opening hours	recurrence rule of openings
	opening duration	time delta
price formation	market mechanism	name of method used for clearing
	additional fields	list of additional fields to base bid
	query available offers	boolean
bid constraints	maximum bid	max allowed bidding price
	minimum bid	min allowed bidding price
	maximum volume	largest valid volume for a single bid
	volume tick size	step increments of volume
	price tick size	step increments of price
specialized config	maximum gradient	max allowed change between bids
	eligible obligations lambda	function checking if agent is eligible

The categories relate to information about the market products, the schedule of market openings and closings, the configuration of the price formation mechanism, as well as common constraints of energy bids used in markets similar to the ontology described in [50]. Additional options for specialized configurations make this a comprehensive model of the relevant configuration options of markets. Thus, for specialized markets an additional field can contain a bid value from a market participant, for example for bilateral over-the-counter contracts. This additional field then restricts the allowed agents that can see and accept the bid. In reality, a market design includes more than one option where trading happens, which is why a market design is described as a list of bidding options (market configs). Here, each market has an individual configuration of opening schedule, a set of market products and trading conditions. This makes it possible for agents to decide, from a list of markets, on which markets they want to participate and how the bids are formulated. The configuration of the bidding agents is independent of market configurations, but they have access to all the relevant information described in the market design. The proposed market abstraction model supports scenarios ranging from single-market models with only one trading option to complex simulations involving multiple interacting markets within a unified agent-based framework. For instance, consider a scenario where bidding agents have the option to participate in a day-ahead market as well as a real-time market. Bidding agents can evaluate market conditions and adjust bidding on both markets accordingly as can be seen in the example in Sect. 4. Based on this idea, an abstraction of energy markets is found and provided which allows modeling all significant characteristics of a single market. The different categories and in particular how bids are modeled are detailed in the next subsections.

3.1 Configuration Categories

The first category of the market configuration is the list of market products, which describes the trading intervals as a list of market products. The description of a market product is derived from the usage in the EPEX trading options [51] and describes the delivery duration, the count of how many deliveries can be traded in one market cycle and the offset of the delivery to the market opening time. For example, the typical day ahead market has only one market product which trades hourly, the next 24 h and bidding starts a day ahead, which looks like this: [(HOURLY, 24, next day)]. In addition, to which time slots can be traded, the opening duration defines the hours how long and how often markets open. This category is closely related to the price formation category, which specifies the clearing method. By providing a freely defined market mechanism for the clearing and defining additional fields on which the market mechanism function can rely, the abstraction covers the modeling of various markets. For example with clearings relying on signals from a grid, as is the case in nodal markets, as well as complex bidding options (block order, all-or-nothing, exclusive orders), Over-The-Counter (OTC) trading and subventions/policies. Within the clearing method, special attention needs to be given to the clearing frequency. Using the technical standard to define recurring events as described in RFC 5545 [52] makes it possible to define arbitrary recurrent schedules in a well-defined way, both being precise and highly configurable.

3.2 Bidding Abstraction

In general, all bidding behavior of energy trading needs to have a defined time frame of delivery with a given volume that has to be delivered according to the market configuration. For example, if the volume unit is "MW", a power of 100 MW can be provided throughout the whole time frame from 2023-06-30 00:00 until 2023-06-30 01:00 resulting in 100 MWh of contracted energy as shown in Table 3. Here, a positive volume indicates generation while a negative volume represents demand, as is typical for sink and source models. Using this abstraction of market offers and orders allows the modeling of all other market behavior similarly by extending the introduced bids through customized behavior. For a better understanding of this important aspect, an exemplary bid is given in Table 3, which contains the default fields each bid must have.

Table 3. Exemplary bid showing mandatory fields used in all markets. The volume is positive for generation while it is negative for demand bids. The sender id contains a unique id of the bidding agent.

start-delivery	2023-06-30 00:00
end-delivery	2023-06-30 01:00
volume	100
price	32
sender id	118

By providing additional fields, complex bidding for block orders as described in [40] can be modeled, which makes conditional negative bidding to skip turnoffs, and a correct representation of power plant bidding possible. The configuration would therefore be extended by an additional identifier "BaseId" and "LinkId", which allows linking multiple blocks to surrounding blocks, as it is used and needed by power plant representations to model the ramping constraints in their bidding behavior [51,53]. This allows a similar representation of linked block bidding as in the European energy market [40]. Of course, the market participant agent needs to adhere to this behavior, so knowledge about this market configuration has to be provided in the list of available markets. On the other hand, the market must respect the additional constraints through linked blocks by respecting an additional constraint in a modified clearing function for each market clearing interval:

$$\sum_{n=0}^{N} n_{\text{used}} \leq (1 + R) * \sum_{n=0}^{N} \text{parent}(n)_{\text{used}} \tag{1}$$

where R is the ramping factor noting how much the power can be increased relative to the parent bid. This can be addressed entirely in the market config without changes to the actual implementation of the market abstraction, which is a key feature in contrast to existing market simulation frameworks. Equation 1 ensures through the inequality that blocks can not be used if the parent block is not used.

3.3   Continuous Trading and Contracts

For continuous auctions, things are different as they are matching suitable bids as soon as the bids reach the market while clearing auctions have fixed clearing intervals based on a recurrence schedule. In continuous trading, agents can also query the available unmatched bids to check the current market price beforehand. This can lead to agents continuously checking the market situation which slows down the simulation. To still provide continuous trading in a simulation, some limitations are needed to guarantee a sufficiently advancing simulation time by implementing minimum steps for the agents and the market. Therefore, a continuous trading auction does not clear its offers on an event base in real-time but through fast clearing actions in intervals of a few minutes in comparison with the 24-h duration of day-ahead markets. Thus, as not all auctions have clearable bids, messages are only sent for accepted bids in continuous markets. This approach to simulating continuous auctions ensures the reproducibility of the scenarios as the order of bidding actions is set by a global clock. While this gives a pseudo-continuity it allows implementing the functionality similar to the usage of fixed clearing intervals and reduces complexity by using a working generalization. Still, the special query functionality to receive unmatched bids from the market is respected in the market config in the parameter "query available offers". Agents can therefore check existing unmatched bids before providing their bidding, as is also the case in existing markets. This new approach for representing continuous trading makes it further possible to simulate additional bidding behavior like OTC trading including complex evaluation of contracts.

Peer-to-Peer/Over-The-Counter Contracts. Most of the actual market actions are happening through OTC trading, which covers a bilateral agreement between two market participants to trade energy [54]. While this can theoretically be settled without any third party involved, often an OTC trading platform is involved, which tracks available offers and bids. For example, Agent-A can send a bid to the market which is only seen by Agent-B. Agent-B can use the aforementioned mechanism to look into unmatched bids of the market and accept the bid from Agent-A. This is using continuous trading in conjunction with additional fields to describe that only some agents are allowed to use the trading option. This means, that the additional fields contain the "ReceiverId" which ensures that each bid contains a field "ReceiverId" additionally to the fields specified in Table 3. In market clearing, a function can be specified that matches these offers only to bids sent by the agent with the respective Id - as is the case with peer-to-peer markets.

Conditional Contracts. Besides contracts with individual participants, subvention mechanisms are often based on a price index or have an unspecified volume, which creates the need for contract logic to be included in the bid.

    The relevance of such long-term investment policies is rising and is commonly implemented through Power Purchase Agreements (PPA) or Contracts for Differences (CfD). At first sight, the concept of long-term contracts with conditions tied to market behavior or unit dispatch seems somewhat different from the typical bidding described before. Yet, continuing the same concept of OTC trading and applying it here allows modeling such contracts in the same way as bids. Providing an additional field to contain the type of contract, makes it possible to handle contracts in a way that different agents can interact and accept offers. The actual logic of a contract has to be provided before the simulation but can be freely defined as a callback function.

Throughout the reduction of the complexity by stepwise addition to previous results, the usage of Market contracts can be seen as an extension of the simple bidding described in Subsect. 3.2. The abstraction is then used to make comparable simulations of different market designs possible. For this, a market design, the unit operators and needed time series data are specified as a model input.

4   Case Study

In the following, a scenario with an EOM is compared to one with an EOM and an additional OTC market. The results of the case study are created using the ASSUME Framework 3which was extended by an implementation of the described market configuration that includes new features for agent-based modeling of energy markets. To assure openness and transparency, the code and results used for this paper were made public on Zenodo [55].

Most market simulations only focus on fixed interval clearing, yet markets with continuous trading are making up large parts of existing trading in future markets and OTC trading [54]. The importance of modeling long-term OTC trading as well as subventions is often weighted against the increased complexity of the seemingly different mechanisms. Using the described common abstraction of bids, it is shown in the following that one can easily integrate different market behaviors in the same simulation, as shown in the example.

4.1   Application of Morphological Box

To create use cases, relevant market designs are derived by using the morphological box. When analyzing the impact on markets, a combination of different scenarios extracted from the morphological box has to be considered. For this reason, we apply the characteristics proposed in the morphological box to define scenarios for modeling the hourly EOM spot as well as an LTM with weekly physical contracts shown in Table 4.

The EOM includes market products for the next single hour, instead of the next 24 h to reduce the complexity of the example. For comparison, an example of a long-term trading option is shown, which uses pay-as-bid as a market pricing mechanism and trades weekly products. The different clearing mechanisms and market products are modeled in the proposed market configuration. The resulting market design is shown in Table 5. The programmatic representation of this market design is used for the showcase in the following section.

Table 4. Application of the Morphological Box for the description of electricity markets: hourly EOM spot and LTM Market.

Characteristic	EOM	LTM
Degree of Competition	Wholesale and retail competition	Wholesale competition
Market Structure	central scheduling and central dispatch	Contracts on Power Exchange
Clearing Mechanisms	Power pool price-based	Physical contract
Price Formation	Marginal Pricing (Pay as clear)	Pay as bid
Pricing mechanisms	Zonal Pricing	Zonal Pricing
Market Products	Hourly Energy Generation	weekly contracts
Market Timeframe	Day-ahead market (DAM)	Forward Market (FM)

Table 5. Configuration of energy markets used in the scenario. The main difference is the opening schedule, the bidding products and the price formation/market mechanism.

	EOM Hourly market	LTM forward market
product type	energy	energy
market products	[(HOURLY, next 1 h, offset 1 h)]	[(weekly, one week, offset 2 h)]
opening hours	every hour	weekly at 24:00
opening duration	1 h	2 h
market mechanism	pay as clear	pay as bid
maximum bid	9999	9999
minimum bid	−500	−500
maximum volume	500	500
additional fields	[baseid, linkid]	none
volume tick size	0.1	0.1
price tick size	0.1	0.1
volume unit	MW	MW
price unit	€/MW	€/MW
query available offers	false	false
maximum gradient	none	none
eligible obligations lambda	none	none

Both inspected cases utilize the same agent bidding behavior which is based on always bidding marginal cost of the power plant. The volume of the bids is decided by their availability of energy generation for the whole bidding period. There are 262 generation units bidding on each market generated from the same input scenario data set. The list of power plants is based on the World Electric Power Plants Database [56] and complemented by data from the German Environment Agency [57], and the Federal Network Agency [58]. The variable renewable energy generation and the inelastic demand for Germany were obtained from SMARD[1]. The fuel prices for marginal cost calculations are obtained from [59–61]. The complete input data is available on Zenodo [55].

4.2   Scenario 1 - EOM only

The first scenario includes a single energy-only market, which has an hourly scheduled opening for the next hour after bidding, as described on the left side in Table 5. A schematic overview of the bidding interval and the opening frequency is shown in Fig. 1a.

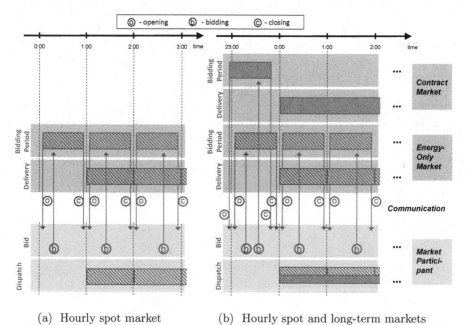

(a) Hourly spot market   (b) Hourly spot and long-term markets

Fig. 1. Schematic overview of the clearing times in the simulation with (a) hourly spot market, (b) hourly spot and the long-term markets.

The market communicates the openings and closings at each hour, while every market participant sends its bids in this time slot. The delivery obligation starts with an offset of one hour to the opening times as described in the third value

---

[1] https://www.smard.de.

of the market products. As the opening duration is also one hour, the delivery starts directly after market clearing. After receiving the result from the energy market, the market participant checks if the requested dispatch is feasible.

4.3 Scenario 2 - EOM with Additional LTM

The above-described scenario is compared to a market design that includes an additional LTM. The agents bid their firm capacity for the product period on each market, which refers to the minimum capacity that can be supplied throughout the entire market product period. In the case of the LTM, a generation load for the whole week is sold or bought. In most weeks renewable generation does not have firm capacity, as there is a time per week when no energy generation is available, so they can not bid on the LTM in the way we have simulated the product duration. A schematic overview including the additional market opening and clearing schedule is shown in Fig. 1b. The market design in this case consists of a list of both markets, as both markets in Table 5 are configured in the simulation.

4.4 Simulation Results

An exemplary power dispatch of the simulation is shown for the generation technology nuclear and hard coal in Fig. 2 for the scenario which includes bidding on the LTM. The traded amount on the LTM can be seen as the lower part of the graph, while the requested amount of hard coal increases in every bidding period of seven days, due to larger demand, while the nuclear firm capacity is fully requested, due to its lower marginal price. Further visualizations for remaining generation technologies from the simulation are available on an open-source dashboard realized with Grafana.

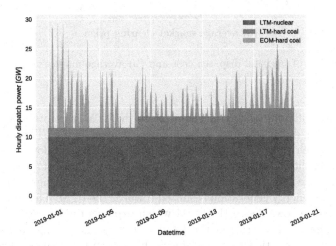

Fig. 2. Traded Electricity for Nuclear and Coal on the LTM and EOM respectively.

Please note that these results showcase the capabilities of the market abstraction framework. The results do not aim to replicate actual market results, due to the reduced complexity in the bidding behavior as well as the market implementation. In this specific case, one can see the change of volume traded on the EOM towards the LTM once it is introduced. The step-wise increment can be seen due to increasing minimum demand in the modeled weeks of January 2019. The total volume traded on both markets stays the same as agents aren't reselling energy on the market.

The impact of the shown dispatch on the total system cost and average market prices can be seen in Fig. 3. The total cost of trading on the LTM, cleared with pay-as-bid, is lower than the EOM if the marginal costs bidding strategies are used. We use these results to explain the behavior of the implemented sequential markets. In another simulation that focuses on replicating realistic bidding more complex bidding strategies which take reselling, portfolio management and long-term market strategies into account, should be implemented.

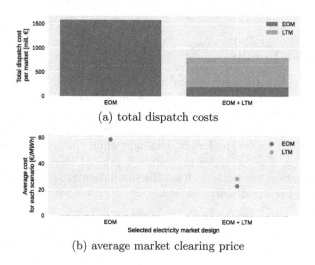

(a) total dispatch costs

(b) average market clearing price

Fig. 3. Overview of (a) total dispatch cost and (b) average market clearing prices for both scenarios.

Due to the different pricing mechanisms at the LTM, the total dispatch cost, shown in Fig. 3a, decreases when more volume is traded on the LTM market using pay-as-bid, which shows that the general market behavior follows the expectation. Figure 3b shows the average clearing price on both markets. Once the LTM is introduced, the average price of the EOM is decreased, as a significant amount of conventional energy generation is shifted towards the LTM. This leaves a much higher share of renewables in the EOM which explains the low average price on the EOM. The average price in the LTM settles as the average marginal cost of conventional generation, as renewables can't bid on this market. The average marginal cost is much lower than the clearing price in the EOM-only example, due to the pay-as-bid pricing which does not set a uniform price for all involved generation plants. This behavior shows the correct functionality of the bidding, but can not be generalized for other bidding strategies.

5 Discussion and Conclusions

Evaluation of agent-based models can be difficult due to the need for correct parametrization and modeling of agent behavior [62]. To facilitate the evaluation process and enable a comparative market analysis, a generalized market abstraction is crucial. In this paper, we propose a novel approach to market modeling in the energy domain. Our study involves an in-depth analysis of existing simulation approaches and ontologies that abstract energy markets. From these sources, we extract a robust methodology for modeling different market designs by defining a comprehensive abstraction that encompasses various market configurations. By bridging the gap between market descriptions in ontologies and their implementation in simulation frameworks, our approach establishes a solid foundation for future comparative studies of market designs. Moreover, we implement our methodology in an open-source framework, empowering other researchers to conduct their market design studies. Finally, we demonstrate the capabilities of our market modeling methodology through the implementation of a multi-market simulation scenario.

While the show-cased multi-market scenario has strong simplifications, it can be adapted to model complex real-world examples with multiple markets. The results for existing markets can be validated through historical data. To assess such real-world examples and analyze the impact of market design changes on market outcomes, it is recommended to incorporate the existing market options described in [53] for an evaluation. For this purpose, the current presentation can be seen as a first step for an extensive market comparison. The demonstration lacks an example of continuous trading and the bidding agent strategies have been simplified to enhance clarity by reducing the complexity of the illustration.

The latter, namely integrating more complex bidding behavior, will be addressed in future research. While we address the market simulation, altering the simulated market design requires corresponding adjustments in the agents' bidding behavior. Determining the optimal bidding strategy for a given market design can, however, be challenging. Reinforcement learning techniques offer a solution by enabling the endogenous creation of bidding strategies that conform to a specific set of market rules. These strategies can be learned through iterations of the simulation, as demonstrated in [63–65]. However, further research is necessary to investigate bidding strategies in greater depth and conduct comparative simulations using publicly available datasets.

Acknowledgments. Kim K. Miskiw and Nick Harder thank the German Federal Ministry for Economic Affairs and Climate Action for the funding of the ASSUME project under grant number BMWK 03EI1052A.

References

1. ENTSO-E: Conclusions from Stakeholder Engagement on 2030 Market Design (2022)
2. Bichler, M., et al.: Electricity markets in a time of change: a call to arms for business research. Schmalenbach J. Bus. Res. **74**(1), 77–102 (2021). https://doi.org/10.1007/s41471-021-00126-4
3. Künzel, T.: Entwicklung eines agentenbasierten Marktmodells zur Bewertung der Dynamik am deutschen Strommarkt in Zeiten eines steigenden Anteils erneuerbarer Energien (2019). https://doi.org/10.5445/IR/1000100456
4. Groissböck, M.: Are open source energy system optimization tools mature enough for serious use? Renew. Sustain. Energy Rev. **102**, 234–248 (2019). https://doi.org/10.1016/j.rser.2018.11.020
5. Pfenninger, S., et al.: Opening the black box of energy modelling: strategies and lessons learned. Energ. Strat. Rev. **19**, 63–71 (2018). https://doi.org/10.1016/j.esr.2017.12.002
6. Borokhov, V.: Antimonopoly regulation method in energy markets based on the Vickrey-Clarke-Groves mechanism. Electr. Power Syst. Res. **209**, 107964 (2022). https://doi.org/10.1016/j.epsr.2022.107964
7. Huang, M., Wei, Z., Ju, P., Wang, J., Chen, S.: Incentive-compatible market clearing for a two-stage integrated electricity-gas-heat market. IEEE Access **7**, 120984–120996 (2019). https://doi.org/10.1109/ACCESS.2019.2936889
8. Azizi, A., Aminifar, F., Moeini-Aghtaie, M., Alizadeh, A.: Transactive energy market mechanism with loss implication. IEEE Trans. Smart Grid **12**(2), 1215–1223 (2021). https://doi.org/10.1109/TSG.2020.3028825
9. Tsaousoglou, G., Giraldo, J.S., Paterakis, N.G.: Market mechanisms for local electricity markets: a review of models, solution concepts and algorithmic techniques. Renew. Sustain. Energy Rev. **156**, 111890 (2022). https://doi.org/10.1016/j.rser.2021.111890
10. Weinhardt, C., et al.: How far along are local energy markets in the DACH+ region? A comparative market engineering approach. In: Proceedings of the Tenth ACM International Conference on Future Energy Systems. E-Energy 1919, pp. 544–549. Association for Computing Machinery, New York (2019). https://doi.org/10.1145/3307772.3335318
11. Sensfuß,F., Genoese, M., Ragwitz, M., Möst, D.: Agent-based simulation of electricity markets -a literature review-. Energy Stud. Rev. **15**(2) (2007). https://doi.org/10.15173/esr.v15i2.507
12. Hansen, P., Liu, X., Morrison, G.M.: Agent-based modelling and socio-technical energy transitions: a systematic literature review. Energy Res. Soc. Sci. **49**, 41–52 (2019). https://doi.org/10.1016/j.erss.2018.10.021
13. Newbery, D.: Efficient renewable electricity support: designing an incentive-compatible support scheme. EJ **44**(3) (2023). https://doi.org/10.5547/01956574.44.3.dnew
14. Gabrielli, P., Aboutalebi, R., Sansavini, G.: Mitigating financial risk of corporate power purchase agreements via portfolio optimization. Energy Econ. **109**, 105980 (2022). https://doi.org/10.1016/j.eneco.2022.105980
15. Roth, A.E., Wilson, R.B.: How market design emerged from game theory: a mutual interview. J. Econ. Perspect. **33**(3), 118–143 (2019). https://doi.org/10.1257/jep.33.3.118

16. Cramton, P.: Electricity market design. Oxf. Rev. Econ. Policy **33**(4), 589–612 (2017). https://doi.org/10.1093/oxrep/grx041
17. Fatras, N., Ma, Z., Jørgensen, B.N.: An agent-based modelling framework for the simulation of large-scale consumer participation in electricity market ecosystems. Energy Inform. **5**(4), 47 (2022). https://doi.org/10.1186/s42162-022-00229-0-0
18. Ma, Z., Schultz, M.J., Christensen, K., Værbak, M., Demazeau, Y., Jørgensen, B.N.: The application of ontologies in multi-agent systems in the energy sector: a scoping review. Energies **12**(16), 3200 (2019). https://doi.org/10.3390/en12163200
19. Battula, S., Tesfatsion, L., McDermott, T.E.: An ERCOT test system for market design studies. Appl. Energy **275**, 115182 (2020). https://doi.org/10.1016/j.apenergy.2020.115182
20. Reeg, M.: AMIRIS - ein agentenbasiertes simulationsmodell zur akteursspezifischen analyse technoökonomischer und soziotechnischer effekte bei der strommarktintegration und refinanzierung erneuerbarer energien. Technischen Universität Dresden (2019)
21. Glismann, S.: Ancillary services acquisition model: considering market interactions in policy design. Renew. Sustain. Energy Rev. (2021). https://doi.org/10.1016/117697
22. Qussous, R., Harder, N., Schafer, M., Weidlich, A.: Increasing the realism of electricity market modeling through market interrelations (2022)
23. Okwuibe, G.C., et al.: Evaluation of hierarchical, multi- agent, community-based, local energy markets based on key performance indicators. Energies **15**(10), 3575 (2022). https://doi.org/10.3390/en15103575
24. Zade, M., Lumpp, S.D., Tzscheutschler, P., Wagner, U.: Satisfying user preferences in community-based local energy markets auction-based clearing approaches. Appl. Energy **306**, 118004 (2022). https://doi.org/10.1016/j.apenergy.2021.118004
25. Santos, G., et al.: Multi-agent simulation of competitive electricity markets: autonomous systems cooperation for European market modeling. Energy Convers. Manage. **99**, 387–399 (2015). https://doi.org/10.1016/j.enconman.2015.04.042
26. Künzel, T., Weidlich, A.: Flexibility as an economic commodity in the intelligent energy system for the efficient integration of renewable energies (2015)
27. Bublitz, A., Ringler, P., Genoese, M., Fichtner, W.: Agent-based simulation of the German and French wholesale electricity markets. In: Proceedings of the 6th International Conference on Agents and Artificial Intelligence - Volume 2. ICAART 2014, pp. 40–49. SCITEPRESS - Science and Technology Publications, Lda (2014). https://doi.org/10.5220/0004760000400049
28. USEF Design Team: USEF - The Framework Explained (2021)
29. Weber, C.: Achievements and challenges in European energy markets. J. Mod. Power Syst. Clean Energy (2023). https://doi.org/10.35833/MPCE.2023.000061
30. Rana, O.F., Stout, K.: What is scalability in multi-agent systems? In: Proceedings of the Fourth International Conference on Autonomous Agents, AGENTS 2000, pp. 56–63. Association for Computing Machinery, New York (2000). https://doi.org/10.1145/336595.337033
31. Frey, U.J., Klein, M., Nienhaus, K., Schimeczek, C.: Self-reinforcing electricity price dynamics under the variable market premium scheme. Energies **13**(20), 5350 (2020). https://doi.org/10.3390/en13205350
32. Schimeczek, C., et al.: AMIRIS: agent-based market model for the investigation of renewable and integrated energy systems. JOSS **8**(84), 5041 (2023). https://doi.org/10.21105/joss.05041

33. Fraunholz, C., Keles, D., Fichtner, W.: On the role of electricity storage in capacity remuneration mechanisms. Energy Policy **149**, 112014 (2021). https://doi.org/10.1016/j.enpol.2020.112014

34. Fraunholz, C., Hladik, D., Keles, D., Möst, D., Fichtner, W.: On the long-term efficiency of market splitting in Germany. Energy Policy **149**, 111833 (2021). https://doi.org/10.1016/j.enpol.2020.111833

35. Krishnamurthy, D.: Psst: an open-source power system simulation toolbox in python. In: 2016 North American Power Symposium (NAPS), pp. 1–6 (2016). https://doi.org/10.1109/NAPS.2016.7747925

36. MISC

37. Santos, G., Pinto, T., Vale, Z.: Ontologies to enable interoperability of multiagent electricity markets simulation and decision support. Electronics **10**(11), 1270 (2021). https://doi.org/10.3390/electronics10111270

38. Santos, G., Pinto, T., Praça, I., Vale, Z.: Iberian electricity market ontology to enable smart grid market simulation. Energy Inform. **1**(1), 1–14 (2018). https://doi.org/10.1186/s42162-018-0018-2

39. Santos, G., Pinto, T., Praça, I., Vale, Z.: Nord pool ontology to enhance electricity markets simulation in MASCEM. In: Oliveira, E., Gama, J., Vale, Z., Lopes Cardoso, H. (eds.) EPIA 2017. LNCS (LNAI), vol. 10423, pp. 283–294. Springer, Cham (2017). https://doi.org/10.1007/978-3-319-65340-2_24

40. Santos, G., Pinto, T., Praca, I., Vale, Z.: EPEX ontology: enhancing agent- based electricity market simulation. In: 2017 19th International Conference on Intelligent System Application to Power Systems (ISAP), pp. 1–6 (2017). https://doi.org/10.1109/ISAP.2017.8071411

41. Booshehri, M., et al.: Introducing the open energy ontology: enhancing data interpretation and interfacing in energy systems analysis. Energy AI **5**, 100074 (2021). https://doi.org/10.1016/j.egyai.2021.100074

42. Blanco, J.M., Rossi, B., Pitner, T.: A comparative study of energy domain ontologies. In: Marchiori, M., Domínguez Mayo, F.J., Filipe, J. (eds.) WEBIST WEBIST 2020 2021. LNBIP, vol. 469, pp. 43–58. Springer, Cham (2023). https://doi.org/10.1007/978-3-031-24197-0_3

43. Tomašević, N.M., Batić, M.Č., Blanes, L.M., Keane, M.M., Vraneš, S.: Ontology-based facility data model for energy management. Adv. Eng. Inform. **29**(4), 971–984 (2015). https://doi.org/10.1016/j.aei.2015.09.003

44. Haghgoo, M., Sychev, I., Monti, A., Fitzek, F.H.: SARGON smart energy domain ontology. IET Smart Cities **2**(4), 191–198 (2020). https://doi.org/10.1049/iet-smc.2020.0049

45. Daniele, L., den Hartog, F., Roes, J.: Created in close interaction with the industry: the smart appliances REFerence (SAREF) ontology. In: Cuel, R., Young, R. (eds.) FOMI 2015. LNBIP, vol. 225, pp. 100–112. Springer, Cham (2015). https://doi.org/10.1007/978-3-319-21545-7_9

46. OFFIS: Mango-Agents - Modular Python Agent Framework, Mango Agents (2023). https://gitlab.com/mango-agents/mango. Accessed 30 June 2023

47. Acosta, R.R., Lehnhoff, S., Gomez, J.M.: An electricity market categorization based on morphological analysis for smart grid development. In: 2022 18th International Conference on the European Energy Market (EEM), pp. 1–7 (2022). https://doi.org/10.1109/EEM54602.2022.9921038

48. Santos, G., Pinto, T., Vale, Z., Praça, I., Morais, H.: Electricity markets ontology to support MASCEM's simulations. In: Bajo, J., et al. (eds.) PAAMS 2016. CCIS, vol. 616, pp. 393–404. Springer, Cham (2016). https://doi.org/10.1007/978-3-319-39387-2_33

49. Salah, F., Flath, C.M., Schuller, A., Will, C., Weinhardt, C.: Morphological analysis of energy services: paving the way to quality differentiation in the power sector. Energy Policy **106**, 614–624 (2017). https://doi.org/10.1016/j.enpol.2017.03.024
50. Santos, G., Pinto, T., Praça, I., Vale, Z.: An interoperable approach for energy systems simulation: electricity market participation ontologies. Energies **9**(11), 878 (2016). https://doi.org/10.3390/en9110878
51. EPEX SPOT: Trading Products | EPEX SPOT (2022). https://www.epexspot.com/en/tradingproducts. Accessed 05 Sept 2023
52. Desruisseaux, B.: Internet calendaring and scheduling core object specification (iCalendar). Request for Comments RFC 5545, 168 p. Internet Engineering Task Force (2009). https://doi.org/10.17487/RFC5545
53. Shah, D., Chatterjee, S.: A comprehensive review on day-ahead electricity market and important features of world's major electric power exchanges. Int. Trans. Electr. Energy Syst. **30**(7), e12360 (2020). https://doi.org/10.1002/2050-7038.12360
54. Bundesnetzagentur: Monitoringbericht 2022 (2023)
55. MISC
56. S.G.M. Intelligence (Firm): World Electric Power Plants Database, March 2017. Version 2. Harvard Dataverse, 9 March 2018. https://doi.org/10.7910/DVN/OKEZ8A, https://dataverse.harvard.edu/dataset.xhtml?persistentId=doi10.7910/DVN/OKEZ8A. Accessed 04 July 2023
57. Redaktionsassistenz, U.B.A.: Datenbank "Kraftwerke in Deutschland". XLS. Umweltbundesamt. https://www.umweltbundesamt.de/dokument/datenbank-kraftwerkein-deutschland. Accessed 04 July 2023
58. Bundesnetzagentur: Kraftwerksliste Der Bundesnetzagentur (Stand: 31. Mai 2022). XLS (2022). https://www.bundesnetzagentur.de/SharedDocs/Downloads/DE/Sachgebiete/Energie/Unternehmen_Institutionen/Versorgungssicherheit/Erzeugungskapazitaeten/Kraftwerksliste/Kraftwerksliste_2022.html. Accessed 13 Nov 2022
59. EEX: Environmental Market Data (2023). https://www.eex.com/en/marketdata/environmentals. Accessed 04 July 2023
60. EEX: EEX Market Data (2023). https://www.eex.com/en/market-data. Accessed 04 July 2023
61. Destatis: Data on Energy Price Trends - Long-time Series to Dezember 2022 (2023). https://www.destatis.de/EN/Themes/Economy/Prices/Publications/Downloads-Energy-Price-Trends/energy-price-trends-pdf-5619002.html. Accessed 04 July 2023
62. Weidlich, A., Veit, D.: Agent-based simulations for electricity market regulation advice: procedures and an example. SSRN J. (2007). https://doi.org/10.2139/ssrn.2951092
63. Wolgast, T., Nieße, A.: Approximating energy market clearing and bidding with model-based reinforcement learning. arXiv: 2303.01772 [cs, eess] (2023). https://doi.org/10.48550/arXiv.2303.01772. Accessed 24 May 2023
64. Sanayha, M., Vateekul, P.: Model-based deep reinforcement learning for wind energy bidding. Int. J. Electr. Power Energy Syst. **136**, 107625 (2022). https://doi.org/10.1016/j.ijepes.2021.107625
65. Yang, L., Sun, Q., Zhang, N., Li, Y.: Indirect multi-energy transactions of energy internet with deep reinforcement learning approach. IEEE Trans. Power Syst. **37**(5), 4067–4077 (2022). https://doi.org/10.1109/TPWRS.2022.3142969

Distributed Resources Remuneration on a Medium Voltage Network with Uncertainty and Seasonal Impacts

Fábio Castro[1,2,3] (ID), Bruno Canizes[1,2,3] (ID), João Soares[1,2,3(✉)] (ID), Marcos J. Rider[4] (ID), and Zita Vale[1,2,3] (ID)

[1] GECAD - Research Group on Intelligent Engineering and Computing for Advanced Innovation and Development, Porto, Portugal
{fadsc,bmc,jan,zav}@isep.ipp.pt
[2] LASI – Intelligent System Associate Laboratory, Guimaraes, Portugal
[3] Polytechnic of Porto, R. Dr. António Bernardino de Almeida, 431, 4200-072 Porto, Portugal
[4] Department of Systems and Energy, UNICAMP, Campinas, Sao Paulo, Brazil
mjrider@unicamp.br

Abstract. The current landscape of the electric world is shifting toward a cleaner and more sustainable pattern. While this is a known fact, there is still very little consideration for how distributed generators (DG) should be compensated when studying the network, whether through planning or operation/reconfiguration. The DG remuneration needs to be considered in modern network studies, especially when there is a high percentage of renewable energy penetration. Another major factor that should be given an adequate amount of importance is the introduction of uncertainty to the data used along the process. Thus, this study applies uncertainty to wind and solar generation and load, with its' degree varying according to the season and daily periods. This study is applied to a 180-bus network in the Leiria district, Portugal, with 42 Wind farms, 33 Photovoltaic (PV) parks, as well as three biomass generators, and a substation belonging to the Distribution System Operator (DSO). The network also has two Energy Storage Systems (ESS) already in place owned by an outside party, but the model allows for the installation of more from the DSO. This study is done from the point of view of the DSO, aiming to minimize the investments and expenditures on their part while fairly remunerating the participants using a two-stage stochastic model. There are 16 main scenarios in this model, the combinations of the four seasons and daily periods. The results are promising with a Payback of 3,02 years.

Keywords: Distributed Resources · Remuneration · Renewable Generation · Optimal Planning · Seasonal Impacts · Uncertainty

1 Introduction

The topic of remuneration of DG is a necessary discussion in modern networks, especially with the network getting more and more complex and unpredictable with an increase in renewable energy sources (RES) penetration. There is a need for solid consideration for these contributors who are part of a more extensive network.

© The Author(s), under exclusive license to Springer Nature Switzerland AG 2024
B. N. Jørgensen et al. (Eds.): EI.A 2023, LNCS 14468, pp. 158–174, 2024.
https://doi.org/10.1007/978-3-031-48652-4_11

Current literature addresses these issues in different ways. A common consensus is that introducing ESS benefits the network by allowing for more flexible handling and management [1].

Regarding remuneration, in [2] the authors offer a new approach that combines several methods and tools to manage uncertainty and overcome the obstacles of unclear data. The goal is to reduce the total involved cost and the number of associated forecasting errors.

Many authors aim to calculate the associated remuneration through Locational Marginal Pricing (LMP), such as [3] in which the authors propose a method to reimburse DG with LMP in distribution systems with radial configurations. Similarly to our research work proposed in this paper, the authors consider both used and unused resources. Bai et al. in [4] aim to give attention to managing congestion and prices while taking into consideration both active and reactive power, also addressing the voltage support through mixed-integer second-order cone programming (MISOCP).

In [5], the congestion is computed ahead of time, and demand response (DR) is calculated to respond as needed. This information is then utilized to determine the relevant remuneration value, which also considers the interactions between the unit to be remunerated and the DSO. Reference [6] adopts a similar strategy, although it is implemented on a network managed mainly by non-RES.

The authors Faria et al. in [7] present a technique to manage resources using an aggregator, to provide various combinations of aggregation and payment schemes. In [8], the authors investigate multiple strategies, including hierarchical and fuzzy c-means clustering. These strategies are utilized to aggregate and monetize energy resources.

Even though the primary focus of the study is on fairly compensating contributors and reducing operational costs, Silva et al. in [9] offer a new stage to the already existing scheduling, aggregation, and remuneration, which is the classification stage. This stage aims to assist the aggregator in operating situations. Similarly, in [10], these authors contribute by striving to grasp precisely how aggregating affects the final values of pay for each contributor. In other words, they are trying to determine how aggregating affects the final pay values.

Although the DG remuneration aspect in the context of network planning is vital, offering the best possible representation of reality, this could be achieved by combining several concerns such as adding the uncertainty to the model, which is very much a necessity in modern planning, as well as ESS [11].

Sarker et al. in [12] prepare for a potential rise in the number of circulating EVs (Electric Vehicles). To adapt to time-varying pricing and offer possible incentives to those who contribute the most to keeping the network within its bounds, the key goal is to maximize the aggregator's profitability while reducing the costs to the customer. The authors establish that boosting EV penetration in contemporary networks is feasible.

Likewise, Ma et al. in [13] employ real-time changes to determine the appropriate incentives to give to the network's demand side. The customers in their suggested model, an improved Arrow'd Aspremont-Gerard-Varet (AGV) mechanism, are penalized or rewarded based on their consumption history. The authors claim that this works very well in raising customers' awareness of their power use and is advantageous to both consumers and providers. Lastly, Kim et al. in [14] investigate how predicting errors affects resource allocation and compensation. In this article, the authors create two ways in retrospect, one flawless and one flawed, and consequently, they evaluate how each method affects the outcomes. These models can accommodate DLMP-based compensation, value stacks, and net metering. According to Kim et al., incorrect foresight results in a financial loss of at least 1.6% in all cases.

Our research paper proposes individual remuneration for each resource across a medium voltage (MV) distribution network with 180 buses, 42 Wind farms, and 33 PV parks. The network also has a substation and three Biomass generators owned by the DSO. Two ESSs are already installed, owned by a third party, allowing the DSO to use 25% of its capacity under contract freely. If the DSO needs to access the remaining 75% of the storage unit, a cost penalty is applied for contract breach. The model allows for the installation of more storage units.

Apart from the individual remuneration of each resource, this work also applies a deep level of uncertainty (daily values), a crucial combination not commonly seen in related literature.

Our proposed advancements with this paper are:

- Advancing the level of uncertainty in similar models to daily values;
- Fair remuneration of DG units individually;
- Intertwining uncertainty, remuneration of DG, ESSs, DG, and EVs with an optimization model, to get the closest we can to a real situation.

This paper is divided into the following topics: 1-Introduction, where relevant literature is analyzed, and briefly explaining the paper's aim. In 2-Considered Methodology, the work method is described, namely the appliance of uncertainty and considerations used in the remuneration process. Here, the optimization model is also explained. In 3-Case study, the specific details of the existing network are discussed more in-depth, and the application of the methodology happens. In 4-Results Discussion the results for the model are exposed. Lastly, in 5-Conclusions, there is a global gathering of the information portrayed in the paper, such as the implications of the results.

2 Considered Methodology

This section provides an overview of the model's definition and application. There is an explanation of how the uncertainty is structured and how the remuneration was decided and applied. Subsection 2.1 aims to explain how the scenarios were defined and distinguished and how the uncertainty was applied to each scenario. Subsection 2.2 aims to explain the proposed optimization model. Subsection 2.3 describes how the values for remuneration were defined and applied.

2.1 Scenario Segmentation and Application

The model consists of 16 main scenarios: all combinations of seasons (Summer, Spring, Fall, Winter) and daily time periods (Morning, Peak, Afternoon, Night). The probability of each of these main scenarios is as exposed in Table 1.

Each of these 16 main scenarios' probability has been calculated as follows in Eq. (1), using Fall Night as an example:

$$Prob_{Fall_{Night}} = \frac{1275}{8760} \times 100\% = 14.54\% \tag{1}$$

Table 1. Scenario Segmentation and Probability

Season (days)	Scenario Probability (%)/Days out of 8760/Scenario Number			
	Morning	Peak	Afternoon	Night
Summer (92)	7.35%/644/(1)*	3.15%/276/(2)	3.15%/276/(3)	11.55%/1012/(4)
Spring (92)	5.25%/460/(5)	3.15%/276/(6)	4.20%/368/(7)	12.60%/1104/(8)
Fall (91)	5.19%/455/(9)	2.08%/182/(10)	3.12%/273/(11)	14.54%/1274/(12)
Winter (90)	4.11%/360/(13)	2.05%/180/(14)	3.08%/270/(15)	15.41%/1350/(16)

(1)*, for example, refers to the scenario number, as such, Summer Morning is scenario (1) from now on

For each of these 16 main scenarios, 50000 individual scenarios were created for wind and solar generation, load, EV, and ESS states, which are then reduced to the corresponding number of hours. For example, the initial 50000 situations are reduced to 1274 for the main scenario Fall Night through a scenario reduction tool (Scenredpy).

The multiplicative factors that help distinguish the scenarios between themselves were found through a collection and analysis of data in Portugal from 2017 to 2022. Load data were extracted from [15] and wind and PV behavior from [16]. Spring Morning was chosen as the base value (unitary load, wind, and PV factor) to enable a direct comparison between scenarios. The results are shown in Table 2.

Table 2. Multiplicative factor for PV/Wind/Load

Season	Multiplicative Factor for PV/Wind/Load			
	Morning	Peak	Afternoon	Night
Summer	1.40/1.00/0.99	3.20/1.60/1.11	2.40/1.00/0.91	0.05/0.80/0.59
Spring	1.00/1.00/1.00	2.60/1.40/1.12	1.40/1.00/0.92	0.05/0.80/0.65
Fall	1.00/1.00/1.03	2.20/1.40/1.16	1.40/1.00/0.93	0.05/0.80/0.65
Winter	0.60/1.00/1.03	1.40/1.40/1.14	1.00/1.00/0.95	0.05/0.80/0.69

2.2 Optimization Model

Our proposed model presents a baseline based on [17] with some changes, namely:

- Three biomass generators are used along the network, belonging to the DSO;
- Two ESSs are already installed (usage is explained in 2.3), on top of allowing the model to install more;
- Instead of approaching the 16 main scenarios with one state per scenario, an hourly approach was implemented, as explained in 2.1;
- There is a consideration for remuneration of all resources (analyzed yearly and for the project's entire lifetime of 30 years) individually, with the model aiming to reduce all associated costs.

The model allows for investments in potential new lines (as seen in Fig. 1) and a redesign of its topology and investments in ESS.

The proposed model is formulated as MILP to find the following decision variables:

- Power required by DSO (substation, biomass, and any ESS to be added apart from the ones in buses 31/87);
- Power generation curtailment of DG;
- Size and location of ESS;
- Optimal network topology;
- Optimal power flow for each line in each sub-scenario;

The model outputs the following information:

- Every associated network-specific cost: new lines, lines' maintenance, expected energy not supplied (EENS), power losses, ESS installation and maintenance, load cut, and power generation curtailment;
- System average interruption duration index (SAIDI);
- System average interruption frequency index (SAIFI);
- Cost of the power required by DSO (substation, biomass, and any ESS to be added apart from the ones in buses 31/87) yearly;
- Remuneration to the networks' third-party generation providers (PV, Wind, ESS buses 31/87);
- Economic analysis as a comparison to the original network.

The model is also subject to the following constraints:

- Power balance;
- Power flow limit;
- Unidirectionality of power flow;
- Insurance of radial topology;
- Avoidance of island creation;
- Substation, biomass, and ESS maximum capacity;
- ESS charge and discharge rate;
- Price adaptation of ESS;
- SAIDI and SAIFI limits;
- Generation and load curtailment limit.

The network initially has two ESS units already applied in buses 31 and 87. A third party owns these and is part of the network through a contract with the DSO, who has control over 25% of the capacity of the unit to charge and discharge as needed, with

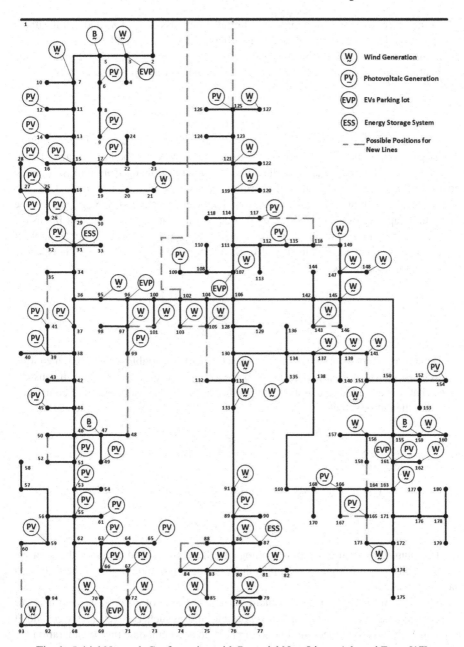

Fig. 1. Initial Network Configuration with Potential New Lines, Adapted From [17].

minimal compensation to the unit's owner. Would the DSO need to access the remaining 75%, there would be compensation to be paid to this third party. The detailed prices are exposed in Subsect. 2.3.

Equations (2)–(4) are implemented to limit the biomass generators and storage units. Equation (2) defines Biomass generation, where $P_{BioMinLimit(b)}$ and $P_{BioMaxLimit(b)}$ are the minimum and maximum Biomass generation, respectively. $P_{Bio(b)}$ is the actual value of generation of each Biomass generator (b). B is the set of biomass generators.

$$P_{BioMinLimit(b,s)} \leq P_{Bio(b,s)} \leq P_{BioMaxLimit(b,s)} \qquad (2)$$
$$\forall b \in \Omega_B, \forall s \in \Omega_S$$

Regarding the storage units, Eqs. (3) and (4) represent the adaptation of price whether the usage is within the contract or not. Equation (3) represents the compliance of contracted values. Here, $St_{Usage(e,s)}$ is the amount of energy flowing from an ESS (can be positive if discharging or negative if charging), for every ESS available, e, be it the two pre-installed or potential new additions, for every scenario studied, s. $St_{MaxCap(e)}$ is the maximum capacity of every ESS used. $St_{Cost(e,s)}$ is the final price to pay for the usage of that specific unit, e, on that scenario, s, and the $St_{PriceInContract}$ is the price to apply if the contract is followed. E is the set of ESSs and S is the set of scenarios. The specific prices are outlined in Sect. 2.3.

$$St_{Usage(e,s)} \leq St_{MaxCap(e)} \times 0.25$$
$$St_{Cost(e,s)} = St_{PriceInContract} \times St_{Usage(e,s)} \qquad (3)$$
$$\forall e \in \Omega_E, \forall s \in \Omega_S$$

Equation (4) represents a breach of contract, where all variables retain their meaning. Regarding $St_{PriceOutContract}$, it is the price to apply to the excess value. It must be noted that this extra value is only to be applied to the excess value past the contracted 25%, not the entire value.

$$St_{Usage(e,s)} \geq St_{MaxCap(e)} \times 0.25 \qquad (4)$$
$$St_{Cost(e,s)} = St_{PriceInContract} \times \left(St_{MaxCap(e)} \times 0.25 \right)$$

$$+St_{PriceOutContract} \times \left(St_{Usage(e,s)} - \left(St_{MaxCap(e)} \times 0.25 \right) \right)$$

$$\forall e \in \Omega_E, \forall s \in \Omega_S$$

The plan is to ensure a radial topology to the network and evaluate the strategy economically while studying the impact that considering remuneration of the resources has on the network.

Since we are looking at the problem through the lens of a DSO, we're aiming to minimize the associated costs as much as possible, and, as such, Eqs. (6)–(10) were added to the already existing objective function in [17], to accommodate the consideration for remunerating these resources. These belong to the second stage of the stochastic model and, as such, would be adapted to the already existing PC$_2$ in Eq. (5), from [17].

$$MinimizePC = PC_1 + PC_2 \qquad (5)$$

Here, PC_1 are the first-stage variables in the two-stage stochastic model ("here-and-now decisions"), and PC_2 are the second-stage variables ("wait-and-see decisions").

Equation (6) represents the total amount to pay for substation generation, as shown:

$$Sub_{TotalGenCost} = P_{Sub(s)} \times Sub_{Price} \qquad (6)$$

$$\forall s \in \Omega_S$$

where, $Sub_{TotalGenCost}$ is the total cost to pay for the amount produced by the substation, $P_{Sub(e)}$ is the total generation for the substation in any scenario, s, and Sub_{Price} is the price explained in Table 3.

Equation (7) represents the remuneration calculation for the biomass generators, as shown:

$$Bio_{TotalGenCost} = \sum_{b \in \Omega_B} P_{Bio(b,s)} \times Bio_{Price} \qquad (7)$$

$$\forall b \in \Omega_B, \forall s \in \Omega_S$$

where $Bio_{TotalGenCost}$ is the total amount to pay for all biomass generators, b, in any scenario, s. $P_{Bio(b,s)}$ is the total amount generated by each biomass generator, and Bio_{Price} follows the prices discussed in Table 3.

Equations (8) and (9) follow the same trend but for PV parks and Wind farms, respectively.

$$PV_{TotalGenCost} = \sum_{pv \in \Omega_{PV}} P_{Solar(PV,s)} \times PV_{Price} \qquad (8)$$

$$\forall pv \in \Omega_{PV}, \forall s \in \Omega_S$$

where $PV_{TotalGenCost}$ is the total amount to remunerate to all contributors for all PV parks, pv, across all scenarios, s. $P_{Solar(PV,s)}$ is the amount of generation for any given PV park in any given scenario, and, again, PV_{Price} follows Table 3.

$$Wind_{TotalGenCost} = \sum_{W \in \Omega_w} P_{Wind(w,s)} \times Wind_{Price} \qquad (9)$$

$$\forall w \in \Omega_W, \forall s \in \Omega_S$$

The same happens with this equation. $Wind_{TotalGenCost}$ is the total amount to remunerate to all contributors for all Wind farms, w, across all scenarios, s. $P_{Wind(w,s)}$ is the amount of generation for any given Wind farm in any given scenario, and, again, $Wind_{Price}$ follows Table 3.

Equation (10) is what is added to PC_2 to be minimized, and it is as follows:

$$Remuneration_{TotalCost} = Sub_{TotalGenCost} + Bio_{TotalGenCost} + PV_{TotalGenCost}$$
$$+ Wind_{TotalGenCost} \qquad (10)$$

Table 3. Prices of each technology to remunerate accordingly.

Generation Source	Regular Usage Price (m.u./MWh)	Excessive Generation Price (m.u./MWh)
Owned and Operated by the DSO		
Substation	55	300
Biomass	45	300
ESS	40	400
Owned and Operated by another Party, which needs compensation from the DSO		
Wind Farms	45	150
PV Parks	45	150
ESS (Buses 31/87, within Contract)	30	150
ESS (Buses 31/87, breach of Contract)	400	1000

*Any ESS that the model decides to install apart from the two that were already in place (buses 31/87) are assumed to be owned by the DSO

2.3 Remuneration of Distributed Resources

Regarding the remuneration of distributed resources, research was conducted to discover the most accurate pricing feasible for each technology, and the data for this study was obtained from various sources [18–25]. A price was determined for the typical use of all technologies, and another price, dubbed the "Excess Price," was established for any surplus energy that was generated but not used. As may be seen in Table 3, the final costs were as follows:

The proposed cost of 300 m.u./MWh for excessive generation follows the study made in [17], where an analysis was made for the values of 100, 200, 300, 400, and 500 m.u./MWh, and 300 was found to be the most suitable. A study will be done to understand the impact of ESSs on total remuneration.

3 Case Study

The proposed methodology will be applied to a real MV network with 180 buses in the Leiria district in Portugal.

As mentioned before, the network has 42 Wind farms, 33 PV parks, and two ESSs owned by participants of the grid, being that the ESSs are partially maneuvered by the DSO under a contract, as previously discussed. The network also has a substation, three biomass generators, and potentially any ESSs the model sees fit to add, all owned by the DSO. These generation units are used to feed 90 loads across the entire network, as well as five EV parking lots. The biomass generators have a maximum capacity of 0.25MW, based on [26].

The proposed analysis will evaluate the project economically for the full 30 years of the project, with the corresponding recuperation factor. In addition, a study will determine how impactful the change in the contracted percentage of ESS usage would be in the economic analysis, with incremental steps of 25%. All the possible ESS conditions that will be studied are as follows in Table 4, although the default state is 25% for the DSO. This study aims to understand the differences that would be caused, such as in the costs.

Regarding the potential of adding new ESSs, the model can place them in buses 15, 66, and 156. It is also allowed to consider adding more capacity to the existing ones on buses 31 and 87, with a corresponding cost.

The discount rate used in the study is 0.05% [27], and since the project has a lifetime of 30 years, there is a capital recovery factor (CRF) of 0.034. There is an imposed limitation to the SAIDI and SAIFI values of at least a 10% reduction from their original actual values of 24.48(h/customer) and 5.98(interruptions/customer), respectively.

Moreover, all corresponding maintenance and applied costs are multiplied by three since it is a three-phase system, and the costs for power losses are assumed as 120m.u./MWh. The economic analysis evaluated the Net Present Value (NPV), Payback, and Internal Rate of Return (IRR).

Table 4. Different possibilities for ESSs

Housing Bus For the ESS	Percentage Owned by The DSO (%)	Percentage Owned by the Network Participant (%)	Current Installed Capacity (MW)	Maximum Possible Capacity (MW)
31	*0/25/50/75/100**	*100/75/50/25/0*	1	5
87			3	5
15/66/156	100	--	--	3

* Corresponding to the five different analyses made

4 Results Discussion

The study's primary optimization model considered the yearly remuneration situation, which consists of 1,245,255 constraints and 2,658,602 variables. It was executed on a computer with an AMD Ryzen 7 5800H processor and 16GB of RAM, operating on Windows 11 Home, modeled with Pyomo's library [28], and solved with Gurobi's Optimization Solver [29], using Python. Table 5 shows the difference in run time and memory allocation caused by considering remuneration, as measured by the tracemalloc library.

In Fig. 2, we show the contribution of each technology to the final model for each of the 16 main scenarios, considering remuneration. After that, the contribution to the total remuneration of each technology (Fig. 3). Since the other situations are variations for analysis purposes, Figs. 2 and 3 refer to the standard case of 25% of ESS contracted usage.

Table 5. Computational Resources for the different situations

Case	Run time (s)	Memory allocation (MB)
Remuneration Not Considered	545	396
Yearly Remuneration	948	792

*The run time and memory allocation are an average of all studies undertaken (different runs for different % of ESS usage allowed within the contract)

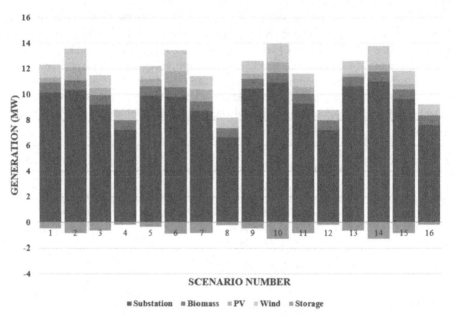

Fig. 2. Generation by technology for each scenario

As seen, a large portion of generation is upheld by the substation.

The three Biomass generators are also used near their maximum capacity since the DSO owns them and does not need to pay anyone for the respective generation, apart from the resources. The variation within scenarios depends on the surrounding circumstances, i.e., negligible PV generation at night requires a different generation pattern, even if there is much less demand to be met.

The model decides not to install any ESS unit and opts not to add capacity to the existing buses (31 and 87). Primarily, the ESS in bus 31 is being used to feed the network (apart from scenarios 12 and 16, which are Fall and Winter at Night). In contrast, the ESS in bus 87 is being charged in all scenarios, where the third-party owner pays the DSO for the corresponding quantity (between 9.000 m.u. and 10.000 m.u., as seen in Fig. 3.

This study could be translated into other networks, with only some minor adaptations, along with the required input changes, meaning that it is versatile in terms of application.

The optimization model is formulated in such a way that it is universal to any network as long as the input data is known.

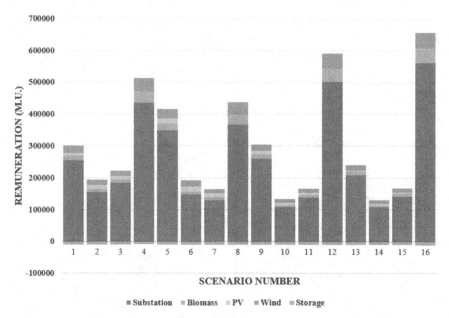

Fig. 3. Remuneration for each technology in each scenario

The final network is shown in Fig. 4. The model opts not to use some lines previously on the network, such as 82–174. It also opts to add some new lines and a new connection to the feeder, where the respective costs for the transformer and connectors and the respective maintenance were considered (1–102).

Since the primary purpose of this model is to reduce the total costs for the DSO, a detailed analysis of the total expenses is made in Table 6.

An economic evaluation was also made to understand how valuable the model is, by evaluating the economic indicators NPV, Payback, and IRR, as previously mentioned, and it is shown in Table 7. The consideration for biomasses and ESS in this network, especially when the DSO owns them, aid the model tremendously economically since the generation needed to meet the demand can come from several places, allowing the model more options. If there were no biomasses, all the generation coming from them would need to be compensated by the substation, resulting in higher EENS and power loss costs derived from the distance the power would need to travel.

The model is economically advantageous compared to the original network, with a relatively short Payback (3,02 years) considering the size of the problem and the investment made.

The economic analysis was conducted based on [17, 30, 31].

The main contributors to the model's total cost are the maintenance of lines, as aspected due to the network dimension and the considered project lifetime (30 years).

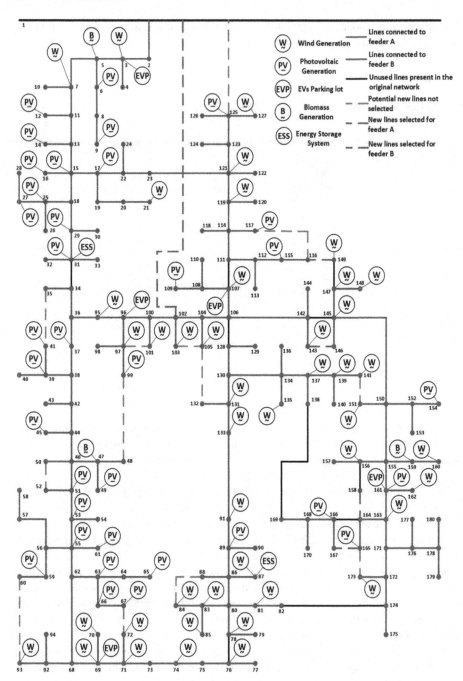

Fig. 4. Optimal Network Topology (Original Network Adapted from [17])

Another strong contributor to the total cost is the amount of power supplied by the substation (the most significant contributor to feeding the grid).

Table 6. Total listing of costs for the current model

Investments	Lines (Including Transformer Cost)	1 257 600 m.u
	ESS	400 000 m.u
	Total Investments	1 657 600 m.u
Expenditures	Excessive Generation	26 887 m.u
	Power Losses	556 580 m.u
	Expected Energy Not Supplied (EENS)	1 280 487 m.u
	Lines Maintenance	8 564 554 m.u
	ESS Maintenance	1 203 755 m.u
	Total Expenditures	11 632 263 m.u
Total Network Planning Costs		13 289 863 m.u
Remuneration (Yearly)	Substation	5 258 321 m.u
	Biomass	389 621 m.u
	Wind	585 655 m.u
	PV	390 621 m.u
	Storages	−157 169 m.u
Total Remuneration Associated Costs		6 467 049 m.u
Total Costs		19 756 912 m.u

Table 7. Economic evaluation of the proposed model

NPV	14 699 358 m.u
Payback	3,02 years
IRR	33,16%

Regarding the study of the percentage of ESS that is contracted to be available to the DSO, it was found that there was a very slight decrease in total cost from 25% to 50% availability. Still, assuming that the contract would also be costlier with an increase in percentage access, 25% seems to be the adequate balance to choose from the DSO in this situation. This essentially means that the amount used of ESS does not change with the accessible percentage, meaning that 25% is enough for the current model.

The failure indicators SAIDI and SAIFI end up at 19,23 h/customer and 2,94 interruptions/customer, respectively.

5 Conclusions

Our world is rapidly shifting toward a clean future, but despite it being necessary, it brings a plethora of issues to address. The uncertainty correlated to RES results in forecasting errors, and a low network flexibility to correct those errors calls for meticulous planning of the network, where it is crucial to consider potential uncertainties correlated to these Wind, PV, and Load values. It is also increasingly needed to study the effects of storage devices since they are seen as a way to allow the network to be more flexible by being dispatchable with immediate effect when needed.

Since our current landscape is shifting toward using more RES, naturally, these resources must be remunerated appropriately. Many current networks are seeing an influx of electricity generation from many directions derived from network contributors, who need to be appropriately reimbursed. Our proposed model is not only appealing economically by optimizing all aspects of the network, such as line placement but is also fair regarding remuneration. With a Payback of 3,02 years and an IRR of 33,16% we can see that we improve the network drastically, especially since the original was not efficient in its topology. The addition of biomass generators and ESSs also proved to be tremendously beneficial, especially regarding the decrease in power loss and EENS related costs, but it also proved to help improve the SAIDI and SAIFI by 21,45% and 50,84%, respectively.

According to the findings of this paper, it is recommended that all modern network planning works consider the remuneration aspect, since it accounts for a significant portion of associated costs, and, as such, must not be ignored.

The present approach is limited in regards to computational time, since it is a significant burden, and also by not yet considering risk assessment.

The current plan is also to implement risk assessment in future work to allow our model to prepare for extreme situations regarding either generation or load, and also multi-period investment.

Acknowledgments. This research has received funding from the National Funds through the FCT Portuguese Foundation for Science and Technology under project UIDB/000760/2020 and UIDP/00760/2020. João Soares has received funding from FCT, namely CEECIND/00420/2022. The authors acknowledge the support provided by the Thematic Network 723RT0150 "Red para la integración a gran escala de energías renovables en sistemas eléctricos (RIBIERSE-CYTED)" financed by the call for Thematic Networks of the CYTED (Ibero American Program of Science and Technology for Development) for 2022.

References

1. Agamah, S.U., Ekonomou, L.: A heuristic combinatorial optimization algorithm for load-leveling and peak demand reduction using energy storage systems. Elect. Power Compon. Syst. **45**, 2093–2103 (2017). https://doi.org/10.1080/15325008.2017.1406017
2. Pérez-Arriaga, J.D.J.I.J.: Improved regulatory approaches for the remuneration of electricity distribution utilities with high penetrations of distributed energy resources. Energy J. **38** (2017). https://doi.org/10.5547/01956574.38.3.jjen

3. Mancera, C.T., Monroy, A.C.: Pricing of distribution networks with distributed generation: application of nodal pricing. In: 2011 IEEE PES Conference on Innovative Smart Grid Technologies Latin America (ISGT LA). IEEE, pp. 1–7 (2011)
4. Bai, L., Wang, J., Wang, C., et al.: Distribution locational marginal pricing (DLMP) for congestion management and voltage support. IEEE Trans. Power Syst. 33, 4061–4073 (2018). https://doi.org/10.1109/TPWRS.2017.2767632
5. Liu, W., Wu, Q., Wen, F., Ostergaard, J.: Day-ahead congestion management in distribution systems through household demand response and distribution congestion prices. IEEE Trans Smart Grid 5, 2739–2747 (2014). https://doi.org/10.1109/TSG.2014.2336093
6. Mercure, J.-F., Salas, P.: On the global economic potentials and marginal costs of non-renewable resources and the price of energy commodities. Energy Policy 63, 469–483 (2013). https://doi.org/10.1016/j.enpol.2013.08.040
7. Faria, P., Spínola, J., Vale, Z.: Methods for aggregation and remuneration of distributed energy resources. Appl. Sci. 8, 1283 (2018). https://doi.org/10.3390/app8081283
8. Faria, P., Spinola, J., Vale, Z.: Aggregation and remuneration of electricity consumers and producers for the definition of demand-response programs. IEEE Trans. Industr. Inform. 12, 952–961 (2016). https://doi.org/10.1109/TII.2016.2541542
9. Silva, C., Faria, P., Vale, Z.: Demand response and distributed generation remuneration approach considering planning and operation stages. Energies (Basel) 12, 2721 (2019). https://doi.org/10.3390/en12142721
10. Silva, C., Faria, P., Vale, Z.: Multi-period observation clustering for tariff definition in a weekly basis remuneration of demand response. Energies (Basel) 12, 1248 (2019). https://doi.org/10.3390/en12071248
11. Wang, W., Yuan, B., Sun, Q., Wennersten, R.: Application of energy storage in integrat-ed energy systems — a solution to fluctuation and uncertainty of renewable energy. J. Energy Storage 52, 104812 (2022). https://doi.org/10.1016/j.est.2022.104812
12. Sarker, M.R., Ortega-Vazquez, M.A., Kirschen, D.S.: Optimal coordination and scheduling of demand response via monetary incentives. IEEE Trans. Smart Grid 6, 1341–1352 (2015). https://doi.org/10.1109/TSG.2014.2375067
13. Ma, J., Deng, J., Song, L., Han, Z.: Incentive mechanism for demand side management in smart grid using auction. IEEE Trans. Smart Grid 5, 1379–1388 (2014). https://doi.org/10.1109/TSG.2014.2302915
14. Kim, J., Bialek, S., Ünel, B., Dvorkin, Y.: Impact of imperfect foresight on the optimal DER deployment, remuneration and policy. Appl. Energy 326, 119885 (2022). https://doi.org/10.1016/j.apenergy.2022.119885
15. DGEG DGEG Estatística. https://www.dgeg.gov.pt/pt/estatistica/energia/eletricidade/pro ducao-anual-e-potencia-instalada/. Accessed 13 Sep 2023
16. REN REN datahub. https://datahub.ren.pt/pt/. Accessed 13 Sep 2023
17. Canizes, B., Soares, J., Lezama, F., et al.: Optimal expansion planning considering storage investment and seasonal effect of demand and renewable generation. Renew. Energy 138, 937–954 (2019). https://doi.org/10.1016/j.renene.2019.02.006
18. BloombergNEF. Cost of New Renewables Temporarily Rises as Inflation Starts to Bite (2022). https://about.bnef.com/blog/cost-of-new-renewables-temporarily-rises-as-inflation-starts-to-bite/. Accessed 13 Sep 2023
19. Armstrong M.: The Falling Cost of Renewable Energy (2021). https://www.statista.com/chart/26085/price-per-megawatt-hour-of-electricity-by-source/. Accessed 23 May 2023
20. WindEurope. Wind energy is the cheapest source of electricity generation (2019). https://win deurope.org/policy/topics/economics/. Accessed 23 May 2023
21. Knoema. A Decade of Change: How Renewables Became Competitive with Fossil Fuels (2021). https://knoema.com/infographics/fmzvyg/a-decade-of-change-how-renewables-bec ame-competitive-with-fossil-fuels. Accessed 23 May 2023

22. NREL. Annual Technology Baseline: Electricity (2022). https://atb-archive.nrel.gov/electr icity/2019/index.html?t=hp. Accessed 23 May 2023
23. Richter, A.: U.S. EIA: Geothermal very competitive on levelized cost of electricty basis. In: THINKGEOENERGY (2016). https://www.thinkgeoenergy.com/u-s-eia-geothermal-very-competitive-on-levelized-cost-of-electricity-basis/. Accessed 23 May 2023
24. Irena. Renewable Power Generation Costs IN 2021 (2021). https://www.irena.org/-/media/Files/IRENA/Agency/Publication/2022/Jul/IRENA_Power_Generation_Costs_2021.pdf? rev=34c22a4b244d434da0accde7de7c73d8. Accessed 23 May 2023
25. LAZARD. Levelized Cost of Energy, Levelized Cost of Storage, and Levelized Cost of Hydrogen (2020). https://www.lazard.com/perspective/levelized-cost-of-energy-levelized-cost-of-storage-and-levelized-cost-of-hydrogen-2020/. Accessed 13 Sep 2023
26. Mittermeier, F.: Operating manual Operating manual HDG K10–33-Content 3 Content
27. CIA. CIA Rates (2023). https://www.cia-ica.ca/publications/rates-and-indexes. Accessed 13 Sep 2023
28. Bynum, M.L., Hackebeil, G.A., Hart, W.E., et al.: Pyomo—Optimization Modeling in Python. Springer International Publishing, Cham (2021). https://doi.org/10.1007/978-3-030-68928-5
29. Gurobi Optimization L (2023) Gurobi Optimizer Reference Manual. https://www.gurobi.com. Accessed 6 May 2023
30. Dai, H., Li, N., Wang, Y., Zhao, X.: The Analysis of Three Main Investment Criteria: NPV IRR and Payback Period (2022)
31. Zativita, F.I., Chumaidiyah, E.: Feasibility analysis of Rumah Tempe Zanada establishment in Bandung using net present value, internal rate of return, and payback period. IOP Conf. Ser. Mater. Sci. Eng. **505**, 012007 (2019). https://doi.org/10.1088/1757-899X/505/1/012007

New Perspectives on Clustering for Demand Response

Kushan Choksi🆔 and Anupama Kowli(✉)🆔

Indian Institute of Technology Bombay, Mumbai, India
anu.kowli@iitb.ac.in

Abstract. Demand response (DR) programs have received significant attention with proliferation of smart meters and increasing need for demand-side flexibility to complement the growing share of renewable generation. A critical element in DR program is the consumer selection; adhoc selection of consumers may not yield any tangible results in actual deployment. Clustering on features derived from smart meter data has shown potential for facilitating the consumer selection for DR. This paper furthers the understanding of this approach by looking at issues associated with the clustering process. Specifically, the paper identifies the problem of defining characteristic profiles for consumers exhibiting multiple consumption patterns. The characteristic profile is a key element for clustering as well as for evaluating behavior consistency. A new method for extracting characteristic profile is presented and metrics for consistency in consumption patterns are redefined. We also propose several useful attributes to quantify the peak load contributions associated with a consumer cluster. We apply the proposed techniques to Dataport smart meter data to bring fresh insights on clustering techniques that segregate consumers based on their consumption and behavioral patterns. We demonstrate how clusters formed using our proposed definition of characteristic profile show bettering clustering consistency. Our results also show how the proposed consistency metrics and peak attributes are useful for capturing the consumer predictability and peak contribution for a more meaningful DR program design.

Keywords: Clustering · Consumer consistency · DR consmumer selection · Peak contribution

1 Introduction

With increased deployment of renewable generation, demand-side flexibility is not just a means to improve electricity market competition but also a source of ancillary services to manage the impact of intermittent renewable power outputs [21]. Last few years have witnessed several demand response (DR) success stories, with most significant demand side flexibility potential demonstrated by curtailment services from commercial and industrial demand segments. Residential loads typically contribute to 25 to 35% of the system load [9] and have also shown promising potential for DR. For example, Austin Energy in Texas, US,

B. N. Jørgensen et al. (Eds.): EI.A 2023, LNCS 14468, pp. 175–191, 2024.
https://doi.org/10.1007/978-3-031-48652-4_12

reported savings of roughly 2.25 million US dollars in avoided generation costs due to all its residential DR programs combined [29]. Therefore, a careful consideration of residential DR is necessary for effective system load management. Residential demand segment typically has large number of consumers and constitutes the largest connected load in any grid. Therefore, it is a vital component of the system supply-demand analysis and effective load management for this segment via tariff design and/or pricing- and curtailment-based DR is necessary for a well functioning system. On the one hand, electricity costs may actually matter more to some residential users as compared to industrial consumers, making them ideal candidates for pricing-based DR schemes. On the other hand, residential users may not have adequate backup unlike industrial and commercial consumers making them more likely to ignore DR curtailment events. Finding the right DR scheme for a residential consumer thus becomes a challenging problem.

Targeting the residential users for DR programs based on pricing schemes and/or curtailment incentives is complicated by two factors. First, the number of consumers being large allows for many sub-optimal choices. Second, the response of consumer(s) can vary widely. The review of several practical implementations of time-of-use (TOU), critical peak pricing (CPP) and real time pricing (RTP) programs in [8] precisely emphasizes these two challenges. In this paper, we address them by proposing data analytics that leverage the advanced metering infrastructure (AMI) being deployed in many countries around the world. AMI facilitates access to smart meter data that can be used towards a meaningful analysis of consumer behavior and allow for a more effective consumer targeting for specific DR schemes.

The problem of consumer classification and/or selection for DR programs using their smart meter data has received increased attention in academia. Several papers use the data to partition the residential consumers into various groups based on commonalities in appliance ownership or similar high consumption patterns or coincidence in time of use of specific appliances so that these groups can be targeted for more effective DR program design. For instance, contributions of individual consumers to system peak can be used for cluster identification [2]. Likewise, the thermal sensitivity of the consumer demands can be characterized and deployed for identifying potential candidates for DR [1]. The grouping itself can be achieved using various clustering/classification techniques as seen in literature – references [10, 28] review several such methods. These include hierarchical techniques (see [6, 19]), centroid-based methods such as k-means and k-medoids (see [16, 17]), density-based approaches (see [14]) and model-based methods (see [27]).

In several clustering schemes mentioned above, consumer clusters are identified based on their representative or characteristic load profiles. Such profiles can be extracted by averaging the daily load profiles of the consumers (see [7]) or averaging consumer load profiles of certain weekdays to avoid effect of weekend and holidays (see [15]). Then, clustering consumers based on such profiles can be implemented taking into consideration the specific DR program in mind

[26]. For instance, clustering can be implemented for peak load and energy loss assessment [5] and DR participant selection [12] as well as design of pricing-based DR program [18] and incentive-based DR program [13]. Since the clusters are based on the similarities among the characteristic load profiles of the constituent consumers, the definition of a characteristic load profile should be carefully considered.

A consumer may exhibit multiple consumption patterns owing to weekends, vacation, variable cleaning schedules, climatic changes, etc. Multi-profile consumers may be defined as a consumers who exhibit multiple consumption patterns – a systematic treatment of such consumers for characteristic load profile definition and clustering applications is missing in the current state-of-art. This paper proposes a new definition for the characteristic load profile of the multi-profile consumers – it is defined as the weighed average of the consumer's multiple profiles instead of the traditionally used mean profile. The weights for the same are computed as the degree of repeatability of the characteristic consumption pattern. It is noted that this adaption ensures that the characteristic profile remains close to the repeatable consumption pattern and improves the consistency quantification for the consumer.

Literature on clustering for DR using smart meter data often focus on improving adequacy measures or similarity index values, which may not be adequate from DR viewpoint. A utility implementing DR among its residential consumers may prefer to rely on consumers with fairly consistent consumption patterns if curtailment contracts are to be offered. In case of a group engaging in such contract, the consistency based inference for clustered consumers may be of interest to the said utility. Additionally, quantitative measures that capture the contribution of the cluster towards system peak and correlation of cluster aggregate consumption with system peak may be useful for quantifying the DR potential of the group. This paper provides quantifiable metrics for consistency and peak demand contribution so that clustering techniques can be re-examined from the DR application point of view.

The quantification of consistency of consumer helps to understand the predictability of consumer [23]. There are few attempts made in literature to quantify consistency. In [12], consistency is quantified using threshold K-means and entropy metrics. However, it requires meta data and is sensitive to threshold value and type of clustering algorithm used. A consistency score suggested in [23] uses average load profile of an consumer – the usual choice of characteristic profile as per [7,15] – and the standard deviation around it, but it is highly sensitive to outliers or abnormalities. More importantly, the algorithm design penalizes any ephemeral load variation in the consumption profile and produces a reduced consistency score for the consumer despite of the profile being *mostly* consistent across the time series. On the contrary, the consistency metric proposed in this work explicitly take into consideration multi-profile behavior of consumers by explicitly considering variations around the weighted average characteristic profile. The approach is thus better suited to capture consistent weekday/weekend/holiday patterns. We also define consistency of a cluster to quantitatively demonstrate its reliability for DR targeting scheme.

Peak demand action can prove to be decisive in relieving grid overload if consumers contributing to the system peak are targeted for DR participation [20]. Hence, clustering and peak analysis has been used for system peak load assessment in [5]. But these approaches do not use peak attributes such as coincidence and correlation to assess the impact of consumer cluster on system peak reduction. This paper extracts peak attributes and correlation values of a consumer cluster in relation to system load and peak. These attributes allow the utility to identify conforming and non confirming group/cluster of consumers so that appropriate consumer clusters can be targeted for peak curtailment or load shifting DR schemes. The paper discusses how the attributes can be derived from data post processing after cluster identification. This provides a comprehensive treatment for the consumer selection problem by including the practical feasibility into clustering-based DR consumer selection approach.

In summary, the paper makes following contributions to the problem of clustering for DR consumer selection:

1. Defining the characteristic profile for multi-profile consumers: we show how clustering results vary considerably with such modeling.
2. Devising cluster consistency and consumer cluster reliability metrics for cluster selection for DR: the metrics explicitly consider multi-profile behavior.
3. Proposing peak coincidence and peak contribution metrics: we discuss how clusters can be selected for DR based on these attributes.

In what follows, we present our analytics, results and concluding remarks.

2   Materials and Methods

A simple, linear methodology is adopted in this paper: data pre-processing, consumer clustering and post-processing for cluster attributes. The data cleaning and structuring steps involved in pre-processing stage, the analytics for consumer clustering and the computation of the consistency metrics and peak attributes for the clusters in the post processing stage is described in the following subsections.

2.1   Data Pre-processing

Data pre-processing is foremost step in any data-driven analysis that ensures data compatibility and deals with missing data. In the context of this paper, this step is divided into data import, data cleaning, missing data replacement, data structuring and data visualization and exploration.

Data Cleaning, Missing Data and Outlier Replacement: For the Dataport smart meter data used in our casestudy, we use the Savitzky Golay filter [24] to filter any high frequency noise in the consumption data. Missing data is replaced using exponential smoothing and seasonal auto regressive integrated moving average (S-ARIMA) forecasting [3] for three and more than three consecutive missing data respectively. Outliers in daily consumption profiles are detected using bands whose limits are formulated based on time and frequency domain approaches by utilizing three mean absolute deviation and median absolute deviation respectively. Any consumer profile that violates the outlier detection band is tagged as outlier. Furthermore, outlier profile tagged for any day consumer is then replaced by its mean consumption profile.

Data Structuring and Extraction of Characteristic Profile: The filtered data is indexed by the consumer id, day and time interval for consumption. Specifically, the term $P_n^d(t)$ is used to denote the consumption of the nth consumer during the tth interval of dth day. Here, $n \in \{1, 2, \ldots, N\}$, $d \in \{1, 2, \ldots, D\}$ and $t \in \{1, 2, \ldots, T\}$, with N being the number of consumers, D representing the total number of days for which data is available and T denoting the number of intervals per day for which the data is reported by the meter. The data structured in this format is the processed to extract the characteristic profiles for the consumers.

A key step in extracting characteristic consumption profile for any consumer is identifying how many representative consumption patterns he exhibits. In this paper, gap evaluation criterion and basic K-means clustering are used to extract this information. Specifically, the number of clusters of a consumer's daily consumption profiles for which maximum gap evaluation is achieved are considered to be number of characteristic profiles for that consumer [25]. To avoid over partitioning, the maximum number of characteristic profiles for any consumer is restricted to K. The optimal choice for K is derived by help of gap evaluation criteria and visualized using dendrogram for hierarchical clustering [11]. The same can be achieved using gap evaluation criteria and Davies Bouldin index [4].

K-means is used to assign $\theta_{nd}^k \in \{0, 1\}$ to the daily consumption profile of the nth consumer for the dth day. This classification is then used to extract the characteristic consumption profile $\left\{ \overline{CP}_n^k(t) : t = 1, 2, \ldots, T \right\}$ as shown as:

$$\overline{CP}_n^k(t) = \frac{\sum_{d=1}^{D} \left(\theta_{nd}^k * P_n^d(t) \right)}{\sum_{d=1}^{D} \theta_{nd}^k} \quad \text{for } k = 1, \ldots K . \tag{1}$$

The probability of consumer n exhibiting the kth pattern is calculated as

$$\pi_n^k = \frac{\sum_{d=1}^{D} \theta_{nd}^k}{D} , \tag{2}$$

while the mean absolute deviation for this pattern in the tth interval is calculated using

$$MAD_n^k(t) = \frac{\sum_{d=1}^{D} \left| \left(\theta_{nd}^k * P_n^d(t) - \overline{CP}_n^k(t) \right) \right|}{\sum_{d=1}^{D} \theta_{nd}^k} . \tag{3}$$

The metrics π_n^k and $\{MAD_n^k(t)\}$ are statistical measures of the repeatability of the consumption patterns for consumer n. Knowing the distribution of the K patterns, the characteristic profile for the multi-profile consumer n can be constructed as

$$\widehat{CP}_n(t) = \sum_{k=1}^{K} \overline{CP}_n^k (t) \, \pi_n^k \, . \tag{4}$$

The profile expressed by Eq. (4) is indeed representative all the K profiles potentially exhibited by consumer n and hence is a more suitable feature to represent his consumption behavior. The results presented in the following section further expand on this concept.

2.2 Clustering Algorithm

The characteristic profiles for the N consumers derived in Eq. (4) are used to cluster them into c classes. Since any clustering algorithm such as K-means or hierarchical may be used, clustering process itself is treated as a black box here. It is modelled as a set of membership vector M_n for n^{th} consumer where

$$M_n = [m_{n1}, m_{n2}, \ldots\ldots m_{nc}] \tag{5}$$

$$\text{with } m_{nx} \in [0,1] \quad \text{and} \quad \sum_{x=1}^{c} m_{nx} = 1 \, . \tag{6}$$

Note that for the hard partitioned clustering schemes like k-mean, k-medoids and hierarchical clustering algorithms, the membership value is discrete such that $m_{nx} \in \{0,1\}$. The cluster id for consumer n is denoted as θ_n and determined using

$$\theta_n = \operatorname{argmax}_x(m_{nx}) \, . \tag{7}$$

After all consumers are clustered, the mean consumption profile for cluster x, denoted by $\{C_x(t)\}$ is obtained using

$$C_x(t) = \frac{\sum_{n=1}^{N} m_{nx} \widehat{CP}_n(t)}{\sum_{n=1}^{N} m_{nx}} \quad \text{for } t = 1, 2, \ldots, T \, . \tag{8}$$

2.3 Data Post Processing

The clusters formed are analyzed to quantify the consistency of the consumer groups. Quantification of peak attributes is also undertaken to determine how useful clusters may be for specific DR schemes.

Consistency Attributes: The consistency metric proposed herein for a consumer is a measure of regularity with which a consumer follows a certain consumption profile over a time series. The mean absolute deviation for consumption pattern k, $k = 1, \ldots, K$ defined in Eq. (3) is used to formulate upper and lower bounds so that a metric $f_n^k(s)$ can be defined to measure the bound violation for sample $s \in \{1, 2, \ldots, S_n^k\}$ and thus measure bound consistency BC_n^k as shown:

$$TUB_n^k(t) = CP_n^k(t) + h \times MAD_n^k(t) \tag{9}$$

$$TLB_n^k(t) = CP_n^k(t) - h \times MAD_n^k(t) \tag{10}$$

$$f_n^k(s) = 0 \quad \text{if } TLB_n^k(t) < P_n^{dk}(t) < TUB_n^k(t) \qquad \text{else 1} \tag{11}$$

$$BC_n^k = \left(S_n^k - \sum_{s=1}^{S_n^k} f_n^k(s) \right) / S_n^k \tag{12}$$

Here, the variable h used in definition of lower and upper bounds $TLB_n^k(t)$ and $TUB_n^k(t)$ takes value $1, 2$ or 3 as desired to signal as the number of standard deviations around the mean to be considered. Then, the overall bound consistency for the consumer is computed as

$$\mathbb{E}\left(BC_n\right) = BC_n^1 \pi_n^1 + \ldots + BC_n^K \pi_n^K . \tag{13}$$

The reliability of a cluster is denoted by RC_x: it is a measure of the aggregate bound consistency of all the consumers in it and is formulated using $\mathbb{E}\left(BC_n\right)$ and m_{nx} as follows:

$$RC_x = \frac{\sum_{n=1}^{N} m_{nx} \cdot \mathbb{E}\left(BC_n\right)}{\sum_{n=1}^{N} m_{nx}}, \tag{14}$$

$$RCM = \frac{\sum_{x=1}^{x=c}(RC_x \sum_{n=1}^{N} m_{nx}}{c}. \tag{15}$$

The second metric RCM is the overall reliability of clusters metric that averages RC_x across all clusters.

Another consistency measure termed as consumer cluster consistency is devised to clock the regularity with each consumer profile is clustered in its respective cluster. The daily profiles of N consumers were clustered for D days to compute instance of nth consumer categorization in cluster θ_n. The cluster of consumer to be selected for any DR opportunity can be achieved using CC_n^x for x^{th} as shown in Eq. (17).

$$U_n^x = (T_p - N_{px}) / T_p \tag{16}$$

$$CC^x = \frac{\sum_{n=1}^{N} U_n^x}{\sum_{n=1}^{N} m_{nx}} \tag{17}$$

$$CCM = \frac{\sum_{x=1}^{x=c}(CC^x \sum_{n=1}^{N} m_{nx}}{c} \tag{18}$$

where T_p is the total number of consumer profiles for which consistency is quantified and N_{px} are the total number of consumer profiles not classified with cluster x. In other words, it is ratio of consumer profiles associated with the specified cluster id to total number of consumer profiles. These attributes allow utility to select fairly consistent consumers or cluster(s) for DR.

Peak Association Attributes: Peak association attributes are extracted in reference to aggregated system profile peak or the peak that would interest DR programs. Traditionally, peaks are defined as highest value of curve. This paper use the definition of peak prominence as the minimum vertical distance that the signal must descend on either side of the peak before either climbing back to a level higher than the peak or reaching an endpoint. This paper defines the peak width as length of half prominent peak vector. Hence, peak attributes are specified as $PA_x^y := (Peakm_x^y, Peakw_x^y, S_x^y, L_x^y))$, where $Peakm_x^y$ and $Peakw_x^y$ are peak magnitude and peak width associated with half prominent peak respectively for y^{th} peak of cluster aggregate $CA_x(t)$ while S_x^y and L_x^y are start and end time stamps of the peak detected. The peak detection uses the findpeaks() function of Matlab with half peak prominence notion.

The definition of critical peak employed in the proposed framework is based on prominence of the highest peak for the aggregate system profile $\{A(t)\}$, which can be computed from the cluster aggregate profile $\{CA_x(t)\}$ as shown:

$$CA_x(t) = \sum_{n=1}^{N} m_{nx}\widehat{CP_n}(t), \tag{19}$$

$$A(t) = \sum_{x=1}^{c} CA_x(t). \tag{20}$$

The critical peak period is assumed as width of half prominent peak for the system profile as shown in the Fig. 1. We use notation $Coin_x^y$ and PO_x^y to denote the coincidence and offset of the yth peak of the aggregated cluster consumption pattern $\{CA_x(t)\}$ with that of the critical peak of the system aggregate profile $\{A(t)\}$. If lc_x^y represents the length of cluster aggregated peak that coincides with system peak and la_x^y is total length cluster peak that includes the coincidence interval and the offset, then

$$Coin_x^y = lc_x^y/la_x^y, \tag{21}$$

$$offset_x^y = \pm(1 - lc_x^y/la_x^y). \tag{22}$$

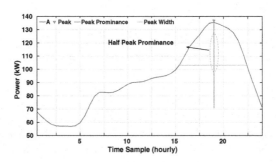

Fig. 1. Peak Identification for the Aggregated Profile A

Here, PO_x^y takes negative values if cluster peak ends after the aggregated profile peak ends and it takes positive values if cluster peak starts prior to aggregated peak. However, if cluster peak starts as well as ends before (or after) the aggregated peak PO_x^y takes positive values. Maximum peak per consumer in a cluster x is denoted by MC_x^y and determined using

$$MC_x^y = \frac{Peakm_x^y}{\sum_{n=1}^{N} m_{nx}}.$$
(23)

The cluster correlation $Corr_x$ is given by

$$Corr_x = \frac{R \sum A(t)CA_x(t) - \sum A(t) \sum CA_x(t)}{\sqrt{[R \sum (A(t))^2 - (\sum A(t)^2][R \sum CA_x(t)^2 - (\sum CA_x(t))^2]}}$$
(24)

where R is number of pairwise distances. Conforming cluster may be defined as a cluster that has high $Corr_x$ with the aggregated consumption pattern and high value of $Coin_x^y$. Whereas, PO_x^y quantifies a degree with which a consumer is non confirming.

3 Results and Discussion

This section discusses the application of methodology developed in the preceding section to the Dataport smart meter data set [22] as a case study for DR program design. The data consists of aggregate, appliance level and circuit level power consumption for 722 houses in US, including residential single family houses, apartments and mobile vehicles. We only use the data set for residential single family consumers over the course of one year (2014). The analysis discussed here does not use device or circuit level consumption pattern to ensure that proposed methodology remains generalized and is not constrained by intrusive data sets.

The results presented here highlight the impacts of data pre-processing such as normalization. Also, the insights that can be drawn from the clusters formed using hierarchical, k-means, k-medoids and SOM clustering are also discussed. In particular, the metrics proposed in the data post processing described in the preceding section are applied to formulate our inferences.

3.1 Effect of Normalization on Clustering Techniques

Since the data analyzed in this paper did not exhibit any trends or noise, detrending and filtering are not discussed in detail here. We only discuss data normalization, which aims at reducing data redundancy and leads to assignment of equal weights to all the features. Normalization is typically used in multi-feature clustering since algorithms based on distance measures are highly sensitive to magnitude variations among different features. However, in case of time series clustering of consumer consumption patterns, the role of normalization is debatable. Using normalized consumption patterns may lead to consumer clusters which show similar consumption times and are hence useful for TOU-, CPP-based DR schemes. Alternately, clustering on actual consumption pattern leads to grouping of consumers with similar magnitudes of power usage that may be helpful for peak rebate type DR programs. We compute the Silhouette score for clusters achieved by different techniques with and without normalization in Table 1. The mean cluster mean profiles $\{C_x(t)\}$ extracted using the four techniques with and without normalization are shown in Figs. 2 and 3.

Table 1. Effect of normalization on clustering performance

Silhouette Score	K-means	K-medoids	HC	SOM
With normalization	0.37	0.38	0.58	0.47
Without normalization	0.31	0.47	0.58	0.29

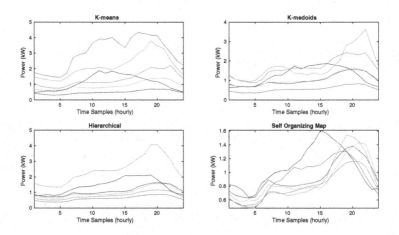

Fig. 2. Cluster mean profiles using normalization

It is evident from the Table 1 and the plots in Figs. 2 and 3 that the cluster mean profiles are sensitive to normalization. For instance, SOM and K-medoids performance vary drastically owing to normalization when compared to effect of normalization on performance of classical K-means and hierarchical clustering. Note that all the results and comparisons portrayed in later sections (unless specified) are presented for the hierarchical clustering technique as it was least affected by normalization and outlier for our database.

3.2   Demographic of Multi-profile Consumers

Three distinct characteristic profiles exhibited by a multi-profile consumer are shown in Fig. 4. Figure 5 shows a histogram of distinct characteristic profiles

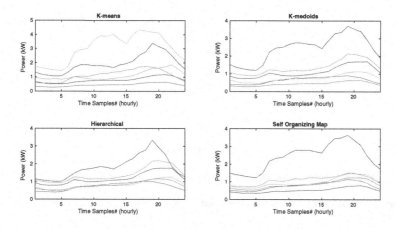

Fig. 3. Cluster mean profiles without using normalization

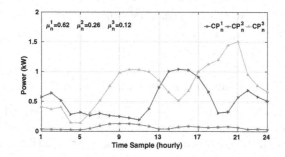

Fig. 4. An example of multi-profile consumer having 3 distinct profiles

exhibited by 100 consumers randomly selected from the Dataport data set. It shows that the number of consumers exhibiting more that two distinct profiles is considerably large. This implies consideration of profiles beyond the weekday-weekend distinction.

Failure to consider the multi profile consumer may introduce skew in results, particularly while capturing consumer consistency and cluster consistency. This is shown in Table 2, where the comparative analysis of reliability and consistency metrics for clustering with the traditional and proposed characteristic profile are tabulated. The proposed characteristic profile registers higher RCM and CCM values as compared to the scores for the profiles proposed in [7] and [15]. Moreover, comparison of characteristic bound violation instance 2.38 times and 1.95 times for [7,15] when compared to that for the proposed $\widehat{CP}_n$. This is a clear indication of the suitability of $\widehat{CP}_n$ for multi-profile consumers to reduce risk of erroneous prediction and estimation.

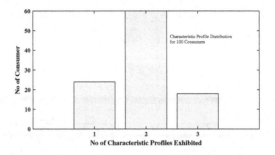

Fig. 5. Distribution of 100 multi-profile consumers from the data

Table 2. RCM and CCM comparison for various characteristic profile extraction

Characteristic Profile	RCM	CCM
Averaged daily [7]	0.631	0.621
Averaged weekday [15]	0.642	0.591
Proposed $\widehat{CP}_n$	0.719	0.702

3.3   Cluster Correlation and Peak Contribution

In order to evaluate the identified clusters from point of view of DR implementation, we compute the peak attributes defined in Sect. 2.3 for each cluster: the values are tabulated in Table 3. Recall that the peak identification adopted in this paper is portrayed in Fig. 1. The metrics tabulated below are computed by comparing the peak coincidence and correlation of the cluster aggregate profiles CA_x's with the system aggregate profile A shown in Fig. 6.

Table 3. Cluster-wise Peak Contribution metric

Cluster (x)	Peak Per Consumer (MC_x^y)	Correlation $(Corr_x)$	Peak Coincidence $(Coin_x^y)$	Offset (PO_x^y)
1	2.22	0.70	1.00	0.00
2	1.21	0.37	0.00	+1.00
3	1.96	0.67	0.42	+0.57
4	1.55	0.97	1.00	0.00
5	1.47	0.83	0.90	−0.10
6	1.44	0.46	0.92	−0.07

Peak contribution metric helps enhancing the usefulness of clustering results for its employment for targeting cluster DR schemes. For instance cluster 1 and 4 would be highly appropriate targets for system peak reduction effort owing to high correlation and peak coincidence. However cluster 2 and 3 may be used for load levelling scheme by contributing load during peak off periods but might not be effective targets for CPP or peak rebate based schemes.

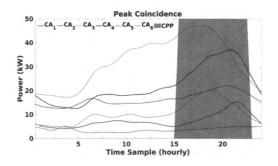

Fig. 6. Critical Peak Coincidence for all CA_x

3.4 Reliability and Consistency of a Cluster

Despite of encouragingly high correlation and peak coincidence of the cluster it is probable that the consumer identified by the cluster may not be having consistent profile or the consumer may vary its profile largely from identified cluster mean profile(s). Hence it is necessary to get a notion of consistency of consumer and reliability of a cluster. Such attributes would provide assurance to the utility about DR selection in terms of planning and consumer consumption behavior prediction. A comparison of cluster consistency and reliability under various clustering techniques is given in Tables 4 and 5 respectively. We note that hierarchical clustering has comparable or higher values of RC_x as well as CC_x. SOM has partially high and low values of RC_x and CC_x, whereas k-medoids has comparative lowest value of RC_x and CC_x. Classical K-means also has comparably higher values of RC_x and CC_x.

Table 4. Cluster Consistency Vs Clustering Techniques

Clustering Technique	Cluster Consistency CC^x					
	x=1	x=2	x=3	x=4	x=5	x=6
K-means	0.77	0.49	0.65	0.70	0.42	0.73
K-medoid	0.76	0.54	0.59	0.66	0.57	0.83
Hierarchical	0.74	0.59	0.72	0.68	0.60	0.89
SOM	0.81	0.43	0.73	0.61	0.55	0.74

Table 5. Cluster Reliability Vs Clustering Techniques

Clustering Technique	Cluster Reliability RC^x					
	x=1	x=2	x=3	x=4	x=5	x=6
K-means	0.83	0.61	0.73	0.78	0.48	0.73
K-medoid	0.81	0.52	0.57	0.71	0.55	0.69
Hierarchical	0.87	0.58	0.81	0.75	0.51	0.90
SOM	0.80	0.69	0.75	0.82	0.39	0.89

3.5   DR Impact Assessment

The DR impact of a cluster is assessed by integration of attributes from peak contribution, reliability and cluster bound consistency to give a clear notion of how the consumer cluster can be exploited DR. The attributes for all clusters are presented in table 6.

Table 6. DR Impact Matrix

Cluster	Consistency Attributes		Peak Attributes			
x	CC_x	RC_x	MC_x^y	$Corr_x$	$Coin_x^y$	PO_x^y
1	0.74	0.87	2.22	0.70	1.00	0.00
2	0.59	0.58	1.21	0.37	0.00	+1.00
3	0.72	0.81	1.96	0.67	0.49	+0.51
4	0.68	0.75	1.55	0.97	1.00	0.00
5	0.40	0.51	1.47	0.83	0.93	-0.07
6	0.89	0.90	1.44	0.46	0.89	-0.11

We note that cluster 1 can be inferred as conforming cluster owing to high *Corr* and *Coin* values. The cluster reliability and consistency are also comparable with other clusters, which suggest that this cluster can be handy selection for any peak pricing or consistent forecast based DR schemes. On the other hand, cluster 2 has exact contradictory values of DR impact attributes, which brands it a potential consumer for load levelling and off-peak rebate DR schemes. It can be inferred from cluster 3 attributes that it has lesser peak coincidence and peak offset value suggest that it tends to consume early peaks and hence can be potentially utilized in peak shifting DR schemes. It may not hamper consumer comport largely as cluster 3 inherently tend to consume early peaks. Interestingly cluster 5 despite having lower consistency attribute values has high coincidence and is a conforming cluster, but it shall serve as low priority option to cluster 1. Cluster 6 is a conforming cluster with high values of consistency attributes with fairly high coincidence but low correlation. This ensures that despite less correlative consumption pattern cluster 6 contributes to the peak period and hence can be used for consistent forecast, peak as well as off peak based DR schemes.

To further identify suitable DR strategies for each cluster, the profiles identified in Fig. 6 can be considered in conjunction with the above metrics. For instance, the consumers exhibiting conforming mean cluster profiles CA_1 and CA_6 with high CCM, RCM and MC_x^y values seem well suited for peak load curtailment programs like CPP or peak hour rebates. Whereas, the consumers in the second cluster with low CCM and high RCM can be incentivized for appliance scheduling/load shifting via TOU pricing. Consumers in clusters 3 and 4 exhibiting profile CA_3 and CA_4 with high CCM and low RCM are best suitable for behavioural change. Lastly, the consumer profile CA_5 with low CCM and low RCM should be avoided due to its poor predictability.

4 Conclusion

The issue of consumer selection for DR programs is critical to ensure that pricing schemes are effective and curtailment contracts are exercised when needed. This paper takes a detailed look at clustering schemes applied to address this issue. A key contribution of this paper is the notion of multi-profile consumers which leads us to propose several new definitions for characteristic consumption profiles, consumer consistency, cluster consistency and consumer cluster reliability. Consumers having higher consistency scores are considered more predictable and the same viewpoint is adopted for clusters to guide DR participant selection. Additionally, attributes such as peak coincidence and peak contribution of the cluster are introduced to provide insights on which specific DR schemes may be suited for a cluster.

This paper allows utility to leverage the smart meter data in an effective manner to aid DR program design. However, this work ignores the use of meta-data which may also provide valuable insights and validate the selection. How to use available meta-data as well extract it (partially or fully) from the available metered data is a future line of work we intend to pursue. Additionally, clustering process itself may be re-looked to get more meaningful consumer groups. Finally, we note that the metrics CC_x and RC_x quantify the confidence for a given consumption profile and hence may be used for risk assessment. We intend to explore this in the context of different DR implementations in future work.

Acknowledgements. This work is supported by Department of Science and Technology (DST), Govt. of India under the Mission Innovation Smart Grid Grant no. DST/CERI/MI/SG/2017/077.

References

1. Albert, A., Rajagopal, R.: Thermal profiling of residential energy use. IEEE Trans. Power Syst. **30**(2), 602–611 (2015)
2. Azaza, M., Wallin, F.: Smart meter data clustering using consumption indicators: responsibility factor and consumption variability. Energy Procedia **142**, 2236–2242 (2017)
3. Cavallini, A., Montanari, G.C.: A parametric approach to the prediction of the time-behavior of harmonic-quantities in electrical networks. In: IAS '95. Conference Record of the 1995 IEEE Industry Applications Conference Thirtieth IAS Annual Meeting, vol. 3, pp. 2226–2232. IEEE, October 1995. https://doi.org/10.1109/IAS.1995.530586
4. Davies, D.L., Bouldin, D.W.: A cluster separation measure. IEEE Trans. Pattern Anal. Mach. Intell. **1**(2), 224–227 (1979)
5. Deepak Sharma, D., Singh, S.N.: Electrical load profile analysis and peak load assessment using clustering technique. In: 2014 IEEE PES General Meeting | Conference Exposition, pp. 1–5, July 2014. https://doi.org/10.1109/PESGM.2014.6938869
6. Faria, P., Spínola, J., Vale, Z.: Aggregation and remuneration of electricity consumers and producers for the definition of demand-response programs. IEEE Trans. Industr. Inf. **12**(3), 952–961 (2016). https://doi.org/10.1109/TII.2016.2541542
7. Figueiredo, V., Rodrigues, F., Vale, Z., Gouveia, J.B.: An electric energy consumer characterization framework based on data mining techniques. IEEE Trans. Power Syst. **20**(2), 596–602 (2005). https://doi.org/10.1109/TPWRS.2005.846234
8. Gyamfi, S., Krumdieck, S., Urmee, T.: Residential peak electricity demand response-highlights of some behavioural issues. Renew. Sustain. Energy Rev. **25**, 71–77 (2013)
9. IEA (2021): Electricity information: Overview, iea, paris. https://www.iea.org/reports/electricity-information-overview
10. Jin, L., et al.: Comparison of clustering techniques for residential energy behavior using smart meter data. In: Workshops at the Thirty-First AAAI Conference on Artificial Intelligence (2017)
11. Jung, Y., Park, H., Du, D.Z., Drake, B.L.: A decision criterion for the optimal number of clusters in hierarchical clustering. J. Global Optim. **25**(1), 91–111 (2003)
12. Kwac, J., Flora, J., Rajagopal, R.: Household energy consumption segmentation using hourly data. IEEE Trans. Smart Grid **5**(1), 420–430 (2014). https://doi.org/10.1109/TSG.2013.2278477
13. Kwac, J., Tan, C.W., Sintov, N., Flora, J., Rajagopal, R.: Utility customer segmentation based on smart meter data: Empirical study. In: 2013 IEEE international conference on smart grid communications (SmartGridComm), pp. 720–725. IEEE (2013)
14. Li, K., Che, J., Wang, B., Zhang, J., Wang, F., Mi, Z.: A meta-heuristic optimization based residential load pattern clustering approach using improved gravitational search algorithm. In: 2018 IEEE Power Energy Society Innovative Smart Grid Technologies Conference (ISGT), pp. 1–5, February 2018. https://doi.org/10.1109/ISGT.2018.8403401
15. Lin, S., Li, F., Tian, E., Fu, Y., Li, D.: Clustering load profiles for demand response applications. IEEE Trans. Smart Grid, 1 (2018). https://doi.org/10.1109/TSG.2017.2773573

16. Madathil, D.K., Thota, R.B., Paul, P., Xie, T.: A static data placement strategy towards perfect load-balancing for distributed storage clusters. In: 2008 IEEE International Symposium on Parallel and Distributed Processing, pp. 1–8, April 2008. https://doi.org/10.1109/IPDPS.2008.4536489
17. Mahmoudi-Kohan, N., Moghaddam, M.P., Sheikh-El-Eslami, M.K., Bidaki, S.M.: Improving wfa k-means technique for demand response programs applications. In: 2009 IEEE Power Energy Society General Meeting. pp. 1–5, July 2009. https://doi.org/10.1109/PES.2009.5275413
18. Mahmoudi-Kohan, N., Moghaddam, M.P., Sheikh-El-Eslami, M., Shayesteh, E.: A three-stage strategy for optimal price offering by a retailer based on clustering techniques. In. J. Electr. Power Energy Syst. 32(10), 1135–1142 (2010)
19. McNamara, P., McLoone, S.: Hierarchical demand response for peak minimization using dantzig-wolfe decomposition. IEEE Trans. Smart Grid 6(6), 2807–2815 (2015). https://doi.org/10.1109/TSG.2015.2467213
20. Olawuyi, N.Y., Akorede, M.F., Femi, E., Ayeni, A.A., Jimoh, R.G.: Real-time demand response algorithm for minimising industrial consumers electricity billing. In: 2017 IEEE 3rd International Conference on Electro-Technology for National Development (NIGERCON), pp. 1061–1066, November 2017. https://doi.org/10.1109/NIGERCON.2017.8281969
21. Paterakis, N.G., Erdinç, O., Catalão, J.P.: An overview of demand response: key-elements and international experience. Renew. Sustain. Energy Rev. 69, 871–891 (2017)
22. Pecan Street Inc., Dataport. https://www.pecanstreet.org/dataport/
23. Rashid, H., Singh, P., Ramamritham, K.: Revisiting selection of residential consumers for demand response programs. In: Proceedings of the 4th ACM International Conference on Systems for Energy-Efficient Built Environments, p. 30. ACM (2017)
24. Savitzky, A., Golay, M.J.E.: Smoothing and differentiation of data by simplified least squares procedures. Anal. Chem. 36(8), 1627–1639 (1964)
25. Tibshirani, R., Walther, G., Hastie, T.: Estimating the number of clusters in a data set via the gap statistic. J. Roy. Stat. Soc. Ser. B (Statistical Methodology) 63(2), 411–423 (2001)
26. Wang, Y., Chen, Q., Kang, C., Zhang, M., Wang, K., Zhao, Y.: Load profiling and its application to demand response: A review. Tsinghua Sci. Technol. 20(2), 117–129 (2015). https://doi.org/10.1109/TST.2015.7085625
27. Yamaguchi, N., Han, J., Ghatikar, G., Kiliccote, S., Piette, M.A., Asano, H.: Regression models for demand reduction based on cluster analysis of load profiles. In: 2009 IEEE PES/IAS Conference on Sustainable Alternative Energy (SAE), pp. 1–7. IEEE, September 2009. https://doi.org/10.1109/SAE.2009.5534840
28. Yilmaz, S., Chambers, J., Patel, M., et al.: Comparison of clustering approaches for domestic electricity load profile characterisation-implications for demand side management. Energy 180(C), 665–677 (2019)
29. Yoon, J.H., Bladick, R., Novoselac, A.: Demand response for residential buildings based on dynamic price of electricity. Energy Build. 80, 531–541 (2014)

Smart Energy Device Management

Distribution Grid Monitoring Based on Widely Available Smart Plugs

Simon Grafenhorst$^{(\boxtimes)}$ ⓘ, Kevin Förderer ⓘ, and Veit Hagenmeyer ⓘ

Institute for Automation and Applied Informatics (IAI), Karlsruhe Institute of Technology, Hermann-von-Helmholtz-Platz 1, 76344 Eggenstein-Leopoldshafen, Germany
simon.grafenhorst@kit.edu

Abstract. The growing popularity of e-mobility, heat pumps, and renewable generation such as photovoltaics is leading to scenarios which the distribution grid was not originally designed for. Moreover, parts of the distribution grid are only sparsely instrumented, leaving the distribution system operator unaware of possible bottlenecks resulting from the introduction of such loads and renewable generation. To overcome this lack of information, we propose the use of widely available smart home devices, such as smart plugs, for grid monitoring. We detail the aggregation and storage of smart plug measurements for distribution grid monitoring and examine the accuracy of the measurements. A case study shows how the average monitoring error in a distribution grid area decreases the more measurement devices are installed. Hence, simple smart plugs can help with distribution grid monitoring and provide valuable information to the DSO.

Keywords: Smart Grid · Distribution Grid Monitoring · Smart Home Measurement Device

1 Introduction

1.1 Motivation

With new loads such as electric vehicle (EV) chargers and new generators such as small PV systems, the demands on the grid are changing rapidly. For example, the distribution grid can only accommodate a certain amount of photovoltaic generation without violating regulatory constraints (hosting capacity [10,23]). Other challenges include the optimized control of distributed energy resources (DER), such as controllable heat pumps or schedulable electric vehicle charging infrastructure, as well as demand-side management (DSM) of smart household appliances. As a result, it is essential that the distribution system operator (DSO) has comprehensive and up-to-date measurement data from the distribution grid. However, the adoption of smart distribution grid infrastructure to monitor the live state of the grid or detect bottlenecks is slow [7]. Many old network infrastructures are still in use. It is neither monitored nor equipped with the necessary

ⓒ The Author(s), under exclusive license to Springer Nature Switzerland AG 2024
B. N. Jørgensen et al. (Eds.): EI.A 2023, LNCS 14468, pp. 195–212, 2024.
https://doi.org/10.1007/978-3-031-48652-4_13

communication infrastructure, and upgrading the infrastructure is costly and time-consuming. Key components in the distribution grid such as transformers and cables, have a life expectancy of about 35 years [6], and monitoring the state of the grid with such old equipment is therefore a challenge. However, smart home devices are becoming increasingly popular. In the US, 35.8 % and in the EU, 23.0 % of households had smart home systems installed in 2021 [21]. Smart plugs can turn power outlets on and off remotely, and some smart plugs also include hardware to measure the power consumption of the connected device and the line voltage of the socket outlet they are plugged into. We hypothesize that sufficiently accurate grid monitoring is possible with the use of smart plugs as measurement devices. This raises two further research questions: What is the accuracy of the measurements and can the accuracy be further improved with software modifications tailored to the voltage measurements?

The contributions of this paper are as follows:

1. It is shown that the measurement inaccuracies of the widely available smart plugs are low enough to be comparable to other distribution grid measurement devices.
2. It is demonstrated how a modified firmware can increase the measurement accuracy and frequency, and the firmware version is released as open source [30].
3. A case study is presented to outline the practicality of using distributed and non-calibrated measurement devices for distribution grid monitoring.

The paper is organized as follows: Sect. 2 summarizes related works on distribution grid monitoring, the development of measurement devices, and the secure communication with Internet of Things (IoT) devices. The method for selecting a type of smart plug to measure voltages and analyzing the data is presented in Sect. 3. The measurement error of the smart plugs with an unmodified open source firmware as well as with a firmware version tailored for voltage measurements is evaluated in Sect. 4. Section 5 presents a case study that illustrates a realistic use case for distribution grid monitoring using smart plugs. The case study is conducted using a grid simulation and a simulation of the smart plugs with the same measurement error as the real devices shown in the evaluation. The results of the case study and the practical applicability of this research are discussed in Sect. 6, followed by a final conclusion in Sect. 7.

2   Related Work

2.1   Distribution Grid Monitoring

To assess the state of the distribution grid, several articles identify accurate voltage measurements at different nodes in the distribution grid as an important prerequisite [3,10]. The p.u. (per unit) value describes the factor between the real voltage and the nominal voltage. There are different standards that define the minimum and maximum p.u. values for different countries. For example, the EN-50160 standard specifies a p.u. of 0.9 to 1.1 as the permissible voltage variation. Therefore, to evaluate the hosting capacity for PV systems in a part of the distribution grid, the minimum and maximum p.u. levels that occur within a predefined period of time need to be known, and thus voltage measurements are needed.

2.2 State of the Art

In the past, the lack of measurement hardware in the distribution grid led to the exploration of simulations based on sparse measurement data and pseudo measurements [1,8,24]. Others have increased the observability of the distribution grid by integrating smart meter data into a state estimation [2,15,16,36]. This enables the generation of a forecasts [25,26] or the detection and localization of faults in the grid [4,35]. Furthermore, network topology reduction techniques can be applied to carry out a grid state estimation with a limited number of smart meters [16]. To increase the accuracy of the state estimation in [2], the unsynchronized measurements of multiple smart meters are filtered and only the most recent measurements are included. Compared to a state estimation that assumes all smart meter measurements are recorded at the same time, the proposed method is more accurate [2]. However, the smart meters require a professional electrician to install, and the majority of meters only take measurements every 15 min [36]. In comparison, the commercially available smart plugs can be installed by anyone and measure the voltage every second with a modified firmware.

Leveraging the Advanced Metering Infrastructure (AMI) already present in the distribution grid saves costs and expenditures at the expense of the timeliness of the data [27], and consequently the accuracy of the grid state estimation at the present time. The lack of measurement hardware also leads to inaccurate load modeling of the distribution grid transformer. To calculate load profiles of the transformer and determine whether new loads could overload the current hardware, AMI can be included in the analysis [19]. Installing monitoring devices on all transformers could also solve this problem, but is not cost effective [19]. To improve the grid model and more accurately estimate the transformer peak load, several other sources of information such as temperature, geographic, customer, and facility management data can also be included. The near real-time optimization of the distribution network with smart grid technology is identified as a significant improvement for the efficient operation of the grid [19].

A smart plug to monitor voltage and frequency in real-time is designed in [9]. The measured values are sent to a smartphone that is connected via Bluetooth. The smartphone then forwards the data to a web server. With their implementation, they demonstrate the feasibility of measuring the voltages at different points in the distribution grid and estimating the live state of the grid based on these measurements. The device is considered a working proof of concept for a low-cost substitute for smart metering hardware, although no measurement accuracy or time delay is specified. Other authors propose the use of specialized voltage meters to monitor the state of the grid [3]. They synchronize their measurements and analyze the grid state with load flow simulations based on a series of snapshots of the grid. Furthermore, the underlying grid model is extended by learning from the differences between the calculated and measured voltages at different nodes. In [11], a smart plug is designed for DSM. They develop a software that switches the connected load on or off depending on the voltage level and show that the load peaks are shaved off when the designed smart plugs are widely distributed in the grid. However, no communication mechanism is implemented, so the measured values cannot be used for a distribution grid monitoring. The hardware is also a prototype design that is not commercially available. To monitor meteorological variables and PV generation, a low-cost data logger device with LoRa wireless communication is developed in [22]. The data is sent to the LoRa Gateway by the data logger and forwarded to a MQTT Broker. The data is stored in the Google Cloud Platform. However, all of these devices are custom-built and cannot be considered widely available, which hinders widespread adoption.

2.3   Implementation Challenges

When integrating IoT devices into an electrical grid to improve the monitoring and control capabilities, a major challenge is network security [17]. The potential number of devices in the grid creates a large attack surface. In addition, critical infrastructure is dependent on an uninterrupted supply of electricity, and attacks on the grid infrastructure could result in huge financial and economic losses [17]. Energy infrastructure is therefore a popular target for cyber attacks. Attacks targeting IoT devices in the electricity grid include Denial-of-Service, Man-in-the-Middle, and Phishing attacks, whereas the latter two types of attacks being easier to execute when communications are not encrypted. Therefore, we encrypt the network communication of the smart plugs in our proposed approach.

An exemplary communication and data management platform is outlined in [5], which collects measurement data from various devices through a variety of interfaces. It also adapts the protocols and stores the abstracted data in a database. The abstraction layer enables the unification of data collected by measurement devices from different vendors and their evaluation in new domains. In addition, by integrating multiple interfaces, it is possible to support multiple versions of software without having to worry about updating interfaces and losing support for older versions of software. To promote the reuse of functionality in [5], auxiliary services are divided into components that are as small as possible. This approach follows the microservice philosophy. Moreover, a microservice-based architecture has the advantages of scalability, autonomy, and rapid deployment of new features [14]. The lightweight technologies that a microservice relies on accelerate the development and deployment process. Deployment on servers using containerization leads to great autonomy of individual services and allows for dynamic allocation of resources [13]. These advantages also lead to the increasing popularity of containerization of applications [13]. To make our ICT structure for data collection and aggregation extensible, we decide to separate the different services and implement them as microservices. This allows us to support other vendors and communication channels without compromising compatibility with the technologies we already support. For example, the implementation of a REST API for data aggregation or the support of other database systems can be realized by implementing independent adapters.

3 Method

Smart plugs are plugs that connect to a Zigbee hub, a LoRaWAN hub, or a WiFi access point. They consist of an outlet that can be turned on and off by smartphone apps or a smart home hub. In addition to a relay to control the outlet and a microcontroller, some smart plugs also contain hardware to measure the power consumption of the connected device and the line voltage of the socket outlet they are plugged into. The measurement data is typically sent to a server of the device manufacturer, allowing customers to monitor the values measured by the smart device via a web service. However, with suitable firmware, some smart devices can connect to IoT gateways other than the manufacturer's server. These gateways can forward the measured data, packaged into standardized messages, to a message broker, thus enabling remote monitoring and logging of the voltage levels and power consumption of connected devices. The data can then be stored as a time series and be used as input data for grid simulations, or be used in real-time to detect congestion, faulty hardware, or to control DSM hardware and distributed generation.

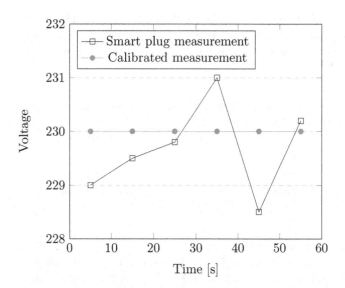

Fig. 1. Smart plug measurements compared to voltage levels measured by a calibrated device

Because these smart home devices are not intended to monitor the grid, the manufacturers of these devices do not provide data on the accuracy of the energy measurements. Furthermore, the accuracy and frequency of the measurements can be modified by modifying the firmware of the smart plugs. We analyze the measurements of the smart plugs with the unmodified firmware and our modified version. The difference between the values measured by a calibrated measurement device and the values measured by the smart plugs is reported as the accuracy of the smart plug. We use the measurements of a Janitza UMG 604EP-PRO power analyzer as a calibrated reference. The measurement error shall not include a constant systematic bias, as we are treating this constant measurement error separately. The measurement error may be due to a change in temperature, interpolation between two measurement points, or insufficient resolution at some point in the measurement process. An example is shown in Fig. 1, where the difference between the calibrated voltage readings and the smart plug measurement is the measurement error.

In addition, smart home devices may be calibrated differently. Due to manufacturing tolerances and environmental differences between the smart home devices, the measured voltage and current levels can vary between devices from the same manufacturer and production batch. We calculate a constant offset bias for all smart plugs separately and remove this offset for each individual smart plug in a pre-processing step of the measured values. This calibration step must also be completed prior to deployment in a live environment.

3.1   Communication Interface

There are several types of smart home devices available. The main difference is the communication interface available, which can be based on WiFi, LoRaWAN or Zigbee. All three interfaces have different strengths and weaknesses as can be seen in the Table 1.

Table 1. Comparison of smart home communication technologies [31]

Protocol	Hub needed	Data Rate	Range
WiFi	no	high	low
LoRaWAN	yes	low	high
Zigbee	yes	medium	medium

For this work, we use WiFi smart plugs. With a customized version of the Tasmota open source firmware [33], it is possible to collect measurements every second and send them directly to a MQTT broker. With further modifications, a slightly higher measuring frequency could be realized, but this caused problems during practical tests. Compared to the LoRaWAN and Zigbee smart devices, no hub or gateway device is required other than the WiFi access point. In the test environment, access points are already in place, so no additional hardware is required, making the deployment of WiFi smart plugs the most practical option. In addition, the higher bandwidth allows for more frequent and comprehensive measurement data. With the smart plug used for testing in this paper, the measurements are available in the simulation in less than one second.

In general, the data sent over WiFi to an access point is not necessarily encrypted. However, the smart plugs evaluated in this paper contain an ESP8266 microcontroller that supports the WPA2 encryption standard. This enables the encryption of the communication between the smart plug and the access point, which protects the transmission of measurements.

The TLS encryption standard is supported by the Mosquitto MQTT broker we use, and the Tasmota firmware for the smart plug also includes basic support for this standard. To enable the ESP8266 to send TLS encrypted packets, a custom version of the Tasmota open source firmware must be compiled that includes the very lightweight BearSSL library. Since the smart plugs are configured with the SSL fingerprint of the MQTT broker and a preshared key, a spoofing attack in which the attacker impersonates the smart plug and sends malicious or false data is not trivially possible.

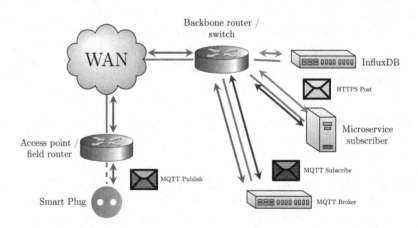

Fig. 2. Network infrastructure between the smart plug and the InfluxDB server

A microservice application is used to subscribe to the MQTT broker. The application creates the adapter between the MQTT messages and the InfluxDB server. Incoming measurement data is mapped to specified fields. This architecture also allows for multiple different measurement devices to write to the same database server, and, in this case, to compare voltage measurements recorded by different devices. In addition, metadata can be added to the measurements so that the voltage data is associated with a power phase, a geographic location, and the manufacturer of the device.

This infrastructure also enables fast integration of new sensors by developing new microservices to map the measurement data messages. Should new smart plugs be introduced that do not support the MQTT protocol, new microservices can be added to inject data into the time-series database without losing support for the existing devices. Furthermore, the addition of other database servers for specific measurement data only requires the development of another microservice and does not require changes to the existing structures. An overview of the resulting networking infrastructure is shown in Fig. 2.

3.2   Measurement Hardware

Besides the communication interface, another difference between the smart plugs is the measurement hardware. Popular energy measurement integrated circuits (ICs) for smart plugs are the Shanghai Belling BL0937 and the Shanghai Belling BL0940 [32]. The smart plugs used for testing in this paper contain the BL0937 IC. The smart plugs used to perform the tests are numerous Nous A1T, Gosund SP1 and Shelly Plug S. However, the same measurement hardware is also included in many other smart plugs, so the measurement accuracy of the plugs is identical. All tested smart plugs share the same measurement characteristics.

The measurements taken by the smart plugs are compared to the values measured by a Janitza UMG 604EP-PRO power analyzer. This power analyzer implements a measurement process according to IEC 61000-4-30 and is connected to an Influx database via TCP/IP.

4   Evaluation

To evaluate the accuracy of the smart plug voltage measurement, two smart plugs are installed in the real-world test environment. In our test setup, the power analyzer is configured to send one measurement value per second. Since the smart plugs contain the same measurement IC, the difference in the measured values is only due to the difference between the modified and the unmodified firmware versions.

First, we analyze the measurements of the smart plug with the unmodified Tasmota open source firmware [32]. With this firmware, the smart plugs output voltage measurements with one decimal place. Therefore one could assume that the error of a measurement is at most 0.1 V. However, due to rounding errors in the unmodified Tasmota firmware, the measurement error is higher. The smart plug only takes voltage measurements in steps of at least 0.2 V, sometimes even only 0.3 V.

In Fig. 3, the measurement error of the smart plug with the unmodified firmware version is plotted in orange and the measurement error of the smart plug with the modified firmware is plotted in blue. Since the unmodified firmware version outputs one measurement value every ten seconds and the modified firmware version outputs one value per second, there are exactly ten times as many measurement values of the modified firmware version in the same time span. The Y-axis values are relative to the total number of measurements.

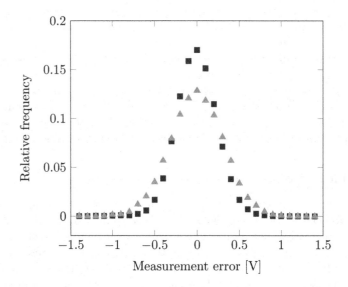

Fig. 3. Relative frequency histogram of the measurement error of smart plugs with the modified firmware (blue) and the unmodified firmware (orange). (Color figure online)

The measurements of the smart plug with the unmodified Tasmota firmware are more spread out compared to the measurements of the measurements with the modified firmware, indicating that the standard deviation of the blue measurements is lower than the standard deviation of the orange measurements. This is indeed the case, as the standard deviation of the smart plug with the unmodified firmware is 0.33 V and the standard deviation of the smart plug with the modified firmware is 0.27 V.

Neither the Anderson-Darling test [20] for normality nor the Shapiro-Wilk test [29] allow us to reject the null hypothesis that the data are normally distributed. The Anderson-Darling test returns a statistic of 0.44 and a critical value to reject the null hypothesis of 0.57, even at a significance level of 15 %. The Shapiro-Wilk test gives a p-value of 0.54. Therefore, we conclude that the measurement error is likely to follow a normal distribution or some other very similar distribution.

5   Case Study: Monitoring the Distribution Grid with Smart Plugs

The use of smart plugs as distributed measurement devices in the distribution grid can enable real-time monitoring of voltage levels, allowing utilities to detect and address issues promptly. However, the measurement error could be an issue for accurate distribution grid monitoring. To further explore the impact of the measurement error and the correlation between the number of measurement devices and the accuracy of the grid monitoring, this section presents a case study of an exemplary distribution grid monitoring.

In the case study, we simulate the power flow in a IEEE 37 bus system. The smart plugs installed in the grid are simulated as well with a measurement error according to our findings in the previous section. An integration of real world measurements into a power flow simulation is not shown in this case study.

5.1   Problem Formulation

Distribution grid monitoring and state estimation are becoming increasingly important for DSOs due to the rise in flexible consumption, distributed generation and the increase of demanding loads such as heat pumps and electric vehicle chargers. However, accurately monitoring the distribution grid and determining the impact of new loads and distributed electricity generation requires a large number of measurement devices. This case study shows how a limited number of smart plugs can provide valuable insight into the voltage levels at different nodes within the distribution grid area. It also outlines the relationship between the number of smart plugs in the grid area and the accuracy of the monitoring.

5.2   Method

To evaluate the benefit of smart plug measurements for grid state monitoring, an IEEE 37 bus system is simulated. We implement the grid simulation using Pandapower, an open-source tool written in Python for modeling and analyzing of power grids [34]. The smart plugs providing the measurements are also simulated. Figure 4 shows an overview of this standardized distribution grid bus system.

The transformer **T** is connected to the 20 kV grid on the primary side and to the 400 V distribution grid on the secondary side. The nodes in the graph represent the houses in the distribution grid. In this power flow simulation, all the houses are placed 40 m away from each other, and NAYY 4 × 150 SE lines are used to connect them. These are the most common lines used in Germany [18] and 40 m is a common distance between neighbors in a rural German distribution grid [12]. We assume that the root mean square (RMS) voltage at the transformer is constant for this simulation model.

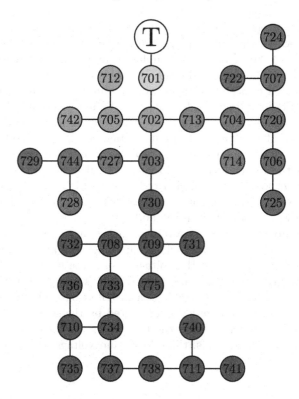

Fig. 4. IEEE bus system 37. Nodes are colored based on the voltage monitoring error. Monitored voltages at white and yellow nodes are similar to the simulated voltages and monitored voltages at the red nodes differ more from the simulated voltages. In this instance, only one smart plug is installed at node 736 and the average monitoring error is about 2.87 V (Color figure online)

To evaluate the impact of the measurement error of the distributed smart plugs on the monitoring of the grid area, we implement several scenarios with different numbers of smart plugs installed in the grid area. We also compare the monitoring results that are based on the smart plugs with the unmodified firmware with the results based on the smart plugs with the modified firmware version. All scenarios are based on the IEEE bus system 37. For each node in the original bus system, we add and connect another node representing the house and the smart plug inside the house. We also add random resistive loads between 0 kW and 6.5 kW with a power factor of 1.0 to the house nodes, representing household appliances and electric vehicle chargers. The DSO sees the total load at the feeder, but does not know where the individual loads are located. The simulated voltage levels are the ground truth against which we will later compare our monitoring results.

The DSO monitors the total load at the feeder level and the voltage level at the outlets where the smart plugs are located. In the case study, we use the voltage levels generated by the simulation as the ground truth. We offset them with random values sampled from a normal distribution with the standard deviation calculated in Sect. 4 to model the measurement accuracy of the smart plugs. This results in voltage levels that could be measured by a DSO in a real world experiment and we call them artificial voltage measurements.

We now attempt to estimate the true voltage levels at all nodes in the bus system 37 from the perspective of the DSO based on the artificial voltage measurements and the feeder load. To do this, we calculate the average load by dividing the feeder load by the number of houses in the grid. We then place this average load at each node in the grid as a starting point. This results in a rough estimate of the voltage levels at all the nodes.

Next, we compare the voltage levels at each house to the artificial voltage measurements recorded by our artificial smart plugs and approximate the loads at these measurement points. If the voltage at a house node is higher than the artificial voltage measurements, the assigned load is increased. If the voltage is lower, the load is reduced. The result is a distribution grid with loads placed at all nodes so that the voltage levels measured by the smart plugs match the true voltage levels. However, due to the inaccuracy we intentionally introduced into the simulated voltage levels, these loads and voltage levels differ from the ground truth.

5.3   Evaluation

In order to evaluate the effect of distribution network metering devices on the quality of monitoring, we compare the artificial voltage measurements generated as described above with the true voltage levels. The nodes in Fig. 4 are colored based on the difference between the true voltage levels and these artificial voltage measurements. Red nodes represent a greater difference between the true voltage levels and the artificial voltage measurements and the lighter the nodes are colored, the smaller the monitoring error is. The voltage error at the feeder is the smallest. This is due to the short length of the line and the small voltage drop across the line between the feeder and the first house. In the grid shown in Fig. 4 only one smart plug is used for monitoring.

In Fig. 5, eight smart plugs are placed in the grid area. It can be clearly seen that the monitoring error is lower at each node in the grid.

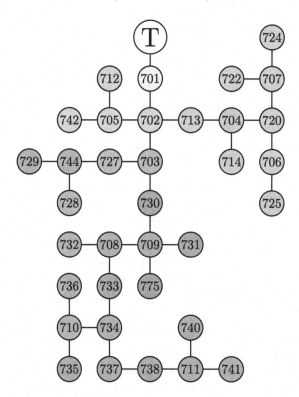

Fig. 5. IEEE bus system 37. Nodes are colored based on the voltage monitoring error. Monitored voltages at white and yellow nodes are similar to the simulated voltages and monitored voltages at the red nodes differ more from the simulated voltages. In this example, eight smart plugs are installed at nodes 736, 706, 709, 711, 742, 722, 725 and 738. The average monitoring error is about 1.04 V and the coloring is consistent with Fig. 4

The correlation between the number of measurement devices in the grid and the average voltage error in a 230 V grid can be seen in Fig. 6.

6   Discussion

The voltage standard deviation observed in the smart plug measurements with the modified firmware of 0.27 V is well within the range of what is considered acceptable in other publications (0.6% in [26] and 0.3% to 0.9% in [15]). Installing multiple smart plugs in the same distribution grid area further improves the accuracy of the measurements, and monitoring multiple phases in three-phase distribution networks would allow asymmetric loads to be detected. This should be evaluated in the future. The smart plugs with the modified firmware version allow for up to one voltage measurement per second, which are available almost immediately for a grid state analysis. In contrast, smart meters often take only

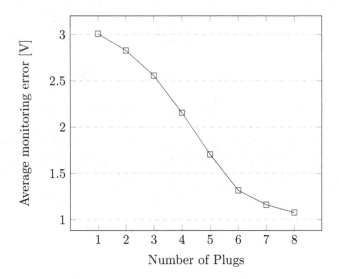

Fig. 6. Correlation between the number of smart plugs in the grid area and the average monitoring error.

one measurement every fifteen minutes and transmit the data at intervals of up to six hours [27]. In addition, the deployment of the smart plugs in a real-world test environment can be completed in minutes by configuring the smart plug and connecting it to a nearby WiFi network, and no electrician is required for installation.

Smart meters are typically installed near to the point of common coupling. Smart plugs, on the other hand, measure the voltage at the outlet to which they are connected to. This means that the voltage drop within the resident's home is included in the smart plug's measurements. This voltage drop depends on the loads within the home's electrical system and is therefore not constant. In order to reduce the voltage drop on the local line, it is necessary to install the smart plug as close as possible to the point of common coupling. In addition, the smart plugs monitor only one phase. However, the load in the distribution grid is predominantly symmetrical [28], which means that the voltage drop is also symmetrical.

The approach of using widely available smart plugs to monitor the distribution grid is mostly limited by privacy concerns and the accuracy of the measurements, especially when compared to the measurements from calibrated smart metering systems or power analyzers. Installing the smart plugs away from the common coupling point further reduces the validity of the measurements, and the constant offset of each device must be determined and compensated for. However, the frequency of the measurements could permit some compensation for these shortcomings, e.g. by means of filters. Another issue for practical implementation in the field is the availability of a WiFi connection to transmit the measurements. Perhaps allowing customers to use the switching function of the smart plug would be an incentive to allow the use of their private WiFi access.

In general, the installation of a custom firmware to monitor the distribution grid voids the warranty of the smart plugs. The manufacturers of the smart plugs would need to provide a software interface to collect measurement data or connect to a custom server in order to use the smart plugs without flashing a custom firmware. Without the manufacturers support for such a feature, the DSO would need to flash the custom firmware before distributing the smart plugs to the customers.

7   Conclusion

In this paper, we determine the accuracy of smart plug measurements by comparing the calculated values with voltage readings from a Janitza UMG 604EP-PRO power analyzer. We use commercially available devices in the present work that are able to connect directly to a WiFi network and transmit the measurement data to a server, eliminating the need for a relay. The voltage measurements of the tested smart plugs with the modified Tasmota firmware have a standard deviation of 0.27 V, which is lower than the standard deviation of the measurements taken by smart plugs with the unmodified Tasmota firmware. The modified firmware is published as open-source. We also describe the network structure and the integration of smart plug measurement data into an existing time-series database. In a case study, a practical use-case for a distribution grid monitoring is outlined and evaluated. It is shown how the average monitoring error in a distribution grid area decreases the more measurement devices are installed. The installation of the commercially available smart plugs does not require an electrician, the hardware is inexpensive, and the individual configuration of the devices is simple. In this light, simple smart plugs can help with distribution grid monitoring and provide valuable information to the DSO.

Future research should evaluate other use cases of smart plugs for a DSO, such as DSM and non-intrusive load monitoring. Furthermore, other types of power measurement ICs in other smart home devices should be evaluated and compared. To complete the monitoring and account for asymmetric loads, it would be relevant to consider two-phase or three-phase distribution systems. And in a real-world implementation of a grid monitoring using smart home devices, the placement of the devices in the grid must be optimized to collect the most useful data.

Acknowledgement. This research has been funded by the German Federal Ministry for Economic Affairs and Climate Action (TrafoKommune project, funding reference: 03EN3008F)

References

1. Akrami, A., Asif, S., Mohsenian-Rad, H.: Sparse tracking state estimation for low-observable power distribution systems using D-PMUs. IEEE Trans. Power Syst. **37**(1), 551–564 (2022)
2. Alimardani, A., Zadkhast, S., Jatskevich, J., Vaahedi, E.: Using smart meters in state estimation of distribution networks. In: 2014 IEEE PES General Meeting | Conference & Exposition, pp. 1–5. IEEE, National Harbor, MD, USA, July 2014. https://doi.org/10.1109/PESGM.2014.6939801. http://ieeexplore.ieee.org/document/6939801/
3. Abart, A., et al.: Power Snapshot Analysis: A new method for analyzing low voltage grids using a smart metering system. vol. 21st. Frankfurt, June 2011
4. Araujo, M.A., Flauzino, R.A., Moraes, L.A., Borges, F.A.S., Spatti, D.H.: Decision trees applied to fault locations in distribution systems with smart meters. In: 2019 IEEE International Conference on Environment and Electrical Engineering and 2019 IEEE Industrial and Commercial Power Systems Europe (EEEIC/I&CPS Europe), pp. 1–6. IEEE, Genova, Italy, June 2019. https://doi.org/10.1109/EEEIC.2019.8783511,https://ieeexplore.ieee.org/document/8783511/
5. Bao, K., Mauser, I., Kochanneck, S., Xu, H., Schmeck, H.: A microservice architecture for the intranet of things and energy in smart buildings: research paper. In: Proceedings of the 1st International Workshop on Mashups of Things and APIs, pp. 1–6. ACM, Trento Italy, December 2016. https://doi.org/10.1145/3007203.3007215
6. Behi, B., Arefi, A., Pezeshki, H., Shahnia, F.: Distribution transformer lifetime analysis in the presence of demand response and rooftop PV integration. Renewable Energy Environ. Sustainability **2**, 27 (2017)
7. Bundesnetzagentur für Elektrizität: Gas, Telekommunikation. Post und Eisenbahnen: Bericht zum Zustand und Ausbau der Verteilernetze **2021**, 62, April 2022
8. Dahale, S., Karimi, H.S., Lai, K., Natarajan, B.: Sparsity based approaches for distribution grid state estimation - a comparative study. IEEE Access **8**, 198317–198327 (2020)
9. Dimitriou, P., Leber, T., Nagele, N., Temmel, L., Tessarek, C.: Voltage and frequency measuring plug: As part of Smart Grids metering system. In: 2014 IEEE International Conference on Smart Grid Communications (SmartGridComm), pp. 350–355. IEEE, Venice, Italy, November 2014. https://doi.org/10.1109/SmartGridComm.2014.7007671
10. Fatima, S., Püvi, V., Lehtonen, M.: Review on the PV hosting capacity in distribution networks. Energies **13**(18), 4756 (2020). https://doi.org/10.3390/en13184756. https://www.mdpi.com/1996-1073/13/18/4756
11. Ganu, T., et al.: nPlug: a smart plug for alleviating peak loads. In: Proceedings of the 3rd International Conference on Future Energy Systems: Where Energy, Computing and Communication Meet, pp. 1–10. ACM, Madrid Spain, May 2012. https://doi.org/10.1145/2208828.2208858. https://dl.acm.org/doi/10.1145/2208828.2208858
12. Kerber, G., Witzmann, R.: Statistische Analyse von NS-Verteilnetzen und Modellierung von Referenznetzen. ew Jg. 107 (2008), vol. 6 pp. 22–26 (2008)
13. IBM Cloud Education: Containerization, June 2021. https://www.ibm.com/cloud/learn/containerization
14. Jamshidi, P., Pahl, C., Mendonca, N.C., Lewis, J., Tilkov, S.: Microservices: the journey so far and challenges ahead. IEEE Software **35**(3), 24–35 (2018)

15. Jia, Z., Chen, J., Liao, Y.: State estimation in distribution system considering effects of AMI data. In: 2013 Proceedings of IEEE Southeastcon. pp. 1–6. IEEE, Jacksonville, FL, USA, April 2013. https://doi.org/10.1109/SECON.2013.6567406. http://ieeexplore.ieee.org/document/6567406/

16. Khan, M.A., Hayes, B.: Smart meter based two-layer distribution system state estimation in unbalanced MV/LV networks. IEEE Trans. Ind. Inform. **18**(1), 688–697 (2022)

17. Kimani, K., Oduol, V., Langat, K.: Cyber security challenges for IoT-based smart grid networks. Int. J. Critical Infrastruct. Protection **25**, 36–49 (2019)

18. Kochanneck, S.: Systemdienstleistungserbringung durch intelligente Gebäude. Ph.D. thesis, Karlsruher Institut für Technologie (KIT), Karlsruhe, December 2018

19. Lo, Y.L., Huang, S.C., Lu, C.N.: Transformational benefits of AMI data in transformer load modeling and management. IEEE Trans. Power Delivery **29**(2), 742–750 (2014)

20. M. A. Stephens: EDF statistics for goodness of fit and some comparisons. J. Am. Stat. Assoc., 9 (1974)

21. Bäckman, M.: Smart Homes and Home Automation, Smart Buildings 9th Edition, April 2022

22. Melo, G.C.G.d., Torres, I.C., Araújo, Í.B.Q.d., Brito, D.B., Barboza, E.d.A.: A low-cost IoT system for real-time monitoring of climatic variables and photovoltaic generation for smart grid application. Sensors **21**(9), 3293 (2021). https://doi.org/10.3390/s21093293. https://www.mdpi.com/1424-8220/21/9/3293

23. Mulenga, E., Bollen, M.H., Etherden, N.: A review of hosting capacity quantification methods for photovoltaics in low-voltage distribution grids. Int. J. Electr. Power Energy Syst. **115**, 105445 (2020)

24. Primadianto, A., Lu, C.N.: A review on distribution system state estimation. IEEE Trans. Power Syst. **32**(5), 9 (2017)

25. Quilumba, F.L., Lee, W.J., Huang, H., Wang, D.Y., Szabados, R.L.: Using Smart meter data to improve the accuracy of intraday load forecasting considering customer behavior similarities. IEEE Trans. Smart Grid **6**(2), 911–918 (Mar2015)

26. Samarakoon, K., Wu, J., Ekanayake, J., Jenkins, N.: Use of delayed smart meter measurements for distribution state estimation. In: 2011 IEEE Power and Energy Society General Meeting. pp. 1–6. IEEE, San Diego, CA, July 2011. https://doi.org/10.1109/PES.2011.6039384

27. Sanchez, R., Iov, F., Kemal, M., Stefan, M., Olsen, R.: Observability of low voltage grids: actual DSOs challenges and research questions. In: 2017 52nd International Universities Power Engineering Conference (UPEC), pp. 1–6. IEEE, Heraklion, August 2017. https://doi.org/10.1109/UPEC.2017.8232008. http://ieeexplore.ieee.org/document/8232008/

28. Schwab, A.J.: Elektroenergiesysteme: Erzeugung, Übertragung und Verteilung elektrischer Energie. Springer, Heidelberg (2017). https://doi.org/10.1007/978-3-662-55316-9. http://link.springer.com/10.1007/978-3-662-55316-9

29. Shapiro, S.S., Wilk, M.B.: An analysis of variance test for normality (complete samples). Biometrika **52**(3/4), 22 (1965)

30. Grafenhorst, S.: Fast + Accurate Voltage Measurements in Tasmota, June 2023. https://github.com/si-gr/Tasmota/commit/0d5170928e4fc09a29421b43731631c5c061f42e

31. Song, Y., Lin, J., Tang, M., Dong, S.: An internet of energy things based on wireless LPWAN. Engineering **3**(4), 460–466 (2017)

32. Tasmota: Tasmota Components, May 2022. https://tasmota.github.io/docs/Components/#tasmota

33. Arends, T., et al.: Tasmota, December 2022. https://github.com/arendst/Tasmota
34. Thurner, L., et al.: Pandapower—an open-source python tool for convenient modeling, analysis, and optimization of electric power systems. IEEE Trans. Power Syst. **33**(6), 6510–6521 (2018)
35. Trindade, F.C.L., Freitas, W.: Low voltage zones to support fault location in distribution systems with smart meters. IEEE Trans. Smart Grid **8**(6), 2765–2774 (2017)
36. Wang, Y., Chen, Q., Hong, T., Kang, C.: Review of smart meter data analytics: applications, methodologies, and challenges. IEEE Trans. Smart Grid **10**(3), 3125–3148 (2019)

Analysis of Electrical Equipment at UNICAMP: Insights from the Inventory Database

Hildo Guillardi Júnior$^{(\boxtimes)}$ (iD)

São Paulo State University, São João da Boa Vista, São Paulo, Brazil
`h.guillardi@unesp.br`

Abstract. Data plays a crucial role in understanding several problems, including those related to electrical micro, smart grids and power consumption. In addition to electrical meters, data can be sourced from different channels such as environmental conditions, user expertise, maintenance history, and inventory registries. This paper introduces a Python-based analysis tool designed to search for equipment categories that exhibit constant power consumption within the asset inventory database of the University of Campinas. The software effectively identifies and categorizes items as air conditioners, refrigerators, computers, uninterrupted power supplies and internet routers, providing detailed insights into their specific characteristics. The tool generates a comprehensive PDF report featuring item discrimination through values, charts, organized and university units. Additionally, the software incorporates identification item lists and logs, aiding in the identification of missing or mismatched data throughout the process. These reports has been utilized to establish internal guidelines for optimizing in power consumption and already help the university to improve its GreenMetric index.

Keywords: Big data · Data analysis · Python language

1 Introduction

Data became an important resource to understanding a problem and it is no exception for micro and smart-grids [1,2]. Such data can be provided not only by electrical or environmental measurements but also by user experience or static databases (DBs) that keep historic of maintenance or registry of equipment into the grid.

As part of asset control, large institutions like companies and universities store them equipment inventory in extensive DBs that specify purchase data (indirectly informing the aging of the equipment), item description (which may include type, power, and other relevant characteristics), manufacturer, model, serial number, etc. The inventories provide valuable information about the electrical power grid of the institution and can be applicable for specialized control and management in a smart-grid scenario [1].

These DBs are usually filled by individuals with knowledge of registry and purchase procedures but without technical backgrounds. As a result, they often

B. N. Jørgensen et al. (Eds.): EI.A 2023, LNCS 14468, pp. 213–223, 2024.
https://doi.org/10.1007/978-3-031-48652-4_14

lack in complete the technical descriptions or the correct physical units that describe the electrical characteristics of a particular item. The challenge of extracting information from these DBs lies in recognizing patterns and mining data while considering user interpretations at the time of filling and potential typing errors. Programming libraries/languages can help in pattern recognize procedure [3,4], but they still require the programmer's understanding of the DB and common fields errors.

This work is the case of the University of Campinas - Brazil (UNICAMP), where inventory data is publicly available according to Brazilian law number 12 527 from November 18, 2011 [5]. At May 28, 2023, the inventory contained 759 990 items divided into 126 units (plus a virtual unit for "available items") and it encompasses a wide range of general categories, such as chairs, tables/desks, cars, and others items with constant power consumption, as: air conditioners, fridges, computers. As additional issue of this DB, the categorization may not be direct expressed into a DB column or it may not be reliable, requiring scraping from existing descriptions and other fields as part of the automated search procedure.

As an institutional initiative, the Sustainable Campus project of UNICAMP (*Campus Sustentável*) [6] aims to develop a living laboratory at UNICAMP focusing on renewable energy [7], losses and fault detection [8,9], energy management in small and smart-grids [10], urban mobility [11] and consumption understanding of the university (Fig. 1). Retrofit and Energy Efficiency in Building is also a area of study and it must be guided by thorough an understanding of the equipment in use.

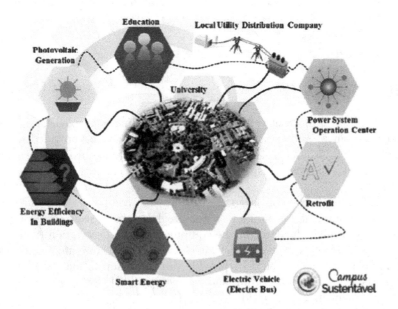

Fig. 1. Study areas of the Sustainable Campus of UNICAMP project [6].

This article presents one aspect of this project, namely the better understanding of the final power usage at UNICAMP by examining all electrical equipment that remains constantly plugged into the grid through an automated procedure of investigation into the asset inventory DB of the university.

The goal of the study is to provide guidelines for improving efficiency in usage and specification processes for such items. This article is organized as follow: Sect. 2 presents the methodology, libraries, and software structure developed to identify, analyze, and generate a report based on the UNICAMP DB inventory. Section 3 shows the results of this analysis based on the May 28, 2023 inventory data. And Sect. 4 concludes by discussing the real impacts of this work at the university.

It is important to highlight that no such analysis has been conducted at UNICAMP until now, and the study is ongoing to assess the full extent of its impacts.

2 Software Development

Analyzing a vast DB can be a tedious and error-prone task due to human factor such as mistyping or overlooking certain items or values. To mitigate these challenges and leverage computational power for repetitive tasks, an automated script or software validated by test examples is crucial.

In the analysis of the UNICAMP inventory, a Python [12] software consisting of 14 164 lines was developed to search for patterns in each asset item description. The software identifies various parameters such as nominal power, item type, the Brazilian National Power Conservation Program Stamp ("PROCEL stamp") [13], which classifies equipment categories based on their efficiency since December 8, 1993, and other relevant parameters. The primary Python packages utilized in this application were:

- Pandas [14,15] for read the exported DB file and generate intermediary file outputs containing all identified items;
- Numpy [16] and ScyPy [17] for statistic evaluation;
- Matplotlib [18] and Seaborn [19] for chart generation;
- WeasyPrint [20] for final report composition;
- Numba [21] to speed-up some software functions evaluation;
- Selenium, [22] used to connect to university services and download the DB.

Figure 2 illustrates the software structure associated with each processing step. The rectangles in the image represents the Python files and libraries that were developed. The software itself can be accessed at https://gitlab.com/hildogjr/unicamp-inventory, and the complete list of dependencies can be found in the Process/requirements.txt file.

The developed software performs five procedures:

1. Connection though Virtual Privacy Network (VPN) and **extraction** of the inventory DB from UNICAMP server (extract_dbs.py) by using the Selenium package as web browser puppeteer. This step is necessary due to access restrictions imposed on downloading the raw DB.

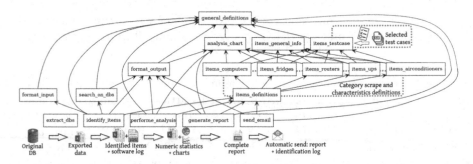

Fig. 2. Hierarchy of the Python software developed libraries and data processing steps.

2. **Identification of the items** by searching for specific description patterns (`search_on_dbs.py`) within the exported DB. It utilizes the item characteristics defined in the `items_definitions.py` file;

3. **Statistic analysis** (`perform_analysis.py`) to evaluate measures such as mean, median, and other statistics for each relevant value of the specified equipment categories and university units. The analysis results are then plotted in charts based on the value **types** (string, float, date, ...) defined in `analysis_char.py`;

4. **Generation of a report file** in PDF format that includes the previously generated charts, tables and units information. The formatting of the report follows the guidelines specified in `format_output.py`;

5. **Send** the report file and the software log to an email group via the Simple Mail Transfer Protocol (SMTP) connection, secured by VPN.

Other files and internal procedures are of the software are described as follow: The `general_definitions.py` file lists general variables and definitions for the software, including the operating system and path definitions.

The `items_*.py` modules contain lists of match and non-match patterns using Regular Expressions [4]. These modules form the core of the software, enabling the identification of items and defining patterns to search for unique item characteristics across DB columns. They also specify the type of analysis to be performed for each item category. The `items_general_info.py` file defines general scraping parameters for all equipment, such as electric power and PROCEL stamp. All these modules are loaded and validated through test scenarios in the `items_testcase.py` file as part of the Continuous Integration and Continuous Delivery (CI/CD) pipeline [23].

Lastly, `format_input.py` contains specific functions to read the exported DB data at the begin of the process and ensure proper data conversion according to the configurations used by the UNICAMP server during exportation.

The software is designed to run into a container or a GitLab repository pipeline to provide automatic reports via email at regular intervals. The configurations for these functionalities can be found in the `Makefile` and `.gitlab-ci .yml` files within the software repository.

3   Results

The developed software was utilized to analyze the information into the DB inventory looking for several types of equipment, including Air Conditioner systems, Computers, Uninterrupted Power Systems (Upss), Refrigerators/Fridges, and Internet Routers, along with their respective subtypes, as shown on Fig. 2. The results of item identification for the UNICAMP database dated of May 28, 2023, and the average purchase year, which provides insights of the equipment aging, are summarized in Table 1. Additionally, the following charts complement this information.

Table 1. Summary of software identification of complete inventory.

Item category	Total quantity	Purchase average year
Air conditioners	13 084	2009
Refrigerators	5681	2006
Computers	34 466	2013
UPSs + power stabilizers (IT)	7420	2007
Internet routers	4967	2014

Figures 3 to 7 show graphical analysis with typification, aging and PROCEL classification for each category of items enrolled at Table 1. On the chart legends, "NO CLASS" marks the item quantity that was not possible to identify the characteristic and "Before procel" on the PROCEL pie chart indicates the items percentage produce before the mandatory PROCEL classification on item manufacture [13].

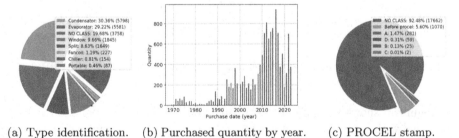

(a) Type identification.   (b) Purchased quantity by year.   (c) PROCEL stamp.

Fig. 3. Classification of all air conditioners equipment at UNICAMP.

Despite the purchase average year of 2009 for **air conditioners** systems (Table 1), Fig. 3 indicates the presence of more the 20 years-old air conditioner equipment and possible not efficient one as pointed by the unregistered classification at Fig. 3c (bellow class A). Also the significant presence of "Window"-type air conditioners, a technology knows as old and less efficient. The "Before procel" counting of 1070 indicates, for sure, purchased item before Dec. 8, 1993, which may deserve a better maintenance attention.

"Condensator" and "Evaporator" numbers discrepancy from Fig. 3a may be caused by mismatched registry procedures. For example, instead of using the word "Split" to register the pair of "Condensator" and "Evaporator" air conditioner systems, or they individual "Condensator"/"Evaporator" words to register each part separately, some air conditioners items have no description or a simple entry such as "air conditioner", or even "Condensator" was used to refer to both parts of the air conditioner system.

Figure 4 presents the results for **refrigeration equipment** other than air conditioners. This category includes common refrigerators, fridges, frigobars, drinking fountains, ice machines and ultra fridges. UNICAMP, being home to one of the most important hospitals in the region and having a significant undergraduate course on Food Engineering, relies on these equipment types for essential purposes. Drinking fountains, in particular, have a significant presence on UNICAMP *campi*, providing drinkable water for employees and students. The PROCEL data of such item (Fig. 4c) indicates a high percentage of unidentified items, suggesting not only the possibility of old equipment but also a lack of attention to filling in such characteristics in the item descriptions within the database.

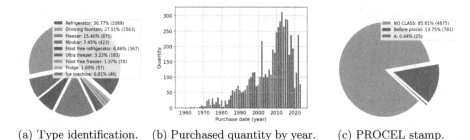

(a) Type identification.   (b) Purchased quantity by year.   (c) PROCEL stamp.

Fig. 4. Classification of all refrigerators/fridges equipments at UNICAMP.

Figure 5b shows the surge of **computer** purchases in the year 2011, which coincided with UNICAMP's efforts to modernize its infrastructure and network. The most prevalent computer type is "Desktop" (Fig. 5a), often accompanied by a higher number of displays, registered apart from computers. This can be attributed to the versatile use of displays as TVs, information displays, or for dual-screen workstation setups. UNICAMP currently has 894 computers dedicated as server equipment to support its internal network and services.

Uninterrupted Power Systems (UPSs) and small auto-transformers power stabilizers for computers also experienced a significant increase in pur-

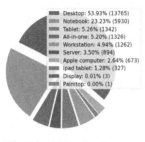

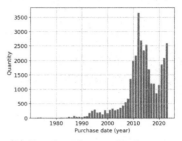

(a) Type identification.   (b) Purchased quantity by year.

Fig. 5. Classification of all registered computers at UNICAMP.

chases during the same period as computers ((Fig. 6b). The majority of these purchases were small stabilizers and offline UPSs, both commonly used for desktop computers. Line interactive, sinusoidal, and online UPSs account for 660 units, representing 8.90% of all UPSs in the asset inventory (Fig. 6a), are typically applicable to provide power backup to critical electronic equipment in Information Technology (IT), network provisioning, and medical facilities. The medical units within the UNICAMP own 3888 of these UPSs, accounting for 52.40% of the total (as compiled in Table 2).

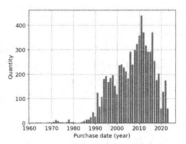

(a) Type identification.   (b) Purchased quantity by year.

Fig. 6. Classification of all UPSs equipment at UNICAMP.

Furthermore, Fig. 7a provides insights into UNICAMP's **internet hardware asset** by categorizing Ethernet routers as "infrastructure" (main network providers), "access point" (Wi-Fi coverage on UNICAMP *campi*, with the largest presence), "service" (dedicated equipment for network and server services such as interconnection and backup), and "common" (general-purpose routers used internally in laboratories and not part of the main network structure). Figure 7b highlights a significant investment by the university in year 2015, likely related to the expansion of the Education Roaming (Eduroam) internal infrastructure [24]. Additionally, there appears to be a possible upward trend in router acquisitions by the year 2020, possibly due to an increase in Wi-Fi coverage.

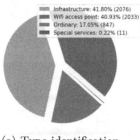
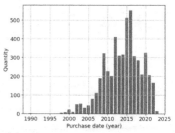

(a) Type identification.   (b) Purchased quantity by year.

Fig. 7. Classification of all internet routers at UNICAMP.

Due to administrative and registration process time for a purchased item, the data for 2022 may be incomplete, and information for 2023 is partial available, making it challenging to draw definitive conclusions for these last two years on any item.

The analysis report generated by the software revealed that the top 10 out of the 116 units at UNICAMP, which are known by consume the most significant amount of electricity bill, accounted for a minimum of 35.52% of items in each analyzed category (Table 2). Notably, these units possess nearly 50% of the air conditioning systems and the are enrolled as follows:

1. CAISM: Women's Hospital "Prof. Dr. José Aristodemo Pinotti" (*Hospital da Mulher "Prof. Dr. José Aristodemo Pinotti"*);
2. CCUEC: Computer Center (*Centro de Computação*);
3. FCM: School of Medical Sciences (Faculdade de Ciências Médicas);
4. FEA: School of Food Engineering (Faculdade de Engenharia de Alimentos);
5. FEM: School of Mechanical Engineering (Faculdade de Engenharia Mecânica);
6. HC: UNICAMP's Clinical Hospital (Hospital das Clínicas da UNICAMP);
7. HEMOCENTRO: UNICAMP's Blood Center (Hemocentro da UNICAMP);
8. IB: School of Biology (Instituto de Biologia);
9. IFGW: School of Physics "Gleb Wataghin" (Instituto de Física "Gleb Wataghin");
10. IQ: School of Chemistry (Instituto de Química).

This group of units are composed by 3 hospital unities (CAISM, HEMO-CENTRO and HC) plus one medical school (FCM), four school heavy based on cooling process (FEA, IB, IFGW and IQ) and the computer center/server administration (CCUEC), which explain the air conditioning and refrigerators presence.

The created software is not restrict to the presented analysis in this paper and it is capable of discriminate data of each of the 116 schools/administrative unit of UNICAMP and extract more data, those result are not included here for simplicity sack but can be found as a semiannual analyses at the public e-mail

Table 2. Total by category of the 10 biggest power consumption units.

Item category	Quantity	Perceptual to total	Purchase avg. year
Air conditioners	6250	47.67%	2008
Refrigerators	3193	58.20%	2006
Computers	12 241	35.52%	2012
UPSs + power stabilizers (IT)	3888	52.40%	2007
Internet routers	2147	43.23%	2014

group dataanalytics-l@unicamp.br and the webpage https://hildogjr.gitlab.io/unicamp-inventory/.

In a significant development, the results generated by the software were utilized to update the GreenMetric World Universities Rankings of UNICAMP. This, along with other university directives, resulted in a significant improvement of 35 positions in the global index in 2021 [25] and a further 10 positions in 2022. These achievements have also provided the basis for the university's current investment in retrofitting air conditioning systems.

4   Conclusions

The application of data mining techniques, leverage by data acknowledgement and regular expressions made possible the analysis of the extensive UNICAMP asset inventory and facilitated quantitative analyses of equipment categories with constant power consumption to obtain periodic university statistics without human interference.

The initial results have highlighted the aging of equipment and underscored the need for better and standardized procedures for updating the inventory. It is exact the case of PROCEL and other characteristics not presented here.

The work presented here has sparked meaningful discussions within the university about the significance of data and the measures required to maintain an accurate and up-to-date inventory database. It also helped to indirectly improve the university green statistics [25].

Acknowledgements. to Research Foundation of the State of São Paulo (FAPESP) for their support through grants #2020/16635-9 and #2021/11380-5. The author also acknowledges the Interdisciplinary Research Activities in Electric Smart Grids (LabREI) of UNICAMP, funded by FAPESP #2016/08645-9, which provided the necessary computational infrastructure for processing the data presented in this paper. Gratitude are extended to the team of the General Directorate of Administration of Unicamp (DGA-UNICAMP) for their valuable contributions in provision of useful information about the data and to the project Sustainable Campus of UNICAMP support group for their efforts in verifying data generated by the software, ensuring its accuracy.

References

1. Bhattarai, B.P., et al.: Big data analytics in smart grids: state-of-the-art, challenges, opportunities, and future directions. IET Smart Grid **2**(2), 141–154(13) (2019), https://digital-library.theiet.org/content/journals/10.1049/iet-stg.2018.0261, publisher: Institution of Engineering and Technology
2. Ghorbanian, M., Dolatabadi, S.H., Siano, P.: Big data issues in smart grids: a survey. IEEE Syst. J. **13**(4), 4158–4168 (2019)
3. Robbins, A.: Sed and awk Pocket Reference: Text Processing with Regular Expressions. O'Reilly Media, Inc. (2002)
4. Stubblebine, T.: Regular Expression Pocket Reference: Regular Expressions for Perl, Ruby, PHP, Python, C, Java and. NET. O'Reilly Media, Inc. (2007)
5. Brazilian Government: Law of access to public interest information (in Portuguese). http://www.planalto.gov.br/ccivil_03/_ato2011-2014/2011/lei/l12527.htm
6. da Silva, L.C.P., et al.: Sustainable campus model at the university of campinas-brazil: an integrated living lab for renewable generation, electric mobility, energy efficiency, monitoring and energy demand management. In: Leal Filho, W., Frankenberger, F., Iglecias, P., Mülfarth, R.C.K. (eds.) Towards Green Campus Operations: Energy, Climate and Sustainable Development Initiatives at Universities, pp. 457–472. Springer (2018). https://doi.org/10.1007/978-3-319-76885-4_30
7. DA Silva, M.K., Narvaez, D.I., de Melo, K.B., Costa, T.S., de Siqueira, T.G., Villalva, M.G.: Comparative analysis of meteorological databases and transposition models applied to photovoltaic systems. Anais da Sociedade Brasileira de Automática 1 (2019)
8. Puma, F.A., Cavalcante, M.M., Ugarte, L.F., Sau, R.G., de Almeida, M.C.: Assessment of loss estimation methods for distribution transformers. In: 2018 13th IEEE International Conference on Industry Applications (INDUSCON), pp. 1274–1279. IEEE (2018)
9. Ugarte, L.F., Sau, R.G., de Almeida, M.C.: On the performance of state estimators in distribution systems under fault conditions. In: 2018 13th IEEE International Conference on Industry Applications (INDUSCON), pp. 799–805. IEEE (2018)
10. Cypriano, J., Pinto, L., Machado, L., da Silva, L., Ferreira, L.: Energy management methodology for energy sustainable actions in university of campinas-brazil. In: IOP Conference Series: Earth and Environmental Science. vol. 257, p. 012034. IOP Publishing (2019)
11. Daniel Filipe Vieira, H.G.: Public transportation passengers accounting at university by IoT device. In: 2022 Symposium on Internet of Things (SIoT) (2022)
12. Van Rossum, G., Drake, F.L.: Python 3 Reference Manual. CreateSpace, Scotts Valley, CA (2009)
13. Brazilian Government: Brazilian National Power Conservation Program - PROCEL (in Portuguese) (1993). http://www.procelinfo.com.br/. Accessed 17 Feb 2021
14. McKinney, W.: Data structures for statistical computing in python. In: Stéfan van der Walt, Jarrod Millman (eds.) Proceedings of the 9th Python in Science Conference, pp. 56–61 (2010)
15. pandas development team, T.: pandas-dev/pandas: Pandas, February 2020. https://doi.org/10.5281/zenodo.3509134
16. Harris, C.R., et al.: Array programming with NumPy. Nature **585**, 357–362 (2020)
17. Virtanen, P., et al.: SciPy 1.0 Contributors: SciPy 1.0: fundamental algorithms for scientific computing in python. Nature Methods **17**, 261–272 (2020)

18. Hunter, J.D.: Matplotlib: a 2d graphics environment. Comput. Sci. Eng. **9**(3), 90–95 (2007)
19. Waskom, M., the seaborn development team: mwaskom/seaborn, September 2020. https://doi.org/10.5281/zenodo.592845
20. CourtBouillon: WeasyPrint: the awesome document factory (2011–2021). https://www.courtbouillon.org/
21. Numba: A High Performance Python Compiler, June 2022. https://numba.pydata.org. Accessed 28 Jun 2022
22. Selenium, June 2022. https://www.selenium.dev. Accessed 28 Jun 2022
23. Patil, A., Soni, M.: Hands-on Pipeline as Code with Jenkins: CI/CD Implementation for Mobile, Web, and Hybrid Applications Using Declarative Pipeline in Jenkins (English Edition). BPB PUBN (2021). https://books.google.com.br/books?id=xTYcEAAAQBAJ
24. Unicamp Computing Center (CCUEC): Instruction 10 (in Portuguese), June 2013. https://www.ccuec.unicamp.br/ccuec/sites/default/files/tutoriais/IN_10_2013_Substituicao_IN_09_2013_Adesao_servico_EDUROAM_.pdf
25. Unicamp advancepositions in the ranking GreenMetric 2021 (in Portuguese), December 2021. https://www.unicamp.br/unicamp/noticias/2021/12/21/unicamp-ganha-posicoes-no-ranking-greenmetric-2021. Accessed 28 June 2022

Power Consumption Analysis as a Detection Indicator for Cyberattacks on Smart Home Devices

Victoria Schorr[1], Nikolai Kamenev[1], Thomas Bleistein[1($\boxtimes$)], Dirk Werth[1], Steffen Wendzel[2], and Thomas Weigold[2]

[1] August-Wilhelm Scheer Institut für digitale Produkte und Prozesse gGmbH, 66123 Saarbruecken, Germany
thomas.bleistein@aws-institut.de
[2] Hochschule Worms, 67549 Worms, Germany

Abstract. The increasing prevalence of smart home devices has created new opportunities for cyberthreats and -attacks, necessitating effective security measures for their protection. This study investigates the potential of using power consumption analysis as an indicator for detecting cyberattacks on smart home devices. Through the examination of power data from a hardware testbed of 10 different devices over a one-month period, distinct groups of devices with varying power consumption patterns during simulated cyberattacks were identified. The findings reveal noticeable changes in power consumption during attacks across all devices, suggesting that monitoring power data could help detect threats and initiate appropriate countermeasures. Moreover, this study provides insights into the limitations and challenges associated with the stated approach and suggests avenues for future research. This study contributes to smart home security by demonstrating the feasibility of using power consumption analysis as an additional layer of protection for IoT devices and their users.

Keywords: Smart home security · Cyberattacks · Anomaly detection · IoT devices · Power consumption patterns · Data analysis

1 Introduction

The increasing digitization and connectivity of ordinary objects have brought profound shifts in our daily lives, work dynamics, communication ways. Smart homes are an example of this development, providing individuals with a convenient and efficient way to control and automate their homes and appliances [1]. The proliferation of internet-connected devices and the valuable data they store, has rendered smart homes susceptible to a range of cyberthreats and -attacks, including Distributed Denial of Service (DDoS), Man-in-the-Middle (MitM), and malware-related attacks. DDoS attacks involve overwhelming a network or website with an enormous amount of traffic, making it inaccessible to users. MitM attacks occur when an attacker intercepts communication between two parties and

B. N. Jørgensen et al. (Eds.): EI.A 2023, LNCS 14468, pp. 224–239, 2024.
https://doi.org/10.1007/978-3-031-48652-4_15

has the ability to manipulate the conversation or steal sensitive information. Malware-related attacks involve the installation of malicious software on a device, granting the attacker potential control over the device, the ability to extract sensitive information, or even execute diverse forms of attacks, including DDoS. In the realm of smart homes, these attacks can have severe repercussions, including compromised privacy, property damage, and even physical harm. For instance, an attacker could exploit a smart lock system, gaining unauthorized and undetected entry. Moreover, as highlighted by Kevin Coleman, manipulating a heating system could lead to fire hazards [2]. To mitigate or detect such attacks, it is imperative to implement appropriate security measures. One promising approach involves analyzing power data generated by smart home devices. By examining power usage patterns, it is possible to pinpoint anomalies that may indicate the presence of an attack. For example, an attacker could manipulate a device to carry out a DDoS attack, which could cause a noticeable surge in power usage. By actively monitoring and analyzing power data, such anomalies can be detected, allowing for the timely response and preemptive measures against potential cyberattacks.

The study analyzes of how the power consumption of different devices connected in a hardware testbed varies or respond to simulated cyberattacks. It aims to answer whether and how cyberattacks are reflected in power metering data. The objective is to investigate the feasibility of using power consumption data to detect hacking attacks and identify patterns on IoT devices and changes in their power consumption. The results may contribute to alternative attack detection approaches, potentially enhancing the overall robustness and effectiveness of existing methods. The motivation for this study is driven by the need to address the following issues:

- Investigating the possibility of detecting hacking attacks through the analysis of power consumption data and comparing this method with detection based on network data.
- Identifying patterns and anomalies in power consumption that could indicate hacking attacks and developing algorithms or models for detecting such patterns.
- Examining the observed changes in power consumption of devices.
- Analyzing the potentials and limitations of using power consumption data for detecting hacking attacks and contributing to the improvement of overall attack detection in interconnected systems.

2 Related Work

As stated by Wendzel et al. [3, 4], the expansion of smart home systems leads to increasing threats, challenges, and vulnerabilities to cyberattacks. In response, researchers have focused on early detection of attacks. This section provides an overview of related works discussing their strengths and limitations, and how this study differs from and builds upon prior works in the field.

Zhao et al. [5] propose a two-layer learning framework for robust anomaly detection in the presence of unreliable anomaly labels. While their focus is on detecting IoT attacks and failures, they do not analyze power consumption patterns of smart home devices statistically.

Zhou et al. [6] directly address cyberattack detection, developing a short- and long-term detection algorithm based on binary logistic regression to learn power consumption patterns and identify anomalies. However, their research considers power data and power consumption within the context of sponsor incentive pricing attacks, rather than the attacks themselves.

Sajeev et al. [7] investigate the impact of cyberattacks on smart home energy management systems under an aggregator system of operation. Their focus is on price attacks and the overall impact on the smart home system, rather than early detection and statistical analysis of attacks.

Bobrovnikova et al. [8] examine the detection of IoT cyberattacks through power consumption patterns and opcode sequences. In contrast, this paper emphasizes the direct examination of power consumption data, conducting actual hacking attacks on a hardware testbed to determine the resulting effects. This approach offers easy integration into existing systems and provides detailed insights into the correlation between cyberattacks and IoT device power consumption, utilizing various statistical methods for accurate interpretation of the results.

Bobrovnikova et al. [8] also mention other approaches based on monitoring the power consumption to detect cyberattacks in different contexts [9–12]. Caviglione et al. [13] present an approach to detect covert data exfiltration from smart phones using power consumption profiles of Android apps.

Yang Shi et al. [14] proposed a detection framework based on power consumption analysis, focusing on a wide range of attacks. However, their work does not measure the real power consumption patterns whilst the simulated cyberattacks. In contrast, this approach involves direct measurement and provides practical results. Additionally, their primary focus is on the accuracy and detection speed of learning algorithms, while this study concentrates on different power consumption patterns of four distinct groups.

Lara et al. [1] investigate anomaly detection in the smart home context, primarily focusing on larger devices and working with hypothetical scenarios. They mention the testing of attack detection limits through anomalies in power consumption as a potential area of further research.

Yan Lim et al. [15] aim to develop a detection algorithm for identifying anomalies in power consumption data recorded by a smart meter. Their research focuses on general anomalies in the context of industrial energy management rather than cyberattacks in the private smart home sector.

In addition, the work by Mottola et al. [16] presents a method for detecting energy attacks by leveraging machine learning and approximate intermittent computing, focusing on the detection of anomalies in energy consumption data of battery less IoT devices. However, the statistical analysis is mainly concerned with the evaluation of the detection system and not with the changed consumption behavior per se, notwithstanding that the system is not concerned with the context of a smart environment.

Pathak et al. [17] also propose a similar approach but focusing on security sensor tampering in office environments.

Chatterje et al. [18] review and compile existing publications on anomaly detection algorithms for IoT devices, but these studies do not necessarily consider cyberattacks. There is also a scarcity of anomaly detection methods that can function without sufficient ground truth data, particularly in private smart home systems with various sensors and data expansion.

3 Methodology

The present work is a contribution to the BMBF-funded research project KIASH (funding code: 16KIS1614). Due to this a hardware testbed with 10 components created for research purposes in the project is used and linked to an intelligent measuring device in order to carry out cyberattacks and to record these in the measured data. The following section is structured in three parts. First, the collection of the power data as well as the structure of the testbed and measurement station are described. Second, the various cyberattacks are explained, and last, the structure of the following analysis is presented.

3.1 Power Data Acquisition

Power data over a period of one month were collected in order to get an assessment of possible measurement errors, updates and the targeted attacks.

The basis for the anomaly detection is given by the power consumption data collected via separately and independently installed smart meters (TP-Link Tapo P110 [19]). These smart meters can handle devices with a maximum power of 3680 W and 16 A of maximum current. The main request on the smart meters is an easy installation for every person, to be used in a broad range of households. It is not necessary to have an accuracy in the range of sub mW, because the focus is to detect cyberattacks with low-cost devices in single households. Regardless the IoT sensors should be stable and precise enough to measure small power consumptions in the range of about 50 mW. For the smart home testbed, a wide range of 10 different smart home devices were installed and connected to the network. Each of the 10 devices was connected to one smart meter and in addition, the power consumption of the whole testbed was monitored with a twelfth smart meter. The used smart home devices are summarized with their connection to the smart meters in Table 1. The measurement and storing of the smart meter data are done using a Raspberry Pi 4 [20]. The smart plugs were connected via an independent network connection completely separated from the network of the smart home devices. The sensor data was collected using the graphical development tool Node-RED [21]. It consists of a server and a web browser-based flow editor. Inside the flow editor, a flow was built up to connect the IoT smart meters and separate the needed power consumption data. Inside the flow the data acquisition was triggered once a second for all sensors. The data was collected and automatically added to a daily log file. The log file consists of the date, timestamp, and the current power consumption for all smart meter sensors in mW. The data was collected over a period of one month to get an assessment of possible measurement errors, updates, and the targeted attacks.

3.2 Simulation of Cyberattacks

Several of today's common IoT based attacks [32–34], such as (D)DoS or brute-force attacks, rely on sending a high number of packets within a short time to exhaust the computing capabilities of IoT devices or to exploit side channels to, e.g., gain user credentials. Even if this type of attack exists since several years, it is still often used against IoT devices [35, 36]. One of the reasons for that fact is that such attacks can be realized easily. If the target is an IoT device, it usually possesses limited processing

Table 1. Smart meter and plug abbreviations, devices and data sheets

Smart Plug	Device	Datasheet
Sensor 1	Printer I "Canon"	[22]
Sensor 2	Google Nest Mini	[23]
Sensor 3	Amazon Alexa Echo Dot	[24]
Sensor 4	Apple HomePod Mini	[25]
Sensor 5	Netamo Weatherstation	[26]
Sensor 6	Bosch Smart Home Controller	[27]
Sensor 7	Phillips Hue Bridge	[28]
Sensor 8	Netamo Alarm System	[29]
Sensor 9	Homematic IP Access Point	[30]
Sensor 10	Netamo radiator thermostat	[31]
Sensor 11	Entire testbed	–

power, i.e., it is not able to handle a larger amount of requests simultaneously. To confirm the assumption that the power consumption of an IoT device increases strong enough to differentiate its power consumption during an ongoing attack, ICMP flooding was conducted. The attack itself sends a high amount of ICMP requests to a remote peer that has to answer the requests.

To this end, the different IoT devices were installed following the device instructions without automatic device actions being configured. Devices were connected to a single network via Wi-Fi, or, if available, through a wired connection. As attacking machine, a Raspberry Pi 3 with hping3 [37] was used.

The attack itself was configured in flood mode, which sends packets to the targeted device as fast as it can without considering ICMP responses.

3.3 Power Data Analysis

Since the study assumed that the power consumption of an IoT device increases during an ongoing attack, metrics like average, minimum and maximum values, standard deviation were calculated. To observe the effects of attack, pre-attack and post-attack values were also considered. The average value before, after and during an attack helped to summarize the behavior of energy consumption of a device under different conditions over a period. The minimum and maximum value during an attack were noted to understand how extreme the values can go in both directions during an attack. This value when compared to average value can help us note the extreme behavior. The graphical representations were generated to notice if the attacks can be easily identified given access to a better visual representation than just numbers. Finally, standard deviation calculation was done to quantify the fluctuation than the average behavior over a period under consideration.

All these statistical tools help to test the assumption by quantification on which this entire study is based.

In summary and based on the explained data analysis the following listed points were viewed concerning days with and without cyberattacks.

- Average and median power consumption of the devices before, during and after hacking attacks
- Minimum and maximum power value of the devices during hacking attacks
- Graphical representation of power consumption before, during and after hacking attacks
- Examining fluctuations in IoT device power consumption due to attacks using standard deviation.

In the overview section of this analysis, visible changes were observed in the power consumption data during the hacking attacks for all devices. Frequently, the power consumption data shifted upward during the attacks, and then normalized once the attacks had ended. When looking at the power consumption data, it was noticed that certain devices showed similar changes their power consumption during an attack, although it is not clear why the devices reacted in this way. The devices could be divided into four groups, in which all devices of a group showed similar reactions to a cyberattack. These device groups and their reactions are explained in the following and then always considered based on a representative device.

Group 1. Devices exhibiting a clear upward change in power consumption during the attacks, followed by normalization. This group includes Apple Homepod, Amazon Alexa, Bosch Smart Home Controller, and Philips Hue.

Group 2. Devices showing small, intermittent spikes in power consumption during the attacks, both upwards and downwards. This group consists of Netatmo Weather Station, Netatmo Thermostat, Netatmo Alarm System, Homematic IP Access Point, and Google Nest Mini.

Group 3. Devices with occasional upward spikes in power consumption during the attacks, such as the Canon Printer.

Group 4. A subset of Group 2 devices that experienced a significant increase in power consumption for several hours following the attack, specifically the Netatmo Thermostat and Netatmo Weather Station.

The statistical analysis revealed that the average power consumption consistently increased during the attacks across all devices. In the subsequent sections, a deeper look into the patterns and trends exhibited by each group and their implications for detecting hacking attacks through power consumption data analysis is taken.

4   Analysis

The following section presents the results of the measurement, statistical analysis, and visual analysis. Table 2 is provided, which includes information about the four groups. The table lists the selected representatives from each group, which are further analyzed in detail. The general power consumption behavior of the four groups during cyberattacks is described both in words and in numerical values. This includes average power consumption before, during, and after a hacking attack, as well as the minimum and maximum consumption values, and their deviation during the attack. Furthermore, it is discussed whether the representative and their power consumption can be utilized to identify cyberattacks.

Following the table, there are plots illustrating the power consumption of the different representatives before, during, and after the cyberattacks. These plots (see Fig. 1 to Fig. 4) visually depict the behavior explained numerically in the previous section.

Table 2. Results of the statistical analysis for the four representatives of the different device groups

	Group 1	Group 2	Group 3	Group 4
Representative	Amazon Alexa	Google Nest Mini	Canon Printer	Netamo Thermostat device
Power consumption behavior under attack	distinct increase in power consumption during attack, rapid return to normal after attack	overall increase during attack, greater variability, and intermittent drops below normal levels	overall increase during attacks, greater variability and intermittent drops return to normal levels after attack	initial increase during hacking attack, followed by stabilization and decrease to level above pre-attack consumption
Average power consumption before attack	902 mW	1,316 mW	1,260 mW	468 mW
Average power consumption during attack	1,385 mW	1,623 mW	1,525 mW	535 mW
Average power consumption after attack	911 mW	1,328 mW	1,260 mW	513 mW
Deviation during attack	69 mW	212 mW	257 mW	191 mW
Min. and max. Power consumption during attack	997 mW 1,541 mW	987 mW 1,943 mW	1,152 mW 1,874 mW	0 mW 812 mW
Hacking attack according to visual and statistical analysis identifiable	more readily identifiable	not that easy to identify	challenging to identify	potentially identifiable, although challenging

4.1   Group 1

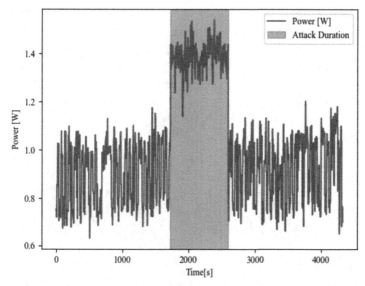

Fig. 1. Exemplary power consumption of group 1 devices 30 min before, during and 30 min after the cyberattack, represented by Amazon Alexa Dot

4.2   Group 2

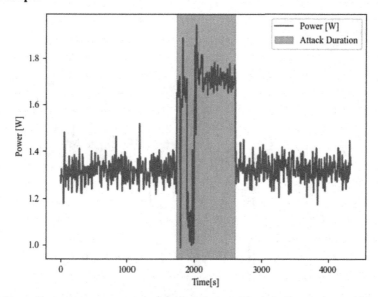

Fig. 2. Exemplary power consumption of group 2 devices 30 min before, during and 30 min after the cyberattack, represented by Google Nest Mini

4.3   Group 3

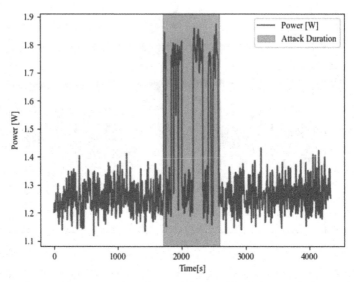

Fig. 3. Exemplary power consumption of group 3 devices 30 min before, during and 30 min after the cyberattack, represented by Canon Printer

4.4   Group 4

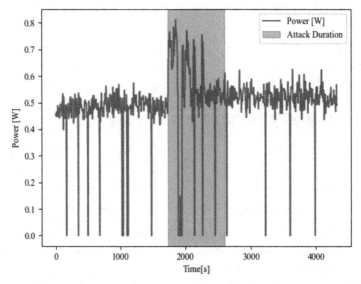

Fig. 4. Exemplary power consumption of group 4 devices 30 min before, during and 30 min after the cyberattack, represented by Netamo radiator thermostat

4.5 Key Metrics and Comparisons

In this section, the key metrics (mean, median, standard deviation, etc.) for each representative example from the four groups are compared, highlighting the similarities and differences in power consumption patterns during and outside of hacking attacks.

Mean Power Consumption During Attacks. When comparing the mean power consumption during the attack for each group, there is a clear increase in power consumption noticeable for all devices. Group 1 devices (e.g., Amazon Alexa) have the highest increase (53.4%), while Group 4 devices (e.g., Netamo Thermostat) show the smallest increase (14.3%). Group 2 devices (e.g., Google Nest Mini) experience a 23.3% increase, and Group 3 devices (e.g., Canon Printer) have an increase of 21.0%.

Standard Deviation During Attacks. The standard deviation during the attacks varies across the different groups.

As seen in Fig. 1 Group 1 devices, such as Amazon Alexa, exhibit a relatively low standard deviation, indicating uniform power consumption during the attack. In contrast, Group 2 (Google Nest Mini) and Group 3 (Canon Printer) devices show higher standard deviations, indicating greater variability in power consumption. Group 4 devices (Netamo Thermostat) demonstrate a standard deviation suggesting variable power consumption patterns.

Post-attack Power Consumption. A notable difference between the groups is the behavior of power consumption after the attack. Group 1 devices (e.g., Amazon Alexa) return to pre-attack power consumption levels, while Group 4 devices (e.g., Netamo Thermostat) maintain elevated post-attack power consumption. Group 2 and Group 3 devices display mixed patterns, with some returning to pre-attack levels and others experiencing fluctuations in power consumption after the attack.

Through Months. It is important to note that the analysis is based on power consumption data of only a few days including the cyberattack, which demonstrates the significant impact of the attack on the device's power consumption, regardless of which group is considered, visible throughout the whole month.

Conclusion. The comparisons of key metrics between the groups demonstrate the varying impact of hacking attacks on power consumption patterns for different smart devices. Group 1 devices show the most consistent response, while Group 4 devices indicate a lasting effect on power consumption after the attack. Group 2 and Group 3 devices display more variable power consumption patterns during and after the attacks. Understanding these differences can be valuable for further investigation into detecting and mitigating the effects of hacking attacks on smart home devices based on their power consumption data.

5 Discussion

5.1 Interpretation of the Results in Context of the Research Question

The primary aim of this research was to investigate the impact of cyberattacks on the power consumption of smart home devices and to determine if power data could be utilized to detect these attacks. This analysis of the 10 different devices, divided into four groups based on their power consumption patterns during the attacks, provides valuable insights into the relationship between cyberattacks and power consumption.

For Group 1 devices, there was a clear increase in power consumption during the attacks observed, followed by a return to normal levels after the attacks ended. This suggests that cyberattacks have a noticeable impact on the power consumption of these devices, and monitoring power data could potentially serve as a means of early detection for such attacks.

Group 2 devices exhibited smaller fluctuations during the attacks, with occasional deviations both above and below the normal power consumption levels. This indicates that while power data might still be useful for detecting attacks on these devices, it may require more advanced statistical analysis or machine learning techniques to differentiate between genuine anomalies and normal variations in power consumption.

Group 3, represented by the Canon Printer, demonstrated occasional spikes in power consumption during the attacks. This suggests that, although power data may not be as reliable for detecting cyberattacks on devices in this group, it could still provide some indications of potential threats when combined with other detection methods.

Lastly, Group 4 devices, such as the Netamo Thermostat, experienced a sustained increase in power consumption after the attacks, indicating that cyberattacks can have long-lasting effects on the energy efficiency of these devices. This finding highlights the importance of not only detecting but also mitigating the impacts of cyberattacks on smart home devices.

In conclusion, this study has demonstrated that power consumption patterns can be indicative of cyberattacks on various smart home devices by examining devices with distinct power consumption behaviors.

5.2 Comparing the Results with Existing Literature

The objective of this paper was to investigate the impact of cyberattacks on the power consumption of smart home devices and determine whether the changes can be used to detect cyberattacks early on. In Table 3, the main focuses in comparison with existing studies are presented. Here, ✓ and ✗ symbols are used to indicate whether a specific topic is addressed in each study. The table shows how this study covers topics not addressed in some of the other studies and how it focuses on different aspects to provide a more comprehensive understanding of the impact of cyberattacks on the power consumption of smart home devices.

From the Table, it is evident that this study is similar or complementary to some existing works in some aspects. Some of the key differences compared to other studies are:

- Yang Shi et al. [14] focused on the same research question, still this work differs from the referenced paper in several ways. While they focused on a wide range of attacks, this paper specialized in one method. Additionally, the power consumption patterns of various devices were measured directly, making this here stated approach more practical and accurate. Also, potentials and limitations of this approach were considered, while the study concentrates on different power consumption patterns of distinct groups rather than the accuracy and detection speed of learning algorithms.

- The shown results confirm Bobrovnikova et al.'s approaches [8], however this study goes beyond by directly examining the power consumption data, conduction real hacking attacks on a hardware testbed, and using statistical methods for accurate interpretation. This comprehensive approach allows a more details insight into the correlation between cyberattacks and IoT device power consumption, contributing significantly to IoT security research.

In summary, this research contributes to the understanding of the impact of cyber-attacks on IoT devices and their power consumption, thereby advancing security in the smart home field.

Table 3. Comparison between this study and other studies with similar topic

Study	Smart environment	Energy-management	Anomaly Detection	Cyberattacks on smart devices	Statistical analysis	Private (Smart Home) or Industrial Usage
This study	✓	✓	✓	✓	✓	private
Bobrovnikova et al.	✓	✓	✓	✓	✓	both
Sajeev et al.	✓	✓	✓	✓	✗	both
Sivanthan et al.	✓	✗	✗	✓	✗	both
Lara et al.	✓	✓	✓	✓	✗	private
Zhao et al.	✓	✓	✓	✓	✗	both
Zhou et al.	✓	✓	✓	✗	✓	private
Yan Lim et al.	✓	✓	✓	✗	✓	industrial
Chatterje & Ahmed	✓	✗	✓	✗	✗	both
Pathak et al.	✓	✗	✓	✗	✗	industrial
Yang Shi et al.	✓	✓	✓	✓	✓	both
Mottola et al.	✗	✓	✓	Energy attacks	✓	neither

5.3 Limitations

In this section the limitations of the analysis are acknowledged, which may impact the interpretation of the results and the generalizability of the findings.

1. Insufficient data: Although this study includes data from 10 smart devices, the sample size is relatively small, limiting the robustness of the conclusions stated in this paper.

A larger sample size with a greater diversity of devices would be beneficial to make more definitive claims about the relationship between hacking attacks and power consumption patterns.

2. Potential biases: This analysis is based on data from a specific hardware testbed, which may not be representative of all smart home devices and their configurations.
3. The hacking attacks: The attacks used in this study might not cover the full range of possible cyberattacks that these devices could face in real world scenarios. In fact, only DDos attacks were used. Moreover, this study focuses on simulated cyberattacks, which might not fully reflect real world scenarios. Therefore, experiments in a live environment would have been needed and might be considered in follow up research.
4. The power consumptions were measured only in standby mode and not during regular operation. Further research should consider different operating modes of the devices.
5. Some smart home devices are not connected to a power supply and utilize batteries or other energy sources, limiting the direct application of this approach.
6. Additionally, it was observed, that different devices may show varying impacts on their power data. Therefore, the devices were grouped into four categories. Nonetheless, it might be necessary to investigate further in future studies to determine the underlying causes.

By acknowledging these limitations, the aim is to provide a transparent and balanced perspective on the findings. Future research should consider addressing these limitations to provide a more comprehensive understanding of the relationship between hacking attacks and power consumption patterns in smart home devices.

6 Conclusion

This study's findings have significant implications for improving smart home security, demonstrating that monitoring power consumption patterns could serve as an additional layer of defense against cyberattacks. It is illustrated that cyberattacks on connected devices can be detected, which is the base to take appropriate countermeasures by analyzing power consumption patterns and might be discussed in further research. The implementation of anomaly detection systems can supplement existing security measures in smart homes.

This investigation studied the impact of cyberattacks on the power consumption patterns of various smart home devices. Through detailed analysis and comparison of power data during attack and non-attack periods, distinct device groups with different power consumption behaviors under cyberattacks were identified. The main findings of this research include:

1. Noticeable increases in power consumption during cyberattacks, followed by normalization after attack cessation.
2. Occasional spikes in power consumption during attacks, with some devices also experiencing temporary decreases.
3. Persistent increases in power consumption post-attacks for certain devices.

This study contributes to existing research on smart home security by providing a novel approach to detecting cyberattacks through power consumption anomalies. By analyzing real-world data from a hardware testbed and applying various statistical methods, valuable insights into the relationship between cyberattacks and the power consumption of IoT devices are offered.

Future research can build on these findings by exploring other potential indicators of cyberattacks in smart home devices, such as irregularities in battery usage patterns or data transmission rates. In addition, researchers can develop more sophisticated anomaly detection algorithms and techniques to minimize false alarms and adapt to evolving smart home devices and their power consumption patterns.

Moreover, to strengthen the study's findings, further studies should address the mentioned limitations and consider real-world testing with a more diverse sample of devices. Also expanding the discussion on potential countermeasures would contribute to the overall impact of the research.

Another possible consideration for the future would be to explore the integration of power consumption analysis with other security mechanisms to create a comprehensive defense framework for IoT devices.

In conclusion, this study illuminates the potential of using power consumption analysis as an extra layer of security in smart homes. By refining and expanding these techniques, this study can contribute to a more secure and resilient smart home ecosystem.

References

1. Lara, A., Mayor, V., Estepa, R., Estepa, A., Díaz-Verdejo, J.E.: Smart home anomaly-based IDS: architecture proposal and case study. Internet of Things (2023)
2. Coleman, K.: Arson by Cyberattack. Fire Engineering. https://www.fireengineering.com/app aratus-equipment/arson-by-cyber-attack/. Accessed 9 May 2023
3. Wendzel, S.: How to Increase the Security of Smart Buildings. Communications of the ACM (CACM) 59/5:47–49. ACM (2016). https://doi.org/10.1145/2828636
4. Wendzel, S., Tonejc, J., Kaur, J., Kobekova, A.: Cyber security of smart buildings. In: Song, H., Fink, G., Jeschke, S. (eds.) Security and privacy in cyber-physical systems: foundations and applications. pp. 327–352. Wiley-IEEE Press (2017)
5. Zhao, Z., et al.: Robust anomaly detection on unreliable data. In: DSN 2019 - 49th IEEE/IFIP International Conference on Dependable Systems and Networks, Portland, Oregon, United States (2019)
6. Zhou, Y., Liu, Y., Hu, S.: Smart home cyberattack detection framework for sponsor incentive attacks. IEEE Trans. Smart Grid 10(2), 1916–1927 (2019)
7. Sajeev, A., Rajamani, H.-S.: Cyber-attacks on smart home energy management systems under aggregators. In: 2020 International Conference on Communications, Computing, Cybersecurity, and Informatics (CCCI), pp. 1–5, Sharjah, United Arab Emirates (2020)
8. Bobrovnikova, K., Lysenko, S., Popov, P., Denysiuk, D., Goroshko, A.: Technique for IoT cyberattacks detection based on the energy consumption analysis. In: Proceedings of IntelIT-SIS'2021: 2nd International Workshop on Intelligent Information Technologies and Systems of Information Security. Khmelnytskyi, Ukraine (2021)
9. Tushir, B., Dalal, Y., Dezfouli, B., Liu, Y.: A quantitative study of DDoS and E-DDoS Attacks on WiFi smart home devices. IEEE IoT J. (2020)
10. Azmoodeh, A., Dehghantanha, A., Conti, M., Choo, K.-K.R.: Detecting crypto-ransomware in IoT networks based on energy consumption footprint. J. Ambient. Intell. Humaniz. Comput. 9, 1141–1152 (2018)

11. Fasano, F., Martinelli, F., Mercaldo, F., Santone, A.: Energy consumption metrics for mobile device dynamic malware detection. Procedia Comput. Sci. **159**, 1045–1052 (2019)
12. Hernandez Jimenez, J., Goseva-Popstojanova, K.: Malware detection using power consumption and network traffic data. In: International Conference on Data Intelligence and Security Conference, West Virginia University Morgantown (2019)
13. Caviglione, L., Gaggero, M., Lalande, J.-F., Mazurczyk, W., Urbanski, M.: Seeing the unseen: revealing mobile malware hidden communications via energy consumption and artificial intelligence. IEEE Trans. Inf. Forensics Secur. **11**(4), 799–810 (2016)
14. Shi, Y., Li, F., Song, W., Li, X.-Y., Ye, J.: Energy audition based cyber-physical attack detection system in IoT. In: ACM Turing Celebration Conference - China (ACM TURC 2019), May 17–19 China (2019)
15. Lim, J.Y., Tan, W.N., Tan, Y.F.: Anomalous energy consumption detection using a Naïve Bayes approach, F1000 Research, Multimedia University Malaysia (2022)
16. Mottola, L., Hameed, A., Voigt, T.: Energy Attacks in the Battery-less Internet of Things. Uppsala University, Sweden (2023)
17. Pathak, A. K., Saguna, S., Mitra, K., Åhlund, C.: Anomaly detection using machine learning to discover sensor tampering in IoT systems. In: ICC 2021 - IEEE International Conference on Communications, Montreal, QC, pp. 1–6, Canada (2021)
18. Chatterjee, A., Ahmed, B.S.: IoT anomaly detection methods and applications: a survey. Internet of Things **19**, 100568 (2022)
19. TP-Link WLAN-Steckdosen - Tapo P110 – Spezifikationen. https://www.tp-link.com/de/home-networking/smart-plug/tapo-p110/#specifications. Accessed 13 Jun 2023
20. Datasheet Raspberry Pi 4. https://datasheets.raspberrypi.com/rpi4/raspberry-pi-4-datasheet.pdf. Accessed 10 May 2023
21. Node-RED Documentation. https://nodered.org/docs/. Accessed 24 May 2023
22. Canon MAXIFY GX7050 Technische Daten. https://www.canon.de/printers/maxify-gx7050/specifications/. Accessed 7 Jun 2023
23. Technische Daten Google Nest Mini. https://store.google.com/de/product/google_nest_mini_specs?hl=de. Accessed 07 Jun 2023
24. Produktseite Amazon Alexa Echo Dot Gen 4. https://www.amazon.de/der-neue-echo-dot-4-generation-smarter-lautsprecher-mit-alexa-blau/dp/B084J4QQFT/ref=sr_1_1?. Accessed 13 Jun 2023
25. HomePod Mini Technische Daten. https://www.apple.com/de/homepod-mini/specs/. Accessed 07 Jun 2023
26. Netatmo Smarte Wetterstation. https://www.netatmo.com/de-de/smart-weather-station. Accessed 07 Jun 2023
27. Bosch Smart Home Controller Technische Daten. https://www.bosch-smarthome.com/de/de/produkte/vorgaengermodelle/controller/. Accessed 07 Jun 2023
28. Produktseite Philips Hue Bridge. https://www.philips-hue.com/de-de/p/hue-hue-bridge/8719514342620#overview. Accessed 13 Jun 2023
29. Netatmo Smart Outdoor Camera With Siren Technische Daten. https://www.netatmo.com/de-de/smart-outdoor-camera-with-siren. Accessed 07 Jun 2023
30. Homematic-IP Produktdatenblatt Access Point. https://homematic-ip.com/sites/default/files/downloads/hmip-hap_140887A0_produktdatenblatt.pdf. Accessed 07 Jun 2023
31. Netatmo Smart Radiator Valves Technische Daten. https://www.netatmo.com/de-de/smart-radiator-valves. Accessed 07 Jun 2023
32. Xenofontos, C., Zografopoulos, I., Konstantinou, C., Jolfaei, A., Khan, M. Choo, K.-K. R.: Consumer, commercial, and industrial IoT (In) security: attack taxonomy and case studies. IEEE Internet Things J. **9**(1), 199–221 (2022)
33. Hoque, N., Bhuyan, M.H., Baishya, R.C., Bhattacharyya, D.K., Kalita, J.K.: Network attacks: Taxonomy, tools and systems. J. Network Comput. Appl. **36**(2), 611–615 (2013)

34. Krishna, R.R., Priyadarshini, A., Jha, A.V., Appasani, B., Srinivasulu, A., Bizon, N.: State-of-the-art review on IoT threats and attacks: taxonomy, challenges and solutions. Sustainability **13**(16), 9463 (2021)
35. Chaganti, R., Bhushan, B., Ravi, V.: A survey on Blockchain solutions in DDoS attacks mitigation: techniques, open challenges and future directions. Comput. Commun. **197**, 96–112 (2023)
36. Singleton, C., et al.: X_Force Threat Intelligence Index 2022. IBM Security (2022)
37. hping3(8) – Linux man page. https://linux.die.net/man/8/hping3. Accessed 16 Jun 2023
38. Sivanathan, A., et al.: Classifying IoT devices in smart environments using network traffic characteristics. IEEE Trans. Mob. Comput. **18**(8), 1745–1759 (2019)

Management Strategies for an EP Device in an Energy Packet Grid

Marcel Weßbecher[1]($\boxtimes$) (iD), Jasper Marianczuk[1], Friedrich Wiegel[1] (iD),
Sophie Xing An[1] (iD), Klemens Schneider[3], Dominik Schulz[2] (iD),
Martina Zitterbart[3] (iD), Marc Hiller[2] (iD), and Veit Hagenmeyer[1] (iD)

[1] Institute for Automation and Applied Informatics (IAI),
Karlsruhe Institute of Technology (KIT), Karlsruhe, Germany
{marcel.wessbecher,friedrich.wiegel,sophie.an,veit.hagenmeyer}@kit.edu
[2] Institute of Electrical Engineering (ETI), Karlsruhe Institute of Technology (KIT),
Karlsruhe, Germany
{dominik.schulz,marc.hiller}@kit.edu
[3] Institute of Telematics (TM), Karlsruhe Institute of Technology (KIT),
Karlsruhe, Germany
{klemens.schneider,martina.zitterbart}@kit.edu

Abstract. The increasing use of renewable energy sources, which are predominantly based on power electronics, and the increasing demand for electricity due to the electrification of the transportation and heating sectors have brought new challenges to traditional power grids. In order to address these challenges, the so called Energy Packet Grid (EP Grid) proposes a novel operating scheme for the power grid that focuses on the control of the power electronic components of the grid and considers the limitations of the grid equipment and power lines. The present article specifically deals with the management of a single Energy Packet Device (EP device) as an active participant within this grid structure. It outlines the challenges associated with managing an EP device and presents three employable control strategies: Three-Step Switching Controller, Probabilistic Range Control, Packetized Energy Management. A simulation environment is created to evaluate the effectiveness of these control strategies. The results of the simulations compare the impact of the different strategies on the operation of EP devices. The primary contribution of this article is the proposal of management strategies for EP devices, highlighting the challenges involved and suggesting solutions to mitigate uncertainty in EP device management.

Keywords: Energy Packet Grid · EP Device Management Strategies · Smart grid · Simulations and Modeling

1 Introduction

With an increasing share of renewable energy sources, the supply side of power grids becomes more decentralized and more power converter-based. This transformation poses new challenges because the power grid was originally designed

B. N. Jørgensen et al. (Eds.): EI.A 2023, LNCS 14468, pp. 240–256, 2024.
https://doi.org/10.1007/978-3-031-48652-4_16

as a top-down architecture with few conventional large power plants based on rotating machines. One major drawback of renewable energy sources is their volatility and an thus their reduced predictability. Therefore flexible loads and storages are needed to match the demand to the actual supply. All these novelties drastically increase the complexity of grid management and control. Moreover, both the topology of the installed power lines and the grid equipment are not designed for massive distributed generation [1,2]. At the same time, there is an increasing energy and power demand because of the electrification of the mobility sector and the heating sector [3].

Also, today's grid control technique with its different levels of control is suited to the physical characteristics of generation systems based on rotating machines, such as primary control and secondary control. Since these characteristics do not necessarily have to be present in power converter dominated systems, it is necessary to adapt the control system to the new conditions. This task is also becoming more dynamic and complex due to the increasing number of measurement data, possible control signals and their communication.

One group of approaches to tackle this challenges are hierarchical control approaches based on decentralized and autonomous control of participants, which then can be aggregated for higher control layers, like in microgrids [4,5] multi-microgrids [6], web of cells and fractal grids [7]. One point where these control approaches do not offer a clear solution is scalability, especially together with management of shared and limited resources like lines and transformers.

Another upcoming approach is motivated by communication networks. Like packet switching helped to overcome similar challenges in such networks, the approach proposes energy packets for the power grid as discrete power flows for a simpler and non-continuous control and management. It was first introduced in [8] and discussed in particular in [9–12]. In these first works, there is no control over the transmitted power, because energy packet transfers are realized by interconnecting capacitors charged with DC voltage requiring an exclusive line usage between the participants.

Since then several approaches were proposed which can be classified as energy packet concepts dependent on the used definition or at least share similarities with the concept. One of those concepts is the so called "Energy Internet" and related designs [12–19]. Beside many similarities to the energy packet concept, like the existence of energy routers, they do not necessarily employ discrete energy packets or use them only partially on a higher system level.

A recently published concept is packetized energy management [20–23] which was applied to thermostats, batteries and electric vehicle charging. It uses a central coordinator that authorizes participants to draw or withdraw an energy packet with a discrete power during a discrete time step. The works show the advantage of efficient grid resource utilization, but do not involve energy routers.

The Energy Packet Grid (EP grid) proposed in [24,25] presents an alternative approach that provides a quantized power flow that takes into account the limitations of grid equipment and lines during power transmission. An Energy Packet (EP) in this concept is a quantized power flow between two pre-negotiated EP devices which exchange a certain amount of energy. The EP device as a key element proposed in [24] and developed in [25] is a power converter combined with a battery storage system as well as control and communication equipment. They are the participants of the EP grid and interconnect either multiple cells of the EP grid or an EP grid cell with a traditional grid. Within each EP cell, a line manager (LM) is involved in the negotiation phase of every EP transfer. The LM evaluates the grid state resulting from the requested transfer and dependent on transmission line constraints and voltage constraints denies or accepts each transfer. For the participants in an EP grid, this means that they can never draw or feed in power without finding a partner for the EP transfer and without the permission of the line manager.

The present article builds on the work described in [24,25] and discusses the challenges of managing an EP device and proposes two potential management strategies as a main contribution. The proposed strategies are also compared with a corresponding strategy from related work by [22,23]. In addition, the approaches to identify the causes that reduce the success rate and reliability of EP device management are developed. The results highlight the need to reduce uncertainty in EP device management, which will be instrumental in improving the success rate. The selection of parameters for the energy packets themselves as well as safety margins for protection devices are also mentioned as key aspects to improve the success rate. As a conclusion, we suggest the integration of forecasting into EP device management as a possible solution to reduce uncertainty. Another possible approach is to make loads and generators, especially those with higher power, interruptible or controllable.

The remainder of the article is organized as follows: Sect. 2 introduces the task of EP device management. Section 3 proposes three control strategies for EP device management. Section 4 describes the implemented simulation environment. Section 5 defines the simulation setup. Section 6 shows the simulation results of the different control strategies. Section 7 compares the results of the control strategies and Sect. 8 concludes the paper.

2   EP Device Management

Conventional loads and generators, or any form of aggregation like a complete household are connected to the EP grid via EP devices. Figure 1 shows a schematic of the power flows in such a household with an EP device. One interface of the power converter of the EP device connects to the EP grid for the exchange of energy packets with the grid. The other interface operates as a grid-forming inverter (GFM), which provides the local AC grid for the household. Since in the context of households, AC connected batteries may already exist in a household and commercial products at least are available, this work considers the battery being connected to the local AC grid instead of being connected directly to the power converter of the EP device. This creates a balance point of loads, generators, battery and power converter, with the last two logically forming the EP device. This balance point in most cases will have to be actively balanced by either the battery, the inverter or a combination of both.

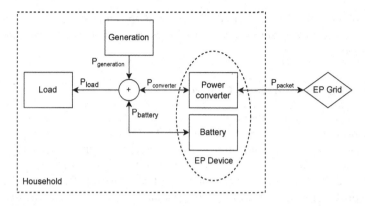

Fig. 1. Generalized overview of power flows in an EP grid household. [24]

In such a case, both sides are affected by a number of physical constraints, so finding an appropriate operating strategy to keep the balance point neutral becomes an a major task, which is the essential part of EP device management. In a traditional grid, the power converter could always supply or feed in needed power within its power limits. But as the EP device and so the power converter is a participant in the EP grid, this gets more complicated. Energy packets need to be requested and can get denied. Thus the EP device can not rely on instantaneous power from the public grid. This means the battery always has to be in a state where it can fullfill the power demand of the local AC grid for a short time in case a packet request gets denied. Otherwise reliable supply can not be guaranteed or components may be damaged. The main task of the EP device management therefore is battery management:

Assume an energy packet is send into the EP grid and the battery is supplying the local grid at its maximum power. In that case, there is no battery power left over to supply additional loads in the household and the power converter is tied to the negotiated transfer. A load increase would lead to an undersupply of the local AC grid with consequences on the voltage and stability issues. Considering non-curtailable generation, this situation also exists the other way round if the generation at the balance point exceeds maximum battery charging power and the power converter is tied to a packet transfer or packet request is denied.

3   Control Strategies and Guard Schemes

Three empirically derived control strategies for EP device management are implemented and compared in the following. As an intuitive approach, Three-Step Switching Controller is used to gain first results. Packetized Energy Management (PEM) is a strategy from related work [22, 23] which faces similar challenges under slightly different constraints. Probabilistic Range Control (PRC) is a modified version of PEM that uses linear functions and omits the state machine to reduce the complexity. At the end of the chapter guard schemes are proposed that can be evaluated in addition to each strategy and are allowed to override the strategy decision under certain conditions, e.g. when hardware constraints are exceeded.

3.1 Three-Step Switching Controller

The first strategy is a Three-Step Switching Controller based on the state of charge (SoC). If SoC is above an upper limit u, a request of sending an EP is made. If SoC is below a lower limit l, a request of receiving an EP is made. This behavior can be described by two probability functions $P_R(x_b)$ for request to receive (cf. Eq. (1)) and $P_S(x_b)$ for request to send (cf. Eq. (2)) an EP. The resulting probability distribution for $l = 0.3$ and $u = 0.9$ is shown in Fig. 2.

$$P_R(SoC) = \begin{cases} 1 & , SoC \leq l \\ 0 & , SoC > l \end{cases} \tag{1}$$

$$P_S(SoC) = \begin{cases} 1 & , SoC \geq u \\ 0 & , SoC < u \end{cases} \tag{2}$$

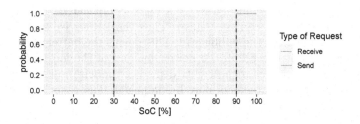

Fig. 2. Three-Step Switching Controller probability curve

3.2 Probabilistic Range Control (PRC)

Probabilistic range control (PRC) adds a desired SoC parameter SOC_{target} which has to be in the interval introduced by the two limits. Between the lower limit l and SOC_{target}, the probability making a request for the receipt of an energy packet linearly decreases from 100% to 0%, like shown in Eq. 3. Between SOC_{target} and the upper limit u, the probability making a request for sending an EP linearly increases from 0% to 100%, like shown in Eq. 4. Figure 3 shows the probability curves for the two request types for an exemplary configuration of $l = 0.4, u = 1, SOC_{target} = 0.8$. PRC can be modified by two extensions: estimation approach (EST) and direction awareness (DIR).

The **estimation approach (EST)** uses the actual SoC and the actual power of the battery to calculate an SoC estimation $SoC_{estimate}$. $SoC_{estimate}$ is the SoC the battery would have at the next strategy decision, assuming constant power of the battery until then. In the decision making of PRC with EST, $SoC_{estimate}$ is used as parameter for the probability functions instead of SoC.

Direction awareness (DIR) which is evaluated after the PRC decision. It cancels a request if the actual power of the battery exceeds a relative threshold compared to the power of the EP transfer that would be requested by PRC. This relies on the assumption that in this situation, the same result as with the packet transfer will be achieved by the actual power of the battery.

$$P_R(SoC) = \begin{cases} 1 & , SoC \leq l \\ \frac{SoC_{target} - SoC}{SoC_{target} - l} & , l < SoC < SoC_{target} \\ 0 & , SoC \geq SoC_{target} \end{cases} \quad (3)$$

$$P_S(SoC) = \begin{cases} 0 & , SoC \leq SoC_{target} \\ \frac{SoC_{target} - SoC}{SoC_{target} - l} & , SoC_{target} < SoC < u \\ 1 & , SoC \geq u \end{cases} \quad (4)$$

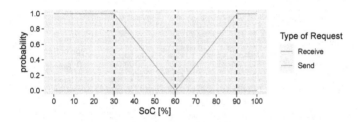

Fig. 3. Probabilistic Range Control (PRC) probability curve

3.3 Packetized Energy Management (PEM)

The third strategy is the Packetized Energy management (PEM) approach for energy storage systems of Almassalkhi et al. [22]. The approach consists of a state machine where each state is associated with two probability functions, similar the probability functions shown before. However in PEM, probability curves are exponential. The general function $P_{R,S}$ is shown by Eq. (5). Depending on request to receive or request to send different functions $\mu_R(SoC)$ and $\mu_S(SoC)$ are used to calculate the individual probability, cf. Eq. (6) and cf. Eq. (7). Between the different states, the parameter M_i of the functions varies to achieve a steeper or flatter curve. States are changed in dependency on the acceptance of the previous request. If a requested is accepted, the strategy assumes that the grid is not fully utilized and switches to a state with functions of steeper probability functions. If a request is denied, the strategy assumes high grid load and switches to a state with flatter probability functions. With this behaviour, the PEM approach tries to adapt the request rate to the actual grid utilization. Like the exemplary probability distribution in Fig. 4 shows, in PEM, the strategy could decide to simultaneously request sending and receiving a packet. As mentioned in [22], this case is ignored and does not result in sending two EP requests because the resulting transfers would cancel each other out.

$$P_{\{R,S\}_i} = 1 - e^{-\mu_{\{R,S\}}(SoC)\delta_c} \tag{5}$$

$$\mu_R(SoC) = \begin{cases} 0 & , SoC \leq l \\ \frac{u-SoC}{SoC-l} \cdot \frac{SoC_{target}-l}{u-SoC_{target}} \cdot M_i & , l < SoC < u \\ \infty & , SoC \geq u \end{cases} \tag{6}$$

$$\mu_S(SoC) = \begin{cases} \infty & , SoC \leq l \\ \frac{SoC-l}{u-SoC} \cdot \frac{u-SoC_{target}}{SoC_{target}-l} \cdot M_i, & l < SoC < u \\ 0 & , SoC \geq u \end{cases} \tag{7}$$

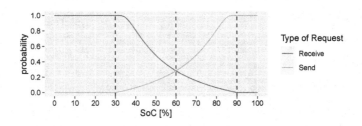

Fig. 4. Exemplary probability curve of Packetized Energy Management (PEM) [22]

3.4   Guard Schemes

In addition to the three strategies shown above, we design guard schemes that try to prevent the EP device management from a bad decision mainly in terms of exceeding hardware limitations. The guards are evaluated after a strategy's decision and have the ability to override them. Whenever a strategy decides to send an EP request, each of the guards has to be fullfilled or otherwise no request will be sent. We implement the battery capacity guard, the battery power guard and the oscillation guard. Requests are canceled by the battery power guard if the actual power situation exceeds the maximum charge or discharge power of the battery. The battery capacity guard cancels requests if the EP transfer based on the actual power situation would lead to exceeding SoC limitations assuming a non-changing power situation. Note that this is not a reliable protection measure because it is evaluated when the decision is made and the power situation can change afterwards, but it prevents the EP device management from requesting transfers that are not feasible at the moment of decision making. Changing power situations are also the reason why both of these guards can be configured with a margin to leave some headroom for fluctuation. The oscillation guard prevents the EP device management from requesting the receipt of an EP if the previous decision was a request to send an EP, or vice versa. Such opposite actions in two consecutive decisions are considered unnecessary and oscillating transfers, because they would not have an impact on the SoC of the battery as the energy sum is zero.

4 Simulation Environment

A simulation environment is implemented to evaluate the different strategies. Algorithm 1 shows the overall simulation process. As inputs there are aggregated load power $P_{load}[t]$ and aggregated generation power $P_{generation}[t]$ for each time step t, and the constant power of each energy packet P_{packet}. For each time step, the simulation calculates the charging power of the battery $P_{battery}$ based on the power of the load, the generation and the converter. If necessary, the generation gets curtailed to reduce charging power. Afterwards, the SoC of the battery gets updated based on the charging power. The discrete-time battery model is a simplified version of the battery model from [22]. It includes standby losses and charging efficiency as well as discharge efficiency. It does not include battery degradation, temperature-specific and SoC-specific behavior. Every k-th time step, the EP device management decides whether an EP should be requested or not and whether it should be received or sent. For that, the decision function shown in Algorithm 2 is called. It calculates a control strategy's decision and afterwards evaluates the guards. At the end, there is a randomized acceptance of the request to model the request acceptance of the Line Manager. If a request is made, not prevented by the guards and gets accepted by the Line Manager, the decision function returns the power of the EP P_{packet} with the correct sign depending on sending or receiving. This value is stored as setpoint of the power converter $P_{converter}$ in the simulation process. Although the decision is only based on the actual power of a single time step, the EP is send over k time steps because the converter power $P_{converter}$ is not modified in the following time steps. Thus, the strategy's decision has an impact on the following $k - 1$ time steps. This provides a fluctuating load and fluctuating generation behavior to the simulation, because those power values change every time step and therefore may lead to an exceeding limit which a strategy should avoid. Without the modeled fluctuation ($k = 1$), a strategy can perfectly adapt to the given power data which in a real world scenario would mean that load power and generation power is constant for the duration of an EP transfer or would be exactly known beforehand. This might be the case when a very short duration for time steps is considered.

Algorithm 1. Simulate

1: **for** $t \in [0, N]$ **do**
2:    **if** $t \bmod k = 0$ **then**
3:       $P_{converter} \leftarrow \text{decision}(SoC, P_{load}[t] - P_{generation}[t], P_{packet})$
4:    **end if**
5:    $P_{battery} \leftarrow P_{load}[t] - P_{generation}[t] + P_{converter}$
6:    **if** $P_{battery} < -P_{battery\_max}$ **then**
7:       $P_{generation}[t] \leftarrow P_{generation}[t] - P_{battery\_max} + P_{battery}$
8:       **if** $P_{generation}[t] < 0$ **then**
9:          $P_{generation}[t] \leftarrow 0$
10:      **end if**
11:      $P_{battery} \leftarrow P_{load}[t] - P_{generation}[t] + P_{converter}$
12:   **end if**
13:   battery.updateSoC($P_{battery}$)
14:   **if** !battery.checkLimits() **then**
15:      fail()
16:   **end if**
17: **end for**

5   Simulation Setup

For the evaluation, data profiles from the Open Power System Data project [26] are used. This data set provides measured time series data for many small enterprises and residential houses that are valuable in modeling household or low-voltage power systems. The data contains solar power generation as well as energy consumption (load) down to the level of a single unit. Specifically, we used the time series for the Residential 1 household (R1) and for the Residential 4 household (R4). For both, data are used for the duration of one year from 2015-12-11 19:00:00 to 2016-12-11 18:59:00 with a time resolution of one minute. We set the interval of strategy decisions to 5 min which corresponds to $k = 5$. The modeled battery has a capacity of 12 kWh and a nominal power of 12 kW. Simulation runs with different batteries show comparable results relative to their capacity. As constant EP sizes for individual simulation runs, we choose 0.05 kWh to 1.4 kWh in increments of 0.05 kWh. In comparison, the average energy consumption per control interval in data set R1 is 0.059 kWh. The upper limit for the EP size corresponds to a power during the control interval of 16.8 kW comparing well to the 16.4 kW maximum grid feed in of the R4 data set. The set of transfer grant probabilities simulating the Line Manager decision is chosen to $\gamma \in \{0.1, 0.2, 0.3, 0.4, 0.5, 0.6, 0.7, 0.8, 0.9, 0.99\}$. For the same set of simulation parameters the individual probability decision at each control step is the same for each strategy so that results are comparable. The lower margin of the battery capacity guard is set to 0.7 kWh and the upper margin to 11.5 kWh. This is an adaption on the used data sets where in a single control step without packet transfers the maximum energy discharged is 0.7 kWh and the maximum energy charged is 0.5 kWh. As a result, at each control step, the made decision will always lead to an assumed upcoming SoC that provides enough stored

---

Algorithm 2. Decision($SoC, power, P_{packet}$)

1: $requestType \leftarrow$ strategyDecsion($SoC, power, P_{packet}$)
2: **if** $requestType = $ NONE **then**
3:     **return** 0
4: **end if**
5: **if** !checkGuardsValid($requestType, SoC, power, P_{packet}$) **then**
6:     **return** 0
7: **end if**
8: **if** !checkTransferGranted() **then**
9:     **return** 0
10: **end if**
11: **if** $requestType = $ SEND **then**
12:     **return** $+P_{packet}$
13: **else**
14:     **return** $-P_{packet}$
15: **end if**

---

energy and free storage capacity to successfully pass the following control step even without a EP transfer. Note that this only tries but can not guarantee the SoC to be within this limit because strategy and guards only know the momentanous power situation at the moment of decision making. The receive power guard safety margin is set to 0 which allows to use the complete available charging power of the battery (12 kW) within the guard. With EP power less than the maximum charge power of the battery, this is always a suitable choice. The packet transfer itself does not exceed maximum charge power in that case and any generation leading to a charge power beyond the limit is curtailed by the simulation at every time step. So there is no need to leave additional headroom by choosing receive power guard safety margin greater than zero.

Choosing a send power guard safety margin is more complicated. The obvious limit would be the maximum discharge power of the battery. But assuming a situation where a strategy fully uses this power, any load increase during the control interval will lead to a failure of the simulation. In contrast to generation, the loads are modeled as uncontrollable and can not be curtailed which makes this scenario very likely to happen. Therefore it can be helpful to choose a send power guard safety margin greater than zero to only plan with some amount of battery discharge power and leaving headroom for changing load behavior.

Figure 5 shows an aggregated evaluation of all simulation runs with the described set of parameters in dependency of the send power guard safety margin. We can see that the success rate of the simulation increases with increasing margin. Accordingly, the fail rate due to exceeded discharge power decreases and the number of triggered send power guards during simulation increases. The figure shows that a margin above 9 kW will not increase the success rate because the fail rate due to exceeded discharge power is zero at this point. For the following evaluation, we thus set the send power guard safety margin to 9 kW leading to an allowed charge power within the guard scheme of only 3 kW.

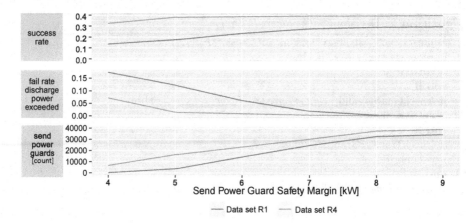

Fig. 5. Combined simulation results of the strategies for different send power guard margins and data sets.

6 Evaluation

In the following, the different strategies are compared based on their success rate, total received energy and total wasted energy. Figure 6 shows the results for data set R1 and Fig. 7 for data set R4. The boxplots of total received energy show the energy that the power converter of a household has received via energy packets in each simulation run with the different parameters. Beside the local generation this is the only supply of the household. The blue dashed line visualizes the energy consumption of the household with preferred usage of the battery and local generation. This is the energy, the households needs from the grid in a traditional grid environment. In the context of EP device management, the received energy is desired to be as close to this baseline as possible. Any additional energy received above the storage capacity (12 kWh) is not consumed and can not be stored. This energy at some point in the simulation had to be fed back to the EP grid and is an indicator for unnecessary transfers. The wasted energy metric combines the surplus energy of unnecessary transfers and the unused energy by curtailed generation. Both of these two effects are undesired behavior and strategies with less wasted energy are preferred. Note that generation sometimes has to be curtailed because the transfer grant probability denies sending an EP and therefore zero wasted energy is not achievable with every simulation configuration. For both data sets, the ranking of the strategies in terms of success rate stays the same with PEM providing the best result, and the variants of PRC being very close. Only the Three-Step Switching Controller provides significantly worse results. In terms of wasted energy, no strategy clearly outperforms the others.

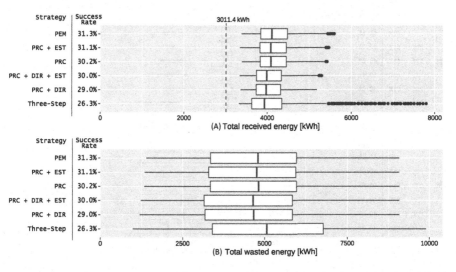

Fig. 6. Boxplot visualization of total received energy (A) and wasted energy (B) for simulation runs with different strategies and different simulation parameters based on R1 data set. The blue dashed line signalizes the possible minimum of received energy. (Color figure online)

Figure 8 shows the simulation results of the different strategies with different packet sizes when using the R1 data set. Sent energy is the energy that the power converter of the household sent into the EP grid. Curtailed energy is the energy of the generation that is not used because of curtailment. The effect that less energy can be sent into the grid if generation is curtailed can be seen clearly in the mirrored course of the two curves. The wasted energy metric shows the same behavior as curtailed energy with an offset. This offset can be assigned to unnecessary transfers where energy was received but had to be sent back to the grid at a later point. To reduce unnecessary transfers and especially to curtail as less generation as possible, a EP size between 0.4 kWh and 0.5 kWh should be used based on the modeled battery. This translates to a 40%–50% saturation of the batteries possible charging power. On the other hand, the success rate and received energy show better values with increasing packet size. However, both curves, especially received energy, flatten towards the end. This makes the proposed packet size a suitable compromise between wasted energy and success rate.

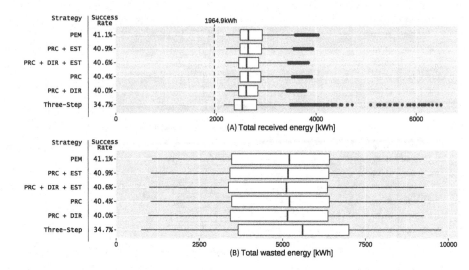

Fig. 7. Boxplot visualization of total received energy (A) and wasted energy (B) for simulation runs with different strategies and different simulation parameters based on R4 data set. The blue dashed line signalizes the possible minimum of received energy. (Color figure online)

7   Discussion

According to the results of the evaluation, it can be concluded that battery power and the send power guards are critical for the success of the strategy. The send power guard prevents the strategy from exceeding the discharge power limit of the battery when a packet shall be sent. The margin is used to deal with power fluctuations during the control interval which of course are not known at the beginning of the interval when packet decision is made. Power fluctuations leading to an increase in discharge power are increasing load power, decreasing generation power and the combination of both. This shows that in contrast to the other parameters that mainly depend on battery properties, the send power margin strongly depends on the data set. The margin of the send power guard for the evaluation is set to 9 kW based on experimental results of R1. This matches quite well with the data set for which during a control interval maximum increase of load power is 7.44 kW, maximum decrease in generation power is 9.6 kW and maximum increase in power demand (sum of load and generation) is 10.38 kW. The fact that a margin of 9 kW is already enough to prevent failures, even if there is maximum fluctuation as high as 10.38 kW, shows that the strategies made the right decision at these control intervals even without the send power guard. Overall the evaluation shows the high impact of the send power guard, but with the margin being an adaption on the data set, it shows that in a real world scenario, the margin should be chosen individually for each household and can not be defined generally.

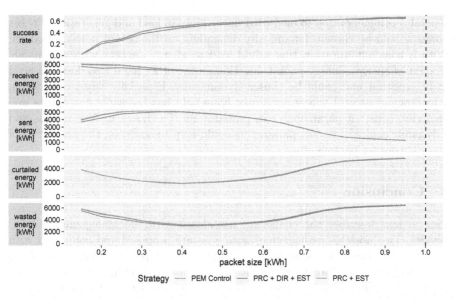

Fig. 8. Combined simulation results for different packet sizes based on R1 data set.

Based on the evaluation, there is no clear strategy to choose for EP device management. PEM and PRC + EST show similar results for the given data set. Without the EST extension, PRC performs worse, which shows that EST is a good extension. This rises the question whether PEM could also benefit from EST. In the simulation, each run uses a constant transfer grant probability. PEM is designed to adapt to grid utilization based on transfer grant decisions. This means it may show better results than PRC, if the transfer grant probability varies during the simulation run, which would also happen in real world. Overall, the success rates of the strategies are not satisfying enough for EP device management because without further measures every strategy with less than 100% success rate would lead to partial power failures in the according household. At this point further analysis of the results and more testing is needed. The evaluation aggregates the results of all simulation runs for the complete set of simulation parameters. Thus bad results due to bad parameter setup, e.g. packet energy, are integrated in the overall results. Also harsh scenarios like low transfer grant probabilities are integrated in the results although it is unclear whether these occur in the real world. This especially includes simulations runs with 10% transfer grant probability where no strategy and parameter set achieved a successful run.

With the constant duration of energy packets in the evaluation and a constant packet energy during each simulation run, the evaluation suggests an EP size leading to a utilization of about half of the batteries maximum power. Whether this is a suitable choice in general or just a fit for the evaluated parameter and data set needs further investigation. It could be possible that it applies as a general recommendation to deal with uncertainty in load and generation. Packet power should be chosen dynamically depending on the actual power situation. With a constant duration this would lead to energy packets with a dynamic amount of energy. Energy packet duration on the other hand also does not need to be constant and could be chosen dynamically. Especially when considering a heterogeneous grid where not every household has the same generators and batteries, constant parameters can probably not be chosen to fit everyone and a dynamic choice of packet parameters could help to adapt on the properties of two EP transfer partners.

8   Conclusion

This article describes the challenges associated with the management of EP devices. Two possible management strategies are proposed and compared with the strategy in the related work by [22]. Approaches that contribute to reducing uncertainty are likely to improve the success rate. Therefore, several methods are possible. One is to integrate forecasting into the EP device management. Another one is making loads and generators, especially the ones with higher power, interruptable or controllable. A major point to improve success rate is the parameter choice regarding the energy packets themselves and also safety margins for guards. The presented results show the trade off between wasted energy and success rate regarding the packet size. A suggestion for packets size dependent on battery power and capacity is given, but is strongly based on the simulation setup where packet size is the only choosable packet parameter. A more freely parameter choice where packet power, packet duration and packet size can be choosen independently from each other and also dynamically during runtime should improve the results, but will need a more complex simulation environment. Free choice of parameter will also help to find suitable parameters that fit for all EP devices in a grid with heterogeneous distribution of loads, generators and batteries.

Acknowledgment. This work was supported by the Helmholtz Association under the program "Energy System Design".

References

1. Coster, E.J., Myrzik, J.M.A., Kruimer, B., Kling, W.L.: Integration issues of distributed generation in distribution grids. Proc. IEEE **99**, 28–39 (2011)
2. Lopes, J.P., Hatziargyriou, N., Mutale, J., Djapic, P., Jenkins, N.: Integrating distributed generation into electric power systems: a review of drivers, challenges and opportunities. Electr. Power Syst. Res. **77**, 1189–1203 (2007)
3. Gupta, R., et al.: Spatial analysis of distribution grid capacity and costs to enable massive deployment of PV, electric mobility and electric heating. Appl. Energy **287**, 116504 (2021)

4. Hatziargyriou, N. (ed.): Microgrids: Architectures and Control. Wiley, IEEE Press, Chichester, West Sussex (2014). http://ieeexplore.ieee.org/servlet/opac? bknumber=6685216
5. Liserre, M., et al.: The smart transformer: impact on the electric grid and technology challenges. IEEE Ind. Electron. Mag. 10, 46–58 (2016)
6. Kampezidou, S., Vasios, O., Meliopoulos, S. Multi-microgrid architecture: optimal operation and control. In: 2018 North American Power Symposium (NAPS), pp. 1–5. IEEE (2018)
7. Kariniotakis, G., Martini, L., Caerts, C., Brunner, H., Retiere, N.: Challenges, innovative architectures and control strategies for future networks: the web-of-cells, fractal grids and other concepts. CIRED - Open Access Proc. J. 2017, 2149–2152 (2017)
8. Toyoda, J., Saitoh, H.: Proposal of an open-electric-energy-network (OEEN) to realize cooperative operations of IOU and IPP. In: Proceedings of EMPD '98. 1998 International Conference on Energy Management and Power Delivery (Cat. No.98EX137), vol. 1, pp. 218–222 (1998)
9. Rojas-Cessa, R., et al.: An energy packet switch for digital power grids. In: 2018 IEEE International Conference on Internet of Things (iThings) and IEEE Green Computing and Communications (GreenCom) and IEEE Cyber, Physical and Social Computing (CPSCom) and IEEE Smart Data (SmartData), pp. 146–153 (2018)
10. Corzine, K. A. Energy packets enabling the energy internet. In 2014 Clemson University Power Systems Conference, pp. 1–5. IEEE, 11–14 March 2014
11. Takahashi, R., Tashiro, K., Hikihara, T.: Router for power packet distribution network: design and experimental verification. IEEE Trans. Smart Grid 6, 618–626 (2015)
12. Monti, A., De Din, E., Müller, D., Ponci, F., Hagenmeyer, V.: Towards a real digital power system: an energy packet approach. In: 2017 IEEE Conference on Energy Internet and Energy System Integration (EI2), pp. 1–6 (2017)
13. Abe, R., Taoka, H., McQuilkin, D.: Digital grid: communicative electrical grids of the future. IEEE Trans. Smart Grid 2, 399–410 (2011)
14. Keshav, S., Rosenberg, C.: How internet concepts and technologies can help green and smarten the electrical grid. SIGCOMM Comput. Commun. Rev. 41, 109–114 (2011). https://doi.org/10.1145/1925861.1925879
15. He, M.M., et al.: An architecture for local energy generation, distribution, and sharing. In: 2008 IEEE Energy 2030 Conference, pp. 1–6 (2008)
16. Nardelli, P.H.J., et al.: Energy internet via packetized management: enabling technologies and deployment challenges. IEEE Access 7, 16909–16924 (2019)
17. Boroyevich, D., Cvetkovic, I., Burgos, R., Dong, D.: Intergrid: a future electronic energy network? IEEE J. Emerg. Sel. Top. Power Electron. 1, 127–138 (2013)
18. Wang, K., et al.: A survey on energy internet: architecture, approach, and emerging technologies. IEEE Syst. J. 12, 2403–2416 (2018)
19. Kouveliotis-Lysikatos, I., Hatziargyriou, N., Liu, Y., Wu, F.: Towards an internet-like power grid. J. Mod. Power Syst. Clean Energy 10, 1–11 (2022)
20. Zhang, B., Baillieul, J.: A packetized direct load control mechanism for demand side management. In: 2012 IEEE 51st IEEE Conference on Decision and Control (CDC), pp. 3658–3665 (2012)
21. Rezaei, P., Frolik, J., Hines, P.D.H.: Packetized plug-in electric vehicle charge management. IEEE Trans. Smart Grid 5, 642–650 (2014)

22. Almassalkhi, M., et al.: Asynchronous coordination of distributed energy resources with packetized energy management. In: Meyn, S., Samad, T., Hiskens, I., Stoustrup, J. (eds.) Energy Markets and Responsive Grids. The IMA Volumes in Mathematics and Its Applications, vol. 162, pp. 333–361. Springer, New York (2018). https://doi.org/10.1007/978-1-4939-7822-9_14

23. Espinosa, L.A.D., Khurram, A., Almassalkhi, M.: Reference-tracking control policies for packetized coordination of heterogeneous der populations. IEEE Trans. Control Syst. Technol. **29**, 2427–2443 (2021)

24. Schneider, K., et al.: Designing the interplay of energy plane and communication plane in the energy packet grid. In: 2021 IEEE 46th Conference on Local Computer Networks (LCN), pp. 331–334. IEEE (2021)

25. Schulz, D., et al.: Hardware realization of participants in an energy packet-based power grid. In: 2022 IEEE 13th International Symposium on Power Electronics for Distributed Generation Systems (PEDG), pp. 1–6 (2022)

26. Data, O.P.S.: Household data: detailed household load and solar generation in minutely to hourly resolution. https://data.open-power-system-data.org/household_data/

Design of Digital Controllers for Grid-Connected Voltage Source Converter Operating as Voltage or Current Source

Claudionor F. do Nascimento[1,2] (ID), Simone Buso[2] (ID), and Wesley Angelino de Souza[3](✉) (ID)

[1] DEE, Federal University of Sao Carlos - UFSCar, Sao Carlos, SP, Brazil
[2] DEI, University of Padova - UNIPD, Padova, PD, Italy
[3] DAELE, Federal University of Technology - Parana - UTFPR, Cornelio Procopio, PR, Brazil
wesleyangelino@utfpr.edu.br

Abstract. Digital controllers for grid-connected voltage source converters GC-VSC offer a noteworthy alternative to traditional continuous-time control systems. A power grid often comprises inverters, grid- forming and grid- following converters, renewable energy source units, and various local loads. Currently, the design of GC-VSC controllers is subject to restrictions and additional considerations following standards and technical recommendations for their control when operating connected or disconnected from a power grid, mainly to maintain the stability of the control system. In this context, this paper presents the design of the GC-VSC digital controllers, using mainly the concepts of dead- beat control. Thus, the main result of this project is to improve the modeling and control of the single- phase GC-VSC using the digital control method. The relative RMS errors of the GC-VSC current and load voltage are $\epsilon_{i_f} = 3.67~\%$ and $\epsilon_{v_o} = 0.01~\%$, respectively, i.e., the controller showed tracking accuracy. Simulation results using MATLAB/SIMULINK are presented to validate the proposed controllers.

Keywords: Grid-Following · Grid-Forming · Dead-beat controller · Digital control · Voltage source converter

1 Introduction

Industrial, commercial, and residential applications of grid-connected voltage source converters (GC-VSCs) based on power electronics, such as battery energy storage systems (BESSs) and photovoltaic systems (PVs), have increased considerably recently, mainly due to the energy transition and variable renewable energy sources (RESs), with the consequent growing demand for distributed energy resources (DERs) [1–3]. Power systems are constantly changing, mainly due to the application of power electronic converters in the distribution system

© The Author(s), under exclusive license to Springer Nature Switzerland AG 2024
B. N. Jørgensen et al. (Eds.): EI.A 2023, LNCS 14468, pp. 257–273, 2024.
https://doi.org/10.1007/978-3-031-48652-4_17

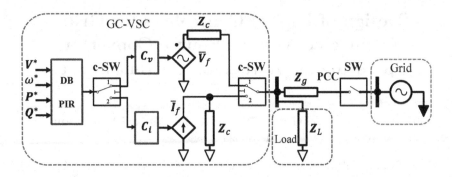

Fig. 1. Basic depiction of single- phase grid with the GC-VSC operation models as GFMVS-VSC or GFLCS-VSC.

[4–6]. GC-VSC in alternating current (AC) grids can be controlled as a grid-forming (GFMVS-VSC) operating in voltage source mode (VS) or grid-following (GFLCS-VSC) operating in current source mode (CS) (Fig. 1) [7–9].

GC-VSC, operating as a GFMVS-VSC, maintains the voltage and frequency at the local load of the power circuit within established limits, in addition to limiting the current within the parameters of the converter [10,11]. Considering the operating mode as GFLCS-VSC, the converter continues feeding the local load, but the grid is responsible for supplying the voltage at the point of common coupling (PCC). In this operation mode, the GC-VSC can inject a current into the grid if there is excess power on the direct current (DC) side [12].

The controllers of the converters have a significant role in order to maintain stability, mitigating power loss, and improving the robustness and dynamic response of the GC-VSC [13,14], considering the purpose of reducing the cost of system implementation [15,16].

Authors of [16] improve the robustness and dynamic response of the voltage source converter (VSC) using a second-order sliding mode control algorithm. This algorithm was applied considering a weak- grid scenario [16].

In [17], the authors presented the control system of a GC-VSC, which enables the enhancement of the stability and resilience of a grid. In [18], a detailed analysis of the operation of grid- connected converters is presented, focusing on GFLCS-VSC, among other configurations. Droop control can be used during the connection to the grid, also allowing the regulation of its output power flow [17,19]. Some researchers use a phase-locked loop (PLL) [20–22] to impose a current through the coupling inductance at PCC, but this issue is not discussed herein.

Authors of [23] present an analysis of the stability of a GC-VSC during transients. The single- loop controller used in this work keeps the amplitude of the supplied voltage within predetermined parameters [23]. However, there is no discussion about the performance of this GC-VSC when there is a need to inject current into the grid.

Currently, there is a growing application of digital controllers [24–26]. Several discretization techniques can be applied to determine the discrete-time model of a GC-VSC [27]. The model definition impacts the digital control system quality.

This paper presents the design of digital controllers applied to a single- phase VSC connected to a local load. Thus, this paper aims to design digital controllers applied in a GC-VSC [10]. The digital control algorithm of the current injected into the grid only starts to operate when the voltage measured at the PCC is equal to the grid voltage with the power switch (SW) closed, which allows the connection of the GC-VSC. The assumptions made throughout this paper are listed as follows:

1. a digital pulse-width modulation (DPWM) based current control is employed in single- phase VSC connected to a local load;
2. a GC-VSC is used to supply electrical power, with voltage and frequency within an appropriate level, only to the local load R_L, i.e., operating as a grid- forming (two control loops using only dead-beat (DB) controllers). This mode of operation occurs when the SW is open (off) and the automatic control switch (c-SW) is set to position 1. Thus, we assume the analyzed circuit is formed only by the inductance L_f in series with the equivalent of the capacitor C_f in parallel with the load R_L. This assumption is valid because we consider that the inductor resistance can be neglected and that the current in the branch formed by L_g and R_g is zero ($i_g = 0$);
3. the GC-VSC operates as a grid- following (three control loops using two DB controllers and one proportional-integral-resonant (PIR) controller) with SW closed (on), which causes the automatic switch c-SW to change to position 2. Thus, the circuit analyzed is formed by R_g and L_g branch;
4. the AC series filter eliminates the harmonics due to the switching;
5. it is assumed that the GC-VSC is lossless;
6. the grid voltage is considered to be ideal.

The paper is organized as follows. Section 2 describes the analysis and modeling of the controller. Section 3 presents the digital controller methods. Section 4 describes the simulation setup, results, and discussions. Section 5 concludes the paper and lists potential future works.

2   Analysis and Modeling of System

Figure 2 shows the power circuit of a GC-VSC with the ideal power semiconductor switches (S_1, S_2, S_3, and S_4), where v_f, v_o, i_f, i_o and i_g are the controlled instantaneous voltage and currents generated and v_g is the voltage at PCC. Note that the inductor L_f and the capacitor C_f form the inductive-capacitive filter (LC-Filter) at the GC-VSC AC side. We consider the GC-VSC DC- side voltage V_{dc} and the grid voltage v_g to be ideal, i.e., without voltage ripple (DC- side) and harmonic distortion (AC- side). The power losses of the GC-VSC are disregarded, but the adverse effects of delay time imposed by the GC-VSC in the current controller are considered in this work [25,28]. The modulation system is

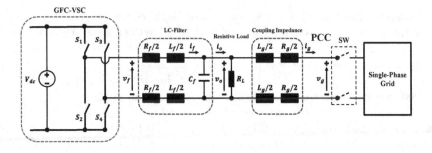

Fig. 2. GC-VSC connected to the single-phase power grid.

Table 1. Power Circuit Parameters.

Parameters	Symbols	Values
DC- side voltage	V_{dc}	450V
Switching frequency	f_{sw}	20kHz
Filter inductance	L_f	1.4mH
Resistance of the Filter	R_f	0.5Ω
AC- side capacitor	C_f	30μF
Coupling inductance	L_g	0.5mH
Resistance of the coupling inductance	R_g	0.25Ω
Load resistance	R_L	26.5Ω
Nominal power	S_o	3k VA
Nominal RMS grid voltage	V_g	230V
Nominal grid frequency	f_g	50Hz

based on the DPWM concept, which is used considering the delay of the digital system. The parameters of the GC-VSC are presented in Table 1 [12].

Figure 3 presents the power circuit at the PCC. The instantaneous current i_f drained from GC-VSC AC- side is composed of the currents of capacitor i_{C_f} and in load node i_o, where i_o is the sum of the currents of load i_L and grid i_g ($i_g = 0$ when SW is open). The GC-VSC AC- side voltage v_f, the load voltage v_o, and the grid voltage v_g are also shown in the circuit. The analysis of this circuit depends on the operation of SW, according to what has already been assumed. Thus, we obtain the mathematical model described in (1) and (2). The models presented in (3) and (4) are obtained by imposing that SW is operating closed, which results in the voltage and frequency at PCC being established by the grid.

$$- v_f + R_f i_f + L_f \frac{di_f}{dt} + v_o = 0 \tag{1}$$

$$i_f - C_f \frac{dv_o}{dt} - \frac{v_o}{R_L} = 0 \tag{2}$$

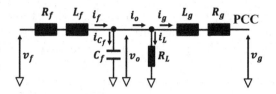

Fig. 3. AC- side equivalent circuit.

$$- v_o + R_g i_g + L_g \frac{di_g}{dt} + v_g = 0 \tag{3}$$

$$i_f - C_f \frac{dv_o}{dt} - \frac{v_o}{R_L} - i_g = 0 \tag{4}$$

Assuming the circuit is disconnected from the grid (SW is open) and applying (1) and (2), the current $G_{i_f}(s)$ and voltage $G_{v_o}(s)$ transfer functions are given by (5) and (6).

$$G_{i_f}(s) = \frac{V_{dc}}{R_L} \frac{1 + sR_L C_f}{1 + \frac{sL_f}{R_f} + s^2 L_f C_f} \tag{5}$$

$$G_{v_o}(s) = \frac{V_f(s)}{I_f(s)} = \frac{R_L}{1 + sR_L C_f} \tag{6}$$

The transfer function of the grid current $G_{i_g}(s)$ in (7) is determined by using (3) and (4), with SW closed.

$$G_{i_g}(s) = \frac{I_g(s)}{V_o(s) - V_g(s)} = \frac{1}{R_g + sL_g} \tag{7}$$

However, the dead-beat (DB) controller design does not require continuous-time transfer functions, such as (5) and (6). It is based on an internal converter model directly built in the discrete- time domain, as described in Sect. 3.

Instead, the transfer function given in (7) is used to design a continuous- time proportional-integral (PI) controller, which is later discretized. One approach step used for the PIR controller design is to obtain the discrete- time equivalent of the continuous- time transfer function of the PI [29]. The PIR controller offers an alternative to the conventional approach based only on the PI, operating directly in the stationary reference frame without coordinating transformations. The resonant part offers a very high gain at the desired AC frequency without using a dq control for disturbance tracking and rejection [30].

3 Digital Controllers

Grid-connected voltage source converter (GC-VSC) control block diagram is depicted in Fig. 4. Note that there are one voltage loop and dual- loop current control block diagram. The voltage v_o is controlled with DB controllers, and the control system limits the local load current i_L. A PIR controller controls the grid current. These controllers are designed in the discrete- time domain.

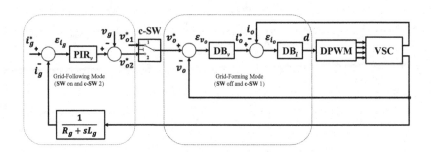

Fig. 4. Loop voltage and current control block diagram.

3.1   Dead- Beat Digital Controller Designs

The design of DB controllers is based on the concept of internal model control, i.e., the discrete- time current generated by GC-VSC is calculated two steps ahead of the measured value, as given in (8) and (9), taking into account the sampling time T_{sw} (switching period $T_{sw} = 1/f_{sw}$). This is to account for the processing time of the control system. DB basically does direct pole allocation with dynamic state feedback in discrete-time systems [24].

$$i_f(k+2) = i_f(k+1) + \frac{\overline{v}_f(k+1) - v_g(k+1)}{L_f}T_{sw} \tag{8}$$

$$i_f(k+1) = i_f(k) + \frac{\overline{v}_f(k) - v_g(k)}{L_f}T_{sw} \tag{9}$$

GC-VSC AC- side average voltage with the respective duty- cycle [$d(k+1)$ and $d(k)$] are given by (10) and (11).

$$\overline{v}_f(k+1) = [2d(k+1) - 1]V_{dc} \tag{10}$$

$$\overline{v}_{inv}(k) = [2d(k) - 1]V_{dc} \tag{11}$$

Considering $i_f^*(k) = i_f(k+2)$ in (8), the duty- cycle is given by (12).

$$d(k+1) = [i_f^*(k) - i_f(k)]\frac{L_f f_{sw}}{2V_{dc}} + \frac{v_g(k)}{V_{dc}} - d(k) + \frac{1}{2} \tag{12}$$

Note in (12) that the current error can be as shown in (13).

$$\varepsilon_{i_f}(k) = i_f^*(k) - i_f(k) \tag{13}$$

Therefore, the duty- cycle is written as in (14).

$$d(k+1) = \varepsilon_{i_f}(k)\frac{L_f f_{sw}}{2V_{dc}} + \frac{v_g(k)}{V_{dc}} - d(k) + \frac{1}{2} \tag{14}$$

GC-VSC controlled voltage at PCC, i.e. at C_f, is given by (15). Note that two steps of generated current $i_f(k+2)$ represent one step of the controlled voltage $v_o(n+1)$, as shown in Fig. 5. Observe also that the sampling interval index k is used, like in $i(k) = i(t)|_{t=kT_{sw}}$, but the interval considered for v_o is n.

$$v_o(n+1) = v_o(n) + \frac{1}{C_f} \left[i_f^*(n) - i_f(n) \right] T_{sw} \tag{15}$$

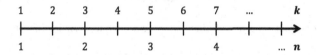

Fig. 5. Discrete-time representation of k and n.

Using (8) and considering $i_L(n) = i_f(n)$, $v_o^*(n) = v_o(n+1)$ and $\varepsilon_{v_o}(n) = v_o^*(n) - v_o(n)$, we have the generated reference current in (16).

$$i_f^*(n) = \varepsilon_{v_o}(n)C_f f_{sw} + i_L(n) \tag{16}$$

3.2   Proportional- Integral- Resonant Digital Controller Design

Figure 6 shows the transfer function $G_{i_g}(s)$ used in the design of the PIR controller. The magnitude M_{i_g} and phase PH_{i_g} of the frequency response of the system, the crossover frequency $\omega_{CR_{i_g}}$ and the $m_{\varphi_{i_g}}$ margins were used to determine the proportional and integral gains of the PIR.

Given that the PI controller function is as shown in (17), the proportional and integral gains are $k_{p_{i_g}}$ and $k_{i_{i_g}}$, respectively [24].

$$PI_{i_g} = k_{p_{i_g}} + \frac{k_{i_{i_g}}}{s} \tag{17}$$

Using the information from the Bode diagram in Fig. 6, we have the PI gains as a function of $\omega_{CR_{i_g}}$, $m_{\varphi_{i_g}}$ and PH_{i_g}, as given in (18). Figure 7 shows the phase- margin $m_{\varphi_{i_g}}$ of the PIR controller.

$$\frac{k_{i_{i_g}}}{k_{p_{i_g}}} = \omega_{CR_{i_g}} \tan\left(PH_{i_g} + 180° - m_{\varphi_{i_g}}\right) \tag{18}$$

The proportional gain value of the PI controller is determined using (19). Thus, the integral gain is determined using (18) and (19).

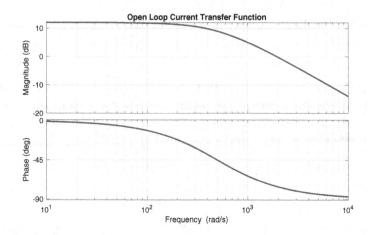

Fig. 6. Bode plot diagram of open- loop grid current transfer function $G_{i_g}(s)$.

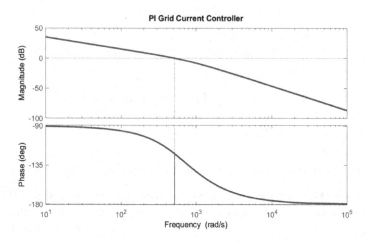

Fig. 7. Bode plot diagram of closed- loop PIR.

$$k_{p_{i_g}} = \frac{1}{1 + \sqrt{\left(\frac{k_{i_{i_g}}}{k_{p_{i_g}}} \frac{1}{\omega_C R_{i_g}}\right)^2}} \qquad (19)$$

We can obtain the discrete time of the PI controller, $PI_{i_g}(z)$, using (17) and the transformation based on step invariance method (ZOH) [29], as given in (20).

$$PI_{i_g}(z) = k_{p_{i_g}} + k_{i_{i_g}} \frac{1}{(1 - z^{-1})f_{sw}} \qquad (20)$$

Resonant (R) filter, $R_{i_g}(z)$, of the digital- based PIR controller is given by (21), with $\omega_o = 2\pi f_g$. Figure 8 shows the block diagram of the PIR controller.

Note that v_g is the feed- forward grid voltage, and v_{o2}^* is the reference voltage generated when SW is closed, i.e., GC-VSC is operating as GFLCS-VSC. The PI controller can guarantee near-zero steady-state error only for DC signals [24]. Since the injected current signal is sinusoidal, the application of the R filter, tuned to the fundamental grid frequency, becomes necessary.

$$R_{i_g}(z) = \frac{k_{R_{i_g}} T_{sw}}{1 + \omega_o^2 T_{sw}^2} \frac{1}{1 - \frac{2}{1+\omega_o^2 T_{sw}^2} z^{-1} + \frac{1}{1+\omega_o^2 T_{sw}^2} z^{-2}} \qquad (21)$$

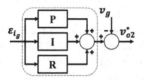

Fig. 8. PIR controller block diagram.

4   Simulation Results

Simulation results obtained from model- based MATLAB/SIMULINK software are presented in this section to verify the effectiveness of the proposed digital controllers. The simulations consider the synchronization between the controllers, the synchronism between the GC-VSC AC- side and the grid, the counters, and the time delay usually encountered in applying a real system.

All tests with the digital controllers were performed using a power circuit based on the GC-VSC, with grid RMS voltage and frequency of $V_g = 230V$ and $f_g = 50Hz$. At the first test, the grid is connected to the PCC (SW closed) at $t = 0ms$, while at $t = 42.5ms$, a negative step of 20% is applied to grid reference current (Subsect. 4.1). In a different test, the GC-VSC operates disconnected from the grid (SW open), but then at $t = 37.5ms$, the circuit is connected by closing SW (Subsect. 4.2). Thus, the GC-VSC was tested both operating as a grid- forming and grid- following during the $200ms$ evaluated. It demonstrates the effectiveness of the controllers that are also automatically switched.

Table 2 summarizes the performance of the three digital control loops of the GC-VSC. Note that the relative errors are dynamic values and the phase errors are static. Total harmonic distortion (THD) is used herein to demonstrate the GC-VSC performance quality using the proposed controllers [31,32]. Performance comparisons between control techniques are presented in [3,33].

4.1   GC-VSC Operating as Grid- Following

Figure 9 shows the grid current i_g imposed through the coupling impedance L_g and the reference current i_g^*, with GC-VSC operating as grid- following (SW

Table 2. Dynamic and static results.

Parameters	Relative RMS Errors (%)	THD (%)	Phase Errors (degrees)
Grid current (i_g)	1.07	0.31	0.90
GC-VSC current (i_f)	3.67	4.92	1.80
Current in load node (i_o)	3.70	0.21	10.35
Load voltage (v_o)	0.01	0.35	0.45

on). The current i_g varies instantaneously after negative step at $t = 42.5ms$. However, it takes at least half a cycle of the grid frequency to enter steady state. This can be seen in the current error shown in Fig. 9. Figure 10 shows details (zoom from result of Fig. 9) of the grid current and current error behaviors. Note that the error grows instantaneously at $t = 42.5ms$, but then it converges to zero. There is a relatively small residual tracking error between the reference signal and the instantaneous average value of the waveform generated by the GC-VSC. This error, measured under steady-state conditions, is due to the delay caused by calculating the duty- cycle in the digital control algorithm [24]. The current THD remains constant at THD = 0.31% before and after the transient, with a relatively small overshoot and fast dynamic response. The distortion of the reference current generated by the digital control algorithm is THD = 0.33%.

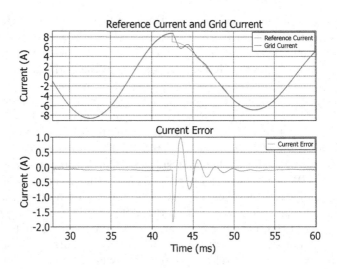

Fig. 9. Controlled grid current.

The current generated by the GC-VSC ($i_f = i_{C_f} + i_L + i_g$) presents a transient but with an instantaneous variation of lower intensity when compared to that of the grid current i_g, as shown in Fig. 11. The voltage v_o at the local load did not show significant variations during the load current variation at $t = 42.5ms$.

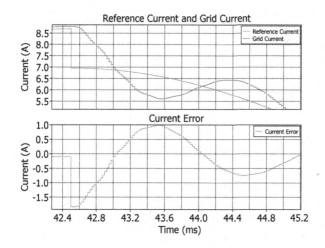

Fig. 10. Controlled grid current (with zoom).

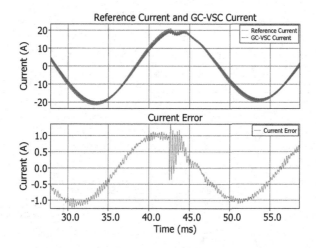

Fig. 11. Controlled GC-VSC current.

However, the effect of the negative step on the reference current i_g^* can be verified in Fig. 12.

4.2   GC-VSC Operating as Grid- Forming or Grid- Following

Figure 13 and Fig. 14 show the signals of the digital controllers designed with the DB concept, considering SW opened. It can be seen in Fig. 13 that the signal of the modulator formed by DPWM, considering N = 700 points in the normalized modulation index, is practically tracking the voltage v_o, which maintains current control. The relative RMS current error is $\epsilon_{i_f} = 3.67\%$, even after the transient with the closing of SW. The current i_f phase error is $\Delta\varphi_{i_f} = 1.80°$. This

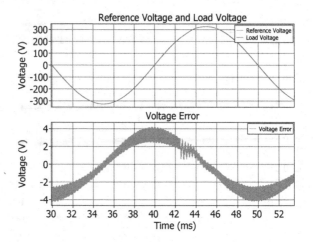

Fig. 12. Controlled voltage at local load.

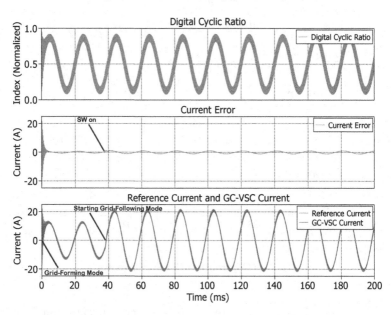

Fig. 13. Current control signals.

result can be verified by comparing the reference current waveform and the one generated by the GC-VSC. Figure 14 presents the current signals, current error, and the comparison between the reference voltages and the voltage controlled by the GC-VSC. The relative RMS voltage error is $\epsilon_{v_o} = 0.01\%$, with the phase error of $\Delta\varphi_{v_o} = 0.45°$, which also demonstrates the effectiveness of the controllers.

Figure 15 shows the PIR controller signals. The reference voltage generated by the controller practically does not change after the closure of SW, in which

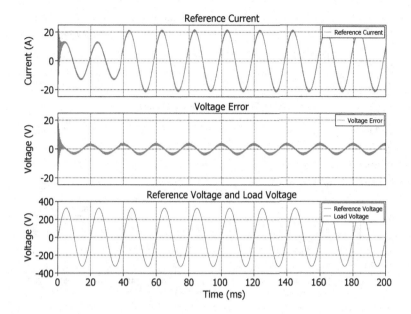

Fig. 14. Voltage control signals.

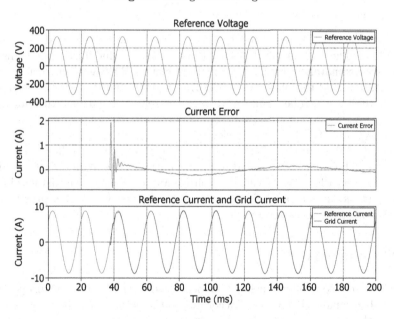

Fig. 15. Grid current control signals.

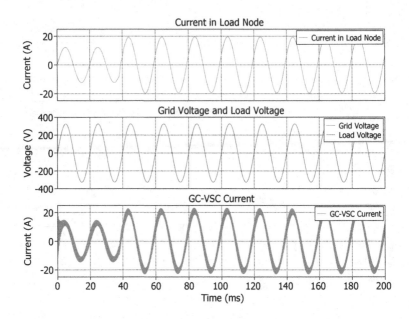

Fig. 16. GC-VSC AC-side voltage and current

only the local load is connected to GC-VSC, i.e., the current is drained only by the load. The current error reaches the maximum value during the transient but is approximately zero soon after. The relative RMS grid current error is $\epsilon_{i_g} = 1.07\%$, and the phase error is $\Delta\varphi_{i_g} = 0.90°$. Thus, it can be seen that the PIR digital controller could also track the reference current with adequate accuracy for the proposed application.

Connecting a GC-VSC to an electrical power grid requires great scientific and technical rigor in the design and development of the controllers, mainly to follow the technical standards and recommendations. The main objective of this work is to feed a local load with the voltage and current waveforms within the design parameters. It can be seen in Fig. 16 that the waveforms provided by GC-VSC meet the proposed design.

5   Conclusions

Digital- based controllers, using two dead-beats (DBs) and one proportion-alintegral- resonant (PIR), acted according to the design, i.e., they were able to follow both the reference current and voltage with relative errors of $\epsilon_{v_o} = 0.01\%$ and $\epsilon_{i_f} = 3.67\%$, respectively. Thus, the approaches used in the design of controllers using the small- signal method in digital systems were effective.

This work is part of a research project that aims to apply these controllers in a three- phase system using the same digital design method. It is also intended to consider the problems inherent to synchronism with a three- phase power grid with unbalanced voltage (and/or current) to improve the effectiveness of the digital controllers considering an application in a low- cost industrial VSC.

In future work, the proposed digital controllers will be implemented for experimental results using the hardware-in-the-loop (HIL) and real scenarios with the implementation on embedded systems. The real- time capability of the controller must be tested at the subsequent development stages.

Acknowledgements. The authors are grateful for the financial support provided by the Sao Paulo Research Foundation (FAPESP) under grant 2022/00317- 3 and grant 2016/08645- 9. We thank our colleagues at the Department of Information Engineering (DEI) at the University of Padova (UNIPD) for their support.

References

1. Rathnayake, D.B., et al.: Grid-forming inverter modeling, control, and applications. IEEE Access **9**, 114781–114807 (2021)
2. Islam, M.M., Muttaqi, K.M., Sutanto, D., Rahman, M.M., Alonso, O.: Design of a controller for grid forming inverter-based power generation systems. IEEE Access **11**, 55755–55770 (2023)
3. Liu, Q., Caldognetto, T., Buso, S.: Review and comparison of grid-tied inverter controllers in microgrids. IEEE Trans. Power Electron. **35**, 7624–7639 (2020)
4. Du, W., et al.: Modeling of grid-forming and grid-following inverters for dynamic simulation of large-scale distribution systems. IEEE Trans. Power Del. **36**, 2035–2045 (2021)
5. Baltas, G.N., et al.: Grid-forming power converters tuned through artificial intelligence to damp subsynchronous interactions in electrical grids. IEEE Access **8**, 93369–93379 (2020)
6. Mitsugi, Y., Baba, J.: Phaser-based transfer function analysis of power synchronization control instability for a grid forming inverter in a stiff grid. IEEE Access **11**, 42146–42159 (2023)
7. Yazdani, S., Ferdowsi, M., Davari, M., Shamsi, P.: Advanced current limiting and power sharing control in a PV based grid-forming inverter under unbalanced grid conditions. IEEE J. Emerg. Sel. Topics Power Electron. **8**, 1084–1096 (2020)
8. Pattabiraman, D., Lasseter, R.H., Jahns, T.M.: Comparison of grid- following and grid-forming control for a high inverter penetration power system. In: Proceedings of IEEE Power Energy Society General Meeting (2018)
9. Lasseter, R.H., Chen, Z., Pattabiraman, D.: Grid-forming inverters: a critical asset for the power grid. IEEE J. Emerg. Sel. Topics Power Electron. **8**, 925–935 (2020)
10. Nascimento, C. F., Diene, O. & Watanabe, E. H. Analytical Model of Three- Phase Four-Wire VSC Operating as Grid-Forming Power Converter under Unbalanced Load Conditions in Proc. of the IEEE Int. Conf. Power Electron. Drive Syst. (2017)
11. Rodríguez - Amenedo, J.L. et al.: Grid-forming control of voltage source converters based on the virtual-flux orientation. IEEE Access **11**, 10254–10274 (2023)
12. Buso, S., Caldognetto, T., Liu, Q.: Analysis and experimental characterization of a large-bandwidth triple-loop controller for grid-tied inverters. IEEE Trans. Power Electron. **34**, 1936–1949 (2019)

13. Cavazzana, F., Caldognetto, T., Mattavelli, P., Corradini, M., Toigo, I.: Analysis of current control interaction of multiple parallel grid-connected inverters. IEEE Trans. Sustain. Energy **9**, 1740–1749 (2018)

14. Petric, I.Z., Mattavelli, P., Buso, S.: Passivation of grid-following VSCs: a comparison between active damping and multi-sampled PWM. IEEE Trans. Power Electron. **37**, 13205–13216 (2022)

15. Xu, J., Qian, Q., Zhang, B., Xie, S.: Harmonics and stability analysis of single-phase grid-connected inverters in distributed power generation systems considering phase-locked loop impact. IEEE Trans. Sustain. Energy **10**, 1470–1480 (2019)

16. Guo, B. et al.: Observer-based second-order sliding mode control for grid- connected VSI with LCL-type filter under weak grid. Electric Power Syst. Res. **183**, 106270. ISSN: 0378–7796 (2020)

17. Rosso, R., et al.: Grid-forming converters: control approaches, grid synchronization, and future trends - a review. IEEE Open J. Ind. Appl. **2**, 93–109 (2021)

18. Rocabert, J., Luna, A., Blaabjerg, F., Rodríguez, P.: Control of power converters in AC microgrids. IEEE Trans. Power Electron. **27**, 4734–4749 (2012)

19. Vasquez, J.C., Guerrero, J.M., Luna, A., Rodriguez, P., Teodorescu, R.: Adaptive droop control applied to voltage-source inverters operating in grid-connected and islanded modes. IEEE Trans. Ind. Electron. **56**, 4088–4096 (2009)

20. Xu, J., Qian, H., Qian, Q., Xie, S.: Modeling, stability, and design of the single-phase SOGI-based phase-locked loop considering the frequency feedback loop effect. IEEE Trans. Power Electron. **38**, 987–1002 (2023)

21. Ciobotaru, M., Teodorescu, R., Blaabjerg, F.: A new single-phase PLL structure based on second order generalized integrator. In: Proocedings of the IEEE Power Electronics Specialists Conference, pp. 1–6 (2006)

22. Silva, S.A.O.D., Campanhol, L.B.G., Goedtel, A., Nascimento, C.F., Paiao, D.: A comparative analysis of p-PLL algorithms for single-phase utility connected systems. In: Proocedings of the European Conference on Power Electronics and Applications, pp. 1–10 (2009)

23. Liu, T., Wang, X.: Transient stability of single-loop voltage-magnitude controlled grid-forming converters. IEEE Trans. Power Electron. **36**, 6158–6162 (2021)

24. Buso, S., Mattavelli, P.: Digital Control in Power Electronics, 2nd edn. Springer Nature, Switzerland AG (2015). https://doi.org/10.1007/978-3-031-02499-3

25. Buso, S., Caldognetto, T., Brandao, D.I.: Dead-beat current controller for voltage-source converters with improved large-signal response. IEEE Trans. Ind. Appl. **52**, 1588–1596 (2016)

26. Diene, O., Rocha, F.P., Nascimento, C.F., Watanabe, E.H.: Model predictive control of grid-connected voltage-source converters operating as STATCOM with unbalanced loads. In: Proceedings of the IEEE International Conference Power Electronics and Drive System (2019)

27. Hori, N., Mori, A., Nikiforuk, P.: A new perspective for discrete-time models of a continuous-time system. IEEE Trans. Autom. Control **37**, 1013–1017 (1992)

28. Benyoucef, A., Kara, K., Chouder, A., Silvestre, S.: Prediction-based deadbeat control for grid-connected inverter with L-Filter and LCL-Filter. Electric Power Compon. Syst. **42**, 1266–1277 (2014)

29. Vatansever, F., Hatun, M.: s-to-z transformation tool for discretization. Gazi Üniversitesi Fen Bilimleri Dergisi Part C Tasarım ve Teknoloji **9**, 773–784 (2021)

30. Busarello, T.D.C., Guerreiro, J.F., Simões, M.G., Pomilio, J.A.:: Hardware- in-the-loop experimental setup of a LCL-Filtered grid-connected inverter with digital proportional-resonant current controller. In: IEEE Workshop on Control and Modelling of Power Electronics, pp. 1–8 (2021)

31. Kim, J., Hong, J., Kim, H.: Improved direct deadbeat voltage control with an actively damped inductor-capacitor plant model in an Islanded AC microgrid. Energies 9 (2016)
32. Parvez, M., et al.: Comparative study of discrete PI and PR controls for single-phase UPS inverter. IEEE Access **8**, 45584–45595 (2020)
33. Elhassan, G., et al.: Deadbeat current control in grid-connected inverters: a comprehensive discussion. IEEE Access **10**, 3990–4014 (2022)

Smart Heating and Cooling System

Digital Twin-Based Fault Detection and Prioritisation in District Heating Systems: A Case Study in Denmark

Frederik Wagner Madsen, Theis Bank,
Henrik Alexander Nissen Søndergaard[(✉)] [ID], Lasse Kappel Mortensen[ID],
and Hamid Reza Shaker[ID]

University of Southern Denmark, Odense, Denmark
heso@mmmi.sdu.dk

Abstract. Faults in district heating systems (DHS) cause sub-optimal operating conditions, which increase energy losses. As DHSs are critical infrastructure for many households in Denmark, these faults should be detected and corrected quickly. A novel model-based fault detection and diagnosis framework has been applied to detect and prioritise faults. The framework uses a bound for normal operation based on the residuals between historical sensor data and simulated properties in a digital twin of the DHS. The faults detected are prioritised based on the fault probability calculated using the Chernoff bound method. A case study on a Danish DHS has proven that the framework can produce a prioritised list of faults that maintenance crews can use to target faults with the highest probability. Furthermore, the digital twin allowed for fault location investigation, which could correlate different faults in the DHS. The framework has the potential for real-time fault detection and diagnosis. However, more precise digital twins need to be developed.

Keywords: fault detection and diagnosis · district heating systems · digital twin · Chernoff bound

1 Introduction

A district heating system (DHS) aims to distribute and provide affordable heat to connected consumers efficiently [4]. In Denmark, the majority of households' heat is supplied by district heating (DH), and a large proportion of total energy use is for hot water use and heating in the EU [6], which makes the DHSs critical infrastructure, and an important domain to improve the energy efficiency of, to lower CO_2 emissions. The complexity of operating a DHS with all the different functions, from heat production and transmission to consumption, leads to faults. These faults result in the DHS operating sub-optimally [4,11,12].

This work is supported by the "Proactive and Predictive Maintenance of District Heating Systems" and "IEA DHC TS4", funded by the Danish Energy Agency under the Energy Technology Development and Demonstration Program, ID number 64020-2102 and 134-22011, respectively.

To ensure the DHSs work efficiently, it is important to detect these faults and remedy them as quickly as possible. However, DH companies mostly perform reactive- and preventive maintenance instead of proactive maintenance. Reactive maintenance strategies often result in faults not being detected quickly enough or are never detected if the system is able to compensate or does not affect the delivery of heat to the consumers (but still wastes energy). Faults leading to the discomfort of consumers are often detected far more quickly. The use of planned maintenance results in inspections being done too often, resulting in a waste of resources. To unleash the full potential of the digitalisation of the DH sector, tools for enabling proactive maintenance via implementing fault detection and diagnosis (FDD) methods are needed. These methods must be able to detect faults in a DHS in a timely and economical manner to reduce waste of energy and time and lowering CO_2 emissions.

Methods for FDD are categorised in [8] into three sub-types: quantitative model-based, qualitative model-based, and process history-based, which all come with advantages and disadvantages. Quantitative model-based, which uses a model based on thorough physical or engineering principles, enhances the precision of the model. However, comprehensive modelling is also a weakness due to the level of complexity and amount of input required to model, which can reduce the scalability of the approach. The method is used in [19], where a DHS is modelled in OpenModelica. The residuals between model output and pressure sensors are compared in a Bayesian Network to determine the possibility of faults and evaluate the system. Another example is [2], in which a simulation of a DHS grid is also created and is coupled with an optimisation problem to detect and identify both thermal and hydraulic faults.

Both quantitative and qualitative model-based FDD have some overlapping elements, and the differences can sometimes be vague. On the other hand, process history-based FDD differentiates itself by only utilising data. This makes the modelling less complex because black-box models require less knowledge of the physics of the system and make it easier to scale to other systems. However, the method requires a lot of good-quality data and, to some extent, computational power. An example of that is the method seen in [14], where three methods of FDD, Hotelling's T^2 and Q statistics, contextual Shewhart chart, and linear regression, are presented. Furthermore, [14] uses an approximation of the Chernoff bound method proposed in [5] to investigate if all three FDD methods agree on the same fault thereby filtering out insignificant alarms for faults occurring in the DHS. Based on the identified literature on FDD in the DHS domain, it is apparent that more research employs data-driven methods compared to model-based methods. Some examples of data-driven research are Sun et al. [15], where they use three clustering methods to identify operation patterns that lead to faulty behaviour in consumers. The use of a gradient boost regressor has been utilised by Månsson et al. [10] to detect faults in DH substations by predicting regular operation. Lastly, the work in [17] utilises cluster analysis and association analysis- to decide rule patterns for the operation of the DH substation. According to a review paper on FDD in DHS [4], many of the data-driven models created will not perform well and are thereby not useful in the real world, due to them being created and trained using laboratory or simulation data. This problem can be alleviated either by using real-world data or by utilising model-based methods. In general, the review paper [4] indicates an overall research gap in the field of FDD in DHSs. This can be in part due to the preconceived idea that DHS work well, even though that is not the case [7], and the use of DH is not as widespread.

A challenge emphasised by the literature is the number of faults different FDD methods will produce [9,13]. A methodology to differentiate between different faults more accurately is important in the decision-making process for making corrective maintenance in DHSs for liability and economic reasons. Paper [19] compares the model's output with sensor data from the system and detects a fault when the sensor data deviates $\pm1\%$ from the model simulation in at least ten consecutive time steps. The fault is then run through a Bayesian Network to diagnose the fault. The Bayesian Network is built upon expert knowledge, strengthening the capability of diagnosing faults. Still, on the other hand, expert knowledge may not be sufficient to identify a correlation between residuals to a fault diagnosis, thereby disregarding a possible fault. The current approach to fault prioritisation is mainly based on expert knowledge to classify the severity of faults and this is extremely time-consuming [16]. Furthermore, according to [16], data-driven methods are not widely utilised for fault prioritisation or even seen in literature at all. Some developments have been made, however. [5] proposed a statistical method of prioritising faults in a telecommunication network using the Chernoff bound method. Using the Chernoff bound method, this statistical approach can identify the probability of a fault occurring in a system without expert knowledge. This methodology has been brought into the energy domain in papers [1,3] using it for FDD in a heat, ventilation, and air conditioning (HVAC) system of a building. Using the Chernoff bound method, the papers were able to categorise the state of urgency into three subsets: low($P < 60\%$), medium($60\% \leq P < 95\%$), and high($P \geq 95\%$). The model-based FDD using the Chernoff bound method proposed in the papers [1,3] showed great potential for FDD in HVAC systems but also the potential for implementation in other energy-system domains such as DHSs.

This paper proposes an FDD framework for DHSs. In summary, it applies Chernoff bound methodology to the residuals between the outputs of a quantitative model of a DH network (digital twin) and real-world sensor data, when the residual is above a predetermined threshold. Chernoff bound provides a fault probability value that can be used by maintenance for better prioritisation of which faults to further investigate. This paper aims to contribute with a framework to the apparent research gap in the literature for FDD in DHSs with a two-fold contribution.

1. A framework is developed by implementing a quantitative model-based FDD approach together with the Chernoff bound method to prioritise faults by their probability. This makes it possible for maintenance crews to only focus on the faults with the highest fault probability, not wasting their time. To the best of our understanding, this has not been done before.
2. The framework's methodology is tested using a case study with real-world data and a digital twin of the DHS.

In Sect. 2, the overall framework for model-based FDD in DHSs is introduced and explained in detail. The next step is in Sect. 3, in which the framework is applied to a case study, and results are presented.

2   Methodology

A novel model-based FDD framework will be presented in this section. The section will describe how sensor data measured in a DHS is processed and simulated in a digital twin for FDD and how the faults are indexed according to their probability. A flow diagram of the framework can be seen in Fig. 1. For the purpose of this work, we adopt the general definition of a digital twin stated by Yu et al. [18] that "a digital twin is a digital (or virtual) representation that looks-like, behaves-like, and connects-to a physical part or system with the goal of improving or optimising decision making for any time horizon."

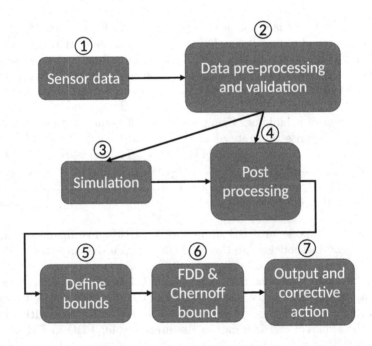

Fig. 1. Flow diagram of model-based FDD framework.

In step 1, the data is collected from the sensors in the DHS. The sensor data is pre-processed to have the right format and units to match the requirements for the data input to the digital twin in step 2. The data validation in step 2 investigates if negative- or NAN-values are present in the data. The data validation also investigates if some measurements violate the physical capabilities of the system or if unexpected repeating patterns can be found in the data, which could indicate sensor faults. Invalidated data must be corrected before further use of the data. In step 3, a digital twin uses some of the data collected by the sensors as boundary conditions to perform quasi-dynamic simulations of the state of the DHS. The digital twin should be a very accurate digital model of the DHS where the pipe configurations, heat loss coefficients etc., are defined. The results from the digital twin are then post-processed together with the unused sensor data for FDD. This model-based FDD framework proposes a univariate statistical approach using a bound of normal operation to detect faults. The bound of normal operation is defined as the root-mean-square error (RMSE) of the residual of one property, e.g., mass flow rate, between the digital twin and the sensor data. With this approach, it is assumed that the majority of the sensors in the DHS are correct and if one sensor deviates more than the bound of normal operation, it is detected as a fault. Furthermore, the bound also represents the modelling error of the digital twin, which allows some deviations from the norm. The RMSE value is calculated using Eq. 1, where N and M are the time steps and sensors, respectively.

$$RMSE = \sqrt{\frac{\sum_{k=1}^{M} \sum_{i=1}^{N} (Y_{ik}^{sensor} - Y_{ik}^{digital\ twin})^2}{N \cdot M}} \tag{1}$$

The RMSE can be interpreted as the standard deviation of the residuals. The r-value, which is the number of standard deviations included, can adjust the size of the bound. The FDD should not raise an alarm if the sensor measurement is within the bound, as seen in Eq. 2.

$$Y_i^{sensor} > Y_i^{digital\ twin} - r \cdot RMSE$$
$$\text{and}\quad Y_i^{sensor} < Y_i^{digital\ twin} + r \cdot RMSE \tag{2}$$

Due to some data having higher numerical values, the data is normalised with maximum scaling (see Eq. 3) before the RMSE value is calculated. The maximum scaling is done by finding the maximum value in the data for one consumer k, which has one column with sensor data and one with simulated data. For each time step i, the data point $r_{i,k}$ is divided by the maximum value $max(r_k)$ giving the normalised data point $n_{i,k}$. Maximum scaling ensures that all data is less than or equal to 1.

$$n_{i,k} = \frac{r_{i,k}}{max(r_k)} \tag{3}$$

In step 6, FDD is carried out using the bound of normal operation. To prioritise which faults have the highest probability and should be investigated by a maintenance crew, the Chernoff bound method from [5] is used. A schematic of the Chernoff bound method can be seen in Fig. 2.

A suspicion is started when the sensor measurements leave the bound of normal operation and end when it enters again. The areas under the curves are used in Eqs. 4 and 5 to calculate the probability of normal- and faulty operation, respectively. As the areas A_O and A_B are used to calculate the probability, the fault probability for a period is correlated to the amplitude and the period.

$$P_{normal\ operation} = P(A_O|A_B) = e^{-\left(\frac{\left(A_B\left(1-\frac{A_O}{A_B}\right)^2\right)}{2}\right)} \tag{4}$$

$$P_{faulty\ operation} = 1 - P_{normal\ operation}$$
$$A_O = Grey\ area \tag{5}$$
$$A_B = Grey\ area + Coloured\ area$$

Lastly, in step 7, the output of the Chernoff bound method is prioritised from highest fault probability to lowest. As proposed in papers [1,3], the faults are categorised into three fault probability indices; high, medium, and low, as seen in Table 1.

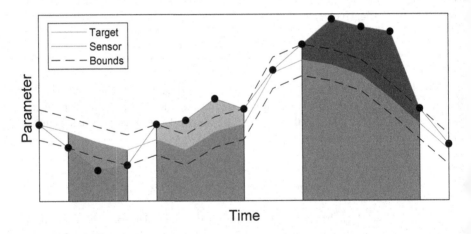

Fig. 2. Chernoff bound schematic. Showcasing the gray and coloured areas used for calculating the probability. The figure does not depict real data.

Table 1. Fault probability indexing levels classifications.

Probability level index	Probability of fault	Colour indication
High	$P \geq 95\%$	Red
Medium	$60\% \leq P < 95\%$	Yellow
Low	$P < 60\%$	Green

3   Case Study and Results

3.1   Description of Case Study

The model-based FDD framework presented will be implemented in a case study with historical data from a suburb of the DHS in Odense, Denmark. The investigation period is from December 2022 to January 2023. A sensor installed at the substation measures supplied and returned energy, mass flow rate, pressure, and temperature at an hourly resolution. At every 648 consumers, a sensor measures the volumetric flow rate, energy consumption, and supplied and returned energy at a daily resolution. Supply and return energy is the supply and return temperature multiplied by the volumetric flow rate. The digital twin of the DHS, developed by a collaboration between Fjernvarme Fyn and Danfoss, was built in the software Leanheat Network (LHN) and will be used to simulate the DHS. LHN simulates hydraulic and thermal conditions based on boundary conditions and optimises pressure-, mass flow rate-, and temperature conditions to minimize pump- and heat production costs. The digital twin will simulate hourly quasi-dynamic simulations, where each hourly simulation will represent the whole day. The boundary conditions imported to the digital twin are the power consumption and return temperature at the consumers, supply temperature and return pressure at the substation, and the pressure change at a critical node defined as 1.33 bar, based on Fjernvarme Fyn's expert knowledge. The sensor data is reformatted to meet the data import requirements for the software. The output from the digital twin, which will be used for FDD, is the supply temperature and mass flow rate at the consumers. Implementing the Chernoff bound method will produce a list of fault probabilities for these two properties with the format as seen in Table 2.

Table 2. Fault probability list of mass flow rate FDD.

Consumer ID	Start	End	Fault probability	Fault probability index
Consumer_345	2023-01-04	2023-01-16	98%	High
Consumer_322	2022-12-07	2022-12-14	84%	Medium
⋮	⋮	⋮	⋮	⋮
Consumer_103	2023-01-05	2023-01-06	16%	Low
Consumer_382	2022-12-15	2022-12-16	16%	Low

3.2   Calibration of Bound Size

As the bound size is defined by $Y_i^{digital\ twin} \pm r \cdot RMSE$, the number of faults found and their probability are directly correlated with the chosen r-value. The investigation of every single fault can be costly and time-consuming. Therefore, tuning the r-value to ensure that a reasonable number of faults with high probability are found is important, disregarding the faults with low probability caused by, e.g., the modelling error. This paper suggests tuning the r-value manually by investigating the framework's output when the r-value is changed. Another approach for automatically tuning the r-value could be the elbow method which is a heuristic method for finding the incremental increase in the r-value with the largest marginal decrease in the number of faults detected. However, the elbow method was not investigated as it is seen as more beneficial for the operator to manually tune the number of faults detected to match the resources available to investigate them. Automatically tuning the r-value could produce an unnecessary amount of faults detected which can be unmanageable to investigate. The proposed manual tuning of the r-value is visualised in Fig. 3 for the mass flow rate and Fig. 4 for the supply temperature, where the number of faults and mean probabilities are shown for each r-value.

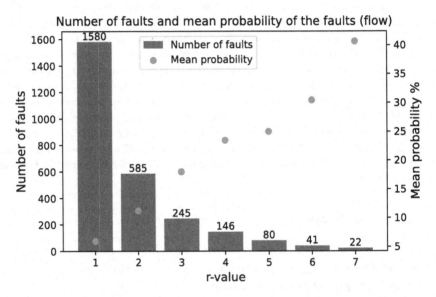

Fig. 3. Incrementally increasing the r-value from one to seven for the mass flow rate FDD.

Figure 3 shows that the number of detected faults decreases with increasing r-value, contrary to the mean probability of the detected faults, which increases with increasing r-value. This illustrates how the size of the bound and the Chernoff bound method are combined only to detect and prioritise the most important faults. For further fault investigation, an r-value of 7 is chosen, which gives 22 faults (13 unique consumers) with a mean probability of 40%.

Looking at supply temperature, the investigation of the r-value shows similar results, seen in Fig. 4. For the further investigation of supply temperature, an r-value of 5 has been chosen, which resulted in 12 faults with five unique consumers and a mean probability of around 50%. R-values larger than 5 seem to decrease the number of faults at a low rate, and it is therefore not seen as necessary to increase the r-value above 5. Another approach is to choose a low r-value and then sort the list of faults, only looking at the high-probability faults.

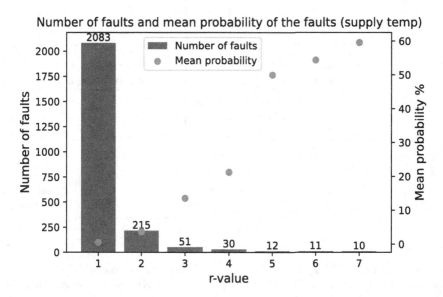

Fig. 4. Incrementally increasing the r-value from one to seven for the mass flow rate FDD.

3.3 Fault Investigation

In Fig. 5, Consumer_239 is showcased, which operates under normal conditions. It can be seen that the sensor- and simulated boundary conditions are equal. Some deviations exist between the measured- and simulated mass flow rate and supply temperature. Still, these small deviations were inside the bound of normal operation and were therefore not detected as faults. The bound of normal operation is not shown in Fig. 5, as the bound was calculated based on normalised data.

From the prioritised list of fault probabilities, regarding the supply temperature FDD, consumer_471 experienced three faults. The operation of consumer_471 can be seen in Fig. 6, and the three faults (grey areas) had a fault probability of 35%, 95%, and 58%, respectively. Correlating the four properties in Fig. 6, the largest deviation in supply and return temperature happens in periods when consumer_471 has no consumption. When there is no consumption,

Properties of Consumer_239

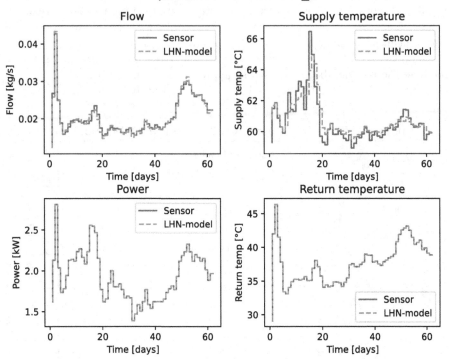

Fig. 5. Consumer_239 shows normal operation conditions, as the residuals between the sensor- and model curves for the four properties are within the bound of normal operation.

the mass flow rate is also 0 kg/s, which may cause the sensor not to measure the supply and return temperature correctly and set it to 0 °C. These boundary conditions can not be simulated accurately by the digital twin, which forces it to change the boundary condition causing this large deviation. This fault may be labelled as a sensor fault and will probably not have damaging effects on the system. However, it can be noticed that the digital twin also changes the return temperature, which is a boundary condition, after the period of no consumption ends by December 2022. In the global property settings in the LHN software, it was defined that the simulation will not allow a $\Delta T \leq 0.5$ °C, i.e., that the consumers cool the DH water less than 0.5 °C. For consumer_471 $\Delta T \geq 0.5$ °C, however, the digital twin still changes the defined return temperature. This action by the digital twin, where boundary conditions were changed, is due to numerical stability in the optimisation problem being solved (confirmed by Danfoss).

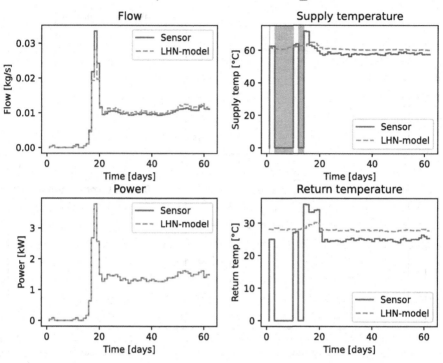

Fig. 6. Consumer_471 shows faulty operation, where the marked grey areas for the supply temperature chart, within the first 15 days, are the three faults.

Consumer_365, presented in Fig. 7, had two faults in the investigation period with 26% and 48% fault probability, respectively, regarding the FDD on mass flow rate. These faults did not rank high on the fault probability indexing. Nevertheless, Consumer_365 is showcased as Fjernvarme Fyn validated that consumer_365 was operating in a faulty condition due to a low cooling efficiency of the consumer installation and that these faults showed particular interest compared to higher prioritised faults. The faults can be seen in Fig. 7, where the simulated mass flow rate spikes twice in the investigation period (grey areas). These spikes are infeasible to occur in the real DHS. The digital twin calculates results by running an optimisation problem, where it tries to match all properties in the pipes and nodes in the system given the set of boundary conditions. These spikes indicate that the boundary conditions for consumer_365 could not be simulated accurately by the digital twin and therefore have a probability of being faulty.

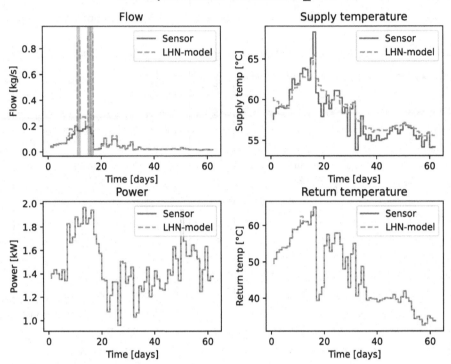

Fig. 7. Consumer_365 shows a faulty operation, where the marked grey areas for the mass flow chart are the two faults.

3.4   Fault Location Investigation

Instead of investigating each fault individually on the list of faults, another approach is to identify the consumers' location and the types of houses on the list. For this investigation, having a digital twin with a geographical user interface is advantageous. Using the two lists of faults obtained by an r-value of 7 for mass flow rate and 5 for supply temperature, the fault location investigation shows that all the detected faults happened in terrace houses. The DHS in the suburb has more terrace houses than single houses, but this indicates that the terrace houses are more prone to operating in faulty conditions. Another interesting result is the location of three out of four consumers in the same terrace house had a fault detected, illustrated in Fig. 8.

The terrace house is located far from the substation and is also the last connection point of that pipeline branch, where the non-faulty consumer is the first one connected. Using this knowledge of the faults' locations can indicate the faults' cause, as similar faults may unlikely occur at three of the four consumers. This could indicate a fault upstream in the pipe network, possibly the pipe going from the main pipe into the terrace house. However, a thorough investigation

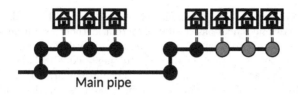

Fig. 8. Three out of four consumers in same terrace house operating faulty.

of the pipes and consumers must be done to find the root of the three faults occurring in the terrace house.

4   Conclusion and Future Work

Faults in district heating systems (DHS) that are not detected quickly enough or not at all, can waste a lot of energy. As DHSs are critical infrastructure for the many Danish households connected, fault detection and diagnosis (FDD) frameworks are of great importance in detecting and correcting these faults. A model-based FDD framework detecting and prioritising faults in a DHS has therefore been developed in this paper. The model-based FDD framework detects faults using a bound of normal operation based on the root-mean-square error (RMSE) of the deviation between a digital twin and the sensors in a DHS, where the r-value could calibrate the number of faults detected, disregarding faults caused by the modelling error. The faults detected were prioritised based on their fault probability using the Chernoff bound method. The prioritised list of faults can be useful for maintenance crews as they can save time and resources by investigating and targeting faults with a high probability. The framework is scalable and can easily be implemented by DH companies with existing digital twins. For future work, the model-based FDD framework should be tested on live sensors, where the benefits of enhanced time resolution of the sensor measurements also could be investigated.

Acknowledgements. We thank Peer Andersen, Lasse Elmelund Pedersen, and the rest of their team at Fjernvarme Fyn A/S for their assistance with the data and the model. Also, thanks to Johan Peter Alsing from Danfoss A/S for assisting us with Leanheat Network.

References

1. Alexandersen, E.K., Skydt, M.R., Engelsgaard, S.S., Bang, M., Jradi, M., Shaker, H.R.: A stair-step probabilistic approach for automatic anomaly detection in building ventilation system operation. Build. Environ. **157**, 165–171 (2019). https://doi.org/10.1016/j.buildenv.2019.04.036
2. Bahlawan, H., et al.: Detection and identification of faults in a district heating network. Energy Convers. Manage. **266**, 115837 (2022). https://doi.org/10.1016/j.enconman.2022.115837

3. Bang, M., Engelsgaard, S.S., Alexandersen, E.K., Skydt, M.R., Shaker, H.R., Jradi, M.: Novel real-time model-based fault detection method for automatic identification of abnormal energy performance in building ventilation units. Energy Build. **183**, 238–251 (2019). https://doi.org/10.1016/j.enbuild.2018.11.006
4. Buffa, S., Fouladfar, M.H., Franchini, G., Lozano Gabarre, I., Andrés Chicote, M.: Advanced control and fault detection strategies for district heating and cooling systems-a review. Appl. Sci. **11**(1), 455 (2021). https://doi.org/10.3390/app11010455
5. Cheung, B., Kumar, G., Rao, S.A.: Statistical algorithms in fault detection and prediction: toward a healthier network. Bell Labs Tech. J. **9**(4), 171–185 (2005). https://doi.org/10.1002/bltj.20070
6. EU: Commission recommendation (eu) 2019/786 of 8 May 2019 on building renovation (2019). https://bit.ly/30nxBs5
7. Gadd, H., Werner, S.: Fault detection in district heating substations. Appl. Energy **157**, 51–59 (2015). https://doi.org/10.1016/j.apenergy.2015.07.061
8. Katipamula, S., Brambley, M.R.: Review article: methods for fault detection, diagnostics, and prognostics for building systems-a review, part II. HVAC&R Res. **11**(2), 169–187 (2005). https://doi.org/10.1080/10789669.2005.10391133
9. Kim, W., Katipamula, S.: A review of fault detection and diagnostics methods for building systems. Sci. Technol. Built Environ. **24**(1), 3–21 (2018). https://doi.org/10.1080/23744731.2017.1318008
10. Månsson, S., Kallioniemi, P.O.J., Sernhed, K., Thern, M.: A machine learning approach to fault detection in district heating substations. Energy Procedia **149**, 226–235 (2018). https://doi.org/10.1016/j.egypro.2018.08.187. 16th International Symposium on District Heating and Cooling, DHC2018, 9-12 September 2018, Hamburg, Germany
11. Pakanen, J., Hyvärinen, J., Kuismin, J., Ahonen, M.: Fault diagnosis methods for district heating substations. VTT Tiedotteita - Valtion Teknillinen Tutkimuskeskus (1996)
12. Sandin, F., Gustafsson, J., Delsing, J.: Fault detection with hourly district energy data: probabilistic methods and heuristics for automated detection and ranking of anomalies. Technical report, Svensk Fjärrvärme AB (2013)
13. Shaker, H.R., Santos, A., Jørgensen, B.: A practical data-driven condition indicator for room-level building diagnostics. Energy Inform. (2021)
14. Søndergaard, H.A.N., Shaker, H.R., Jørgensen, B.N.: Automated and real-time anomaly indexing for district heating maintenance decision support system. SSRN Electron. J. (2023). https://doi.org/10.2139/ssrn.4344182
15. Sun, W., Cheng, D., Peng, W.: Anomaly detection analysis for district heating apartments. J. Appl. Sci. Eng. **21**, 33–44 (2018). https://doi.org/10.6180/jase.201803_21(1).0005
16. Webert, H., Döß, T., Kaupp, L., Simons, S.: Fault handling in industry 4.0: definition, process and applications. Sensors **22**(6), 2205 (2022). https://doi.org/10.3390/s22062205
17. Xue, P., et al.: Fault detection and operation optimization in district heating substations based on data mining techniques. Appl. Energy **205**, 926–940 (2017). https://doi.org/10.1016/j.apenergy.2017.08.035

18. Yu, W., Patros, P., Young, B., Klinac, E., Walmsley, T.G.: Energy digital twin technology for industrial energy management: classification, challenges and future. Renew. Sustain. Energy Rev. **161**, 112407 (2022)

19. Zimmerman, N., Dahlquist, E., Kyprianidis, K.: Towards on-line fault detection and diagnostics in district heating systems. Energy Procedia **105**, 1960–1966 (2017). https://doi.org/10.1016/j.egypro.2017.03.567. 8th International Conference on Applied Energy, ICAE2016, 8-11 October 2016, Beijing, China

Virtual Sensor-Based Fault Detection and Diagnosis Framework for District Heating Systems: A Top-Down Approach for Quick Fault Localisation

Theis Bank, Frederik Wagner Madsen, Lasse Kappel Mortensen$^{(\boxtimes)}$ ⓘ,
Henrik Alexander Nissen Søndergaard ⓘ, and Hamid Reza Shaker ⓘ

University of Southern Denmark, 5230 Odense, Denmark
lkmo@mmmi.sdu.dk

Abstract. For district heating systems (DHS) to operate cost-effectively, avoid disturbances of loads, and increase overall energy efficiency, faults in DHSs must be detected, located, and rectified quickly. For this purpose, a novel digital twin-based fault detection and diagnosis framework with virtual sensor employment have been developed. The framework defines virtual sensors measuring the mass flow rate in points in the DHS where sensors are absent by using the existing sensors in the system. Faults in the virtual sensors are detected when deviations occur between the calculated and digital twin-simulated mass flow rate using a bound of normal operation, allowing some degree of modelling error. To define which virtual sensors are of interest, a novel Specialised Agglomerative Hierarchical Clustering algorithm will be used. A case study on a DHS of a suburb in Odense showed how the framework was able to locate faults with a top-down approach and could indicate whether the fault was local or due to upstream faults. The framework has the potential to be implemented in real-time monitoring of a DHS.

Keywords: Fault detection and diagnosis · District heating systems · Digital twin · Virtual sensor · Machine learning

1 Introduction

In Denmark, a large share of households uses district heating (DH) for hot water use and space heating. The objective of a district heating system (DHS) is to distribute cost-effective heat to consumers efficiently [2]. As hot water use and space heating are a large proportion of total energy use in the EU [5], the DHSs are critical infrastructure, which means it is a relevant domain to improve energy efficiency and thereby lowering CO_2 emissions. The vast amount of functionalities required for the operation of the DHS makes it complex and failure prone. To guarantee the DHS works efficiently, these faults need to be detected and corrected quickly, as the faults result in suboptimal operating conditions of the DHS [2,9,12].

© The Author(s), under exclusive license to Springer Nature Switzerland AG 2024
B. N. Jørgensen et al. (Eds.): EI.A 2023, LNCS 14468, pp. 292–307, 2024.
https://doi.org/10.1007/978-3-031-48652-4_19

Currently, most DH companies perform reactive- and preventive maintenance, whereas proactive maintenance is rarely used. With a reactive maintenance strategy, it is difficult to detect faults quickly. It may also lead to faults never being detected, e.g., if the DHS can compensate for the fault and still deliver heat, but this will still waste energy. Preventive maintenance often leads to a waste of resources due to redundant maintenance. To utilise the still ongoing digitalisation of the DH sector by implementing proactive maintenance, diagnostic tools using automatic fault detection and diagnosis (FDD) methods are of great interest. Developing such tools and methods to detect faults expeditiously and affordably in a DHS would reduce the energy and time waste and furthermore reduce CO_2 emissions.

In [6], three sub-types are used to categorise different FDD methods: quantitative model-based, qualitative model-based, and process history-based, where all three have certain advantages and disadvantages. An advantage of the quantitative model-based method is the utilisation of a very precise model, which is built on the basis of thorough physical or engineering principles. On the other hand, the precise model is also a disadvantage of the method because of the level of complexity and required amount of input needed to build the model, which can lead to reducing the scalability of the approach. [19] models a DHS in OpenModelica, and uses the output of the model together with pressure sensors to calculate residuals. A Bayesian Network is then used to compare these residuals, calculate fault probability, and evaluate the system. [1] also uses a qualitative model-based approach, where a DH pipe network is simulated together with an optimisation problem, used to detect both thermal and hydraulic faults.

While the difference between quantitative- and qualitative model-based methods can be vague due to overlapping features, the process history-based method differs a lot. This category covers data-driven approaches, that do not necessarily require knowledge about the complex physics of the DHS system, and offers great scalability. On the other hand, these methods may require vast amounts of correct data, which can be hard to obtain. Furthermore, they can have high computational demands.

Generally, for the domain of DHS, data-driven FDD is more researched compared to model-based approaches. A data-driven method is seen in [14], which utilises three FDD methods: Hotelling's T^2 and Q statistics, contextual Shewhart chart, and linear regression, enabling to check if all methods agree on detected faults. More examples of data-driven approaches are seen in [8,10,15,16]. [15] identifies operations patterns by three clustering methods, [8] predicts normal operation of DH substations with the use of gradient boosting regressor, and [16] finds rule patterns for the operation of a DH substation using cluster- and association analysis.

This paper utilises a quantitative model as DH companies often have thorough knowledge about their pipe network regarding configuration, dimensions, and heat transfer coefficients, which can be used to set up a digital twin (DT) in industry-specialised software. Software, that supports geographical information systems also allows the operator to locate and correlate faults quickly on a map.

[9,12] argues that previously FDD frameworks for DHS were old and not sufficiently advanced for the move towards Industry 4.0. Though more methods are being developed, as we have highlighted, there is still a general lack of research on FDD in the DHS domain, as is also emphasized by [2]. For these reasons and to support the move towards Industry 4.0, the framework proposed in this paper integrates data from modern residential smart heat meters alongside substations' sensor data to operationalise a digital twin of a real DH network for improved monitoring and proactive maintenance.

One way of utilising a digital twin of a DHS is through the ability to calculate certain properties everywhere in the system. This can be used together with virtual sensors and thereby enabling fault detection by comparing the results from the digital twin and the virtual sensors. For the energy systems domain, virtual sensors have been developed in different applications, such as heat, ventilation, and air conditioning (HVAC) systems of buildings and in residential buildings in a DHS. [7] uses physical relations inside the HVAC to establish virtual sensors, which enables FDD and introduces cost-efficient redundancy. In [17], virtual sensors are established by grey-box modelling, which estimates heating loads in residential buildings in the absence of sensors. To the best of the authors' knowledge, using virtual sensors and a digital twin to locate faults in the pipe network of a DHS has not been done before.

The contribution of this paper to the apparent research gap in the literature for FDD in DHSs is two-fold. Firstly, a digital twin-based FDD framework utilising virtual sensors is developed, which can detect and locate faults in a DHS. To the best of our knowledge, this has not been done before. Furthermore, the FDD method makes use of a novel Specialised Agglomerative Hierarchical Clustering algorithm that validates discovered clusters with information about virtual sensors. Secondly, the framework is tested by implementing it on a case study with real-world sensor data and a digital twin of a DHS.

In Sect. 2, the different steps of the framework are presented, and in Sect. 3, the framework is implemented on a case study, and results are shown.

2   Methodology

This section will present a novel digital twin-based FDD framework using virtual sensors for DHSs.

The framework will utilise sensor measurements and a digital twin to detect faults in virtual sensors in DHSs. Faults in this context are abnormalities and deviations between measured- and digital twin simulated data. Faults can be located in the DHS to correlate possible multiple faulty consumers in an area. Locating and correlating faults in a specific area will enable a maintenance crew to focus resources on local related faults instead of individual faults at consumers. This may lead to the use of fewer resources and achieve better system performance. The unsupervised nature of the framework means it does not require historical maintenance records or fault characteristics. This both strengthens the framework's applicability as it has fewer requirements for implementation than would otherwise be the case, but it also comes at the cost of weakened diagnosis capabilities.

The framework, seen in Fig 1, is divided into eight steps and shows how sensor measurements in the DHS are simulated in a digital twin, how data is processed, and how virtual sensors and consumer clusters are used to perform FDD on pipes in the system. For the purpose of this work, we adopt the general definition of a digital twin stated by Yu et al. [18] that "a DT is a digital (or virtual) representation that looks-like, behaves-like, and connects-to a physical part or system with the goal of improving or optimising decision making for any time horizon".

In the first step of the framework, data is collected from sensors at the individual consumers and at sub-stations. In step two, this data is processed and formatted together with a thorough investigation of the data, finding abnormalities and physics-violations, to validate it. Invalidated data is reconstructed in step 2. In the third step, some of the sensor data is imported as time series to a digital twin as boundary conditions, which can run quasi-dynamic simulations showing the state of the DHS. The proposed FDD framework exploits the increasing modelling error in the digital twin, which occurs due to faults or when the boundary conditions indicate abnormal operation at an individual consumer, to detect deviations between the sensor- and digital twin data The

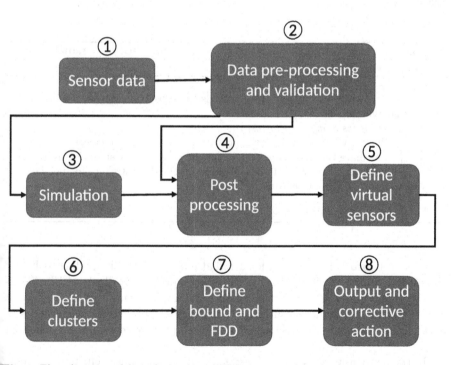

Fig. 1. Flow diagram of digital twin-based FDD framework with virtual sensor employments.

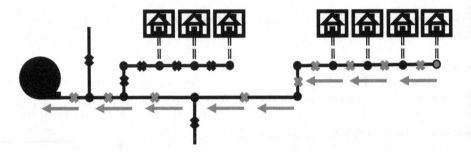

Fig. 2. Virtual sensors are represented as crosses, and nodes connecting pipes and consumers are represented as dots. The arrows show the shortest route from the red end node to the sub-station. (Color figure online)

desired output from the digital twin is consumer properties and the mass flow rate in the pipes used later for the FDD and fault location. The results from the digital twin are formatted and validated in step four for the further use of the data.

The virtual sensors employed in the DHS, in step five, will hold the mass flow rate in the pipes. A pseudocode for the virtual sensor calculation is seen in Alg. 1.

Algorithm 1: Pseudocode for virtual sensors in pipes of a radial pipe configuration.

---

for *all end nodes in the system* **do**
  Find the shortest route of pipes towards the substation using the Dijkstra algorithm [4];
  for *all nodes along the shortest route* **do**
    Place a virtual sensor in the upstream pipe the node connects to;
    Calculate the mass flow rate in the virtual sensor by summing up the total mass flow rate at the consumers in the downstream pipe network from the virtual sensor;

Filter out virtual sensor duplicates;

The pseudocode in Alg. 1 is for a radial pipe configuration, which is by far the most common configuration in DHSs. The approach is illustrated in Fig. 2, where crosses represent the virtual sensors in the pipes and dots are the nodes connecting the pipes and consumers. Applying this approach to all end nodes in a radial pipe network will ensure that all pipes in the system will have a virtual sensor.

In the sixth step, clusters of consumers are defined. These clusters will indicate which virtual sensors are of interest and can be used for FDD. Figure 3 shows how consumers along a small residential street connected to a main pipe can be clustered into one large cluster (blue area) and two smaller sub-clusters (green area). The virtual sensors of interest are shown in Fig 3 (black and red crosses). Larger clusters are divided into smaller sub-clusters as this allows for detecting and locating faults from a top-down approach. E.g. in Fig 3, if a fault occurs in the large cluster (black virtual sensor), then the sub-clusters (red virtual sensors) are investigated. Here a fault might only be detected in one of the sub-clusters, which narrows down the fault location.

Performing FDD on the individual consumers in the sub-cluster can indicate the final location of the fault. If only one consumer in the sub-cluster is operating in a faulty condition, that consumer will probably be the cause of the deviation in the virtual sensors. On the other hand, if multiple consumers operate under faulty conditions, the probability of similar faults at each consumer might be low and can therefore indicate faults in the upstream pipe network.

This paper proposes the use of a Specialised Agglomerative Hierarchical Clustering algorithm, which is a modification of the standard Agglomerative Hierarchical Clustering algorithm for which some of the earliest mentions are from Sibson [13] and Rohlf [11]. The specialized approach views the pipe network as a graph and uses the bottom-up hierarchical clustering method to cluster consumers in close proximity. The extension of the algorithm is proposed to avoid wrongly defined clusters, i.e., clusters of consumers that have no corresponding virtual sensor. This logic is defined as: If c represents a set of consumers, and $V(c)$ is a boolean representation of whether a virtual sensor exists that only aggregates information for the consumers in the set c, then a cluster produced with Agglomerative Hierarchical Clustering, which groups the consumers in set c, is accepted if and only if $V(c) = 1$. The extension of the clustering algorithm can be seen as a filter that eliminates clusters without a corresponding virtual sensor.

The Specialised Hierarchical Agglomerative Clustering algorithm is presented in Algorithm 2. C is a set of clusters at all hierarchical levels, R is a set of the indices of a cluster's children, and H is a set of distances between the children

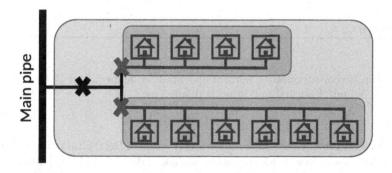

Fig. 3. Hierarchical clustering of consumers. The diagram shows one large cluster and two sub-clusters with their representing virtual sensors (black and red crosses). (Color figure online)

of a cluster. In this setting P is a set of the individual consumers, and $x_k \in X$ denote the consumers downstream of the virtual meter point k. N_c is the number of clusters, which reduce by 1 each time two clusters are agglomerated and it defines when the algorithm is done, i.e., when all points are agglomerated into 1 cluster. The distance between two points is the shortest distance along the pipes of the network, calculated with the Dijkstra algorithm [4]. The distance function denotes yields the maximum distance between all points of the two input clusters (complete linkage).

Algorithm 2: Specialised Hierarchical Agglomerative Clustering

---

Given: *A set of points to cluster* $P = \{p_1, ..., p_n\}$*, a set of potential clusters* $X = x_1, ..., x_k$*, and a distance function* $d(c_1, c_2)$ *Populate the set of clusters,* C *with the points in* P;

$C \leftarrow \{\}$;

H *denotes the distance between the children of each cluster and* R *denotes the indices of the children of each cluster, both of which are empty for leaf clusters*;

for $i \leftarrow 1$ **to** n **do**

> $C \overset{+}{\leftarrow} \{p_i\}$;
>
> $H \overset{+}{\leftarrow} \{\}$;
>
> $R \overset{+}{\leftarrow} \{\}$;

$Z \leftarrow C$;

$N_c = |C|$;

while $N_c > 1$ **do**

> $a, b = \underset{i,j}{\operatorname{argmin}}\, d(z_i, z_j)$ where $i \neq j$ **and** $\{z_i, z_j\} \subseteq X$;
>
> $C \overset{+}{\leftarrow} \{z_a, z_b\}$;
>
> $Z \overset{+}{\leftarrow} \{z_a, z_b\}$;
>
> $R \overset{+}{\leftarrow} \{a, b\}$;
>
> $H \overset{+}{\leftarrow} d(z_a, z_b)$;
>
> $Z \overset{-}{\leftarrow} \{z_a\}$ **and** $\{z_b\}$;
>
> $N_c \mathrel{-}= 1$

Return C, R, and H

In step seven, a bound of normal operation is defined, and FDD is carried out. The bound of normal operation is defined as,

$$Target \cdot (1 \pm \beta) \tag{1}$$

The target in Eq. 1 is the simulated property value in the digital twin, and β is a ratio parameter of how much deviation is allowed due to small modelling errors. Faults are detected by investigating at each time step if the virtual sensor is outside the bound of normal operation simulated in the digital twin. Consecutive out of bound detections will be defined as one faulty event. Faults may arise as a consequence of different events or phenomena, abnormal boundary conditions, such as very low cooling efficiency, can increase modelling error and may be detected using the proposed method. Lastly, in step eight, the detected faults are located with a top-down approach using the hierarchical clusters, and corrective and maintenance actions can be initiated.

3   Case Study and Results

3.1   Description of Case Study

The digital twin-based FDD framework with virtual sensor employments presented will be implemented in a case study in a suburb of Odense, Denmark. The DHS operator, Fjernvarme Fyn, provided historical data and a Leanheat Network (LHN) model for the DHS, which was developed in collaboration with Danfoss, the developer of the software. The LHN model constitute the digital twin of the system.

LHN simulations are performed by hydraulic and thermal condition simulations and pressure and temperature optimisations, minimising pump- and heat production costs, based on defined material properties and boundary conditions at the substation and individual consumers. Simulation results from LHN provides properties at all nodes and pipes in the DHS [3].

Figure 4 shows the DHS of the suburb implemented in LHN, all 648 connected consumers are supplied via the substation. The DHS in the diagram has only radial connections because it is only operated in a radial manner, which is typically for DHSs. Nevertheless, most DHSs have meshed connections for redundancy, e.g. for when faults happen.

The implementation of the framework on the case study results in a list of abnormalities, of which two are analysed to find the possible roots of the abnormalities. Due to not having a maintenance record, a more quantitative method of analysing the abnormalities could not be performed, where the abnormalities could have been compared with the maintenance record thereby confirming or denying them.

The data, from December 2022 to January 2023, contains consumer sensor measurements on a daily resolution at the 648 consumers and sensor measurements on an hourly resolution at the substation. Consumer data contains the energy consumption, volumetric flow rate and supplied and returned energy, which is the supplied and return temperature multiplied by the volumetric flow rate. The substation data contains supplied and returned energy, mass flow rate, pressure, and temperature.

The data will be formatted to have the correct units and a time series format for the model. The model will simulate hourly quasi-dynamic simulations representing the whole day, where the boundary conditions for the model will be return temperature and energy consumption at the consumers, supply temperature and return pressure at the substation, and pressure change at a critical node assumed to be 1.33 bar based on expert knowledge. The output from the model will be the mass flow rate in all the pipes of the network and consumers, which will be used for the later FDD and fault location investigation. This case

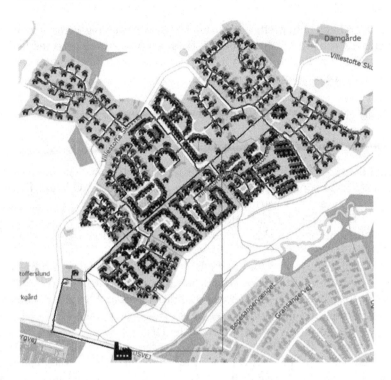

Fig. 4. Visualisation of DHS implemented in the LHN model. The substation located at the bottom supplies the 648 consumers through the pipe network, which represents the real configuration of the DHS. Red dots represent the nodes connecting the pipes and black houses represent the individual consumers. (Color figure online)

study will focus on two consumer clusters in the DHS, which will be divided into sub-clusters, to showcase the capabilities of the framework.

3.2   Consumer Clustering

To enable the monitoring of the DHS by a top-down approach, the consumers need to be clustered in several clusters and sub-clusters. This section will show how a cluster of seven consumers is defined (Cluster 1) using the proposed Specialised Agglomerative Hierarchical Clustering algorithm.

The bottom-up clustering method begins at the lowest level, i.e., each consumer is a cluster, which can be seen in the dendrogram in Fig. 5. Using the geographical data from the model, the method iteratively looks at the defined distance matrix of the edge (pipe) lengths and joins the two closest clusters into one cluster, until only one cluster is left. After the clustering, the dendrogram is used to define the number of sub-clusters by defining a distance threshold. For this clustering, a distance threshold of 60 m is chosen. This resulted in one overall cluster (blue) with two sub-clusters (orange and green), as seen in Fig. 5, but the distance threshold is ultimately a tuneable hyperparameter. Also in general, a series of distance thresholds must be selected to account for more upstream clusters.

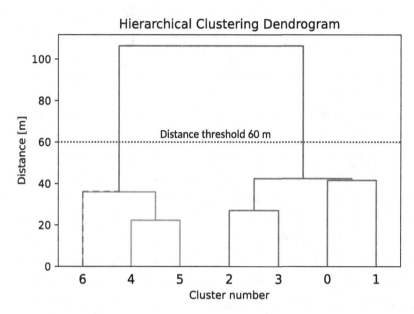

Fig. 5. Dendogram of Cluster 1; initially, all consumers are considered individual clusters. At each iteration, the two closest clusters are joined. The horizontal red dotted line shows the distance threshold is set to 60 m (Color figure online) and defines the two sub-clusters. Consumer 6 is connected with a dotted blue line, representing that the logic-based rule constraint rejects consumer 6 from the clusters containing consumers 4 and 5 as no virtual sensor exists that aggregates all three of them.

The graph representation of the seven consumers (Fig. 6), which is used to define the distance matrix, indicates that the orange sub-cluster is wrongly defined due to the locations of the virtual sensor, which is corrected with the extension of the algorithm. In the dendrogram (Fig. 5), the orange sub-cluster holds three consumers, but the virtual sensor only holds two of them. The logic-based rule extension of the Agglomerative Hierarchical Clustering will indicate that there is no virtual sensor which holds consumers 4, 5, and 6 and therefore disregards this cluster. Going one level down in the hierarchical clustering (Fig. 5), the logic-based rule will accept the sub-cluster containing consumers 4 and 5 and reject consumers 6, as there is a virtual sensor which holds consumers 4 and 5.

A second cluster (Cluster 2) located in another part of the DHS was also made. This cluster contains 13 consumers and was divided into three sub-clusters, two sub-clusters with four consumers and one with five (Sub-cluster 2.1, 2.2, and 2.3).

Graph representation of 7 consumers

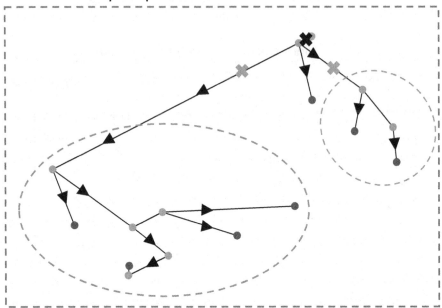

Fig. 6. Cluster 1 contains seven consumers (blue dots), nine nodes (red dots), and 11 pipes (black lines) represented as a graph. The virtual sensors of interest are defined as red and black crosses, where the belonging clusters are represented as dotted lines (blue, green, and orange). Black arrows show the direction of forward flow in the pipes. (Color figure online)

3.3   Fault Investigation and Location

This section will present the detected faults in the virtual sensors and locate the faults with a top-down approach using the hierarchical consumer clusters defined. The parameter β defines the size of the bound and must be calibrated to produce an appropriate number of faults, as there is a direct connection between the size of the bound and the number of faults detected. The bound of normal operation used in this paper is introduced in Eq. 1, with $\beta = 0.3$.

Figure 7 illustrates the mass flow rate in the virtual sensors supplying Cluster 1 and Sub-cluster 1.1 and 1.2. Figure 7 shows that a large deviation in Cluster 1 occurs between the modelled mass flow rate and the calculated mass flow rate in the virtual sensor. This resulted in three fault detections (grey marked areas in Fig. 7). Going one level down in the hierarchy of the consumer clusters, it is evident that the fault in Cluster 1 is due to a fault occurring in Sub-cluster 1.1, as Fig. 7 shows faults detected in Sub-cluster 1.1 and not in Sub-cluster 1.2. FDD was done at the individual consumer level at last and showed that only one consumer was operating in a faulty condition. This may lead to the conclusion

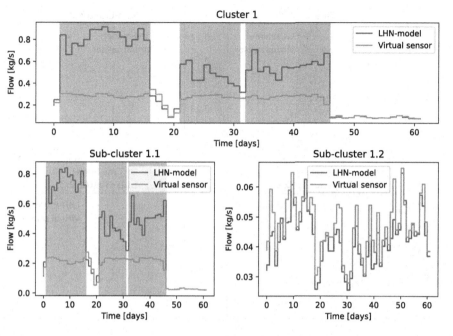

Fig. 7. Cluster 1; Shows the mass flow rate in the virtual sensors supply Cluster 1 and Sub-cluster 1.1 and 1.2. Grey marked areas represent faults detected. (Color figure online)

that it is a local fault at the consumer or its service pipe and is possibly not due to a fault in the upstream pipe network.

Figure 8 shows a consumer cluster of another part of the DHS. Cluster 2 contains three terrace houses with 13 individual consumers in total. Cluster 2 is located far away from the sub-station, and the consumers are the last connected to the pipe branch. Sub-cluster 2.1, 2.2, and 2.3 contains four, five, and four individual consumers, respectively. Figure 8 shows that two faults were detected in Cluster 2 (grey marked areas).

Investigating the three sub-clusters of Cluster 2, in Fig. 8, shows faults were detected only in Sub-clusters 2.2 and 2.3. Notice that some of the faults in Cluster 2 and Sub-cluster 2.2 and 2.3 happen in the same time span, indicating a correlation of the faults. An investigation of the individual consumers in the two faulty sub-clusters showed that faults only were detected at one out of five consumers in Sub-cluster 2.2 and at three out of four consumers in Sub-cluster 2.3.

A visualisation of Cluster 2 and its sub-clusters can be seen in Fig. 9. As faults were both detected in Sub-cluster 2.2 and 2.3, the location of the fault could be upstream in the pipe network from Sub-cluster 2.2. A precise location

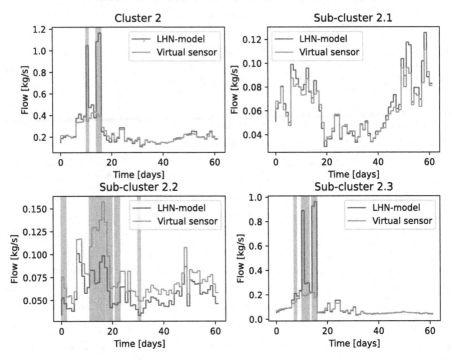

Fig. 8. Cluster 2; Shows the mass flow rate in the virtual sensors supply Cluster 2 and Sub-cluster 2.1, 2.2, and 2.3. Grey marked areas represent faults detected. (Color figure online)

of the fault or multiple faults can be difficult to determine and will have to be found by a thorough investigation.

One possibility could be a fault had occurred in the pipe between Sub-cluster 2.1 and 2.2 as faults were detected in both sub-clusters downstream from Sub-cluster 2.1. This fault could be due to pipe leakage or damage to the pipe insulation, among other things. A fault in this pipe could be the reason for the faults detected further downstream in the pipe network and would have a cascading effect of introducing multiple faults.

Another scenario could be that a fault had occurred in the pipe between Sub-cluster 2.2 and 2.3 and that the single fault detected in Sub-cluster 2.2 is due to a local fault at the faulty consumer. It is unlikely that the faults at three out of four consumers in Sub-cluster 2.3 are due to local faults, which increases the possibility of a fault had occurred further upstream in the pipe network, possibly the main pipe going into the terrace house.

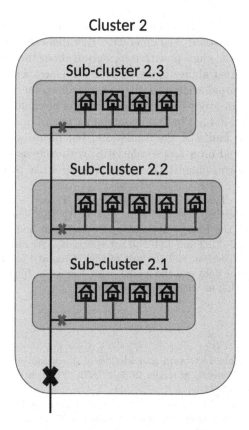

Fig. 9. Visualisation of the pipe network configuration of Cluster 2 and Sub-Cluster 2.1, 2.2, and 2.3. The blue area represents Cluster 2, and the black cross is its virtual sensor. Green areas represent the sub-clusters, and red crosses their virtual sensor. (Color figure online)

3.4   Conclusion and Future Work

Faults occurring in the complex domain of DHSs must be detected, and corrective actions must be made to ensure the cost-effectiveness of the system, avoid disturbance of loads, and lower the overall energy losses and CO_2 emissions of the system. To target these objectives and locate faults, this paper proposes a digital twin-based FDD framework with virtual sensor employments to detect, locate faults in DHSs

The framework defines virtual sensors in the DHS's pipes measuring the mass flow rate, where real sensors are absent, by summing up the total mass flow rate at consumer sensors downstream in the pipe network from the virtual sensors. Faults were detected by the framework by investigating residuals between the calculated and digital twin-simulated mass flow rate in pipes using a bound of normal operation defined as $Target \cdot (1 \pm \beta)$, where the ratio parameter (β) can be calibrated.

To define which virtual sensors are of interest and should be monitored, this paper proposes a Specialised Agglomerative Hierarchical Clustering algorithm that validates discovered clusters with information about the virtual sensors. The framework shows a great ability to detect faults in places where real sensors are absent, and it uses a top-down approach to narrow down the location of the fault. Faults found in the case study of this paper could not be confirmed and diagnosed since Fjernvarme Fyn did not have a maintenance record of abnormalities at the locations of detected faults by the framework. For future work, the framework should be implemented on a large-scale DHS, with a focus testing how well it generalises and performs quantitatively, using metrics like precision and recall.

Acknowledgements. This work is supported by the "Proactive and Predictive Maintenance of District Heating Systems" and "IEA DHC TS4", funded by the Danish Energy Agency under the Energy Technology Development and Demonstration Program, ID number 64020-2102 and 134-22011, respectively. We also thank Peer Andersen, Lasse Elmelund Pedersen, and the rest of their team at Fjernvarme Fyn A/S for their assistance with the data and the model. Also, thanks to Johan Peter Alsing from Danfoss A/S for assisting us with Leanheat Network.

References

1. Bahlawan, H., et al.: Detection and identification of faults in a district heating network. Energy Convers. Manage. **266**, 115837 (2022). https://doi.org/10.1016/j.enconman.2022.115837
2. Buffa, S., Fouladfar, M.H., Franchini, G., Lozano Gabarre, I., Andrés Chicote, M.: Advanced control and fault detection strategies for district heating and cooling systems-a review. Appl. Sci. **11**(1) (2021). https://doi.org/10.3390/app11010455
3. Danfoss: Concept guide: Leanheat network concept and modeling elements(2021). Accessed 9 Sept 2023
4. Dijkstra, E.W.: A note on two problems in connexion with graphs. Numer. Math. **1**(1), 269–271 (1959)
5. EU: Commission recommendation (eu) 2019/786 of 8 May 2019 on building renovation (2019). https://bit.ly/30nxBs5
6. Katipamula, S., Brambley, M.R.: Review article: methods for fault detection, diagnostics, and prognostics for building systems-a review, part ii. HVAC&R Res. **11**(2), 169–187 (2005). https://doi.org/10.1080/10789669.2005.10391133
7. Mattera, C.G., Quevedo, J., Escobet, T., Shaker, H.R., Jradi, M.: A method for fault detection and diagnostics in ventilation units using virtual sensors. Sensors (2018). https://www.mdpi.com/1424-8220/18/11/3931
8. Månsson, S., Kallioniemi, P.O.J., Sernhed, K., Thern, M.: A machine learning approach to fault detection in district heating substations. Energy Procedia **149**, 226–235 (2018). https://doi.org/10.1016/j.egypro.2018.08.187, 16th International Symposium on District Heating and Cooling, DHC2018, 9-12 September 2018, Hamburg, Germany
9. Pakanen, J., Hyvärinen, J., Kuismin, J., Ahonen, M.: Fault diagnosis methods for district heating substations. VTT Tiedotteita - Valtion Teknillinen Tutkimuskeskus (1996)

10. Pedersen, A.S.H., Ustrup, S.E., Mortensen, L.K., Shaker, H.R.: Data valida-
    tion for digitally enabled operation maintenance of district heating systems. In:
    2022 International Conference on Electrical, Computer, Communications and
    Mechatronics Engineering (ICECCME), pp. 1–7 (2022). https://doi.org/10.1109/
    ICECCME55909.2022.9988721
11. Rohlf, F.J.: Single-link clustering algorithms (1987)
12. Sandin, F., Gustafsson, J., Delsing, J.: Fault detection with hourly district energy
    data: probabilistic methods and heuristics for automated detection and ranking of
    anomalies. Tech. rep., Svensk Fjärrvärme AB (2013)
13. Sibson, R.: SLINK: an optimally efficient algorithm for the single-link cluster
    method. Comput. J. **16**(1), 30–34 (1973). https://doi.org/10.1093/comjnl/16.1.
    30
14. Søndergaard, H.A.N., Shaker, H.R., Jørgensen, B.N.: Automated and real-time
    anomaly indexing for district heating maintenance decision support system
    (preprint). SSRN Electron. J. (2023). https://doi.org/10.2139/ssrn.4344182
15. Sun, W., Cheng, D., Peng, W.: Anomaly detection analysis for district heating
    apartments. J. Appl. Sci. Eng. **21**, 33–44 (2018). https://doi.org/10.6180/jase.
    201803_21(1).0005
16. Xue, P., et al.: Fault detection and operation optimization in district heating sub-
    stations based on data mining techniques. Appl. Energy **205**, 926–940 (2017).
    https://doi.org/10.1016/j.apenergy.2017.08.035
17. Yoon, S., Choi, Y., Koo, J., Hong, Y., Kim, R., Kim, J.: Virtual sensors for esti-
    mating district heating energy consumption under sensor absences in a residential
    building. Energies (2020). https://www.mdpi.com/1996-1073/13/22/6013
18. Yu, W., Patros, P., Young, B., Klinac, E., Walmsley, T.G.: Energy digital
    twin technology for industrial energy management: classification, challenges
    and future. Renew. Sustain. Energy Rev. **161**, 112407 (2022). https://doi.org/
    10.1016/j.rser.2022.112407, https://www.sciencedirect.com/science/article/pii/
    S136403212200315X
19. Zimmerman, N., Dahlquist, E., Kyprianidis, K.: Towards on-line fault detec-
    tion and diagnostics in district heating systems. Energy Procedia **105**, 1960–
    1966 (2017). https://doi.org/10.1016/j.egypro.2017.03.567, 8th International Con-
    ference on Applied Energy, ICAE2016, 8-11 October 2016, Beijing, China

Digitalization of District Heating and Cooling Systems

Dietrich Schmidt$^{(\boxtimes)}$ (iD)

Fraunhofer Institute for Energy Economics and Energy System Technology IEE,
Joseph-Beuys-Strasse 8, 34117 Kassel, Germany
`dietrich.schmidt@iee.fraunhofer.de`

Abstract. District heating and cooling (DHC) networks are often run with a small number of sensors and actuators to provide the necessary supply and to maximize economics based on a predetermined high ecologic performance. With better knowledge of the demand and flexibility options, it is feasible to optimize heat generation and network functioning overall. Improved network management based on real-time measurement data and the incorporation of new digital business processes is made possible by a greater deployment of information and communication technology. Clarifying the role of digitalization for various components within district heating and cooling systems is necessary for ongoing growth, as is promoting opportunities for the integration of digital processes into DHC systems. Digital technologies are expected to improve the efficiency and system integration of additional renewable sources while also making the entire energy system smarter, more reliable, and more efficient. Future district energy systems could be able to completely optimize their plant and network functioning while empowering the end user thanks to digital applications. However, there are still more difficulties to be overcome, including issues with data privacy and security as well as issues with data ownership. The research findings from the IEA DHC Annex TS4 on "Digitalization of District Heating Systems – Optimized Operation and Maintenance of District Heating and Cooling Systems via Digital Process Management" are presented and discussed in this publication. https://www.iea-dhc. org/the-research/annexes/2018-2024-annex-ts4.

Keywords: Digitalization of district heating · operation and maintenance · business processes and models

1 Introduction

It is thought that the widespread adoption of digital technology would make our energy systems smarter, more efficient, and more reliable. The utilization of cutting-edge digital technology and procedures also creates new commercial opportunities and is predicted to result in a considerably higher integration of renewable energy sources into the systems [1]. The DHC Annex TS4 initiative is aimed to promote the possibilities of integrating digital processes into DHC schemes in this context. This necessitates a clarification of the function of digitalization for various aspects of the district heating and cooling system's

B. N. Jørgensen et al. (Eds.): EI.A 2023, LNCS 14468, pp. 308–313, 2024.
https://doi.org/10.1007/978-3-031-48652-4_20

operation and maintenance. Additionally, these technologies' applications are shown in close collaboration with a number of industrial partners. Additionally, issues including data privacy and security, as well as queries regarding data ownership, are addressed [2]. The overall structure of the internationally cooperative work of Annex TS4 within the Technology cooperation program on District Heating and Cooling (DHC) of the International Energy Agency (IEA) is given in this article. The initiative offers a forum for the sharing of research findings from both national and international activities. In this approach, information on the digitalization of district heating and cooling systems is gathered, compiled, and presented.

2 Digitalization in District Heating

District heating and cooling (DHC) networks are often operated with a limited number of controls, such as regulating supply temperatures or network pressure, to ensure supply and maximize economic and ecological performance. However, in traditional network operations, there is a lack of detailed information about supply and utilization structures. By gaining more knowledge about demand and flexibility options, such as energy storage, it becomes possible to achieve peak shaving and reduce the use of expensive peak boilers. This leads to efficient heat generation and improved overall network functioning. Previous projects have demonstrated the integration of diverse heat sources, including solar thermal energy and power-to-heat applications that function in electricity markets. The increased use of information and communication technology enables better network management through real-time measurement data and the incorporation of new business models. This has resulted in the emergence of businesses offering products and services like smart meters or digital analysis platforms, which contribute to enhanced network efficiency. Overall, by harnessing the potential of advanced technologies and integrating renewable energy sources, DHC networks can optimize their performance, reduce costs, and promote sustainability in heating and cooling systems.

The particular significance of digitalization in district heating systems arises from the fact that it is a need for cutting-edge low-temperature, or "4th generation," heat networks [4, 5] that incorporate variable and renewable heat sources. Therefore, digitalization has the potential to make heat networks more efficient, dependable, better suited for the integration of lower temperatures, such as through the optimal use of heat pumps or CHP units, and more profitable, such as through the reduction of expensive fossil fuel consumption or through the reduction of transmission losses.

Digitalization in district heating systems is demanding a

- Large number of sensors present in the network,
- An automated recording, transfer, and storage of data
- Automated analyses of data
- The use of analyses beyond automated billing to optimize the network operation.

3 The International Cooperation in IEA DHC Annex TS4

The project DHC Annex TS4 aims to raise awareness of the potential for incorporating digital technology into district heating and cooling systems. The project's primary areas of attention include new business model potential based on digital technology and the legal environment for using things like data, for example. Additionally, a description of how digitalization affects many aspects of system operation and maintenance is provided. A tight partnership between industry and research teams demonstrates how these technologies and procedures are implemented.

The initiative aims to provide insights and information on how the district heating sector and system suppliers are impacted by digitization. It emphasizes the state of the art, points out obstacles, and offers goals, targets, and suggestions for each of the district heating systems' targeted levels:

- Level of sector coupling or integration of numerous sources of production
- Building and consumption levels
- Distribution level
- Legal level
- Economic and business level

The project considers the full energy chain, from production/generation through distribution to end usage and particularly consumer (secondary side systems).

The main objectives of DHC Annex TS4 are to:

- Raise awareness among the various stakeholders and users of the benefits of implementing digital processes; and
- Provide a current overview of the digitalization of district heating schemes in terms of R&D projects, demonstrators, and case studies.
- Consider non-technical factors such as business models, legal considerations, and policy instruments when evaluating barriers and enablers to digitalization processes in district heating and cooling schemes.

All research efforts that are the focus of this activity are organized into so-called subtasks (ST) in order to achieve the goals outlined above (Fig. 1).

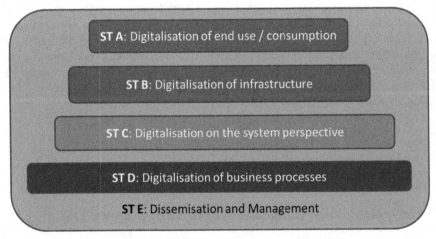

Fig. 1. Working structure of the IEA-DHC Annex TS4, including different subtasks (ST).

Within the group of participants from industrial partners and from research organizations, the main interest areas for the digitization of district heating systems were identified, and this working structure is built on those areas. The following provides a more thorough description of various working groups.

3.1 Digitalization of End Use/Consumption

This working item's goal is to create and demonstrate techniques for improving the operation of heating systems in buildings in order to lower supply and return temperatures as well as peak loads. These approaches are based on data from energy meters.

Heat cost allocators on radiators, space heating sub-energy meters, household hot water systems, and the main energy meter on the district heating supply to individual buildings are all migrating to digital and wireless technology. Therefore, in addition to the yearly data used for the heating bills, they may also give hourly data on the actual functioning of the heating systems in buildings. This new circumstance serves as the foundation for the creation of approaches that will lower the operating temperatures of heating systems and boost the overall efficiency of the heating supply.

3.2 Digitalization of Infrastructure

This working item considers the infrastructure viewpoint for district heating systems' digitization procedures. In order to increase system performance and assist the planning procedures for system extensions, etc., the modeling of the complete supply and network system is particularly important. The application of digital twins for DHC networks is crucial in this situation. It is also necessary to handle benefits and use cases from a system viewpoint, at the component level, and as controller-in-the-loop/hardware-in-the-loop. Focus is placed on reviewing current implementations of digital twins in district heating networks in terms of tangible benefits, real-world experiences, and lessons learned, as well as the techniques and data employed. Additionally, the methods for creating digital twins are categorized according to the system boundaries that have been selected, the level of detail or time interval, and the model features as physical/data driven model or static/dynamic. Focusing on methodologies and needs is the main challenge in this work using digital twins for simulation-related objectives.

3.3 Digitalization on the System Perspective

Here, the emphasis is on the digitalization of district heating from a systems perspective, i.e., how digitalization can be used to improve the sustainability and efficiency of district heating networks, as well as how district heating networks can benefit the overall energy system. Operational optimization and analytics are the main areas of attention in this work item. Operational optimization is here defined as active interaction with the network, i.e. real interventions in the operation of the network. Think of modifying the control of temperatures or flow rates in the network in order to achieve a certain objective on the network or energy system scale (e.g. peak shaving or increasing the share of renewable energy in the energy system). These interventions could happen on the supply side e.g. control of storage (small, large, seasonal), sector coupling through CHPs, HPs, or production portfolio management. The analytics tasks do not seek to actively interfere with the network's normal operation. However, these tasks involve analyzing network performance in order to increase the network's effectiveness and sustainability.

3.4 Digitalization of Business Processes

It is well acknowledged that digitalization is a vital technology for developing low-temperature district heating networks with a large proportion of renewable energy sources. Examining the commercial worth of digitalized district heating systems and calculating their economic potential and return on investment are the goals here. Digitalization can handle the escalating complexity brought by, for example, sector coupling, by having an influence on the whole district heating and cooling value chain from manufacturing and distribution to buildings and end-users. Digitalization can also help the new economic models that district heating will need to become more appealing than individual heat sources. Issues with data security and other legal obligations will be taken into consideration.

3.5 Knowledge Transfer, Dissemination, Management

This work item has been focused on gathering and disseminating data on ongoing and completed activities within this activity. This has involved things like creating an information portal and planning a ton of lectures and workshops. The major product will be a guidebook that compiles the results of the work completed within this activity. Nine nations contributed constantly to the initiative via industry and research partners.

4   Conclusions

With readily available and quickly evolving digital solutions that can utilize data from the field and from multiple sources (market pricing, weather predictions, etc.) to accomplish effective design and efficient operations, digitalization is the key to managing the ensuing complexity successfully. Therefore, an important strategy to enable the decarbonization of the energy system is district heating and cooling. However, DHC systems have to be changed in order to realize their potential since it has grown increasingly complicated as a result of a variety of production methods, remote sources, and sector coupling. When the value chain is considered as a whole, high performance is attained. Particularly, the economic potential of buildings and consumers has not yet been completely realized. The challenges of data security and privacy, as well as concerns about data ownership, must be addressed, and solutions must be developed, in order for digital processes to be more widely integrated. So that the necessary rapid transformation has real-world business models, products, and services that are ready for the market. The strong communication between the scientific community and system producers, utilities, and service providers is the project's greatest asset [7]. Detailed results are in the final report of TS4, available via the project homepage (see above).

Acknowledgment. The outline of the IEA DHC Annex TS4 work presented here was developed cooperatively by all contributors from various countries. The authors and all participants would like to thank the several national funding organizations and corporate partners who supported funding this study.

References

1. Pozzi, M., et al.: Digitalisation in District Heating and Cooling Systems – a Tangible Perspective to Upgrade Performance. DHC+ Platform c/o Euroheat & Power, Brussels (2023)
2. Schmidt, D.: Digitalization of district heating and cooling systems. In: Proceedings of the 17th International Symposium on District Heating and Cooling, 06–09 September 2021, Nottingham, United Kingdom (2021)
3. Männistö, J., Grönberg, A.: The Impact of Digitalisation in District Heating. Deloitte and Touche Oy, Group of Companies (2016)
4. Schmidt, D., Kallert, A. (ed.): Low Temperature District Heating Design Guidebook. Final report of IEA DHC Annex TS1 Low Temperature District Heating for Future Energy Systems, AGFW-Project Company, Frankfurt/M. (2017)
5. Lund, H., Wiltshire, R., Svendsen, S., Thorsen, J.E., Hvelplund, F., Mathiesen, B.: 4th Generation district heating (4GDH) integrating smart thermal grids into future sustainable energy systems. Energy **68**, 1–11 (2014)
6. AGFW: Bringing Focus into Digitalisation in District Heating. AGFW AGFW-Project Company, Frankfurt/M. (2019). (in German)
7. Schmidt, D.: Digitalisation of district heating. In: EUROHEAT&POWER International, Brussels, Belgium, vol. 2020, no. 2, pp. 28–30 (2020)

Field Implementation of a Predictive Control Strategy in District Heating Systems: A Tale of Two Demonstration Sites

Etienne Saloux[1]([✉]) [ID], Jason Runge[1], and Kun Zhang[1,2] [ID]

[1] CanmetENERGY, Natural Resources Canada, Varennes, Québec, Canada
etienne.saloux@nrcan-rncan.gc.ca
[2] École de Technologie Supérieure, Montréal, Québec, Canada

Abstract. District heating systems have become increasingly complex by integrating even more efficient technologies to help decarbonize the built environment. However, the full potential of such systems has yet to be reached due to inadequate controls. Predictive control has emerged as a promising solution to leverage operational data, modelling capabilities and various forecasts (weather conditions, price signals, carbon intensity) to optimize district energy system operation in real time. This paper discusses practical hurdles and lessons learned from the implementation of an artificial intelligence (AI)-based model predictive control (MPC) strategy in two Canadian district heating systems. These systems are equipped with natural gas boilers, which supply space and water heating through a steam network. This AI-based MPC strategy builds upon district heating demand forecasting models and data-driven boiler performance curves to optimize boiler thermal outputs that minimize greenhouse gas emissions. Practical hurdles include the usual suspects – data collection and preparation, communication with the control system, equipment maintenance – but also unexpected aspects such as weather forecast access issues and partial application of the recommendations. Lessons learned deal with the adoption of the proposed strategy, the potential for performance improvement of multi-boiler district heating systems, and the scalability and generalization to more complex systems.

Keywords: Boiler Efficiency · District Heating · Field Demonstration · Load Forecasting · Model Predictive Control

1 Introduction

District heating and cooling systems enable the integration of a wide range of technologies at a large scale, including boilers (biomass, electric, natural gas), combined heat and power, heat pumps, renewable energy systems (e.g. solar collectors), waste heat recovery and thermal energy storage devices (water tanks, geothermal) [1, 2]. It has resulted in complex integrated energy systems, whose optimal operation has yet to be reached. On the other hand, with the advent of the digital age, operational data has been increasingly available whereas data-driven modelling capabilities are becoming

© Crown 2024
B. N. Jørgensen et al. (Eds.): EI.A 2023, LNCS 14468, pp. 314–327, 2024.
https://doi.org/10.1007/978-3-031-48652-4_21

more powerful with the continuous emergence of new machine learning and other artificial intelligence (AI) techniques [3]. In this context, model predictive control (MPC) has appeared as an effective solution to leverage available operational data, modelling techniques and various sources of forecasts –such as weather conditions, price signals, carbon intensity– in order to optimize the operation of district energy systems [4]. However, well-documented real-world demonstration projects remain relatively scarce. Two compelling examples could still be mentioned. The STORM controller aims to exploit flexibility from building thermal inertia and was implemented in two demonstration sites to reduce peak loads [5]. Results showed a decrease of 3.1% in Rottne (Sweden) and 7.5–34% in Heerlen (The Netherlands). The second example is the smart controller developed as part of the TEMPO project [6]. This controller aims to reduce peak loads and return temperatures in district heating networks and was tested in a peripheral branch of an Italian district heating system (Brescia). An average peak load reduction of 34% was obtained for this case study.

This paper presents the development and implementation of a MPC strategy for multi-boiler district heating systems. Such systems (i.e. only relying on natural gas, oil or diesel) represent approximately half of all installed systems in Canada [7] and provides high potential for replicability. Section 2 describes the two demonstration sites and presents the MPC strategy, from the modelling to the implementation results. Section 3 discusses practical hurdles encountered during the development and implementation phases, as well as the lessons learned throughout the project and the potential for generalization to more complex district heating and cooling systems.

2 Development and Implementation of a Model Predictive Control Strategy

2.1 Description of Demonstration Sites

The district heating system under study is composed of several natural gas boilers that generate steam and supply space heating and domestic hot water to a district, characterized by different types of buildings. Boilers are operated alone or in combination with other boilers.

The first demonstration site is located in the province of Ontario (Canada); the second one is located in the province of Québec (Canada). For both sites, the central heating plant is composed of 3 non-condensing boilers (boiler capacity of 11.7–22.2 MW for site #1 and of 18.2–19.6 MW for site #2). The control system records and stores weather conditions, operating conditions and boiler consumption and production. By Canadian law and regulations, the operators must turn on and off the boilers manually for large capacity natural gas boilers. Therefore, they decide in the morning which boilers to run and at what power for the rest of the day, and adjust according to specific requirements or issues (e.g. boiler maintenance or repairs). In site #1, if two boilers are in operation, one boiler provides a base load and the second one fulfills the peak (denoted "base-peak"). In site #2, the load is equally distributed among boilers (denoted "equal load") but could be operated using "base-peak" method.

2.2 Control-Oriented Models

The control-oriented model is two-fold: 1) one model forecasts the district heating demand for the next 24 h based on machine learning techniques; 2) another model estimates boiler efficiency based on part-load ratio performance curves. Both models are calibrated with operational data and rely on hourly averaged values.

The heating demand model consists of a tree-based machine learning (XGBoost) model fed by an appropriate input dataset, composed of weather conditions (outdoor air temperature), time index inputs (hour of the day, cosine function of the hour of the day, cosine function of the scaled heating demand, weekends) and an occupancy variable (work hours derived from heating demand patterns). More information can be found in [3]. The accuracy was evaluated by considering weather forecasts as inputs; CV-RMSE (coefficient of variation of the root mean square error) of 8.7% was obtained for site #1 and of 11.7% for site #2 [3].

The boiler model was inspired from the National Energy Code of Canada for Buildings (NECB) [8] and expresses the energy efficiency (η_{boil}) as a function of the boiler part-load ratio (i.e. *PLR*, ratio of thermal and nominal load) as follows:

$$\eta_{boil} = \frac{a}{\frac{b}{PLR} + c + d \times PLR} \tag{1}$$

where a, b, c and d are parameters calibrated with operational data. Figure 1 shows the boiler performance curves.

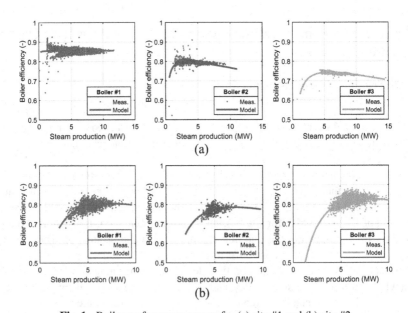

Fig. 1. Boiler performance curves for (a) site #1 and (b) site #2.

To remove transient operation [9], the efficiency was calculated such that the boiler has been in operation for 2 h and remains in operation for 2 h. In site #1, three levels of efficiency are observed (75%, 80%, 85%). In contrast, site #2 shows similar efficiency for all boilers (around 80%). CV-RMSE of 1.0–1.4% were found for boilers in site #1, and of 2.2–2.4% for boilers in site #2.

2.3 Predictive Control Strategy and Decision Support Tool

The predictive control strategy aims to leverage modelling capabilities and weather forecasts to support operators' decision-making about which boilers to run and at which thermal power for the coming day. The MPC strategy targets the minimization of natural gas consumption of all boilers over 24 h by optimizing the hourly thermal output of each boiler. The optimization routine consists of a brute force method that explores all possible combinations, from which the optimum is extracted. The load distribution is determined by "base-peak" approach for site #1, and by "base-peak" and "equal load" methods for site #2.

Since operators need to manually turn on and off boilers, automatic control is not possible and the output format of the MPC strategy must be adjusted to enable implementation. A PDF report was automatically generated to help operators make informed decisions. This report is generated once a day in the morning (around 7am) and provides the recommendations from 8am to 7am the next day. It is up to the operators to decide whether or not to apply the strategy throughout the day, based on their own technical constraints and considerations.

The automatic report generation works as follows. CanMETEO, Python, Windows Task Scheduler and Outlook were used as software platforms. Weather forecasts are retrieved using CanMETEO [10] and adjusted to match the evaluation period. Historical data is retrieved and used to train the control-oriented models in Python. The optimization routine is then run, and recommendations are extracted to build the MPC report in Python. Finally, this report is automatically created and sent to the operators via email (Outlook). These tasks are synchronized using Windows Task Scheduler.

An example of this report for site #1 is displayed in Fig. 2. The report contains several pages. The first page provides forecasted outdoor air temperature and district heating demand (a figure and a summary table with min/max values), as well as the first recommendation, which is the optimum based on energy efficiency. The recommendation consists of a figure showing the heating load forecast and the contribution of each boiler, and three tables providing boiler general information (nominal capacity, load range at which the boiler has been operated in the past), operational style (estimated boiler load and efficiency for the recommended operation) and system performance (energy use estimates for the central heating plant based on operational style). It aims to provide critical information for applying the recommendation, compare proposed operational conditions with historical data and display potential savings to encourage adoption. Plain text descriptions for each figure and table were also added to facilitate adoption. Additional pages were generated to provide the optimum of specific scenarios in case the operators are unable to run the most efficient scenario: only boilers #1 and #3 can be in operation (e.g. due to maintenance on boiler #2); only boilers #2 and #3 can be in operation; least efficient scenario (for performance comparison purposes). The last page aims to gather daily performance and operators' feedback on the proposed recommendations or technical issues encountered. For each scenario, energy, economic and GHG emissions savings are provided for the coming day. For site #1, the reference scenario represents the least efficient situation (the least efficient boiler is also the most reliable one) to encourage adoption. For site #2, the reference scenario was estimated based on historical data to compare with expected system performance under normal operation.

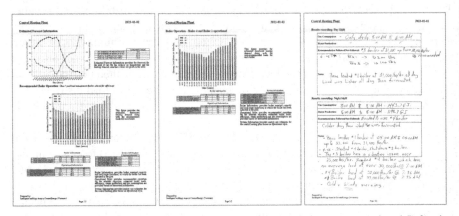

Fig. 2. MPC output report example containing the recommendations (pages 1, 2 and 5) for site #1.

2.4   Implementation Results

To evaluate the implementation results, a baseline model was developed to determine what would have been the performance if MPC was not implemented. It generally consists of an energy signature model that calculates daily energy usage usually as a function of outdoor conditions (e.g. heating degree days, outdoor air temperature) [11, 12]. In this case, daily gas consumption of the central heating plant is estimated as a function of daily heating demand (which is assumed to be equal to the daily total steam production) to specifically track energy efficiency variations. Results showed CV-RMSE of 4.4% for site #1 and 5.3% for site #2, respectively, and are displayed in Fig. 3.

For site #1, results were divided into three categories based on whether the recommendations were 1) followed, 2) partially followed (e.g. the base power was slightly different from what was recommended) or 3) not followed (e.g. technical issues). Figure 3 shows that the MPC performance was almost consistently lower than the baseline when the recommendations were followed and/or partially followed.

For site #2, the recommendations were either 1) followed or 2) not followed. In contrast with site #1, Fig. 3 shows that the daily gas consumption was on average lower than the baseline but some occurrences led to higher consumption. Savings for both sites were confirmed by a statistical analysis.

Table 1 shows the energy savings obtained for both sites during the implementation period. For site #1 (48 effective days), a 2.8% reduction was obtained, which represents in absolute terms, savings of $ 19,975 CAD and 77 t CO2eq (daily average of $ 416

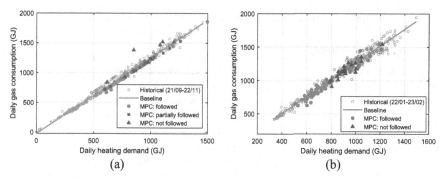

Fig. 3. MPC implementation results showing daily gas consumption vs. daily steam production for (a) site #1 and (b) site #2.

CAD and 1.6 t CO2eq). For site #2 (67 effective days), a reduction of 1.3% is observed, representing savings of $ 10,268 CAD and 45 t CO2eq (daily average of $ 153 CAD and 0.7 t CO2eq).

Table 1. MPC implementation results for site #1 (Feb 2 – Apr 27, 2023) and site #2 (Feb 15 – May 28, 2023).

Performance metric	Difference between MPC and reference case	
	Site #1 (48 days)	Site #2 (67 days)
District heating demand	0 GJ	0 GJ
Gas boiler consumption	- 1,502 GJ (- 2.8%)	- 903 GJ (- 1.3%)
Average system efficiency	2.28%	1.07%
Total energy costs	- $ 19,975 CAD (- 2.8%)	- $ 10,268 CAD (- 1.3%)
Total GHG emissions	- 77 t CO2eq (- 2.8%)	- 45 t CO2eq (- 1.3%)

3   Field Implementation: Practical Hurdles and Lessons Learned

This section tackles practical hurdles faced during the development and implementation phases and lessons learned from this implementation project. In a nutshell, practical hurdles consisted in data-related (access, quality, pre-processing, etc.) and communication (ability to retrieve data and send control commands) issues as well as weather forecast access and uncertainty, equipment maintenance, operational issues and partial application of the recommendation. Lessons learned are related to the adoption of the MPC strategy, the potential of such a strategy (model retraining, performance improvement) and the transition towards decarbonization. They are summarized in Table 2 and discussed in the following sub-sections.

Table 2. Practical hurdles and lessons learned from implementation.

Hurdles and lessons learned	Description
Practical hurdles during development phase	- Data access, availability and quality - Data pre-processing - Data privacy and security - Communication with the control system
Practical hurdles during implementation phase	- Access to weather forecasts - Uncertainty of weather and heating load forecasts - Partial application of the recommendation - Equipment maintenance and operational issues - Baseline and performance evaluation
Lessons learned	- Adoption of the data-driven predictive control strategy - Performance improvement potential - Model training and major operation changes - Transition towards decarbonization

3.1 Practical Hurdles During the Development Phase

Every approach dealing with operational data always comes with the same obstacles: *real world data is messy and challenging*. Most of the practical hurdles faced during the development phase are data-related and can be grouped in the following categories. Eventually, these hurdles could be expressed in terms of monetary amounts and additional efforts are required to prepare datasets before being further used for any applications.

Data Access, Availability and Quality. Data acquisition can be difficult, and comes with its own hurdles (e.g. hardware and software issues, communication problems), ultimately resulting in gaps in the datasets. Data was not necessarily stored for an appropriate period of time and was not accessible in real-time. In site #1, different trend logs characterized the same variable, but their size varied from one to another (a few days up to 2 years). In site #2, steam production was available for several years whereas gas consumption was only available for 8 months.

There was low documentation on measuring instruments (e.g. sensor type, technical specifications, last time sensors were calibrated, measurement uncertainty), or on what was exactly measured (e.g. location of steam meters). It has resulted in tremendous detective work on some of the data to find out what was inside and its extent.

People might even be unaware of the extent of the data they have. Data volumes could vary considerably: we have had plentiful data which are critical for controlling the plant but not necessarily useful for modelling purposes and advanced controls; conversely, small amounts were really critical for the strategy. In site #1, we received 1,300 + csv files with limited descriptive names and redundant information. For instance, steam production for a given boiler was recorded in klbs/hr, kJ/s, MJ/s (several variables for each unit) and with totalizers (hourly, daily, monthly). In site #2, we only received the variables we were interested in, but not always in the same format. Moreover, both sites are actually equipped with four boilers, but one of them is barely used; therefore, little data was available to derive performance curves and they were excluded from the analysis.

Data quality varied significantly, and variables did contain missing values, erroneous and questionable values, unknown units, as well as miscalibrated data. In site #1, the outdoor air temperature sensor is located in the turbine of a cogeneration unit, which is not used anymore, and showed constantly higher values compared to other weather data sources. In site #2, the steam production was characterized by two variables, which showed different values for the same period of time. Furthermore, the steam production is measured in Mg/h but was stored in kW; the internal conversion process remains unclear but might not take into account the effect of steam pressure changes, which have occurred in summer.

Data Pre-processing. The large amount of data obtained came in a variety of different structures and formats, and could combine different data sources. Such a process required laborious processing through various software and tools. Data did not come on nicely aligned time stamps, and was usually available at different times and different time-steps. Data synchronization was thus challenging for both sites. In site #1, efforts were mainly spent on the selection of the appropriate trend logs, and their synchronization, whereas in site #2, different data sources (steam production and gas consumption from two different control systems; weather data from other sources) needed to be synchronized.

Once the data has been synchronized, it still needs to be cleaned for analysis and modelling purposes. This task was partially done manually due to the lack of advanced data cleaning tools. Outlier detection based on statistical distribution might remove peak loads that actually occurred whereas it failed in detecting specific situations; for instance, a value that remains constant for a while, and steam production values, which were not relevant due to pressure changes.

Data pre-processing in real-time could be even more difficult since these steps must be automated and back-up plans must be elaborated if the data happens to be not available. Fail-safes were required for instance in case of missing weather forecasts.

Data Privacy and Security. People are required by law to protect data and they must develop an appropriate data infrastructure for this purpose; however, this can make data sharing more challenging. People may be reluctant to share their own data due the uncertainty of what data they are storing and how it will be used. This was not issue in both sites thanks to operators' and engineers' engagement.

Furthermore, access to real-time data can be even more challenging due to the higher risks of data breaches and the increased need for cybersecurity. In this project, communication was subject to stringent requirements, such as the automatic procedure for generation and sending of emails in a safe and secure manner, which needed to be approved by the IT department.

Communication with the Control System. Another major roadblock was the ability to connect to the control system and the data storage device, and the ability to automatically retrieve operational data and send control commands. In addition, Canadian regulations oblige operators to turn on and off the boilers manually for large capacity gas boilers. Therefore, the MPC strategy output needed to be formatted as a decision support system and aimed to assist operators in their daily routine, rather than automatically controlling the system. The MPC strategy output was shared as a report, which was continuously tailored for operators as part of an on-going learning process. They might have required additional information, not initially shown in the report (e.g. show more scenarios), or in the opposite, more compact results (e.g. reduce the level of details in the results, remove unnecessary scenarios).

3.2 Practical Hurdles During the Implementation Phase

Once the barriers of the development phase have been overcome and the control strategy has been developed, a series of additional hurdles have still been encountered during the implementation phase and led the provided recommendations to be either partially followed or not followed at all. These hurdles are discussed below with no particular order.

Access to Weather Forecasts. Weather forecasts were retrieved through numerical weather prediction files generated by the Canadian Meteorological Centre and postprocessed using the software tool CanMETEO [10]. These GRIB files are readily available on the web and weather forecasts are organized according to specific Canadian geographical zones and locations. However, this file organization has been modified by the Canadian Meteorological Centre during the implementation phase (url, geographical zone distribution), and we needed to adjust the retrieval process accordingly, resulting in losing one week of implementation.

Uncertainty of Weather and Heating Load Forecasts. In site #1, general operators' feedback in the early days of the implementation was pinpointing differences between forecasted weather conditions and heating loads, and actual on-site measurements (e.g. colder weather than forecasted, warmer than forecasted, load higher all day than forecasted). During the development phase, we estimated the load forecast accuracy (i.e. using heating load model along with weather forecasts) to be 8.7% and 11.7% for sites #1 and #2, respectively, which is already pretty good. Our impression is that the perception of operators was to obtain high-quality forecasts that almost perfectly match actual demand. However, weather forecasts by intrinsic nature come with an uncertainty whereas load forecasting model adds up additional uncertainty due to model inaccuracy. Figure 4 shows outdoor air temperature forecasts and measurements for the implementation phase for both sites. Standard deviations of 2.5 °C and 2.6 °C were obtained along with mean values of -0.6 °C and -0.6 °C, for sites #1 and #2 respectively, which is in accordance, although a bit higher, with previous studies (standard deviations of 2.2–2.3 °C) for site #2 [3] and for two other locations in Canada [13]. The week without forecasts in Fig. 4 corresponds to the week when GRIB files were reorganized.

Partial Application of the Recommendation. The inaccuracy of heating load forecasts has affected the decision-making of which boilers to use and at what power. More specifically, it was the case when only one boiler was recommended to operate whereas the actual load was higher than expected or the operators were not confident that one boiler would be enough to take the load. However, for site #1, it also happened that the load distribution was not exactly followed (e.g. the recommended base load was 26

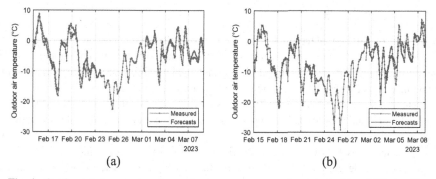

Fig. 4. Outdoor air temperature forecasts vs. measurements for: (a) site #1 and (b) site #2.

klbs/hr whereas it was actually operated at 29–32 klbs/hr). Similarly, it happened that the recommendation was followed during the day but not necessarily at night. For site #1, the predictive control strategy was also only implemented during workdays (Monday to Friday), not during weekends. Finally, it happened that the feedback report was not filled out, such that we could not know if the recommendation was followed. For all these observations, the rationale behind remains unknown.

Equipment Maintenance and Operational Issues. The central heating plant has undergone normal equipment maintenance during the implementation phase. Operators have reported for instance: boiler maintenance, boiler chimney repairs, boiler vibration and noise check, boiler safety valve maintenance, boiler chemicals management. In these cases, some boilers could be off for a few hours up to a few days. The demonstration sites have also been subjected to power failure and electrical repairs (high tension electrical switching order).

Baseline and Performance Evaluation. The implementation of a new control strategy always comes with an appropriate methodology to gauge past and current performance in order to evaluate savings. This methodology is essential to decide whether the strategy was effective or not. In this work, the baseline model allows to calculate the daily natural gas consumption as a function of the daily steam production, in order to grasp boiler performance, regardless of outdoor air conditions. Other models (e.g. different modelling techniques or different inputs) and time resolutions (e.g. hourly values, monthly values) might have led to different results. It is worth mentioning that for both sites, baseline models were also developed to evaluate daily steam production and daily gas consumption as a function of daily average outdoor air temperature. It was found that the daily steam production has increased by 10.7% (site #1) and 3.7% (site #2) compared to the baseline model, most probably due to changes in some of the buildings' operation, so did the daily gas consumption. Nevertheless, the system did perform more efficiently (see Fig. 3) despite this increased gas consumption when normalized with weather conditions.

3.3 Lessons Learned

Adoption of the Data-Driven Predictive Control Strategy. The proposed approach is a first step towards increased utilization of data to support district heating and cooling operation. Data analysis can already bring invaluable insights on system operation by providing an accurate picture of the current operation, which could be helpful to assist operators in their daily routine and transfer knowledge and experience to new operators. For instance, load profile analysis provides a better understanding of system schedules (based on load increase and decrease), energy usage and peak demand. Data-driven performance curves show actual boiler energy efficiency and could identify anomalies or performance degradation that could be further investigated and addressed. Eventually, such a data-driven approach allows to build operators' confidence for projects with more complex systems; it includes retrofits with a new electric boiler, optimization of time-varying energy costs.

After the implementation of the MPC strategy, the main feedback from our collaborators was that the operators were willing to apply the recommendations when it was possible. The operators are experienced technicians and managers, and they are proud in efficiently operating and maintaining their facility for years. The predictive control strategy has helped them be even more aware of energy efficiency and economic considerations by displaying potential savings they could further obtain. If the plant was already well operated, it has strengthened operators' confidence in their approach. Moreover, it is worth mentioning that the operators were engaged at the very beginning of the project. Since the automatic control of the district heating system was not allowed (see Sect. 3.1), they were kept in the loop during the whole process in order to tailor the predictive control strategy output to their needs and preferences, thus facilitating adoption.

After this implementation phase, the question of tool maintenance has gained more importance in the discussion with the operators. Simply said, how to go from a research project to a more robust and reliable tool? This topic has come with its own questions, which have yet to be answered. It includes among others: software development and maintenance in case of technical issue, MPC strategy reliability in the long term, access to operational data for model retraining, funding acquisition and involvement of collaborators.

Model Training and Major Operation Changes. The proposed predictive control strategy significantly relies on operational data to forecast the district heating demand and the central heating plant performance. To this purpose, up to years of data could be used for modelling (see Sect. 3.1). Nevertheless, this data must be representative of current operation to obtain accurate predictions. Therefore, major changes in operation (e.g. increased or reduced heating demand, boiler performance degradation) must be considered during the modelling phase. This project was started during the COVID-19 pandemic and an important consideration was to better understand how the pandemic has affected both district heating system and individual buildings operations. Based on data analysis, the district heating demand did not significantly change because of the COVID-19 pandemic for both sites, which could be due to the nature of these specific district systems. Nonetheless, it is worth mentioning that building schedules were adjusted during the pandemic for site #1 (daytime period from 6am-6pm to 4am-10pm), which was still captured by the district heating demand model (through the "work hour" variable [3]). In the case of major operational changes, datasets used for model training must be adjusted accordingly to account for actual operation. Adaptive learning could be helpful in this regard to rely on the most recent data.

Performance Improvement Potential. In general, the effectiveness of a new control strategy strongly depends on how the system has been operated in the past. If the system has already been well operated, low energy savings are expected; conversely, if the system operation shows several flaws, more savings could be achieved.

Moreover, the potential performance improvement depends on the energy efficiency of each natural gas boiler. Site #1 shows boilers with different energy efficiency levels (from 73% up to 85% for steam production between 3 and 12 MW) and more savings could be expected if the usage of low efficient boilers can be reduced to maximize the high efficient boiler operation (e.g. maximum of 12% efficiency increase). On the other hand, site #2 shows boilers with similar performance (e.g. efficiency between 78 and 83% for steam production between 5 and 10 MW), which reduces the potential for energy savings (e.g. maximum of 5% efficiency increase). These observations were confirmed with the implementation results: higher savings were obtained for site #1 (2.8%) compared to site #2 (1.3%). A similar study on multi-boiler system operation optimization has been conducted by Gunay et al. [14] using simulation. Boiler energy efficiencies were ranging between 65% and 85% (for part load ratio between 20% and 100%) and simulation results demonstrated 4% savings, which is in accordance with site #1 implementation results. Replication of this approach should focus first on boiler performance curves to grasp the potential of such a strategy.

Finally, it is worth mentioning that these savings were obtained during operation at no additional capital cost since no measuring devices nor new equipment were installed. Therefore, although savings in % are modest, the strategy still demonstrates relatively high return on investment (ROI). Preliminary estimates show annual savings of 89,000 $ and 340 t CO2eq for site #1, and 33,000 $ and 140 t CO2eq for site #2. This case study has demonstrated the potential of advanced controls to improve performance and work is underway with our partners to replicate the approach to other sites.

Transition Towards Decarbonization. This project is a first step towards decarbonization of district energy systems and aims to improve the way these systems are operated. Natural gas boilers will not go away overnight, and we still need to operate them more efficiently during this transition period. The proposed control strategy builds upon data-driven models and allows to minimize GHG emissions by improving the current efficiency of the multi-boiler system. Nonetheless, it was built with a mindset to be scalable to similar systems and extendible to next generation systems for which operation can be much more complex and potential savings (GHG emissions, energy costs) much higher. Indeed, these multi-boiler systems may rely on steam-based networks (this is the case for both sites), which have shown limitations in performance improvement unless a major and costly retrofit occurs. Retrofits include partial or full conversion of steam to water network, the installation of new equipment such as electric boiler, heat pumps, renewable energy systems or thermal energy storage devices. The proposed control strategy aims to be easily adaptable to these new technologies and builds the foundations for more complex hybrid energy systems in more complex situations (dynamic tariffication, peak demand management, dynamic electric grid's carbon intensity, etc.). District energy system electrification would also bring new challenges such as resiliency, which could also be tackled to some extent with such a predictive control approach.

4 Conclusions

This paper has presented the development and implementation of a predictive control strategy in two demonstration sites in Canada. This strategy tackles the operation of multi-boiler district heating systems and optimizes boiler thermal outputs for the next 24 h to minimize total natural gas consumption. Implementation results showed reductions of 1.3% and 2.8% for both sites, which represent savings of 45–77 t CO_2 eq and $ 10,268–19,975 CAD for a 2–3-month period.

Nonetheless, the implementation was not straightforward and has faced different obstacles. During the development phase, most of the hurdles were data-related; real world data is messy and challenging. It includes difficult access to data and communication issues, low documentation on measuring instruments or what was exactly measured. Data cleaning has also required substantial efforts to address missing, erroneous and questionable values, unknown units and miscalibrated data. During the implementation phase, weather forecasts were not accessible for a week; the recommendations were not necessarily followed by the book; and the central heating plant has undergone equipment maintenance. Overall, the MPC strategy was well adopted, and the proposed data-driven approach has highlighted benefits of an increased utilization of data to support district heating and cooling operation. Expected savings vary from one site to another, which is mainly due to the original control strategy, and the energy efficiency of each boiler. This project paves the way for decarbonization of district energy systems and future work includes the application of the MPC strategy to similar sites in Canada, and the development of a more generalized approach, applicable to more complex systems in more complex situations.

Acknowledgments. The authors gratefully acknowledge the financial support of Natural Resources Canada through the Greening Government Fund. The authors would like to thank our external partners for sharing their experience, providing data and feedback, and implementing the proposed strategies. Internal and external reviewers are also acknowledged for their useful comments.

References

1. Lund, H., et al.: The status of 4th generation district heating: research and results. Energy **164**, 147–159 (2018). https://doi.org/10.1016/j.energy.2018.08.206
2. Buffa, S., Cozzini, M., D'Antoni, M., Baratieri, M., Fedrizzi, R.: 5th generation district heating and cooling systems: a review of existing cases in Europe. Renew. Sustain. Energy Rev. **104**, 504–522 (2019). https://doi.org/10.1016/j.rser.2018.12.059
3. Runge, J., Saloux, E.: A comparison of prediction and forecasting artificial intelligence models to estimate the future energy demand in a district heating system. Energy **269**, 126661 (2023). https://doi.org/10.1016/j.energy.2023.126661

4. Saloux, E., Candanedo, J.A.: Model-based predictive control to minimize primary energy use in a solar district heating system with seasonal thermal energy storage. Appl. Energy **291**, 116840 (2021). https://doi.org/10.1016/j.apenergy.2021.116840

5. Van Oevelen, T., Vanhoudt, D., Johansson, C., Smulders, E.: Testing and performance evaluation of the STORM controller in two demonstration sites. Energy **197**, 117177 (2020). https://doi.org/10.1016/j.energy.2020.117177

6. Van Oevelen, T., Neven, T., Brès, A., Schmidt, R.-R., Vanhoudt, D.: Testing and evaluation of a smart controller for reducing peak loads and return temperatures in district heating networks. Smart Energy **10**, 100105 (2023). https://doi.org/10.1016/j.segy.2023.100105

7. Canadian Energy & Emissions Data Centre: District Energy in Canada (2019). https://www.sfu.ca/content/dam/sfu/ceedc/publications/facilities/CEEDC%20-%20District%20Energy%20Report%202019.pdf

8. National Research Council of Canada: National Energy Code of Canada for Buildings 2020, Fifth Edition (2020)

9. Saloux, E., Zhang, K.: Data-driven model-based control strategies to improve the cooling performance of commercial and institutional buildings. Buildings **13**, 474 (2023). https://doi.org/10.3390/buildings13020474

10. Natural Resources Canada: CanMETEO, English/French. https://www.nrcan.gc.ca/energy/software-tools/19908

11. Cotrufo, N., Saloux, E., Hardy, J.M., Candanedo, J.A., Platon, R.: A practical artificial intelligence-based approach for predictive control in commercial and institutional buildings. Energy Build. **206**, 109563 (2020). https://doi.org/10.1016/j.enbuild.2019.109563

12. Saloux, E., Cotrufo, N., Candanedo, J.: A practical data-driven multi-model approach to model predictive control: results from implementation in an institutional building. In: Presented at the 6th International High Performance Buildings Conference, Purdue, May 24–28 (2021)

13. Candanedo, J.A., Saloux, E., Hardy, J.-M., Platon, R., Raissi-Dehkordi, V., Côté, A.: Preliminary assessment of a weather forecast tool for building operation. In: Presented at the 5th International High Performance Buildings Conference, Purdue, July 9–12 (2018)

14. Gunay, H.B., Ashouri, A., Shen, W.: Load forecasting and equipment sequencing in a central heating and cooling plant: a case study. ASHRAE Trans. **125**, 513–523 (2019)

Assessment of Residential District Cooling System Based on Seasonal Consumption Data

Madhan Kumar Kandasamy[1]($\boxtimes$) (iD), Vishal Garg[2] (iD), Jyotirmay Mathur[3] (iD),
Srinivas Valluri[4], and Dharani Tejaswini[1] (iD)

[1] International Institute of Information Technology - Hyderabad, Hyderabad, India
madhan.kandasam@research.iiit.ac.in
[2] Plaksha University, Mohali, India
[3] Malaviya National Institute of Technology - Jaipur, Jaipur, India
[4] Synergy infra–Consultants Pvt Ltd., Hyderabad, India

Abstract. Residential District Cooling Systems (DCS) are crucial for maintaining thermal comfort in urban areas, making it imperative to understand occupant cooling behavior as it significantly influences DCS operation. While several studies have investigated cooling behavior within small user groups through on-site measurements or surveys, these often fall short in representing the broader population. In this study we considered 387 homes in Hyderabad, which has a DCS connection for chilled water supply. Operational data spanning three months across different seasons were meticulously selected to assess the residents' behavior for the cooling demand. In order to better facilitate the operation of the residential DCS, user load profile and system performance were analyzed using real world data for different seasons in the year. Our findings revealed notable disparities in DCS electrical consumption, with summer usage being 1.9 times higher than the monsoon period and 2.7 times higher than the winter period. Furthermore, a strong positive correlation emerged between outdoor temperature and thermal energy usage by the residents. On average, the daily thermal consumption per residence during winter, summer and monsoon is 3.3 kWh$_{th}$, 35.1 kWh$_{th}$ and 10.4 kWh$_{th}$ respectively. Interestingly, the probability of a residence using AC during the day for the winter, summer and monsoon seasons are 0.07, 0.41 and 0.18 respectively.

Keywords: District cooling system · Residential AC usage · seasonal data · Air conditioning · Load profile

1 Introduction

Rapid urbanization has led to a surge in urban populations, posing increased risks and detrimental environmental effects. In the years 2021–2022, the residential apartment market sales have increased by 41% across top 8 cities in India [1]. Due to less green spaces and water bodies, built environment in cities is getting warmer and making people vulnerable to rising temperatures. In response, demand for space cooling in the building

B. N. Jørgensen et al. (Eds.): EI.A 2023, LNCS 14468, pp. 328–337, 2024.
https://doi.org/10.1007/978-3-031-48652-4_22

has been viewed not only as a luxury but also a critical element in promoting health, well-being, and productivity. In India, apart from fan and air coolers, room air conditioners have 7–9% penetration in residential sector which would significantly increase over the next decade [2]. This heightened demand necessitates cleaner, more energy-efficient technologies and environmentally friendly cooling solutions. According to International Cooling Action Program (ICAP) reports, per capita energy consumed for space cooling in India stands at 69 kWh compared to the world average of 272 kWh$_e$. With the growing demand for space cooling in the country, it is a great opportunity to implement meaningful and resourceful interventions for the future of cooling technologies.

Generally, space cooling in hot regions is characterized by large seasonal and daily variations which puts a heavy load on the electricity grid. The cooling load for most of the residences is met through window units like split air conditioning or evaporative air coolers. These systems are mostly predefined sizes catering to common markets. Unfortunately, these systems contribute to negative environmental impacts by releasing greenhouse gases and excess heat into the environment. They also affect the aesthetics of the building and create a noisy environment while running. In contrast, central air conditioning like District Cooling Systems (DCS) uses environment friendly refrigerant and water-cooled chillers to reduce environment impacts. This type of air conditioning provides reliable service and can be equipped with energy efficient equipment's to reduce electricity consumption.

The load profile is a crucial element for designing and operating DCS in an efficient manner. By evaluating cooling load and system size more accurately, DCS can provide more economic and environmental benefits. Surprisingly, much of the research surrounding DCS has focused on design and optimization based on theoretical calculations, often unable to utilize real world data [3, 4]. The fundamental reason why theoretical values and operating values frequently diverge is because human behavior and other real-world elements which are not considered while developing. To bridge this gap, a study was conducted based on data from the Hong Kong Polytechnic University campus, analyzing actual hourly cooling and electricity usage data [5]. Using a simulation model, this study evaluated the energy efficiency of DCS and individual cooling systems under various operating modes. The study shows that depending on the control technique employed, the payback period varies from 6.4 to 10.4 years.

Recognizing that user behavior significantly influences system effectiveness, demand load evaluation and management which have assumed greater importance. Comparative investigations between DCS and traditional cooling systems in residential buildings have demonstrated considerable benefits in reducing peak demand and operational costs [6, 7]. The energy efficiency and applicability of centralized AC systems in residential buildings will be significantly impacted by the load pattern and load ratio [8]. Notably, the dispersed nature of residential structures necessitates larger pumps to supply cooling to scattered zones, resulting in lower energy efficiency due to the dispersion of cooling loads [9].

The objective of this paper is to assess the occupant behavior and real-world factors in designing and operating efficient residential cooling systems, ultimately contributing to sustainable urban living. In this study we considered 387 homes in Hyderabad, which has a DCS connection for chilled water supply. The operational data of three months from different seasons were chosen to study the residents' behavior for the cooling demand. The cooling consumption of residences and electrical consumption of DCS were used. In order to better facilitate the performance of the residential DCS, cooling load of different season were analyzed.

2 Methodology

The aim of this study is to provide a comprehensive understanding of residential DCS to understand the actual energy consumption, occupant AC usage pattern and influence of outdoor temperature. The study is conducted in three steps: data collection, data preparation and analysis. The DCS system and the building details was already studied in the case study paper [10]. This paper is an extended analysis of the case study comparing the seasonal variation over the course of a year.

2.1 Residence and DCS Characteristics

The case study is a residential building located in Hyderabad, the capital city of Telangana, India. The city experiences an arid climate, consisting primarily of dry and hot days. As depicted in Fig. 1, cooling demand is very high from March to June, followed by a moderation from July to October. The building consists of five towered apartments with 387 residences and six common areas. The residence areas vary in size from 180 m^2 to 250 m^2, contributing to a total built-up area of 1,04,344 m^2. Since 2015, the building has been equipped with a centralized cooling system boasting a total cooling load of 13,641 kW$_{th}$, serviced by water cooled chiller and a thermal storage system.

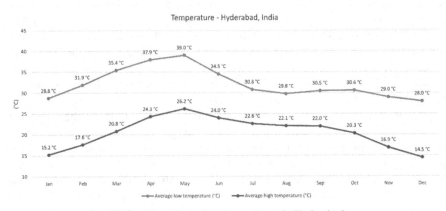

Fig. 1. Monthly outdoor temperature in Hyderabad.

2.2 Data Collection

Data collection involves two types of meters were used to gather thermal and electricity consumption data. The meter connections and its specifications are comprehensively detailed in the previous case study [10]. Each residence is installed with BTU meter through which AC consumption is measured. Electrical energy from chillers and other equipment is measured through the smart three-phase energy meter. Data was stored in a Building Management System (BMS) which is then used by the maintenance office for billing purposes. Data was collected for three different seasons: Winter (January 2023), Summer (May 2022), and Monsoon (September 2022). Detailed description of the data is given in Table 1. AC consumption data contains thermal energy usage in both residences and common spaces for cooling. Electricity consumption of DCS includes meter readings from chillers, brine chiller, pumps, and cooling towers.

Table 1. Description of the data

Type of data	Time period	Data units	Data points	Data interval
AC usage	May 2022, September 2022, & January 2023 (92 days)	kWh_{th}	3.47 million points	15 min
Electricity usage	May 2022, September 2022, & January 2023 (92 days)	kWh_e	0.04 million points	15 min

2.3   Data Preprocessing

Irrelevant data apart from DCS meter and residence meter were removed including the house id. Microsoft excel was used for the processing and analysis of data. Missing data in the dataset were found to be within permissible limit. Thermal data and electricity data was recorded in kWh_{th} and kWh_e units at 15-min interval. Given the data is in time series format, simple moving average method was used for the interpolation of the missing data. This process used the same time hourly values from adjacent 3 days of the missing data. If the adjacent day was also missing, values from adjacent time slots were utilized. Using the meter reading, the value from the interpolation were adjusted according to the missing reading values. The author believes the average value of hourly representation of the data will explain the outcome more clearly. The day is divided into four segments: early morning (12 AM to 6 AM), morning (6 AM to 12 PM), afternoon (12 PM to 6 PM), and night (6 PM to 12 AM).

3   Results and Discussion

This section aims to explain the relationship between the thermal use behavior of residents and electrical load of DCS across 3 different seasons (summer, winter, and monsoon). To understand the behavior of residents, a detailed analysis of the thermal data with a focus on seasonal variation was conducted.

3.1 DCS Energy Usage

Understanding the electrical consumption of the DCS is crucial in improving its efficiency. The hourly electrical load during different time period of the typical day in a month is shown in Table 2. Figure 2 explains the hourly effect of the electrical load of DCS during these three seasons. During the summer and monsoon periods, there is a peak in electrical demand during sleeping hours, as the cooling load is met by chiller. In contrast, during winter, thermal energy storage was used for 19 days to supply chilled water for cooling. The charging occurs over a span of around 3 to 4 h in the evening, followed by discharge during the remaining period. This results in a consistent electricity demand from early morning to afternoon. In summer, due to hot outdoor weather conditions there is a peak in electricity demand during lunch time. The daily average electrical load during winter, summer and monsoon is 2,158 kWh$_e$, 5,910 kWh$_e$ and 3,139 kWh$_e$. The average hourly load for the winter, summer and monsoon seasons are 90 kWh$_e$, 246 kWh$_e$ and 131 kWh$_e$. The maximum hourly load during the months of winter, summer and monsoon are 469 kWh$_e$, 481 kWh$_e$ and 253 kWh$_e$. For the annual electricity usage, two major peaks are observed: one during nighttime and another during the afternoon period. Notably, summer electrical consumption is 1.9 times higher than the monsoon period and 2.7 times higher than in winter period.

Table 2. Hourly average electrical load (kWh$_e$) at given time period.

Time period	Winter	Summer	Monsoon
Early morning	64	330	151
Forenoon	58	200	125
Afternoon	61	212	117
Night	177	243	131

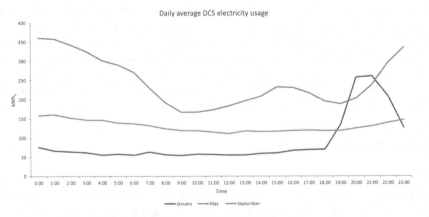

Fig. 2. Daily average DCS electricity usage.

3.2   AC Energy Usage

People prefer different comfort conditions despite being in the same physical environment. Understanding the thermal consumption at different periods of the day and comparing it to different seasons will help us understand the thermal behavior of residents. From Table 3, the thermal load during summer afternoon is higher than the forenoon which is not the case for winter and monsoon season. The graph in Fig. 3 shows the daily average AC usage by the residents. The daily average thermal load during winter, summer and monsoon is 1,269 kWh$_{th}$, 13,565 kWh$_{th}$ and 4,021 kWh$_{th}$, respectively. The average hourly thermal load during the day for the winter, summer and monsoon seasons are 53 kWh$_{th}$, 565 kWh$_{th}$ and 168 kWh$_{th}$. The maximum hourly thermal load during the day in winter, summer and monsoon seasons are 262 kWh$_{th}$, 1199 kWh$_{th}$ and 541 kWh$_{th}$. Notably, during summer, the first peak is 2.9 times higher than the second peak, while in winter it is 5.7 times higher and in monsoon it is 3.2 times higher. The summer AC consumption is 3.4 times higher than monsoon period and 10.7 times higher than the winter period.

Table 3. Hourly average thermal load (kWh$_{th}$) at given time period.

Time period	Winter	Summer	Monsoon
Early morning	99	840	266
Forenoon	46	426	134
Afternoon	24	450	105
Night	42	545	165

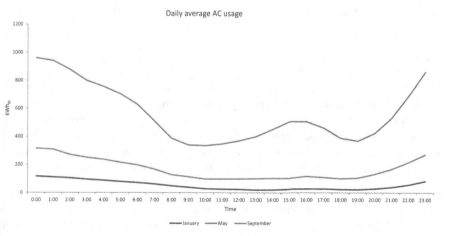

Fig. 3. Daily average AC usage.

3.3 Residence AC Use Pattern

In this section, we will discuss the characteristics of the occupant behavior and provide insights into the operation schedule of the DCS.

Probability

Interestingly, some residents use AC during all the seasons despite the outdoor temperature is comfortable for the average human. Figure 4 illustrates the usage probability of AC during different time periods in a typical house. The average probability of a residence using AC in a day for the winter, summer and monsoon seasons are 0.07, 0.41 and 0.18 respectively. Figure 4 indicates that most residents use AC from midnight to early morning throughout all seasonal months. In summer, people using AC during post lunch has increased more than winter and monsoon due to peak outdoor temperature.

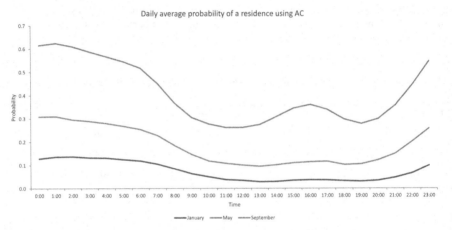

Fig. 4. Daily average probability of a residence using AC.

Load

The study of a typical residence for the AC usage is necessary to understand the AC usage behavior and to provide suitable measures to increase the system efficiency. In Fig. 5, the average of hourly thermal energy plotted against the number of days AC used for each residence for different seasonal months. In this analysis, the hours where the AC was not used throughout the month were removed. The hourly average thermal load during winter, summer and monsoon is 1.8 kW_{th}, 3.2 kW_{th} and 2.2 kW_{th}. In winter and monsoon months the overall load varies a lot due to fewer residents using AC.

Influence of Outdoor Temperature

Figure 6 reveals the average daily thermal usage as a function of the average outdoor temperature for three months. This figure illustrates a clear positive correlation between outdoor temperature and thermal usage. As the outdoor temperature increases AC usage in residences also increases. Thermal energy consumption by residents is more scattered in summer compared to winter and monsoon months. More residents use AC to bring down the room temperature and use mechanical ventilation to maintain the room comfort.

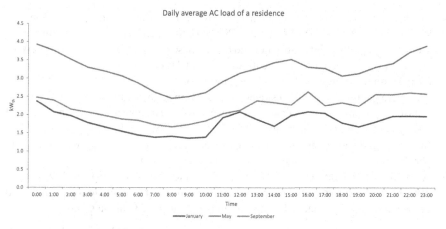

Fig. 5. Daily average AC load of a residence.

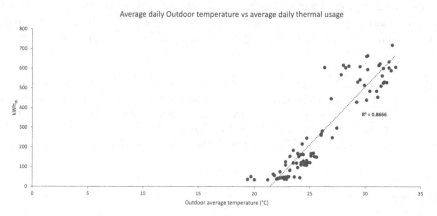

Fig. 6. Average outdoor temperature vs average daily thermal usage.

4   Conclusion

The operational data of three months from different seasons were chosen to study the residents' behavior for the cooling demand. By analyzing the operational data, the cooling load profile of residences and electrical load profile of DCS were identified for different seasons throughout a typical day.

• The average hourly load during the day for the winter, summer and monsoon seasons is 90 kWh$_e$, 246 kWh$_e$ and 131 kWh$_e$, respectively. The maximum hourly load during the months of winter, summer and monsoon are 469 kWh$_e$, 481 kWh$_e$ and 253 kWh$_e$. Summer electrical consumption of DCS is 1.9 times higher than the monsoon period and 2.7 times higher than the winter period. There is a substantial seasonal and hourly variation in electrical demand for air conditioning on the grid.

- The average hourly thermal load during the day for the winter, summer and monsoon seasons is 53 kWh$_{th}$, 565 kWh$_{th}$ and 168 kWh$_{th}$, respectively. The maximum hourly thermal load for the winter, summer and monsoon seasons are 262 kWh$_{th}$, 1199 kWh$_{th}$ and 541 kWh$_{th}$. There is a significant variation in AC consumption among residences during summer compared to winter and monsoon.
- The average probability of a residence using AC in a day for the winter, summer and monsoon seasons is 0.07, 0.41 and 0.18, respectively. The hourly average thermal load during winter, summer and monsoon is 1.8 kW$_{th}$, 3.2 kW$_{th}$ and 2.2 kW$_{th}$, respectively. In winter and monsoon, AC consumption primarily occurs during early morning period, possibly due to residents' accustomed behavior at nights.
- As outdoor temperature rises, AC usage in residences also increases. The thermal energy used by the residents is more scattered in summer compared to winter and monsoon months, primarily because more people using AC in the summer.

These findings will greatly assist policymakers in establishing benchmarks and evaluating solutions for the masses. They will also aid engineers in designing DCS especially for the residential users by providing inputs such as cooling demand profiles for different seasons. If an analysis of chiller's water temperature and the individual electrical load of other equipment's were measured, it would provide valuable insights into the efficiency of the DCS.

Acknowledgements. We thank Synergy Infra Consultants (Pvt) Ltd. for helping us with the data collection. We extend our thanks to the homeowners who voluntarily participated in the study. This research was jointly funded by Department of Science and Technology, India (DST) and Engineering and Physical Sciences Research Council, UK (EPSRC) under the India-UK partnership grant for Residential Building Energy Demand in India (RESIDE).

References

1. PropertyPistol: Residential sales in India's top 8 cities reached a nine-year high (2022). https://www.propertypistol.com/blog/residential-sales-in-indias-top-8-cities-reached-a-nine-year-high-2022/. Accessed 18 Sept 2023
2. MoEFCC: India Cooling Action Plan. MoEFCC, Government of India, New Delhi (2019). http://www.ozonecell.com/viewsection.jsp
3. Chow, T.T., Au, W.H., Yau, R., Cheng, V., Chan, A., Fong, K.F.: Applying district-cooling technology in Hong Kong. Appl. Energy **79**, 275–289 (2004). https://doi.org/10.1016/j.apenergy.2004.01.002
4. Nagota, T., Shimoda, Y., Mizuno, M.: Verification of the energy-saving effect of the district heating and cooling system—simulation of an electric-driven heat pump system. Energy Build. **40**, 732–741 (2008). https://doi.org/10.1016/j.enbuild.2007.05.007
5. Gao, J., Kang, J., Zhang, C., Gang, W.: Energy performance and operation characteristics of distributed energy systems with district cooling systems in subtropical areas under different control strategies. Energy **153**, 849–860 (2018). https://doi.org/10.1016/j.energy.2018.04.098
6. Jing, Z.X., Jiang, X.S., Wu, Q.H., Tang, W.H., Hua, B.: Modelling and optimal operation of a small-scale integrated energy based district heating and cooling system. Energy **73**, 399–415 (2014). https://doi.org/10.1016/j.energy.2014.06.030

7. Al-Qattan, A., ElSherbini, A., Al-Ajmi, K.: Solid oxide fuel cell application in district cooling. J. Power Sour. **257**, 21–26 (2014). https://doi.org/10.1016/j.jpowsour.2014.01.099

8. Zhou, X., Yan, D., Shi, X.: Comparative research on different air conditioning systems for residential buildings. Front. Archit. Res. **6**, 42–52 (2017). https://doi.org/10.1016/j.foar.2016.11.004

9. Deng, G., Yan, D., Yu, R.: Case studies: the effect of occupant behaviors on evaluating the adaptability of district cooling system. Presented at the ASim Conference 2012 (2012)

10. Kumar, M., Garg, V., Mathur, J., Valluri, S.: A case study of AC usage in residential district cooling system using operational data. Energise (2023)

Author Index

B. N. Jørgensen et al. (Eds.): EI.A 2023, LNCS 14468, pp. 339–340, 2024.
https://doi.org/10.1007/978-3-031-48652-4

Printed in the United States
by Baker & Taylor Publisher Services